Political Parties and Electoral Change

Political Parties and Electoral Change

Party Responses to Electoral Markets

Edited by

Peter Mair, Wolfgang C. Müller and Fritz Plasser

SAGE Publications
London • Thousand Oaks • New Delhi

SAGE Publications Ltd
1 Oliver's Yard
55 City Road
London EC1Y 1SP

SAGE Publications Inc.
2455 Teller Road
Thousand Oaks, California 91320

SAGE Publications India Pvt Ltd
B-42, Panchsheel Enclave
Post Box 4109
New Delhi 110 017

British Library Cataloguing in Publication data

A catalogue record for this book is available from the British Library

ISBN 0-7619-4718-3
ISBN 0-7619-4719-1 (pbk)

Library of Congress Control Number available

Typeset by C&M Digitals (P) Ltd., Chennai, India
Printed in Great Britain by TJ International, Padstow, Cornwall

Contents

Notes on Contributors

Luciano Bardi is Professor of Comparative Politics and International Relations at the University of Pisa. He is author and co-author of numerous books and articles on European Union politics and institutions and of several essays on Italian parties and on the Italian party system, as well as co-editor of *Italian Politics. Mapping the Future* (1998) and editor of *Forma partito e sistemi di partito tra due secoli* (2004).

Lars Bille is Associate Professor of Political Science at the University of Copenhagen. He is the author of *Partier i Forandring* (1997) and *Fra Valgkamp til Valgkamp* (1998) and co-editor of *Partiernes Medlemmer* (2003). His English language publications include articles in *West European Politics* and *Party Politics*.

Kris Deschouwer is Professor of Political Science at the Free University of Brussels. He is author of *Organiseren of Bewegen. De evolutie van de Belgische partijstructuren sinds 1960* (1993), *De wortels van de democratie* (1996) and co-author of *Culture, Institutions and Economic Development. A Study of Eight European Regions* (2003), and co-editor of *Party Elites in Divided Societies* (2001). His articles have appeared in *European Journal of Political Research*, *West European Politics*, *Regional and Federal Studies*, *Environmental Politics* and in many edited volumes, including *Party Organizations* (1992), *How Parties Organize* (1994) and *Political Parties in Democratic Societies* (2002).

Andrew Knapp is Senior Lecturer in French Studies at the University of Reading. He is author of *Le Gaullisme après de Gaulle* (1996) and of *Parties and the Party System in France: a Disconnected Democracy?* (2004), and co-author, with Yves Mény, of *Government and Politics in Western Europe* (3rd edition, 1998) and, with Vincent Wright, of *The Government and Politics of France* (4th edition, 2001).

Peter Mair is Professor of Comparative Politics at Leiden University in the Netherlands, and is co-editor of *West European Politics*. He is co-author of *Representative Government in Modern Europe* (3rd edition, 2000) and author of *Party System Change* (1997). He is co-editor of *The Enlarged European Union* (2002).

Michael Marsh is an Associate Professor in the Department of Political Science, Trinity College, University of Dublin. He has written extensively on parties and elections, both in Ireland and elsewhere. He is the co-author of *Days of Blue Loyalty: the Politics of Membership of Fine Gael* (2002), co-editor of *How Ireland Voted 2002* (2003), and co-director of the 2002 Irish election study. His articles have appeared in journals such as *European Journal of Political Research*, *Party Politics*, and *Electoral Studies*.

Wolfgang C. Müller is Professor of Political Science at the University of Mannheim and previously taught at the University of Vienna. He is senior author of *Die österreichischen Abgeordneten, Individuelle Präferenzen und politsiches Verhalten* (2001) and co-editor of *Policy, Office, or Votes? How Political Parties in Western Europe Make Hard Decisions* (1999), *Coalition Governments in Western Europe* (2000) (both with Kaare Strøm), and *Delegation and Accountability in Parliamentary Democracies* (2003) (with Kaare Strøm and Torbjörn Bergman).

Karina Pedersen is Assistant Professor of Political Science at the University of Copenhagen. She is the author of *Party Membership Linkage. The Danish Case* (2003).

Fritz Plasser is Professor of Political Science at the University of Innsbruck. He is author of *Parteien unter Stress* (1987), co-editor of *The Austrian Party System* (1989), *Wählerverhalten und Parteienwettbewerb* (1995), *Wahlkampf und Wählerentscheidung* (1996), *Das österreichische Wahlverhalten* (2000), *Wahlverhalten in Bewegung* (2003) and several other books. His English language publications include *Global Political Campaigning* (2002) as well as articles in *West European Politics*, *Harvard International Journal of Press/Politics* and edited volumes.

Susan E. Scarrow is Professor of Political Science at the University of Houston. She is author of *Parties and Their Members* (1996), editor of *Perspectives on Political Parties* (2002), and co-editor of *Democracy Transformed?* (2003). Her articles have appeared in such journals as the *European Journal of Political Research*, *Comparative Political Studies*, *Party Politics*, and *German Politics*.

Peter A. Ulram is Director of the Department for Political Research at the Fessel + GfK Institut and Associate Professor at the University of Vienna. He is author of *Hegemonie und Erosion* (1990), co-author of *Das österreichische Politikverständnis* (2002), and co-editor of *Wahlverhalten in Bewegung* (2003). His English language publications have appeared in *West European Politics*, *Party Politics*, and in edited volumes.

Paul Webb is Professor of Politics at the University of Sussex. His research interests focus on representative democracy, particularly party and electoral politics. The author or editor of several volumes, including *The Modern British Party System* (2000) and *Political Parties in Advanced Industrial Societies* (2002), he is a co-editor of both *Party Politics* and *Representation*.

List of Figures

List of Tables

ONE Introduction: Electoral Challenges and Party Responses

Peter Mair, Wolfgang C. Müller,
and Fritz Plasser

The problem

Voter loyalties to political parties in western democracies are generally in decline. This has already become part of the conventional wisdom, and it is easily sustained by a large and varied volume of cross-national electoral research. To be sure, this decline is not equally prevalent in each and every country, at least in terms of its extent and pace; nor is it even true for each and every party in any given polity. Nonetheless, with all of the caveats that such generalizations demand, we feel we are on sure ground in asserting that it is the erosion of voter loyalties, rather than their strengthening or even stabilization, that has most clearly marked the western political environment over the past 20 years. We also feel on sure ground in asserting that this decline in voter loyalties has constituted one of the most powerful challenges facing the many individual parties that seek support in contemporary electoral markets. Accordingly, we have set out in this book to investigate how political parties have perceived the sometimes radical changes which have taken place within their electoral markets, and how they have responded to these changes. Where possible, we have also sought to explore some of the consequences that follow from the responses that the parties have chosen to make.

This volume is organized around the analysis of the experiences within a number of specific countries in Western Europe, with the primary focus resting always on the individual parties within these countries. As is evident, the question of party responses can be answered empirically only at the level of the individual party, and hence the chapters in this volume constitute multiple case studies of how individual parties have dealt with the challenge of electoral change. We have limited the analysis to Western Europe not only to enhance the comparability of these multiple case studies and hence to facilitate more generalizable conclusions, but also because it is here that we find some of the most established and firmly rooted political parties in the world, and therefore also those that are likely to be most thrown off balance by major electoral dealignment.

While recent years have witnessed quite a large outpouring of research on the decline of voter loyalties to political parties and on the fluctuation in their electoral support,[1] surprisingly little attention has been paid to the question of how political parties have responded to this decline, particularly from a comparative perspective. The changing nature of party systems has provoked a lot of scholarly interest through the years, of course (see, for example, Daalder and Mair 1983; Mair and Smith 1990; Pennings and Lane 1998; Broughton and Donovan 1999; Webb *et al.* 2002), and a focus on party organizational change has also recently been highlighted (e.g. Katz and Mair 1992, 1994, 2002; Dalton and Wattenberg 2000: Part II). In addition, we have seen the beginnings of a renewed interest in party functions (Dalton and Wattenberg 2000; Webb *et al.* 2002) and election strategies and campaigning (Bowler and Farrell 1992; Butler and Ranney 1992; Swanson and Mancini 1996; Norris 2000; Plasser with Plasser 2002). With the partial exception of an interesting collection of studies edited by Alan Ware (1987), however, a specific concern with the question of how parties perceive their changing electoral environments and how they learn to cope with these changes has largely gone untouched.

Of course, not all of the changes that political parties have gone through in the last two or three decades may be directly related to changes in the electoral markets as such (Strøm and Svåsand 1997). Other factors of influence include technological change, which allows new opportunities and modes of communication to become available to party campaign strategists; institutional change, as for example can be seen in the increasingly frequent examples of reforms to electoral laws or parliamentary structures; change in the status of parties, as for example when parties become subject to new regulatory systems or when they begin to acquire financial subsidies from the state; and changes in the political environment more generally, such as occurs when new patterns of coalition formation prove possible, or when new options for alliances and cooperation present themselves (for a valuable recent overview, see Luther and Müller-Rommel 2002). At the same time, however, at least some of these changes lie at least partly within the control of the parties, and in this sense these may also be at least indirectly associated with electoral change – particularly if electoral dealignment may have made life easier for some of the parties while making it more difficult for others. Accordingly, when we examine how parties have coped with the new electoral uncertainties, we will also pay attention to any institutional changes or to shifts in inter-party alignments that might be seen to constitute part of these responses. Before going on to map out a menu of these possible responses, however, we will first outline some of the key elements that might be involved in electoral change itself.

Changes in electoral markets

Changes in the electoral market obviously take very different forms and involve quite different sets of parameters. Indeed, a substantial share of the political science literature of the past two or three decades has been devoted to identifying what precisely is changing at the electoral level within the advanced industrial democracies, and how these changes might best be understood – in terms both of their origins and of their impact. The details of these debates need not concern us here. What is useful, however, and what can help us to appreciate the full range of responses that can be associated with the various political parties in the different European systems, is to specify the major categories of electoral change, and to link these to some of the key problems which then confront the parties (for a similar but more extended overview, see Dalton 2002).

Social structural change

The first and perhaps most visible form of electoral change which has been highlighted in recent years is that which derives from social structural change. This perspective takes as its starting point the traditional loyalties that have existed between specific social groups, such as blue-collar workers or farmers, on the one hand, and specific political parties, such as socialist or agrarian parties, on the other. It is economic development that has created these groups in the first place, and it is economic development again which is now associated with their disaggregation. More specifically, electoral change is linked to the numerical decline in traditional core party clienteles, and in particular to the declining electoral weight in recent years of farmers, the petty bourgeoisie, and the working class. In contrast, the share of white-collar employees in both the private and public sectors has increased dramatically, and what is most relevant here is that this 'new middle class' is considered to lack a *prima facie* loyalty to any political party. Thus, other things being equal, the changing class structure is seen to lead to a growth in the 'available electorate'. On the one hand, this obviously presents an opportunity for those parties that previously lacked strong support from specific social groups. On the other hand, those parties that were traditionally tied to specific social clienteles now find themselves facing a shrinking 'natural' support base. This need not necessarily spell the decline and decay of these parties, however. For although it was usually stable, their traditional electoral support on its own was often too narrow to permit the parties to achieve their political ambitions. Hence the numerical decline of their core groups may sometimes offer these parties the final stimulus that they require in order to break out of their previous electoral ghettos.

Structural dealignment

While the social structural change perspective proceeds from assumptions about cohesive social groups and about group loyalty to specific political parties, structural dealignment implies that these social groups lose their cohesion, with significant segments eventually turning their back on the parties they previously endorsed. Thus, for example, Catholics may no longer vote for

Christian democratic parties, and blue-collar workers may no longer express a preference for social democratic or communist parties. Indeed, it may even be the case that group members begin to vote for the party which was previously the principal opponent of their 'natural' representative or for parties which have only recently emerged, such as Green parties or neo-populist parties (see, for example, Kitschelt with McGann 1995). If these new patterns of support were to become stabilized, we could then speak of realignment; were they to remain relatively unpredictable, we would then speak of dealignment (Flanagan and Dalton 1984). There is little consensus in this discussion, however. While many authors have emphasized a decline in class and religious voting, and have pointed to the growth of what Franklin *et al.* (1992: 411–13) refer to as 'the particularization of voting choice' (see also Crewe and Särlvik 1983: ch. 3; Robertson 1984; Crewe 1983; Dalton *et al.* 1984; Dalton 2002), others have used a narrower definition of social class in order to indicate that the sense of decline has been exaggerated (see Heath *et al.* 1991; Goldthorpe 1996; Evans 1999).

Nevertheless, what is more or less agreed by all scholars is that parties can no longer take their traditional support for granted. Confronted by either a shrinking base of core voters, or by a more fragmented and instrumental constituency, these parties are obliged to develop new responses and new strategies. They may seek to undo the changes that confront them; or they may seek to adapt their appeals to a world in which traditional loyalties appear increasingly a thing of the past. Either way, and even within a context of relatively stable electoral outcomes, parties have become more aware that their support is more and more contingent, and hence that they have to work much harder and more carefully even to maintain their existing following.

Decline in party identification

The notion of party identification refers to voter alignments at the individual rather than group level, and, as initially developed in voting studies in the United States, seeks to measure the degree of psychological attachment to a specific political party. Typically, party identification was believed to be established at a relatively young age, and to become more pronounced over the individual's lifetime (Converse 1969). Moreover, the stronger the party identification, the more likely it was that the individual would remain a loyal partisan voter (Campbell *et al.* 1960: 120–8). If changes in the individual's party identification did occur, then this was likely to be associated with changes in his or her social circumstances, as, for example, might be the case when marriage, a new job, or a change of neighbourhood exerted a pressure on the individual to conform to the political values of a new environment (Campbell *et al.* 1960: 149–50). Although this notion of party identification is intuitively appealing, its usefulness within the context of the typical West European multi-party system has often been questioned. Moreover, unlike in the United States, the measurement of party identification in Europe has been frequently contested and many attempts at measurement have proved consistent neither across nations nor across time (for a good overview of this discussion, see Schmitt and Holmberg 1995: 96–100; for a recent attempt to propose a more standardized European measure, see Sinnott 1998).

Yet, despite all of the pitfalls involved in such comparisons, most authors do now accept that party identification in the majority of West European democracies has in fact declined (Schmitt and Holmberg 1995; Biorcio and Mannheimer 1995; Dalton and Wattenberg 2000; Dalton 2002: 183–9; Dalton *et al.* 2002). What this also implies is that there has been a growth in the size of the 'available electorate', and this in turn implies that many political parties will have become more vulnerable. In contrast, parties that traditionally lacked a sizeable number of identifiers may have experienced an enhancement of their competitive position. In any case, although a decline in the general levels of party identification need not automatically lead to changes in electoral behaviour, it is likely to have a profound impact on party behaviour. In particular, parties that recognize that the psychological ties between voters and specific parties are no longer as strong as they once were may be willing to take more risks when competing in the electoral market.

Changes in value orientations

Since the 1970s, an enormous body of literature has dealt with changes in citizens' value orientations, with the increase in post-material (or, more recently, post-modern) values receiving particular attention (see, for example, Inglehart 1977, 1990, 1997; Scarbrough 1995). But there is also ample recent evidence to suggest that those values which have accounted for the traditional divides in Western Europe have not wholly lost their relevance. As Knutsen (1995a) and many country studies have shown, for example, orientations along the religious–secular and the left–right materialist dimensions remain decisive for large numbers of voters when making their party choice. Moreover, while secularization is a more or less general European phenomenon, changes along the left–right materialist dimension have neither been uniform across all countries nor unidirectional in their effect (Jagodzinski and Dobbelaere 1995; Knutsen 1995b). Given the decline in social structure as an explanatory variable, however, van Deth and Scarbrough (1995: 527–8) tend to reflect the consensus among scholars in arguing for the increased 'primacy' of values as an explanation of political change in Western Europe. These latter authors conclude their wide-ranging analysis by emphasizing the problems which these changes pose for modern governments, in that 'the "new" value orientations bring new issues on to the agenda whilst the persistence of "old" orientations indicates that many of the old issues, especially the classic issues of inequality, are still not resolved'. They go on to add that 'modern governments have to find support among electorates which are more diverse in orientation. This makes it more difficult to put together the kind of broad consensus necessary to mount major policy initiatives' (van Deth and Scarbrough 1995: 535).

Admittedly, this situation is probably more difficult for governments – the major point of reference for van Deth and Scarbrough – than for political parties as such, at least as long as these remain within the electoral arena. After all, governments have to find working majorities that will allow them to survive and to govern effectively, while political parties as such may satisfy themselves with winning minorities of the electorate (which may or may not become part of a parliamentary majority or government coalition at a later stage of the game). That said, the spectacular increase in the 'heterogeneity of "value types"' (van Deth and Scarbrough 1995: 536) tends to make even this task more difficult, and tends to reduce the size of each of these minorities. The individual parties are therefore also obliged to cope with this new heterogeneity, and this means that they have to be more careful than ever in defining their target groups and, with the next election in mind, also in forming parliamentary or governmental coalitions.

Issue competition

In this perspective, political parties do not depend on 'natural' changes in the electorate but are seen instead to bring about these changes themselves. The requirement is that they identify new and winning issues, and that they then popularize these issues and position themselves accordingly. In this perspective, the parties' electoral alliances remain stable as long as the issue agenda and its underlying cleavages are also stable (Carmines 1991). Political parties which do not attract enough voters seek to remedy this failing by turning to new issues. If these issues appeal to new voters and do not divide the party's existing constituency, they can then lead to relevant shifts in the electorate (Riker 1986: 1). However, only a few issues can work in this way, and hence Riker (1986: 1) has ascribed an 'artistic creativity of the highest order' to those politicians who 'invent the right kind of new alternative' (see also Schattschneider 1960). In practice, of course, many new issues are simply organic extensions of old issues, and hence they may serve to reinforce existing conflicts and thereby to petrify existing electoral alliances (Carmines and Stimson 1993: 156). Moreover, even if a party does succeed in finding an issue which is not already part of the generic ownership of another party, this does not necessarily guarantee an impact on existing electoral alliances, since 'the vast majority of new issue proposals are bound to fail, striking an unresponsive chord in the mass public and leaving the current majority party's coalition intact' (Carmines and Stimson 1993: 154). Research on opinion formation suggests that voters as a rule do not have fixed positions in respect of (many) issues (Zaller 1992), and while they relate issues to their values, these themselves are often inconsistent. As Stimson (1995: 183) suggests, 'each citizen has a range of views, depending on which consideration is consulted, not a single fixed one, and that range tends to be large'.

According to this perspective, political parties are under permanent pressure. Those that fall short of satisfying their electoral ambitions will tend to search for new issues, but will often find themselves frustrated in this attempt. Parties that currently do well, however, have no reason to rest on their laurels. In order to avoid future defeat, these parties have to defend the importance of their old issues as well as to monitor developments that may bring new issues on to the agenda. They also therefore have to think ahead and to learn how to approach these issues in order to appeal to a large enough section of the electorate. These problems tend to become even more complex when two other considerations are borne in mind. First, when parties are obliged to think beyond the electoral arena alone and to consider the impact these issues and their respective positioning will have on future patterns of coalition formation. Secondly, when parties have to face the growing challenge posed by alternative agenda-setters, such as the new and often unpredictable social movements, as well as the increasingly important but also autonomous mass media. In the past, it can be argued, parties tended to have greater control over the political agenda, in that they also controlled a substantial component of the means of political communication. Nowadays, however, they are forced to confront a much greater diversity of agenda-setters, and in this sense they may be seen to be more re-active than pro-active.

Fluctuations between government and opposition parties

Changes in the electoral support for individual parties, as well as changes in the electoral market more generally, are also often explained by the relative status of incumbency and opposition. What is still unclear, however, is whether one is particularly to be preferred over the other, at least in electoral terms (see Rose and Mackie 1983). According to one set of hypotheses, for example, government parties should do well because of their capacity to manipulate the economy, their privileged media access, and, in most countries, their capacity to determine the date of elections (Strøm and Swindle 2002). Governing parties are also believed to benefit from their access to patronage. The opposing view, which predicts a negative incumbency effect, rallies even more arguments behind it. According to this view, government parties should suffer by being identified with all of the shortcomings of the administration, and will be punished for unpopular (though often necessary) policies. They will also receive more critical media attention. Although the empirical record tends to support this negative incumbency thesis (Rose and Mackie 1983; Müller and Strøm 2000), there are nevertheless important variations. In Ireland, for example, every single election between 1973 and 1997 brought about a change of government. In Germany, on the other hand, the advent of the Red–Green coalition in 1998 marked the first complete alternation in power since 1949, with most of the intervening elections even resulting in gains for the then governing coalitions (Mitchell 2000; Saalfeld 2000). Moreover, there is much within-country variation in the electoral fortunes of government and opposition parties, and most actors are neither automatically punished nor rewarded for either of the two roles.

What is perhaps most important here, however, is that the boundaries between government and opposition can become blurred. Contemporary governments in Western Europe sometimes tend to change through reshuffling, with parties which were in opposition joining others which were in government to produce new sets of alliances, and with many new parties, most notably Green parties, gaining access to office for the first time. Parties are therefore faced with new challenges in the division of government and opposition roles, and are increasingly obliged to develop their strategies in a much more flexible fashion. For this reason also, they find themselves observing the electoral markets more closely, and having to devote more time to interpreting the often confused and confusing signals that are sent by these markets (Sarcinelli 1998).

Crisis of party

A crisis of party would obviously reflect the most fundamental source of changes in the electoral markets. The notion of a 'crisis of party' is itself multi-faceted (Daalder 1992, 2002), of course, and within the increasingly voluminous literature devoted to this theme it has been taken to mean almost anything. For our purposes, what is important here is when the parties that make up a party system are seen to fail to perform the functions considered essential to political parties in a democratic polity. In this context, the linkage function is clearly crucial (Lawson and Merkl 1988), in that parties serve principally to link the citizenry to the political institutions and the decision-making processes and to permit these to function in an accountable fashion. Hence, if citizens feel unable to choose a party that will allow them to express their political preferences and to exercise a meaningful influence in the polity, we may indeed face a 'crisis of party'. This problem may be exacerbated by high barriers to entry, thus making it difficult to revive 'party' by introducing new competitors. One possible consequence of such a crisis would be a decline in electoral participation: if *all* politicians are rascals, it does not really make sense to vote one set of them out of office only to allow an alternative set to take their place. Standard indicators of electoral volatility and the erosion of partisan affiliation might also be symptomatic of such a crisis, but, as with changing levels of voter turnout, these may in fact occur for wholly different reasons, and, in any case, it is often difficult to distinguish such symptoms from those associated with the evidently less dramatic processes of electoral dealignment (e.g. Reiter 1989: 327). On the other hand, if we can find over time the development of more cynical views on political parties as well as an increasing share of negative voters, that is voters who end up voting for what they regard as the lesser evil, then this would perhaps indicate, or at least make more plausible, the notion of a crisis of party.

While empirical work has tended to be sceptical concerning a general crisis of party in Western Europe (Reiter 1989; Andeweg 1996; Poguntke 1996), signs of such a crisis became more evident in the 1990s (Mair 1998). The recent

Italian case is obviously the most prominent example of such a claim, but it also seems that similar trends can be seen in other countries, and most particularly in Austria and Belgium. What is also striking is the extent to which neo-populist parties and/or parties of the extreme Right, in Austria, the Netherlands, and Belgium, as well as in France, have linked their familiar anti-immigrant platforms to a more generalized assault on what they see as the failings of the established political class. Parties which claim to recognize signs of a crisis of party in their polity will have every incentive to respond to this phenomenon, and the attempts by individual parties to regain credibility in these circumstances will also depend on other parties being successful in this respect. Responses may therefore range from party-specific solutions, such as the abandonment of 'brand names' that are associated with a bad reputation, or even the abandonment of the label of 'party' as such (it is interesting to note, for example, that none of the major 'parties' in contemporary Italy now labels itself as a 'party'), to more system-wide responses, such as may be seen in various institutional reforms or in a variety of changes to the electoral system.

Party responses

Parties obviously have a large menu to choose from when determining how they will respond to the various electoral changes, and among the different polities, as the subsequent chapters testify, and even among the different parties in any given polity, a wide range of responses can be seen. In an effort to bring some initial clarity to this otherwise complex pattern, this section will attempt to map out the range of dimensions along which party responses can be arrayed, and to include within these some of the more typical examples of the party strategies which make up these responses.

Before that, however, two qualifications need to be underlined. First, if we are to assess how parties respond to changes in the electoral markets, we must first understand how parties have perceived these changes. Perception necessarily precedes response, and however compelling the evidence of change might be to the outside observer, it is also possible that this has simply passed unnoticed by the party strategists themselves. Alternatively, what may seem largely irrelevant or ephemeral to the outside analyst may have proved a matter of great import to the parties concerned. These varying perceptions may even extend to the difference between victories and defeats, in that what the observer might view as having been a largely successful strategy may be seen as a relative failure by some of the protagonists involved. For example, it is difficult to interpret the various institutional and electoral reforms that were introduced by the new British Labour government in its first years of office as indicative of contentment with what appears to have been an overwhelming electoral victory. If anything, they are more symptomatic of a sense of vulnerability, which, at first sight, might seem difficult to reconcile with a party that had recently received such a record parliamentary majority.

Perceptions therefore matter, and one of the key problems which was faced by the authors of the analyses included in this volume was precisely that of identifying how the parties themselves perceived the changes that were so apparent to the authors.

Secondly, while the changes in electoral markets may be classified and catalogued, and while the full range of possible responses by parties may be mapped out in advance, not all of these will acquire a similar weight in each different system, or even in each different party. Although this volume is devoted to the common ground of Western Europe, the institutional and party systemic characteristics of the various polities differ quite markedly. Moreover, within these polities, the parties also differ, and hence their perception of changes, as well as their responses, are likely to vary quite significantly. Indeed one of the more important questions which can be addressed to this volume as a whole concerns the extent to which both perception and response vary by country as opposed to by party type or by party family. In this sense it is also interesting to observe how particular changes are deemed to pose problems in certain countries or for certain parties, but not in others, and how in some cases these changes cause parties difficulties, whereas in others they simply mark opportunities.

The non-response

For both of these reasons, we sometimes witness parties simply choosing not to respond to what we can identify as 'objective' changes in the electoral market. On the one hand, the parties may be unaware of these changes, or of their import. On the other hand, and perhaps more commonly, they may simply deny their significance. There may be good grounds for such a non-response. In less competitive systems, for example, the ebb and flow of a party's electoral support may make little difference in the long term, unless, that is, this implies the risk of a sustained decline. In other words, parties can get used to living with a (limited) degree of electoral change. Parties may also find themselves in strategically pivotal positions, and hence need not necessarily rely on sustaining or even increasing a given level of electoral support in order to remain a key actor in government. Among the various analyses that are included in this volume, we can find quite a number of examples of parties which might easily be deemed complacent, and which, at various points in time, simply brush off the experience of electoral loss or the sense of electoral vulnerability. Either this is seen to make little difference in practical terms – the party will still remain in government, for example – or it is seen as a temporary phenomenon, with what is lost on the electoral swings being capable of later recovery on the roundabouts. What we also witness, of course, and this is sometimes the most interesting phenomenon, is a rude shattering of such complacency, and a sometimes frantic if belated attempt to respond to changes which have already become well established.

Organizational responses

Party organization

When parties do choose to respond to changes in the electoral markets it is often by first seeking to reform their internal organization. Among the most obvious kinds of change at this level is a renewed emphasis on organizational profession-alization, by which the 'amateurs' (who are recruited from the mass organization) are replaced by 'professionals' (who are employed on the basis of expertise) (Mancini 1999). Such changes are often associated with a belief that there is nothing inherently wrong with the party; rather, it is simply failing to adequately communi-cate its message. We see these reforms applying in particular to such fields as cam-paigning, media relations, and the more technocratic aspects of organizational reform (e.g. computerization). Improved mass media relations are also obviously important here. A second approach to organizational reform may involve either decentralization (moving party decision-making closer to the supporters on the ground) or centralization (basing party decisions more on professional experience, e.g. pollsters, media experts, etc., and hence nationalizing electoral strategy). Parties may also respond to changes in the electoral markets by introducing changes in their internal power distribution. These can include new methods of candidate selection which are introduced with the intention of recruiting more attractive candidates and/or to afford more leeway to the party leadership.

Candidates

In a related vein, parties may respond to changes in the electoral markets by recruiting different types of candidates, as for example when parties place more emphasis on nominating media personalities rather than candidates who are drawn from the party organization itself. They may also simply change their candidates more frequently. On the one hand, parties may apply a trial and error strategy, proving more willing to deselect sitting MPs who do not conform to the parties' expectations, particularly in a context where new challenges are presented by the electoral market. On the other hand, the recruitment of new faces may be seen as advantageous in itself. This may help the party to cope with more a volatile electoral environment, for example, and it may also help stave off potential problems which derive from anti-party sentiment. In other words, the parties may be keen to demonstrate a greater openness to society at large, and a greater willingness to engage in party renewal. We may therefore find that turnover among candidates and MPs tends to increase, even leaving aside the inevitable turnover which follows from electoral defeat.

Strategic responses *vis-à-vis* voters

Political parties may also respond to the new electoral uncertainties by rethink-ing their electoral target groups. This may involve appealing to new groups of voters – either newly defined groups, as for example often followed in the wake of the repoliticization of women's issues in the 1970s – or to existing groups which were previously seen as falling largely outside the party's electoral catchment area. Analytically, we may distinguish between the *replacement* of old target groups by new ones, and the *addition* of new target groups. Alternatively, parties may decide not to appeal to new groups of voters but instead to aim at an *intensification* of their ties to their traditional target voters. What does seem clear from the analyses in this volume and elsewhere is that parties still think largely in terms of groups of voters rather than individual voters. Voter choice may have become more particularized (Franklin *et al*. 1992: 406–31), but, albeit sometimes in a very narrow sense, party electoral strategies continue to be built upon appeals to categories of citizens – the young, the old, single parents, working mothers, the new urban middle class, and so on. Where contemporary responses differ from traditional strategies is first, in this very narrowing of the target group involved; secondly, in rarely taking the support of any one group for granted; and thirdly, in often attempting to build a broad base of support by aggregating these specific group appeals.

Strategic responses *vis-à-vis* other parties

Political parties may respond to changes in electoral markets by redefining their relations with their other competitors (cf. Sjöblom 1968: 180–2). In particular, they may reconsider which specific parties they see as their main competitors. At the tactical level, parties may decide to concentrate on targeting enemies in their campaigns (negative campaigning). In this case, parties are still primarily interested in winning votes, although targeting is also likely to have an impact on inter-party relations once the votes have been counted. Political parties may also apply the opposite strategy, attempting to make friends and allies among some of the other parties. This may range from mutual non-aggression pacts during election campaigns, to electoral alliances (with or without the prospect of forming government coalitions after the elections), to party mergers. Two contextual features are obviously relevant here. The first concerns the electoral system, since with certain systems (such as the German additional member system, the French double ballot system, or the Irish single transferable vote) electoral agreements can yield a substantial gain in terms of the distribution of parliamentary seats. The second is the increased flexibility and even promiscuity which is apparent in coalition formation, and which now affords each party a greater range of strategic options (Mair 1997: 223). Indeed, provided that there are enough parties in the party system, individual parties can apply all of these strategies simultaneously.

Programmatic, ideological, and policy-oriented responses

It also goes almost without saying that political parties may respond to changes in the electoral markets by changing their policy positions. One obvious option here is to try to follow the moves of voters on the various dimensions which structure party competition. Parties may try to incorporate 'Green' issues in their programmes and policy positions, for example, or they may try to reposition themselves in terms of the classic left–right materialist dimension (cf. Müller 1994). More generally, and as with the targeting of groups of voters, parties may move between a more sectorally specific approach and a catch-all approach. Alternatively, parties which had already transformed themselves into catch-all parties in the earlier postwar period may later come to believe that a catch-all strategy is no longer viable under the changed conditions of party competition, and they may therefore choose to concentrate more on their traditional core groups and on their 'classic' policy positions. Another option, of course, would be to push the catch-all strategy to its extreme, abandoning all commitments to relatively coherent programmes, and following instead the mass media agenda in trying to build more *ad hoc* issue coalitions.

What also has a strong bearing on programmatic and policy position-taking (as well as on party organization and party–voter linkages) is the party's relationship with interest groups. One of the important features of Kirchheimer's (1966) notion of the catch-all party was that this type of party would begin to build up relations with a *variety* of interest groups. The complement to this process would be the weakening of the traditional ties to specific interest groups, as for example occurs when social democratic parties develop an arm's-length approach to trade unions. Unlike trade unions, however, there are many interest groups in Western Europe which are not in decline, and hence links to these groups can begin to prove advantageous to the parties. The new social movements are of obvious relevance here, as are many of the more *ad hoc* public interest protest movements, and parties will often attempt to win additional support by piggy-backing on their popularity. Although such groups are not necessarily accessible to all parties, they can appeal to two or more parties (Dalton 1994: ch. 9), and hence they may offer a new source of contention in the competing party strategies.

Institutional responses

Party responses to electoral change and uncertainty may also take the form of the promotion of institutional reform (Müller 2002). To begin with, parties may seek to change the rules of the electoral game, which, in Sartori's (1968: 273) terms, involves tackling 'the most specific manipulative instrument of politics'. As Taagepera and Shugart (1989: 4) later put it, when compared to other components of political systems, 'electoral systems are the easiest to manipulate with specific goals in view'. The same purpose can be served by more indirect means. These include manipulating the rules of state party finance and party access to public sector media. As Katz and Mair (1995) have suggested, the established parties may opt to use these and other resources of the state in order to shield themselves from the consequences of electoral defeat and from threats posed by the electoral market more generally. Institutional change may also be of a less manipulative kind, however. Parties feeling pressures from the electoral market may respond by attempting to further democratize their polities, for example. As Scarrow (1997: 468) has noted of the German case, 'politicians have many reasons to support changes that are symbolically benevolent ("extending democracy") and financially costless'. Regardless of the motivation, however, it is only very rarely that parties can hope to effect such changes through unilateral action (Müller 2002: 270–82). These proposals are usually advanced on the basis of an all-party – or, at least, multi-party – consensus, which itself often derives from a sense of widespread party crisis, and hence they need not necessarily be seen to promote a particular partisan advantage. In the recent British case, for example, it is interesting to note that Labour's various and far-reaching proposals for constitutional change have been deliberately developed in cooperation with the Liberal Democrats.

The plan of the book

All of these various responses, as well as others which are too specific to incorporate within this general mapping, can be witnessed in the country-based studies that are included in this volume. In order to keep the project more manageable we have deliberately not aimed at covering the full range of democracies in Western Europe. Rather, we have selected eight countries for illustrative and in-depth coverage. These countries include the four 'major' democracies (Britain, France, Germany, and Italy) as well as four smaller democracies. With respect to the second category, we have aimed at both a reasonably broad geographic coverage and a selection of intuitively interesting cases – Austria, Belgium, Denmark, and Ireland. Nor have we aimed at completeness in terms of party coverage in each of these eight countries. Instead we have opted for a middle way somewhere between the in-depth case study of a single party and a more general 'party system' approach. In practice, this means that we have asked the individual authors to focus on just two to three key parties. Naturally, the chapters concentrate on the 'established' parties, which are parties with an organizational identity of their own, which have long played an important role within the system concerned. At the same time, however, each chapter does include sufficient background material to allow the reader to place these parties in their party systems and institutional environments.

Each of the subsequent chapters follows a more or less common structure. The chapter begins with an outline of the basic features of the party system and those of the parties involved (their electoral strength, the patterns of government coalitions, etc.). This is followed by a summary of the key changes in the electoral markets in which we have been obliged to steer a middle way between presenting data which are strictly comparable throughout all countries and making use of data which are available only for specific countries. Each of our contributors has compiled a standard table which presents electoral results (percentage of votes, number of seats) for the time period covered in the chapter as well as the following standard measures or indices: electoral fractionaliza-tion (Rae 1971), the effective number of parties (Laakso and Taagepera 1979), total electoral volatility (Pedersen 1979, 1983), and turnout (as a percentage of the potential total electorate).[2] Most chapters contain a table on voter loyalties. If available, this table includes the following data: party identification (macro partisanship, i.e. voters who are closer to one party than to others or who iden-tify with one party), the intensity of party identification (i.e. potential voters with strong, moderate, or weak party identification), party shifters (i.e. voters who have voted for different parties in two subsequent elections), non-partisans or anti-partisans (i.e. potential voters who do not like any of the parties running in elections or who reject the whole range of parties which make up the party system), and negative voters (i.e. voters who vote for the lesser evil or who do not have positive feelings towards any party but vote against a particular party or group of parties). While it has proved impossible to report consistent cross-national data on most of these measures, our contributors have tried to compile data that are consistent within each country or, where necessary, have docu-mented changes in the wording of questions. Some chapters also contain a sum-mary table on the changing party composition of government, listing the party composition and changes in party affiliation of the head of government.

As noted above, our concern in dealing with changes in the electoral markets is not only with the nature of these changes, but also with how the parties have perceived these changes. This is obviously a necessary link between measuring the objective changes in the electoral environment and the parties' responses to these changes (cf. Müller 1997; Müller and Strøm 1999). Where possible, therefore, the chapters aim at the reconstruction of party perceptions: When did the parties perceive changes in the electoral markets as a relevant phenomenon? How were these changes perceived – as a threat or as an opportunity? How much attention did the parties give to these changes in the electoral markets? Were there different opinions within the parties about the relevance of these phenomena and the need to respond? Were there different opinions within the parties about the appropriate response strategies? And to what extent do the parties in any given system, or even across different systems, learn from one another?

In addition, each chapter attempts to distinguish between changes which appear to affect only one party as opposed to those which affect some or all parties, and in this way party responses and potential electoral threats are seen within the context of the party system as a whole, as well as being potentially comparable across countries. As is more than apparent in the various chapters, changes that bode very ill for a party in one country might well be simply ignored by a party in another country, while within a given country even potentially generalized changes may be read – and hence responded to – very differently by the different parties. In this sense, a party's position within its party system, as well as the character of the party system itself, constitutes a very powerful intervening variable. Finally, the bulk of the individual chapters is devoted to an analysis of how the selected parties have responded to the changes which have taken place in the respective electoral market. In conducting this analysis, the authors of the chapters have proceeded from the general mapping of potential party responses that is presented above. They also attempt to go beyond this by assessing the degree of success or failure associated with these strategies.

What follows, therefore, is an in-depth analysis of the ways in which parties have perceived the changes in their electoral markets, and of the ways in which they have sought to respond to these changes. Each chapter offers a rounded picture of the development of party strategies in contemporary Western Europe, whether these be electoral strategies, governmental strategies, organizational strategies, or, as is the case even for some of the more established traditional parties, simply survival strategies. What follows is an insight into how parties interact with one another, and with the voters, and by providing this the chapters offer a valuable understanding of the nature of contemporary West European party systems and the likely scenarios for their future development.

Notes

1 See, *inter alia*, Pedersen (1983), Dalton *et al.* (1984), Crewe and Denver (1985), Franklin *et al.* (1992), Schmitt and Holmberg (1995), Biorcio and Mannheimer (1995), Dalton and Wattenberg (2000), Dalton (2002), Mair (2002).

2 The Pedersen index has been calculated according to the operational rules adopted by Bartolini and Mair (1990: 311–12).

References

Andeweg, Rudy (1996). 'Élite–Mass Linkages in Europe: Legitimacy Crisis or Party Crisis?' In Jack Hayward (ed.), *Élitism, Populism, and European Politics*. Oxford: Clarendon Press, pp. 143–63.

Bartolini, Stefano and Peter Mair (1990). *Identity, Competition, and Electoral Availability. The Stabilisation of European Electorates 1885–1995*. Cambridge: Cambridge University Press.

Biorcio, Roberto and Renato Mannheimer (1995). 'Relationships between Citizens and Political Parties.' In Hans-Dieter Klingemann and Dieter Fuchs (eds), *Citizens and the State*. Oxford: Oxford University Press, pp. 206–26.

Bowler, Sean and David Farrell (eds) (1992). *Electoral Strategies and Political Marketing*. Basingstoke: Macmillan.

Broughton, David and Mark Donovan (eds) (1999). *Changing Party Systems in Western Europe*. London: Pinter.

Butler, David and Austin Ranney (eds) (1992). *Electioneering: A Comparative Study of Continuity and Change*. Oxford: Clarendon Press.

Campbell, Angus, Philip E. Converse, Warren E. Miller, and Donald Stokes (1960). *The American Voter*. New York: John Wiley.

Carmines, Edward G. (1991). 'The Logic of Party Alignments.' *Journal of Theoretical Politics* 3: 65–80.

Carmines, Edward G. and James A. Stimson (1993). 'On the Evolution of Political Issues.' In William H. Riker (ed.), *Agenda Formation*. Ann Arbor, MI: University of Michigan Press, pp. 151–68.

Converse, Philip E. (1969). 'Of Time and Partisan Stability.' *Comparative Political Studies* 2: 139–71.

Crewe, Ivor (1983). 'The Electorate: Partisan Dealignment Ten Years On.' *West European Politics* 6 (4): 183–215.

Crewe, Ivor and Bo Särlvik (1983). *Decade of Dealignment*. Cambridge: Cambridge University Press.

Crewe, Ivor and David Denver (eds) (1985). *Electoral Change in Western Democracies*. London: Croom Helm.

Daalder, Hans (1992). 'A Crisis of Party?' *Scandinavian Political Studies* 15: 269–88.

Daalder, Hans (2002). 'Parties: Denied, Dismissed, or Redundant? A Critique.' In Richard Gunther, José Ramón Montero, and Juan Linz (eds), *Political Parties. Old Concepts and New Challenges*. Oxford: Oxford University Press, pp. 39–57.

Daalder, Hans and Peter Mair (eds) (1983). *Western European Party Systems. Continuity and Change*. London: Sage.

Dalton, Russell J. (1994). *The Green Rainbow. Environmental Groups in Western Europe*. New Haven, CT: Yale University Press.

Dalton, Russell J. (2002). *Citizen Politics*. Chatham, NJ: Chatham House.

Dalton, Russell J. and Martin P. Wattenberg (eds) (2000). *Parties without Partisans*. Oxford: Oxford University Press.

Dalton, Russell J., Scott C. Flanagan, and Paul Allan Beck (eds) (1984). *Electoral Change in Advanced Industrial Democracies. Realignment or Dealignment?* Princeton, NJ: Princeton University Press.

Dalton, Russell J., Ian McAllister, and Martin Wattenberg (2002). 'Political Parties and their Publics.' In Kurt Richard Luther and Ferdinand Müller-Rommel (eds), *Political Parties in the New Europe*. Oxford: Oxford University Press, pp. 19–42.

Evans, Geoffrey (ed.) (1999). *The End of Class Politics? Class Voting in Comparative Context*. Oxford: Oxford University Press.

Flanagan, Scott C. and Russell J. Dalton (1984). 'Parties under Stress: Realignment and Dealignment in Advanced Industrial Societies.' *West European Politics* 7 (1): 7–23.

Franklin, Mark, Tom Mackie, Henry Valen, *et al.* (1992). *Electoral Change. Responses to Evolving Social and Attitudinal Structures in Western Countries*. Cambridge: Cambridge University Press.

Goldthorpe, John H. (1996). 'Class and Politics in Advanced Industrial Societies.' In David J. Lee and Bryan S. Turner (eds), *Conflicts about Class: Debating Inequality in Late Industrialism*. London: Longman.

Heath, Anthony, Roger Jowell, John Curtice, Geoff Evans, Julia Field, and Sharon Witherspoon (1991). *Understanding Political Change. The British Voter 1964–1987*. Oxford: Pergamon Press.

Inglehart, Ronald (1977). *The Silent Revolution*. Princeton, NJ: Princeton University Press.

Inglehart, Ronald (1990). *Culture Shift*. Princeton, NJ: Princeton University Press.

Inglehart, Ronald (1997). *Modernization and Postmodernization*. Princeton, NJ: Princeton University Press.

Jagodzinski, Wolfgang and Karel Dobbelaere (1995). 'Secularization and Church Religiosity.' In Jan W. Van Deth and Elinor Scarbrough (eds), *The Impact of Values*. Oxford: Oxford University Press, pp. 76–119.

Katz, Richard S. and Peter Mair (eds) (1992). *Party Organizations*. London: Sage.

Katz, Richard S. and Peter Mair (eds) (1994). *How Parties Organize*. London: Sage.

Katz, Richard S. and Peter Mair (1995). 'Changing Models of Party Organization and Party Democracy: The Emergence of the Cartel Party.' *Party Politics* 1 (1): 5–28.

Katz, Richard S. and Peter Mair (2002). 'The Ascendancy of the Party in Public Office.' In Richard Gunther, José Ramón Montero, and Juan Linz (eds), *Political Parties. Old Concepts and New Challenges*. Oxford: Oxford University Press, pp. 113–35.

Kirchheimer, Otto (1966). 'The Transformation of Western European Party Systems.' In Joseph LaPalombara and Myron Weiner (eds), *Political Parties and Political Development*. Princeton, NJ: Princeton University Press, pp. 177–200.

Kitschelt, Herbert with Anthony J. McGann (1995). *The Radical Right in Western Europe.* Ann Arbor, MI: University of Michigan Press.

Knutsen, Oddbjørn (1995a). 'Party Choice.' In Jan W. Van Deth and Elinor Scarbrough (eds), *The Impact of Values.* Oxford: Oxford University Press, pp. 461–91.

Knutsen, Oddbjørn (1995b). 'Left–Right Materialist Value Orientations.' In Jan W. Van Deth and Elinor Scarbrough (eds), *The Impact of Values.* Oxford: Oxford University Press, pp. 160–96.

Laakso, Markku and Rein Taagepera (1979). '"Effective" Number of Parties.' *Comparative Political Studies* 12: 3–27.

Lawson, Kay and Peter H. Merkl (eds) (1988). *When Parties Fail.* Princeton, NJ: Princeton University Press.

Luther, Kurt Richard and Ferdinand Müller-Rommel (eds) (2002). *Political Parties in the New Europe.* Oxford: Oxford University Press.

Mair, Peter (1997). *Party System Change. Approaches and Interpretations.* Oxford: Oxford University Press.

Mair, Peter (1998). 'Representation and Participation in the Changing World of Party Politics.' *European Review* 6: 161–74.

Mair, Peter (2002). 'In the Aggregate: Mass Electoral Behaviour in Western Europe, 1950–2000.' In Hans Keman (ed.), *Comparative Democratic Politics.* London: Sage, pp. 122–40.

Mair, Peter and Gordon Smith (eds) (1990). *Understanding Party System Change in Western Europe.* London: Frank Cass.

Mancini, Paolo (1999). 'New Frontiers in Political Professionalism.' *Political Communication* 16: 231–45.

Mitchell, Paul (2000). 'Ireland: From Single-Party to Coalition Rule.' In Wolfgang C. Müller and Kaare Strøm (eds) (2000). *Coalition Governments in Western Europe.* Oxford: Oxford University Press, pp. 126–57.

Müller, Wolfgang C. (1994). 'Political Traditions and the Role of the State.' *West European Politics* 17 (3): 32–51.

Müller, Wolfgang C. (1997). 'Inside the Black Box: A Confrontation of Party Executive Behaviour and Theories of Party Organizational Change.' *Party Politics* 3: 293–13.

Müller, Wolfgang C. (2002). 'Parties and the Institutional Framework.' In Kurt Richard Luther and Ferdinand Müller-Rommel (eds), *Political Parties in the New Europe.* Oxford: Oxford University Press, pp. 249–92.

Müller, Wolfgang C. and Kaare Strøm (eds) (1999). *Policy, Office, or Votes? How Political Parties in Western Europe Make Hard Decisions.* Cambridge: Cambridge University Press.

Müller, Wolfgang C. and Kaare Strøm (eds) (2000). *Coalition Governments in Western Europe.* Oxford: Oxford University Press.

Norris, Pippa (2000). *A Virtuous Circle. Political Communications in Postindustrial Societies.* Cambridge: Cambridge University Press.

Pedersen, Mogens N. (1979). 'The Dynamics of European Party Systems: Changing Patterns of Electoral Volatility.' *European Journal of Political Research* 7: 1–26.

Pedersen, Mogens (1983). 'Changing Patterns of Electoral Volatility in European Party Systems, 1948–1977: Explorations in Explanations.' In Hans Daalder and Peter Mair (eds), *Western European Party Systems: Continuity and Change.* London: Sage, pp. 29–66.

Pennings, Paul and Jan Erik Lane (eds) (1998). *Comparing Party System Change.* London: Routledge.

Plasser, Fritz with Gunda Plasser (2002). *Global Political Campaigning. A Worldwide Analysis of Campaign Professionals and Their Practices.* Westport, CT: Praeger.

Poguntke, Thomas (1996). 'Anti-Party Sentiment – Conceptual Thoughts and Empirical Evidence: Explorations into a Minefield.' *European Journal of Political Research* 29: 319–44.

Rae, Douglas W. (1971). *The Political Consequences of Electoral Laws.* New Haven, CT: Yale University Press.

Reiter, Howard L. (1989). 'Party Decline in the West. A Sceptic's View.' *Journal of Theoretical Politics* 1: 325–48.

Riker, William H. (1986). *The Art of Political Manipulation*. New Haven, CT: Yale University Press.

Robertson, David (1984). *Class and the British Electorate*. Oxford: Basil Blackwell.

Rose, Richard and Thomas T. Mackie (1983). 'Incumbency in Government: Asset or Liability?' In Hans Daalder and Peter Mair (eds), *Western European Party Systems: Continuity and Change*. London: Sage, pp. 115–37.

Saalfeld, Thomas (2000). 'Germany: Stable Parties, Chancellor Democracy, and the Art of Informal Settlement.' In Wolfgang C. Müller and Kaare Strøm (eds), *Coalition Governments in Western Europe*. Oxford: Oxford University Press, pp. 32–85.

Sarcinelli, Ulrich (1998). 'Parteien und Politikvermittlung. Von der Parteien- zur Mediendemokratie.' In Ulrich Sarcinelli (ed.), *Politikvermittlung und Demokratie in der Mediengesellschaft*. Opladen: Westdeutscher Verlag, pp. 273–96.

Sartori, Giovanni (1968). 'Political Development and Political Engineering.' In John Montgomery and Albert O. Hirschman (eds), *Public Policy XVII*. Cambridge, MA: MIT Press, pp. 261–98.

Scarbrough, Elinor (1995). 'Materialist–Postmaterialist Value Orientations.' In Jan W. Van Deth and Elinor Scarbrough (eds), *The Impact of Values*. Oxford: Oxford University Press, pp. 123–59.

Scarrow, Susan E. (1997). 'Party Competition and Institutional Change. The Expansion of Direct Democracy in Germany.' *Party Politics* 3: 451–72.

Schattschneider, E. E. (1960). *The Semi-Sovereign People*. New York: Holt, Rinehart and Winston.

Schmitt, Hermann and Sören Holmberg (1995). 'Political Parties in Decline?' In Hans-Dieter Klingemann and Dieter Fuchs (eds), *Citizens and the State*. Oxford: Oxford University Press, pp. 95–133.

Sinnott, Richard (1998). 'Party Attachment in Europe: Methodological Critique and Substantive Implications.' *British Journal of Political Science* 28: 627–50.

Sjöblom, Gunnar (1968). *Party Strategies in a Multiparty System*. Lund: Studentlitteratur.

Stimson, James (1995). 'Opinion and Representation.' *American Political Science Review* 89: 179–83.

Strøm, Kaare and Lars Svåsand (eds) (1997). *Challenges to Political Parties. The Case of Norway*. Ann Arbor, MI: University of Michigan Press.

Strøm, Kaare and Swindle, Stephen M. (2002). 'Strategic Parliamentary Dissolution.' *American Political Science Review* 96: 575–91.

Swanson, David L. and Paolo Mancini (eds) (1996). *Politics, Media, and Modern Democracy*. Westport, CT: Westview Press.

Taagepera, Rein and Mathew Soberg Shugart (1989). *Seats and Votes*. New Haven, CT: Yale University Press.

Van Deth, Jan W. and Elinor Scarbrough (1995). 'Perspectives on Value Change.' In Jan W. Van Deth and Elinor Scarbrough (eds), *The Impact of Values*. Oxford: Oxford University Press, pp. 527–40.

Ware, Alan (ed.) (1987). *Political Parties. Electoral Change and Structural Response*. Oxford: Basil Blackwell.

Webb, Paul, David M. Farrell, and Ian Holliday (eds) (2002). *Political Parties in Advanced Industrial Democracies*. Oxford: Oxford University Press.

Zaller, John R. (1992). *The Nature and Origins of Mass Opinion*. Cambridge: Cambridge University Press.

TWO   Party Responses to the Changing Electoral Market in Britain

Paul Webb

Since 1970 many of the traditional orthodoxies about the British party system have come under challenge. This challenge is based on various interconnected developments that have emerged during this period. These include a number of high volatility general elections; partisan and class dealignment; the emergence of nationalist cleavages in Scotland and Wales, which have threatened to fragment the national political culture; the erosion of two-party electoral domination; the apparent fracturing of the postwar policy consensus by the early 1980s; and the growing chorus of criticism levelled at the damaging iniquities of the electoral system and the adversarial 'winner-takes-all' political mentality that was, for many commentators, closely associated with it.

How have the major parties responded to this challenge? This study will focus on their organizational and strategic responses to the erosion of partisan support. In essence, I shall be arguing that the onset of partisan dealignment has produced a more extensive process of party competition for votes, and this shift in the environment in which British parties operate has fostered their development into organizations which loosely approximate classic models of the electoralist party (Kirchheimer 1966; Panebianco 1988). Thus, both major parties in Britain are now similar to the extent that: (1) they have been obliged by the erosion of partisan loyalty to focus increasingly on competing for support among 'available' voters, rather than reinforcing traditional appeals to 'voters of belonging'; (2) they have relatively high levels of leadership autonomy; (3) they have thoroughly professionalized their approaches to election campaigning and political marketing; (4) they have looser relations with specific interest groups than hitherto.

Electoral dealignment and the erosion of voter loyalties

The British party system between 1945 and 1974 was strongly two-party in character.[1] A number of key features characterized the operation of the system in this period. First, Labour and the Conservatives absorbed the overwhelming majority of votes cast at general elections, their combined support not dipping below 87.5 percent until February 1974 (see Table 2.1). Secondly, elections produced single-party majorities. This was true of all general elections during the period 1945–70, though majorities did vary in size, and the narrow victories achieved in 1950 and 1964 prompted further elections shortly after the original polls. Thirdly, there was alternation in government. Between 1945 and 1970, the Conservatives and Labour each won four elections. Moreover, the Conservatives were in power for thirteen years and Labour for twelve. This is not to say that the swing of the electoral pendulum was precisely metronomic: the Conservatives' thirteen-year spell in power comprised a single unbroken incumbency between 1951 and 1964, while Labour's experiences in government occurred either side of this period. Nevertheless, the changes of government took place regularly enough to constitute a pattern of genuine alternation. Fourthly, the reasonably lengthy periods in office enjoyed by both parties also contributed an element of stability to the development of public policy, it being widely acknowledged that this period saw a broad consensus around Keynesianism and the development of a comprehensive welfare state.

The impression of a frozen party system that successfully expressed and channelled all significant political demands was undermined after 1970 as a series of new social and political challenges beset the major parties. These challenges were either based on issues and political conflicts that potentially cut across existing patterns of electoral alignment, or had the effect of generally undermining the electorate's trust in both major parties. Typical of the latter challenge was the broad issue of relative national economic decline, which became increasingly vexed from the mid-1960s and has remained on the agenda ever since (see Gamble 1985; Sked 1987; Coates 1994; Hutton 1995). The widespread perception of weak economic performance almost certainly undermined the confidence of large parts of the electorate in both major parties (see Webb 1996).

Moreover, long-established class-based alignments have been tested by new conflicts which cut across the class cleavage. These include the sectoral cleavage, which is contingent upon the development of the activities and responsibilities of the state since 1945 and has fostered a number of interconnected lines of differentiation between public and private sectors (Dunleavy 1979, 1980; Dunleavy and Husbands 1985); and the (re)emergent centre–periphery cleavages which have given rise to the phenomena of Scottish and (to a lesser extent) Welsh nationalism since 1970 (Miller 1983). We might also note that the capacity of the issue of European integration to further dislocate voters from parties should not be overlooked; although there is little direct evidence that such an effect has occurred yet, it is clearly an increasingly vexed question in British politics and we should not be blind to its potential (Evans 1999).

The February 1974 general election provided a new scenario for the postwar British party system and seemed to many observers to signify, amongst other things, the onset of new levels of electoral instability. It was characterized by the return of a minority Labour government and a surge in third party support. The Liberals in particular made progress, achieving 19.3 percent of the vote, a

Table 2.1 British general election results since 1945

	Conservative		Labour		Lib/Lib.Dem.*		Others		Fract.	Effective number of parties	Volatility	Turnout
	Vote	Seats	Vote	Seats	Vote	Seats	Vote	Seats				
1945	39.8	213	48.3	393	9.1	12	2.7	22	0.60	2.52	NA	72.8
1950	43.5	299	46.1	315	9.1	9	1.3	2	0.59	2.40	3.9	83.9
1951	48.0	321	48.8	295	2.5	6	0.7	3	0.53	2.13	7.2	82.6
1955	49.7	345	46.4	277	2.7	6	1.1	2	0.54	2.16	2.4	76.8
1959	49.4	365	43.8	258	5.9	6	0.9	1	0.56	2.28	3.2	78.7
1964	43.4	304	44.1	317	11.2	9	1.3	0	0.60	2.53	6.0	77.1
1966	41.9	253	47.9	363	8.5	12	1.7	2	0.59	2.42	4.2	75.8
1970	46.4	330	43.0	287	7.5	6	3.1	7	0.59	2.46	5.9	72.0
1974 (Feb.)	37.8	297	37.1	301	19.3	14	5.8	23	0.68	3.13	14.5	78.8
1974 (Oct.)	35.8	277	39.2	319	18.3	13	6.7	26	0.68	3.16	3.0	72.8
1979	43.9	339	37.0	269	13.8	11	5.3	16	0.65	2.87	8.1	76.0
1983	42.4	397	27.6	209	25.4	23	4.6	21	0.71	3.45	11.6	72.7
1987	42.3	376	30.8	229	22.6	22	4.4	23	0.70	3.33	3.2	75.3
1992	41.9	336	34.4	271	17.8	20	5.8	24	0.67	3.03	5.2	77.7
1997	30.7	165	43.3	419	16.8	46	9.3	21	0.69	3.21	12.3	71.5
2001	31.7	166	40.7	413	18.3	52	9.3	28	0.69	3.25	2.6	59.5

*Liberal–SDP Alliance in 1983 and 1987. 'Fract' refers to Rae's fractionalization of the vote index (Rae 1971). 'Effective number' refers to Laakso and Taagepera's index of the effective number of parties in a system (calculated by vote rather than number of seats: Laakso and Taagepera 1979).

postwar high and a considerable leap from the 7.5 they won in 1970. As a result, the Conservatives and Labour together only managed to win 75 percent of the popular vote, a notable fall from the levels achieved at previous elections. While the disproportional effects of the electoral system continued to limit the parliamentary representation of minor parties, at the level of the electorate the party system began to take on a more fragmented appearance after 1974, as indicated by a rise in both the fractionalization index and effective number of parties (see Table 2.1). The emergence of minor parties from this time has presented Labour with a particular problem, in that parties such as the Liberal Democrats (and, prior to 1988, their predecessors, the Liberals and the Social Democratic Party [SDP]) and the Scottish National Party (SNP) have occupied similar ideological territory (which is to say, broadly centre-left and libertarian). This has served to generate a greater variety in the patterns of party competition found at constituency level, and in so doing especially intensified the pressure on Labour, by presenting it with challenges from both right and left (Webb 2000: 78–9).

There are further indications confirming the growth of electoral instability after 1970. For example, Pedersen's (1979) index of net volatility (Table 2.1), though not presenting evidence of any kind of secular trend since 1945 as a whole, does show how the elections of February 1974, 1979, 1983 and 1997 were relatively high-volatility affairs compared to the postwar norm. More to the point, if we can take these to be the only high-volatility elections in the post-war era, then it is notable that they all occur in the post-1970 period. However, partisan erosion within the electorate can be more directly gauged by measuring levels of partisan commitment. Whilst the proportion of partisan identifiers did not alter radically after 1964, the strength with which partisanship was expressed certainly appeared to shrink considerably. Thus, in the period from 1964 to 1970 the proportion of 'very strong' partisans in the electorate was stable at around 44 percent, but this fell to an average 26 percent in the two elections of 1974. This downward trend continued so that by 1987 less than one-fifth of the electorate claimed a very strong partisan allegiance (see Table 2.2). It is notable, moreover, that while the overall proportion of electors maintaining a Conservative Party identification held up relatively well during the 1980s, both major parties were subject to this loss of very strong partisans. This is highly significant for the question of voter loyalty, for very strong partisans are considerably more likely to vote for 'their' party than other members of the electorate are at general elections. That is, those who still retain clear partisan identities and loyalties are far less susceptible to the game of party competition in the short span of an election campaign. In this light, it is possible to suggest that only those lacking definite partisan commitment constitute the real voter market around which parties can conduct their competitive strategies. This is confirmed by the 1997 British Election Survey data, which show that some 95 percent of 'very strong' partisans voted for the party for which they declared an allegiance; by contrast, only 88 percent of 'fairly strong' partisans did so, and just 78 percent of 'not very strong' partisans (n = 2667). Clearly, very

Table 2.2   Voter loyalties in Britain, 1964–2001 (percent)

	1964	1966	1970	1974 (ave.)	1979	1983	1987	1992	1997	2001
With partisan identification	93	91	90	90	90	86	86	86	91	84
Identifying with Conservatives	38	35	40	35	38	38	37	35	30	22
Identifying with Labour	43	46	42	40	38	32	30	33	46	45
Total Cons. + Labour identifiers	81	81	82	75	76	70	67	68	76	67
Very strong identifiers	44	44	42	26	22	26	19	17	16	15
Fairly strong identifiers	38	38	37	40	46	38	40	40	42	46
Not very strong identifiers	11	9	11	14	23	22	27	29	33	38
No identification	7	9	10	10	10	14	14	14	9	16
Party shifters[†]	18	NA	16	24*	22	23	19	19	25	25

[†]"Party shifters" refers to the overall percentage of electors eligible to vote at consecutive elections who switch parties from one election to the next.
*The 1974 figure is for the February election only.

Sources: Crewe 1992: 143; Crewe *et al.* 1995: 47; Heath *et al.* 1991: 20; British Election Studies 1987, 1992, 1997, 2001. I gratefully acknowledge the ESRC Data Archive for supplying the 1987–97 data sets, and the Directors of the British Election Study (BES) for the 2001 data set.

strong partisanship virtually precludes the possibility of electoral 'disloyalty', but anything less than this leaves greater scope for effective party competition. In short, and inevitably so for a party losing four consecutive general elections, Labour certainly faced the more serious problems after 1974, but even during an era of electoral dominance, the Conservatives were not immune to the phenomenon of partisan erosion. The outcomes of the 1997 and 2001 elections confirm this point and suggest that it is the Conservatives who currently confront the most serious problems of partisan erosion.

Overall, the growth of dealignment and electoral choice in many constituencies means that the UK's electoral market has become more 'open' than it was in 1970. This is not necessarily to say that electoral competition is more *intensive* now, but rather that it is more *extensive*. Viewed from an aggregate-level perspective the outcome of general elections in the UK has always depended on the inter-party battles fought in the minority of seats which are 'marginal'; from an individual-level perspective, the outcome has always been defined by competition for the support of those voters whose electoral choices are not shaped by predetermined partisan loyalties or habits. In effect, these are two different perspectives on the open or available sector of the electoral market-place, and there is no reason to believe that the contest for available voters has not always been very keen. But what has changed over time is the sheer size of this sector: a greater proportion of voters are dealigned and more constituencies are marginal.[2] Hence, the extension of the electoral market-place in the UK.

Party perceptions

How did the parties themselves perceive the phenomenon of partisan erosion and its causes? There is little doubt that they are broadly aware that party competition in the electoral market-place has become more extensive since 1970, and that there has been a need for a higher level of sophistication and flexibility. While the parties do not always use the same data as professional academics, they have for some time exploited to the full a growing body of their own privately commissioned opinion research data which will often convey similar messages about rates of electoral loyalty and volatility.

It is helpful to emphasize that the parties' organizational and strategic responses to partisan erosion depend largely upon their perceptions of what causes it. A variety of theses has been advanced to help explain partisan erosion, including the new 'cognitive mobilization' which is supposedly built upon the twin pillars of expansion of higher education and mass access to television, and deemed by some to facilitate the growing political independence of electors (Barnes *et al.* 1979; Dalton 2001: 31–4). That is, voters become better able to assess information about public affairs without having to rely on party cues (thanks to the role education plays in developing their intellectual skills), at precisely the time that they have far greater access to independent sources of non-partisan information (from the broadcast media). If true, this may go a long way towards explaining the growing difficulty that parties have in controlling the changing issue agenda of politics. More to the point, however, it helps us understand why both major parties in Britain have adopted newly 'professionalized' approaches to political marketing via the televisual medium. As we shall see, parties have responded to the growth of more open electoral competition in Britain partly by perceiving voters as relatively independent political actors who must be communicated with chiefly through the medium of television.

The cleavage changes we discussed above could in themselves, of course, also constitute an important source of electoral instability. In particular, many commentators have interpreted partisan dealignment as a direct corollary of class dealignment in voting patterns; given that partisan and class identities were so closely bound together in the two-party, two-class system, it is inevitable that the weakening of one must affect the other. Quite why class dealignment has occurred – and indeed, the extent to which it has occurred – has been a vexed question in British political science since the 1970s (for an insight into the debate about class dealignment in Britain see Crewe 1983; Heath *et al.* 1985, 1987; Crewe 1986; Dunleavy 1987). The emergence of new centre–periphery and sectoral cleavages can in itself go some of the way towards explaining class dealignment since such cleavages cut directly across class identities. In addition, a number of other factors have been suggested, from the embourgeoisement of the increasingly affluent working class after 1960 (Abrams *et al.* 1960; Goldthorpe *et al.* 1968), to the growth of mixed-class households (Marshall *et al.* 1988: 134), and the physical decomposition of class-typical communities (Hobsbawm 1981).

This phenomenon of class dealignment has particularly exercised the minds of Labour's strategists. While writers like Herbert Kitschelt have taken pains to emphasize that such social trends need not necessarily consign left-of-centre parties to a path of inevitable electoral decline and marginalization (Kitschelt 1993, 1994), there is no doubt that Labour's leaders and strategists have been acutely aware of the shrinking of its traditional 'core' constituency since the 1960s at least. This awareness has been closely linked to broad internal debates about party policy and strategy, and since the mid-1980s the centre Left's interpretation has gradually reassumed its customary dominance within the party, though in the early 1980s a more radical left-wing view temporarily held sway. Generally speaking, this radical position was based upon a definite class ideology, while the centre Left or social democratic position tends to emphasize the need for class alliances founded on a broad social appeal. In the 1960s Harold Wilson famously asserted that this social breadth would transform Labour into the 'natural party of government'. We shall examine this question of strategic response in greater detail below.

It should be said that questions of strategic manoeuvring and the breadth of electoral appeal have become increasingly bound up with the emergence of minor parties since 1970. For there is little doubt that centre parties, which in truth are centre Left parties in the British case (that is, either social democratic or social liberal: Jones 1996), have become serious competitors of Labour in particular. This was amply illustrated by the 1983 election: when Labour's leadership shifted the party's policy and image sharply to the left, the new SDP–Liberal Alliance (now the Liberal Democrats) benefited electorally by occupying the ideological territory vacated by Labour. The result of this was that Labour's new leadership came to regard the subsequent election in 1987 not as a battle for control of the government – victory was already ceded – but as a battle for control of the opposition (Hewitt and Mandelson 1989: 54; Gould *et al.* 1989: 86). That is, the party's strategists perceived the very real threat of Labour being permanently supplanted by the Alliance as a major party, a perception which conditioned Labour's ideological response. More recently, Labour's strategy *vis-à-vis* the Liberal Democrats suggests an increasingly coalitional approach to dealing with minor parties. After the 1997 election Tony Blair created a special inter-party cabinet committee on constitutional reform on which both Labour and Liberal Democrat politicians sat. Moreover, Lib–Lab coalitions eventually emerged in the newly devolved (and proportionally elected) administrations in Scotland and Wales.

In recent years, the Liberal Democrats have come to pose an increasing strategic challenge for the Conservatives. Mired in a seemingly inescapable electoral depression, the Tories find themselves under serious pressure from the Liberal Democrats, often their main competitors in battles at constituency level. The Liberal Democrats talk openly of seeking to replace the Conservatives as the main party of opposition to Labour, and believe they can do so by distancing themselves from the governing party in a variety of ways (for instance, withdrawing from the joint cabinet committee and criticizing it over the war in

Iraq and for poor performance on public services). Note that this stance does not entail an ideological move to the centre Right (into classic Conservative territory), so much as an attack on Labour over 'valence issues'. Though Labour might be the primary focus for such criticism, it is a strategy designed principally to displace the Conservatives by attracting disaffected former Tory voters (Webb 2003).

And it is not only the Liberal Democrats who have complicated life for the major parties. The emergence of centre–periphery cleavages has also required a response. Thus, intensified centre Left competition from Scottish and Welsh nationalists has generated an addition to Labour's policy agenda in the shape of a commitment to new forms of devolved government for Scotland and Wales. This first became apparent in the 1970s when the minority Labour government led by Jim Callaghan sought to appease SNP and Plaid Cymru parliamentarians by holding referendums on devolution proposals. But the need to restrict the advance of the nationalists – especially in Scotland – did not diminish with Labour's return to opposition during the 1980s and 1990s. Indeed, if anything, it increased as the SNP replaced the Conservatives as the second party north of the border. In this context, it is not surprising that Labour's commitment to devolution deepened in the long period of opposition between 1979 and 1997; back in power, the party wasted little time in piloting legislation through parliament which established a Scottish Parliament in Edinburgh and a Welsh Assembly in Cardiff.

The process of adaptation in the era of partisan erosion and more open electoral markets has entailed organizational change as well as policy development. For Labour it should be noted, such development has not followed a simple linear pattern since the 1970s. For many years, the best that professional political marketing had to offer was eschewed by the party. In part this flowed from sheer financial necessity, since Labour has rarely been in a position to match the Tories for resources, but in part too it reflected a visceral distrust of sharp-suited marketing professionals. This sentiment was never so prevalent within the Conservative Party, and Labour has therefore faced the greater challenge in adapting. The disastrous 1983 election campaign – ideologically pure, but weak in terms of party, leadership and policy images, and amateurishly marketed – marked the nadir of Labour's postwar electoral fortunes, and it most clearly embodied the problems that the party faced in coming to terms with the new era. Between the elections of 1983 and 1987, the party took the first steps towards electoral-professional adaptation under the leadership of Neil Kinnock. After another election defeat, the pace of reform picked up. It continued after the subsequent election defeat of April 1992, and achieved a resounding endorsement in the triumphant outcome of the May 1997 election. These reforms, as we shall see, embrace shifts in policy, organizational change and modified relations with external organizations, but at this stage it is interesting to presage our analysis by stating clearly that this process of adaptation (some might say transformation) has been quite deliberate and self-conscious. The painful experience of four consecutive general election defeats, and nearly two decades' exclusion from national office engendered a determination on the part of one leader after another (Kinnock, the late John Smith and then Tony Blair) to effect the reforms that they believed to be necessary, and the impact of a number of key party strategists, advisers and professional consultants has now been well documented (see, for instance, Hughes and Wintour 1990; Webb 1992; Shaw 1994), and indeed, frequently parodied, so emblematic have they become. Their impact on policy development (as well as presentation), organizational centralization, the standardization and professionalization of campaigning, and even the party's relationship with its affiliated trade unions, is clear for all to see.

The Conservatives have generally effected a far smoother transition to the modern era of open competition. Despite their obvious connections with propertied classes and social elites, since the time of Benjamin Disraeli the party has also been capable of sustaining a broad popular appeal. This has been founded largely on its status as the party of the nation (and empire). Moreover, there is evidence to suggest that it has long since been open to the idea of exploiting all the latest techniques of mass communication and campaigning (see p. 32 below). And there is no doubt that one of the party's defining characteristics in the twentieth century has been its commitment to the pursuit of power. All of this means that the Conservative Party was for a long time essentially an organization that was well placed to adapt to the challenge of declining voter loyalty and heightened party competition. In a sense, it was not required to change anything fundamental in the way it perceived the game of politics or the pursuit of power: it was always primarily a vote-maximizing and office-seeking organization, and throughout its history has demonstrated a willingness to adapt policy and strategy in order to achieve these goals. Moreover, it was demonstrably able to fashion electoral appeals which spoke to a broad social constituency.

This is not to deny that it too appeared vulnerable in the 1970s, and that changes were deemed necessary by the new leadership team gathered around Margaret Thatcher. We have already noted, for instance, the decline in highly committed partisanship that affected the Tories as much as Labour at the time. Thus, while 50 percent of Conservative identifiers claimed their allegiance was 'very strong' in 1970, only 29 percent did so in 1974, and just 16 percent by 1992 (Crewe *et al.* 1995: 47). This emphasizes the contingent nature of support that even an electorally 'dominant' party manages to sustain in the modern era. In addition, it must not be overlooked that the Conservatives lost four out of the five general elections held in the decade between 1964 and 1974. That party strategists perceived a need for policy development and greater sophistication in political marketing is certain, and they duly succeeded in forging the changes required to deliver a generation in power. What is interesting about the changes wrought under Thatcher is that they contrast with Labour to the extent that strategic debate was conditioned less by the perception of class cleavage decomposition than by that of national policy failure. As I have implied, in seeking to maintain its political relevance in the 1950s, the Conservative Party became a willing partner to the Keynesian-welfarist-mixed economy consensus which endured over a quarter of a century or more. Yet by the mid-1970s the party's strategists saw that the Tories as much as Labour had become electorally vulnerable as a result of the various manifestations of failure which by then had afflicted the consensus policy model (stagflation, growing public debt, industrial unrest and an unpopular public sector). The Thatcherite response was consequently driven by the need to distance the party from the established policy consensus. Aided by the temporary implosion of the opposition, this strategic and organizational response was enough to earn the party a widely admired reputation as an electoral force. It is ironic, therefore, that at the time of writing the Conservative Party is confronted by one of the most profound crises in its history, a crisis which will require skilled leadership, organizational reform and finely balanced policy adaptations. It is perhaps more ironic still that its famed pragmatism and flexibility in pursuit of broad popular appeal now seems to have given way to a sectarian ideological impulse which distances it from the median voter (Webb 2003).

Party organizational responses to partisan erosion and electoral dealignment

The major parties in Britain have been obliged to adapt to the challenge of partisan erosion at two main levels: organization and policy. In this section I shall focus on the first of these, and in the next I shall consider the second. In a sense there is a connection between the two, in that party organizational reforms have often been motivated by the desire to enhance the policy-making autonomy of the leadership. This means that organizational reform can impinge on policy development. One way of understanding this is through the lens of party competition theory. In the simplified logic of most models of party competition, political parties are understood as unitary actors, though in reality of course this is seldom true. Thus, even if party leaders do have a clear notion of the policy positions their parties need to adopt in order to achieve vote-maximizing or office-seeking objectives, they may well be thwarted by the vagaries of intra-party conflict. Seen in this light, the organizational reforms brought on by the era of extended electoral competition have often been about the attempt to make the parties more 'unitary' by enhancing the autonomy of the leaders at the expense of backbenchers and extra-parliamentary actors. In this way leaders afford themselves the capacity for maximum strategic flexibility in playing the game of party competition. In tension with this, however, has been the growing pressure from grass-roots movements and groups (such as the Campaign for Labour Party Democracy in the 1980s and the Conservatives' Charter Group) for the democratization of intra-party affairs. Thus, it is not hard to find examples of organizational changes which have served to empower members in recent years, but it is important to understand that such reforms have rarely enhanced membership power in the sphere of policy-making. Party leaders wish to reserve this domain to themselves as far as possible, in order to maximize their scope for strategic manoeuvre when playing the game of party competition. This growing autonomy of leaders is an important aspect of a more candidate-centred, 'presidential' style of leadership that has been emerging (Poguntke and Webb, 2005, forthcoming).

Prior to the 1997 general election, organizational response was most obvious in the case of Labour, for whom such reform has been almost as significant a component of the party's 'modernization' process as programmatic change itself. Indeed, it could be argued that modernization is not far short of transformation of the party into an 'electoral-professional' organization (Panebianco 1988). There are a number of organizational strands to this transformation.

First, Labour's leaders since Neil Kinnock (1983–92) have sought to *enhance their autonomy* to manoeuvre according to the demands of party competition. In part this has been effected through decisive actions designed to emphasize their authority on issues of great symbolic significance (Kinnock's battle to expel Trotskyist entryists in the 1980s; John Smith's campaign to reform the role of affiliated trade unions in the party in 1993; Tony Blair's rebellion against the traditional constitutional commitment to public ownership of industry in 1995); and in part it has been achieved through the creation of new party organs and agencies which serve as powerful devices of strong leadership. These agencies have been most obvious in the field of election campaign strategy and management (Hughes and Wintour 1990; Webb 1992). However, more radical innovations emerged in the 1990s, including the new policy commissions and a National Policy Forum (NPF) which have further reduced the real policy role of the (formally sovereign) annual party conference. In early 1997 the leadership introduced a set of proposals designed to take this approach to reform much further. Deriving from interaction between the party's National Executive Committee (NEC) and the Cranfield School of Management, *Labour into Power* (Labour Party 1997) proposed a new two-year 'rolling programme' for policy formulation. While these proposals (endorsed by the 1997 annual conference) certainly allow for input by individual members, local branches and their representatives, the rolling programme approach enshrines a powerful role for the leadership. The main institutional vehicle for the leadership in the policy-making process is the Joint Policy Committee (JPC), which comprises members drawn from the government and the NEC. The JPC shapes the initial agenda and terms of reference for detailed consideration by policy commissions and the NPF; the results of policy deliberation are then fed back to the JPC and/or NEC at a number of points in the process, and the latter drafts the final policy recommendations which go before conference (Labour Party 1997). Thus, although the party conference remains nominally sovereign, its agenda is fundamentally determined by a process of which the party elites are likely to remain in control. To be sure, this is not necessarily a system that offers the membership a *less* meaningful policy role than hitherto. The leadership may well find that the various provisions for rank-and-file input serve to delimit the parameters within which policy innovation can take place; indeed, this is something it might even welcome, but the point is that the leadership leads with respect to policy, and at least as much as it ever did.

Furthermore, in 1996 Blair introduced a referendum of all party members on what he promised would become the main features of the forthcoming election manifesto. This device, rarely deployed hitherto, offered members the chance to state a simple 'yes/no' answer to the question of whether they would support the overall package of policies likely to be included in the formal manifesto. The referendum followed a national series of 'Road to the Manifesto' rallies and events at which the leadership campaigned for its position in the spring and summer of 1996. The position was emphatically endorsed by the membership, but the process itself was not without its critics. Indeed, it is hard to avoid the conclusion that there was something of the plebiscitary model of democracy about the whole exercise: the 'charismatic leader' bypassed the constitutional organs of policy-making, including the party's formal legislature, in order to address directly the mass membership, offering it a crude choice between support and opposition for something that was relatively bland and uncontentious to the progressive mind. Many radically minded critics would argue that while what was on offer was not necessarily in itself unsupportable, there was a real problem over what was excluded from the package. This exercise in plebiscitary democracy was not repeated prior to the 2001 election, but then the party leadership always has greater authority when in office rather than opposition.

Secondly, a growing *professionalization* of the way that the party markets itself has been apparent, and this has increasingly been perceived to be critical to Labour's electoral prospects. This professionalization has entailed the use of senior party employees with professional backgrounds in the mass media, advertising or public relations (Webb and Fisher 2003); a commitment to far greater investment in and reliance upon the findings of opinion research (especially in opposition); and a more standardized approach to national campaigning, with overarching emphasis on the requirements of televisual communication (Shaw 1994: chs 3, 6; Scammell 1995; Kavanagh 1995; Lees-Marshment 2001). In the 1997 election campaign the professionalization of Labour's political marketing reached new heights (Webb 2000: 157–8), though in the years since New Labour came to power this development has attracted criticism from those who regard it as symptomatic of a party lacking clear political convictions. That said, it is clear that in the wake of Tony Blair's adamant insistence that the UK should support America's war in Iraq, even in the face of hostile public opinion, some of these assertions look simplistic, to say the least. Apparently, the exigencies of government leave less scope for focus group influence than do those of opposition.

Thirdly, there have been a number of moves to *enhance the roles and rights of individual party members* since the late 1980s (for instance, in candidate selection and leadership election, not to mention the 'Road to the Manifesto' referendum). Though these moves clearly constitute significant steps towards party democratization, we should not overlook the fact that they were almost certainly designed initially as a method by which the parliamentary leadership could dilute the influence of constituency activists who were perceived to be radical – which brings us back to the theme of leadership control once again. Although a genuine desire to offer new incentives to ordinary members has been evident, it has been tempered by the aforementioned concern not to cede too much policy-making initiative to the rank and file.

To reiterate, then, growing leadership autonomy and the professionalization of political marketing have been key elements of Labour's organizational response to the problem of partisan erosion, and approximate closely to Panebianco's model of the electoral-professional party which recognizes the need for certain kinds of transformation if it is to adapt successfully to the reality of an increasingly competitive and fluid market for votes.

Until the electoral débâcle of 1997, the Conservative Party indulged far less in the business of organizational reform simply because it has had far less obvious need to do so. Its internal structure and distribution of power was always such that the leadership was afforded a good deal of autonomy, though we should take care not to represent it as irretrievably authoritarian (Kelly 1989). It has long been the orthodox view that the Conservative Party is essentially an oligarchy – if not a monarchy – with few formal pretensions to internal demo-cracy. The leader has often been referred to as the font of policy and authority within the party. This would seem to befit a party with cadre-caucus origins and a long history of defending a non-egalitarian social and political order.

Following the shock of the 1997 election defeat, however, the leader's first reflex was organizational rather than policy-oriented. In part this no doubt reflects the persisting sense of division and confusion which the party found itself in with regard to policy. But there was also a real conviction, emanating from the new leader William Hague and running through all levels of the Conservative Party, that its organizational structure, constitution and campaign operations had been left behind by Labour's own innovations in these respects. For many Conservatives Labour had therefore set a standard to be consciously emulated. Few, if any, would have suggested that such reform was a sufficient condition of the party's future revival, but none would have doubted that it was a necessary condition. Thus, Hague's *Fresh Future* reforms were suffused with the rhetoric of participation and democratization, as they declared the bold intention to 'build the single greatest mass volunteer party in the Western world' (Conservative Party 1998: 1). They introduced, among other things, a national membership structure (something hitherto lacking), new rights of involvement in leadership selection for individual members, and a number of reforms in the area of party finance (see Conservative Party 1997; Webb 2000: 195–9).

With respect to political marketing, the Conservatives were the original pioneers of the art in a British context. Indeed, this readiness to adapt to the needs of professional political marketing is hardly a new feature of the party (Cockett 1994: 577). The Conservatives have shown a willingness to employ professional agencies since the 1920s, but the era of partisan erosion and the arrival at the helm of Margaret Thatcher in the 1970s generated a new degree of investment in these methods. The role of the Saatchi and Saatchi advertising agency has attracted an enormous amount of attention over the years, and is widely regarded as having heralded a new age of professionalization in British political campaigning (although it took Labour the best part of a decade to follow suit). While parties had used advertising professionals before, the Saatchis were original in being the first to assume full-time control of all aspects of publicity and opinion research, and in being paid a retainer between elections. This enabled them to work with the leadership on long-term campaign strategies. Their sustained relationship with the party was later supplemented by the introduction of new public relations and marketing approaches to the staging of annual conferences, direct mailing of targeted supporters, telephone canvassing and computer-aided communications.

Policy and strategy responses to partisan erosion and electoral dealignment

What of programmatic adaptation in the era of intensified electoral competition? Until 1970, rates of class and partisan alignment were relatively stable and high in Britain, which tends to suggest that the major parties were able to follow 'sectoral' strategies of party competition designed to appeal to the traditional class-linked identities of supporters in the electorate. In fact, this was always a simplification of reality, given the usual distribution of voter preferences in Britain (essentially bell-shaped in left–right terms, as we shall see) and the dominant two-party pattern of competition which was entrenched by the effects of the electoral system. It is evident, for instance, that the Conservative Party's remarkable record of electoral success in the twentieth century was contingent upon its capacity to forge an appeal to a large section (generally around one-third) of the working class. In order to maintain this appeal in the 1950s and 1960s the party was obliged to adapt to the new realities of the popular welfarist and full employment programme that Labour championed in the era of postwar reconstruction. Similarly, Labour had cause and ample opportunity to reflect on the limits of a narrow class-constrained strategy when the Conservatives succeeded in keeping them out of power between 1951 and 1964. This was the first time that Labour's strategists were concerned about the possible structural decline of the working class, or at least, of its distinctive way of life (Abrams *et al.* 1960; Goldthorpe *et al.* 1968). Thus, when Harold Wilson became Prime Minister in 1964, Labour was already a party aware of the need to maintain – or even to build – a broad social appeal if it was to assume the desired role of 'the natural party of government'. This was reinforced by the phenomenon of class and partisan dealignment in the 1970s and 1980s: if parties such as Labour were to avoid a fate of inevitable and structurally determined decline, then they would clearly have to be prepared to think hard about competitive strategy, and to find ways of maintaining inter-class electoral appeals – a classic dilemma for class-left parties (Esping-Andersen 1985). The

Kirchheimer (1966) model of the catch-all party seemed to be of obvious relevance.

This was all the more true for the fact that in Britain the simple Downsian logic of party competition has often seemed highly apposite. Many discussions of the country's dominant pattern of two-party competition seem to conform to a single-peaked normal distribution of voter preferences, as does the basic Downsian model (Downs 1957). Moreover, other competitive strategies are either irrelevant in the British case, or are compatible with the Downsian vote-maximizing strategy, and therefore do not undermine it. For instance, the vote-maximizing and office-seeking goals that parties might have to choose between under conditions of multi-party competition and multi-polar voter preferences become compatible with one another. In multi-polar competition, a party locating itself near the median voter will certainly be pursuing a rational office-seeking strategy by aiming to become the 'pivotal' party crucial to the formation of any coalition government, but it will not necessarily be locating itself in the best ideological space for maximizing its vote (see Kitschelt 1994: 125–8). A further strategy open to parties under conditions of multi-polar competition is that which Kitschelt refers to as the 'oligopolistic' manoeuvre in which major parties deliberately move away from the median voter in the short term in order to obliterate significant competitors which threaten to outflank them; however, this is simply irrelevant in Britain given that since 1945 there have been no significant competitors to the left of Labour or to the right of the Conservatives, and the system has therefore lacked centrifugal pulls on the major parties.

It might be argued that models based on the ideological proximity of parties to the median voter are generally irrelevant, since there is evidence to suggest that electoral behaviour is more strongly conditioned by valence considerations. That is, voters are driven by evaluations of the performance of governing parties (or projected performance of opposition parties) in respect of policy goals which enjoy a wide degree of consensus. Macro-economic performance is the most obvious and heavily researched of these valence considerations (Fiorina 1977). However, we cannot afford to dismiss parties' strategic manoeuvres in policy space. While it is certainly true that valence issues do matter to British voters – and probably more so in the context of these class-dealigned times – broad political principles matter too, and to a considerable extent (Webb 2000: Table 5.1). Indeed, even for voters who are primarily orientated towards parties and their leaders in valence terms, ideological factors are probably not irrelevant, for parties seen as 'extreme' will lack credibility. That is, such competitors for office are unlikely to be trusted to govern in a competent or wise manner. This being the case, we may assume that it is safe to discuss the development of party strategies in the era of partisan erosion in terms of the basic logic of Downsian competition: British two-party competition takes place in the context of voter preferences which are single peaked, and ranged along an ideological dimension which is overwhelmingly, though not exclusively, defined by the conflict between socialism and capitalism (Webb 2000: ch. 4). In this light, what are the main features of major party competition during the era of partisan erosion?

Perhaps the most widely held view of party ideological development in contemporary Britain is that the relatively high degree of policy consensus which existed between the major adversaries until the 1970s was fractured as both Labour and the Conservatives became more extreme in the early 1980s, only for a period of reconvergence – albeit further to the right along the ideological spectrum – to emerge after 1990. Moreover, Labour's renewed pursuit of the median voter has brought the party even closer to the left-of-centre Liberal Democrats on many issues, a situation which creates possibilities both for greater competition and/or cooperation between the two. How have these developments occurred, and how do they reflect responses to eroding voter loyalties?

When the erosion of voter loyalties first started to become evident during the 1970s, it was undoubtedly the Conservatives who were best placed to exploit certain shifts in voter opinion which characterized the period. Thus, in the decade following 1974 Ivor Crewe noted 'a spectacular decline in support for the collectivist trinity of public ownership, trade union power and social welfare' (Crewe 1985: 138), even among Labour supporters. Between 1974 and 1979, for example, there was a virtual doubling of the percentage of the electorate in favour of more privatization of state-owned industry, mirrored by a corresponding decline in the percentage preferring further nationalization. Similarly, between February 1974 and 1979 the proportion of voters regarding trade unions as 'too powerful' increased from two-thirds to three-quarters, while the numbers feeling that the provision of state welfare had 'gone too far' increased from one-third to one-half of all electors (Webb 2000: 128).

It is not easy to determine the extent to which the new Thatcherite agenda of privatization, trade union emasculation and welfare retrenchment which was evolving throughout this period was a conscious strategic response to the erosion of partisan loyalty on the part of the Conservative Party. To some degree it may simply have been a happy, but unsurprising coincidence of party and voter attitudinal shifts, given the growing problems of the Labour governments of 1974–79. On the other hand, the Conservative Party must take some credit, for either reacting to the changes it perceived in the electorate, or possibly even for actively stimulating those changes. After all, as the Labour government's leading critic in the late 1970s, the Conservative leadership was able to articulate a position on issues such as the way in which the Callaghan administration handled the economy and the unions; the financial liabilities and industrial strife associated with the nationalized industries; and the spiralling welfare costs and taxes of the day. These lines of criticism provided an obvious point of reference for public discontent and a potential catalyst for opinion change at the mass level.

Indeed, the question of the 'preference-shaping' capacity of British parties was accentuated by the accession to power of the Conservatives in 1979. Commentators on the Left and Right alike gave considerable attention to the thesis that the Conservatives sought to exploit state power by introducing policies which would undermine some of the key structural bases of Labour's electoral support. In particular, the Thatcher governments' 'popular capitalism' measures (for instance, the sale to tenants of publicly owned housing, and the mass flotations of equity in state-owned corporations) were held to have altered decisively the economic interests of some of Labour's most traditional supporters, and thereby to have succeeded in changing the structural constraints within which party competition operates. If true, this would constitute a highly significant piece of strategic and long-term thinking by a party reacting to the new electoral market-place which was opening up in the context of partisan erosion. Research suggests that the popular capitalism strategy could have boosted the Conservative Party's share of the vote by as much as 1.2 percent in 1992, and assuming these effects to have been evenly distributed throughout the country (a considerable but a necessary simplification), this could well have made the difference between majority and minority governing status (Garrett 1994: 118–21).

Nevertheless, we must take care not to exaggerate the Conservative Party's capacity for strategic manipulation of the electorate, for there is considerable evidence to suggest that, despite its acknowledged professionalism in opinion research, the party has actually drifted away from the median voter on a number of key issues. In fact, this was already becoming evident in the 1980s. For instance, by 1983, the shock of the recession of 1980–81 (in which one-third of the manufacturing capacity of the country was eliminated) was enough to reorientate voters' minds on the issue of welfare benefits, and by 1987 there were clear signs that the allure of both privatization and the assault on the unions was waning. Indeed, by 1992 there was, for the first time in decades, a majority perception that unions were not too powerful, and an overwhelming majority opposed further privatization (Webb 2000: 128). Of course, these changes do not necessarily mean that the electorate as a whole changed its mind about the shift against the 'collectivist trinity' in the early 1980s: as many commentators have suggested, it could simply be that voters recognized and welcomed the achievements of the Thatcher governments but felt that enough was enough by the mid- or late 1980s. Ivor Crewe even speaks of a 'crusade that failed' to engender an enduring shift in popular attitudes (Crewe and Searing 1988).

Clearly, however, the right-wing thrust of public policy was maintained by Conservative governments after the mid-1980s. The privatization programme continued (after a brief respite occasioned by the stock market crash of October 1987), and while trade union legislation and welfare reform was rather more limited after this time, Britain also witnessed such innovations as the introduction of new forms of market-type mechanisms in the health service, local government and the civil service. In narrow vote-maximization terms, this almost seemed to bespeak a perverse contempt for the distribution of public opinion. And if it constituted an heroic attempt to shape preferences, then opinion research suggests that it failed singularly. So the question must be asked, how did the Conservatives manage to win national parliamentary elections in 1987 and 1992?

There are two persuasive explanations. The first is the personal electoral appeal of the Conservative Party's leaders: Margaret Thatcher had a distinct advantage over Michael Foot in 1983 and Neil Kinnock in 1987, as did her successor John Major over Kinnock in 1992. The second reason is perhaps even more important: the Conservative Party's enduring reputation for competence at economic management. There is a growing body of literature on the impact of the economy on voting behaviour in Britain, and David Sanders has demonstrated how the Conservatives have fared well both in terms of voters' sociotropic and egocentric evaluations (Sanders 1993).

However, these advantages disappeared after 1992. Opinion research suggested that John Smith, during his brief leadership of Labour prior to his untimely death in May 1994, and subsequently Tony Blair, consistently outshone John Major in the voters' eyes. Labour's advantage in this respect became even more pronounced when the hapless William Hague succeeded John Major as Conservative leader in 1997; and nothing has changed Blair's relative advantage in this respect until the impact of an unpopular war in Iraq. Moreover, after the débâcle of 'Black Wednesday' when Major and his Chancellor of the Exchequer, Norman Lamont, struggled in vain to maintain sterling within the European ERM (September 1992), the party's reputation for economic competence plummeted (Sanders 1996: 223 and Figure 9). Notwithstanding the reduction in interest rates, taxation and unemployment, the continuing low rate of inflation, and the growth in housing prices which were trumpeted in the run-up to the May 1997 election, the Conservatives were unable to convince enough electors of their revived economic competence (Sanders 1997). With these crucial advantages gone (and the visible internal disunity it suffered over vexed questions of the UK's relationship with the EU), the party could hardly afford the luxury of alienating itself from the median voter on the defining issues of left–right location, and content analysis of election manifestos does suggest that the Conservatives made a modest shift back towards the ideological centre ground in 1992 and 1997 (Webb 2000: 113). If anything, however, it responded to election defeat in 1997 by lurching further right again. In a sense, there is an echo of what happened to Labour after the 1979 election here. Thus, just as intra-party conflict led Labour to adopt a position which conformed to no apparently logical strategy of party competition in 1983 (that is, neither vote-maximizing, nor office-seeking, nor oligopolizing – see p. 38 below), so the Conservatives were pushed by their radical right into adopting a mirror image of this position after the election of 1997. Any attempt by party 'modernizers' (shorthand for those who want a less Thatcherite stance on economy, social morality and Europe) to modify Conservative rhetoric or policy still tends to provoke a furious response from the party's 'traditionalist' right (Walters 2001). As a result the party finds itself much further from the median voter than either Labour or the Liberal Democrats (Webb 2003). In short, the party has (perhaps temporarily) let slip from its grasp the key assets which afforded it such an effective response to the initial erosion of voter loyalties – leadership autonomy and strategic clear-sightedness.

The Labour Party experienced an ideological odyssey of its own after 1979. In the aftermath of electoral defeat, it is now widely accepted that the party leadership lurched notably leftwards, and ended up issuing a lengthy and, by most accounts, highly radical manifesto for the 1983 general election. This promised withdrawal from the European Community, the imposition of import controls, reflation of the economy, extensive nationalization of industry, new forms of industrial planning and state support, more generous welfare provision and unilateral nuclear disarmament. As with the Conservatives in 2001, Labour's strategy in 1983 was manifestly irrational. The leftward lurch could not be justified as part and parcel of an oligopolistic response to the threat posed by a significant competitor to the party's left; even more obviously, given the rightward shift of the electorate on most of the key issues at that time, it did not constitute a logical vote-maximizing or office-seeking approach (Kitschelt 1994: 178–81). Most probably, it constituted an heroic (some would say fool-hardy) attempt to catalyse a leftward shift in voter attitudes. As in the case of the Conservatives nearly two decades later, this lack of a rational competitive strategy arose from a severe breakdown in party cohesion, which made it virtually impossible to construct a clear unitary strategy.

After Neil Kinnock was elected party leader in the autumn of 1983, however, the party embarked on a long process of ideological and organizational 'moderni-zation' which succeeded in overturning much of this radical charter for 'social-ism in one country'. Indeed, by 1992 the party felt able to assert that 'at the core of our convictions is belief in individual liberty' (Labour Party 1992: 7), and it was made very plain that the proper economic role of the state was to facilitate the smooth working of the market, rather than to replace it. It followed, among other things, that a notably cautious approach to renationalization of public util-ities was promised, while the stark anti-Europeanism of 1983 gave way to an unprecedented enthusiasm for the European project (Webb 1993). Since then a willingness to countenance new forms of thinking that break the mould of Labour Party tradition has also been apparent in the domains of transport, education and social policy.

Content analysis of the 1987–2001 election manifestos confirms that the key feature of Labour Party policy development over this period was a gradual shift back to the centre Left ground of British politics (see Webb 2000: 113; Bara and Budge 2001). In short, after the hiatus of the early 1980s, Labour slowly re-established a classic vote-maximizing/office-seeking strategic approach. The reasons that this approach did not result in electoral victory in either 1987 or 1992 essentially mirror those discussed above in the context of Conservative success on those occasions; valence evaluations (that is, the party leader and Labour's reputation for economic incompetence) limited the extent of its elec-toral revival. Added to which there was the problem that the party faced growing competition on the centre Left as the Alliance/Liberal Democrats con-solidated their own appeal. By the mid-1990s, however, Labour's process of 'modernization' appeared far more likely to achieve the desired electoral break-through. The Conservatives' growing internal disarray and severe economic difficulties following the 1992 election fostered persisting and massive opinion poll leads for Labour, and Tony Blair's personal popularity was far greater than

John Major's or William Hague's. In essence, Labour's strategists performed a classic piece of rational choice manoeuvring after the mid-1980s. Gradually, they sought to neutralize the impact of key issues on which the Tories held an advantage (such as taxation and privatization) by adopting similar positions themselves, while emphasizing those issues on which Labour came to hold an advantage ('sleaze', competence and leadership qualities).

In conclusion, a number of points arise from this discussion of party policy development in the era of open electoral competition. First, the need for maximum flexibility to manoeuvre in ideological space is paramount now that so many voters' minds can apparently be changed in the run-up to, and during the course of, election campaigns. Secondly, the basic logic of party competition in Britain remains similar to that which held in the 1950s: in policy terms at least, it is largely about vote-maximizing by finding a location relatively close to the median voter on a predominantly left–right dimension of competition. However, two things should be noted about this basic truth of British politics. First, the left-right dimension may predominate, but it does not tell the whole story. Whether by coincidence or design, it is interesting to observe that just as the Conservatives became both more right-wing and more authoritarian under Thatcher (Gamble 1988), so Labour shifted in a similar direction, albeit from a radically different starting point, after 1983. The new Labour government's commitments to be 'tough on crime and tough on the causes of crime'; to introduce 'fast-track justice' for young offenders; to establish a curfew on young children; to legislate against anti-social neighbours; to curb 'aggressive begging', and so on, all illustrate the undercurrent of social discipline in its rhetoric and policy. The second point is that, while I am not proposing that relative proximity to the median voter is a *sufficient* condition of electoral success in the country, it would seem to be a *necessary* condition for the major parties. Parties do not always follow the strict logic of Downsian competition, and when they falter it usually reflects a period of intra-party turmoil in which the capacity to set and follow a cohesive strategy is undermined. But it must be emphasized that ideological proximity to the median voter only tells part of the story: it has become increasingly important in the context of partisan erosion for parties and their leaders to compete by fostering a reputation for governing competence and credibility. Thus, the main parties in Britain now expend considerable efforts on creating images of unity, competence and good leadership. These have perhaps become the most distinguishing tactical responses to the erosion of party loyalties. Finally, it is worth adding that the parties have apparently done little to try to re-establish the long-term loyalties and allegiances of voters. For the Conservatives, we can only really point to the flirtation with popular capitalism; for Labour, the most obvious initiative was not linked directly to policy development, but came in the form of a revival of individual party membership during the 1990s. However, the increase from around 300,000 to 400,000 members since 1994 did not prove an enduring phenomenon (Webb 2000: 221). Overall, we might sum up major party competition in Britain in the era of open competition by suggesting that it conforms to what Richard Rose and

Ian McAllister once called a model of 'centripetal instability'. This refers to a model in which there is fluidity of voter intentions and behaviour, but 'while there is great movement, it is that of voters moving around in a circle … centripetal competition brings voters and parties closer' (Rose and McAllister 1983: 159).

External relations (1): state–party linkages

How have major party relations with external organizations altered as part of a strategic response to the erosion of partisan loyalty? The most striking inter-pretation of the way in which established parties more generally seek to shore up their positions in the context of a more fluid and unpredictable electoral market-place is the cartel party thesis, and this also may be of relevance here. According to Katz and Mair (1995: 16), parties with access to state resources and power have a clear advantage in maintaining their own position and deny-ing such power to others. These authors suggest that contemporary political systems are often characterized by an 'interpenetration of party and state' and by a degree of 'collusion' between ostensibly competing parties which is in fact designed to facilitate their survival.

When considering this thesis in the context of Britain it is interesting to note that it held only to a very limited extent for much of the period until the mid-1970s, but the pressure of events seems to be rendering it gradually more applicable. In 1974 the Labour government introduced the legislation that provided for what is still the main form of state financial subvention paid to parties in Britain – the 'Short Money' that opposition parliamentary parties receive. This money is far from generous in comparative international terms (Webb 1994: 123), but it might be regarded as the first sign of the establishment of a defensive cartel strategy designed to help bolster the organizational infra-structure of the major parties in an era of growing electoral uncertainty. More recently, a major inquiry into party funding has produced a new regulatory settle-ment in which the stick of stricter laws on party finance is accompanied by the carrot of greater state support (Webb 2001). Although the extension of state funding is so far modest, the prospect that this will go significantly further at the behest of the new state Electoral Commission is beginning to seem more persuasive (Watt 2001). This has much to do with the acute financial crises which both major parties have suffered in recent years. In June 2002, the Labour and Conservative Party chairmen and the Liberal Democrats' treasurer jointly issued an appeal for further state funding to support a range of party activities, including e-democracy, the training of local councillors, and connections with overseas parties. Later in the year, a number of prominent New Labour figures, including Charles Clarke, Robin Cook and Peter Mandelson, argued that greater state funding was required to re-establish the independence and credibility of parties. In October, the Institute for Public Policy Research published a report in which it revived a proposal for tax relief on small donations to parties – made by the Neill report on party funding in 1998 but subsequently rejected by the government. However, we cannot yet be certain that the parties will definitely act as a cartel in this matter. At the time of writing, the Labour government is known to be unhappy about pressing ahead with greater state funding if it lacks a cross-party consensus, and there are indications that a revival in Conservative finances is prompting the Tories to oppose new subventions on the grounds that they are about to re-establish their traditional financial superiority over their opponents (Webb 2003).

Further potential for the exploitation of state resources by parties is provided by the 'quangocracy'. The major parties – especially if they have been in government for an extended period of time – are well placed to dominate the nomination of non-elected appointees to the welter of state-funded agencies known as quangos (Heywood 1994: 18).[3] By the late 1980s, critics (including the then Labour opposition) had come to regard the Tories' prolonged sojourn in office as having presented the ruling party with an opportunity for the brazen exploitation of this system of patronage. This, it was claimed, created a network of 'unaccountable power' for the party's placemen and women (Jenkins 1995). Many concurred with Anthony King's (1992: 224) view that this was a growing problem in an increasingly centralized and unitary state 'in which there are no autonomous centres of political power apart from national government'. In a context in which local government had been deprived of power; there was no Bill of Rights, or codified constitution; no Freedom of Information Act; relatively strong party discipline inside parliament; and a 'winner-takes-all' adversarial elite political culture, displaying little inclination for bipartisan consensus-building, the exploitation of the spoils of office by the Conservatives helped to ensure that party penetration of the state could remain high, even if party penetration of society was being ratcheted back. The seeming exclusion of opposition party nominees encouraged Labour's newfound hostility to the quango system at the time. This is the context in which Labour's programme of constitutional reform (incorporating, amongst other things, devolution, local government reform, human rights and freedom of information legislation) should be understood. Nevertheless, the quangocracy remains in place as a source of patronage for the parties to utilize. In short, while the cartel party argument cannot be pushed too far in the case of Britain, it can be said that the major parties have extended their exploitation of state resources since 1970, even if this has been at the price of closer legal regulation of their affairs.

External relations (2): interest group–party relations

If the cartel party idea has gradually become relevant in interpreting changing relationships between British political parties and external organizations, Otto Kirchheimer's much older catch-all thesis (1966) also remains informative.

Kirchheimer wrote in the context of the 'end of ideology' debate which absorbed commentators during the early 1960s and, perceiving an attenuation of ideological conflict in western societies, he claimed that the emerging catch-all party was turning more fully to electoralism, trying to exchange effectiveness in depth for a wider audience and more immediate electoral success. Kirchheimer argued that the catch-all transformation affected party ideology, organization and external relations. Specifically, this latter aspect of his model turned on the de-emphasis of links with exclusive social classes or denominational clienteles, in favour of recruiting voters among the population at large; and the securing of access to a variety of interest groups rather than to exclusive groups.

With regard to Britain it has long been recognized that the Conservatives have been successful in constructing a cross-class appeal based on nationalism and populism (Barnes 1994: 329, 336–7). Labour, however, only began consciously to engage with the need to broaden its appeal after 1960. Even then, the organic connection that it shared with the trade union movement that founded the party remained largely intact, although the nature and extent of the link has provided substance for a perennial debate.

After the election defeat of April 1992 this debate once again surfaced within the publications of the party and the general media, and alarm was felt by many in the party about the direction which Labour's post-mortem took when the National Executive established a working group on party–union relations in June 1992. This eventually generated proposals for reform that were endorsed at the annual conference in September 1993. Although many trade union leaders themselves favoured a degree of reform, some of the proposals proved contentious. Nevertheless, the then leader John Smith and the National Executive persevered and won a knife-edge vote in dramatic circumstances at the 1993 conference. These reforms had the effect of reducing the voting power of unions at the party's annual conference, and in processes of candidate selection and leadership election.

This episode in party–union relations was interesting for reviving a long-standing debate in which two main positions have often been discernible: the first one is that the time has come for the party and the unions to 'divorce' each other in a formal sense (Sassoon 1993), while the second is that the two halves of the Labour movement in Britain should retain their constitutional relationship, while nevertheless reforming it (Minkin 1991). It is important to emphasize that, given the continuing (if diminishing) financial significance of the unions for Labour, divorce has not been a serious option without a substantially enhanced degree of state funding for political parties (Webb 1995). This makes the recent evolution in the system of regulation and subvention for parties in the UK all the more intriguing.

It should also be said that New Labour's leadership has taken pains to maintain a certain distance from union interests and demands; this is best summed up in Tony Blair's frequent refrain that the unions will only get 'fairness, not favours' from the government. Certainly, there has been no return to the pre-1997 legal position on industrial relations. Neither should the significance of the party head office's move away from its former premises at Walworth Road (south London) in the mid-1990s be overlooked, for these were built and leased to Labour by a consortium of affiliated unions a decade earlier; prior to that the party had shared the premises of the Transport and General Workers' Union. Symbolically and practically, the move exemplified New Labour's desire to become more independent of the unions.

At the same time, there are also signs that some unions may be intent on asserting their independence of the party. This is evident in the hostility of major public sector unions to the Blair government's plans for reform of public services, and in the reduction of financial donations to the party by some of these same unions (Milne and Wintour 2001). By 2002, this behaviour was having an impact on the party, and in September 2002 Labour's general secretary, David Triesman, sought but failed to negotiate a 'stability pact' that would guarantee that a minimum of 30 percent of the party's funding would come from the unions – it was 66 percent a decade ago – for the next three years. Subsequently, he warned that Labour and the affiliated unions were 'sleep-walking' towards the catastrophe of divorce – the old spectre that has some-times come back to haunt many in the British labour movement.

In short, the Kirchheimer/Panebianco model seems broadly appropriate to Labour now. While policy has clearly been designed to have a relatively broad appeal since the 1960s, it was only the experience of repeated electoral failure after 1979 that forced a substantial rethink of the party-union relationship. Allied to a (so far) modest growth in reliance on the state for funding, vote-maximizing policy strategy, the expansion of leadership autonomy and the pro-fessionalization of the way in which it markets itself, this signifies that the British Labour Party is consciously moulding itself to the requirements of an era of intensive and extensive open electoral competition.

Conclusion

It is evident that the major parties in Britain have adapted to modern conditions of party competition in the era of partisan dealignment and a more 'open' electoral market. This adaptation has involved not only policy change, but also shifts in the internal distribution of power, altered relationships with external organiza-tions and the professionalization of political marketing. It is equally evident, on reviewing the evidence, that the process of adaptation has perforce been greater in the case of the Labour Party up to the present.

The Conservative Party by its very nature has been well adjusted to the pur-pose of winning elections. This is true at the levels both of ideology and of organization. Ideologically, the essence of British Conservatism lies in the twin desires to occupy power and to maintain some system of unequal property relations in society. This has usually rendered the party uniquely flexible, and some com-mentators have even argued that the pragmatism arising from this makes it very difficult to pin down a distinctive Conservative 'ideology' (Barnes 1994: 315). From our point of view, however, the important feature of this is that it highlights the way in which the office-seeking impulse has defined the party, and marks it out as inherently flexible and electoralist in the long term. Organizationally, we have already noted the relatively high degree of autonomy that the Conservative Party leader has always enjoyed; certainly, s/he is encumbered by few formal rules and regulations when it comes to policy adjustments, a key requirement of the modern electoral-professional party in the era of heightened electoral competition. Moreover, while the Conservatives have undoubtedly long been regarded as the party of business interests, they have never been openly and organically tied to business organizations in the way that Labour has been linked to the trade unions. These characteristics have ensured that the party was always 'catch-all' in terms of its electoral appeal. Given its early willingness to embrace the latest in modern campaigning and communications techniques, this also means that the British Conservative Party was quickly attuned to the need for electoral-professionalism as the erosion of partisan loyalties intensified the competitiveness of national elections. That said, growing internal disharmony and ideological sectarianism, organizational decay and a certain complacency born of apparent electoral invincibility have at least temporarily undermined the Tories, who are now confronted by a major task of political and organizational adaptation.

For Labour things have not always been quite so straightforward. The party shared few of the obvious advantages of the Conservatives. For a start, even in the 1970s it was saddled with a more clear-cut class ideology, though many have noted the pragmatism with which Labour leaders in power have interpreted this. In the second place, Labour leaders have not been able to exercise quite the same degree of internal autonomy in developing party policy and strategy, given the formal constitutional constraints imposed on them. This is true notwithstanding McKenzie's (1956) famous assertion that the formal account of Labour's internal democratic structure exaggerates the real differences between it and the Conservatives. Moreover, the apparent capacity of party leaders to override internal party opposition has always been contingent on the sustained support of the leaderships of key union affiliates, and while this has generally been assured, as an historical fact, it has not always been guaranteed (even when Labour has been in power). No Conservative leader has operated under this kind of pressure.

Consequently, of the two major parties, Labour has faced – until recently – the greater task in adjusting to the requirements of a new era of extensive and open electoral competition. After Neil Kinnock became leader the compulsion to adapt became overwhelming as one general election defeat followed another. As we have seen, the necessary adaptation (some would say revolution) in ideology, organization and external relations has taken place and transformed the party into an exemplar of the modern electoral-professional competitor. The challenge before today's Conservative Party is to emulate its major rival's lengthy, often painful, but ultimately successful process of adaptation.

Notes

1 I am, of course, referring here to the party system in Britain, and in this analysis I will not be treating the separate (and more fragmented) party system that has developed in Northern Ireland, and that is currently represented in the British Westminster parliament in the form of the Unionist Party, the Democratic Unionist Party, the Social Democratic and Labour Party, and Sinn Fein.

2 As a broad indication of constituency marginality, on average some 38 percent of constituencies were won on a minority of the vote cast between 1945 and 1970, whereas 49 percent were in the elections from February 1974 to 1997 (calculated from Rallings and Thrasher 2001: 86).

3 Quango is an acronym for 'quasi autonomous non-governmental organization' and is a domain of more than 13,000 non-ministerial public bodies whose members are appointed by government ministers.

References

Abrams, Mark, Richard Rose, and Rita Hinden (1960). *Must Labour Lose?* Harmondsworth: Penguin.

Bara, Judith and Ian Budge (2001). 'Party Policy and Ideology: Still New Labour?' In Pippa Norris (ed.), *Britain Votes 2001*. Oxford: Oxford University Press.

Barnes, John (1994). 'Ideology and Factions.' In Anthony Seldon and Stuart Ball (eds), *The Conservative Century: The Conservative Party since 1900*. Oxford: Oxford University Press, pp. 315–45.

Barnes, Samuel, Max Kaase *et al*. (1979). *Political Action: Mass Participation in Five Western Democracies*. Beverly Hills, CA: Sage.

Coates, David (1994). *The Question of UK Decline: Economy, State and Society*. Hemel Hempstead: Harvester Wheatsheaf.

Cockett, Richard (1994). 'The Party, Publicity and the Media.' In Anthony Seldon and Stuart Ball (eds), *The Conservative Century: The Conservative Party since 1900*. Oxford: Oxford University Press, pp. 547–77.

Conservative Party (1997). *Blueprint for Change: A Consultation Paper for Reform of the Conservative Party*. London: Conservative Party.

Conservative Party (1998) *Fresh Future*. London: Conservative Party.

Crewe, Ivor (1983). 'The Electorate: Partisan Dealignment 10 Years On.' In Hugh Berrington (ed.), *Change in British Politics*. London: Frank Cass, pp. 183–215.

Crewe, Ivor (1985). 'Great Britain.' In Ivor Crewe and David Denver (eds), *Electoral Change in Western Democracies: Patterns and Sources of Electoral Volatility*. Beckenham: Croom Helm, pp. 100–50.

Crewe, Ivor (1986). 'On the Death and Resurrection of Class Voting: Some Comments on *How Britain Votes*.' *Political Studies* 34: 620–38.

Crewe, Ivor (1992). 'Partisan Dealignment Ten Years On': In David Denver and Gordon Hands (eds) *Issues and Controversies in British Electoral Behaviour*. Hemel Hempstead: Harvester Wheatsheaf, pp. 141–7.

Crewe, Ivor and Donald Searing (1988). 'Mrs. Thatcher's Crusade: Conservatism in Britain. 1972–1986.' In Barry Cooper, Allan Kornberg, and William Mishler (eds), *The Resurgence of Conservatism in Anglo-American Democracies*. Durham, NC: Duke University Press, pp. 285–303.

Crewe, Ivor, Neil Day, and Anthony Fox (1995). *The British Electorate: A Compendium of Data from the British Election Studies, 1963–92*. Cambridge: Cambridge University Press.

Dalton, Russell J. (2001). 'The Decline of Party Identifications.' In Russell J. Dalton and Martin P. Wattenberg (eds), *Parties without Partisans: Political Change in Advanced Industrial Democracies*. Oxford : Oxford University Press, pp. 19–36.

Downs, Anthony (1957). *An Economic Theory of Democracy*. New York: Harper and Row.

Dunleavy, Patrick (1979). 'The Urban Basis of Political Alignment: Social Class, Domestic Property Ownership and State Intervention in Consumption Processes.' *British Journal of Political Science* 9: 409–33.

Dunleavy, Patrick (1980). 'The Political Implications of Sectoral Cleavages and the Growth of State Employment.' *Political Studies* 28: 364–83, 527–49.

Dunleavy, Patrick (1987). 'Class Dealignment Revisited: Why Odds Ratios Give Odd Results.' *West European Politics* 10: 400–19.

Dunleavy, Patrick and Christopher Husbands (1985). *British Democracy at the Crossroads*. London: Allen and Unwin.

Esping-Andersen, Gosta (1985). *Politics against Markets: The Social Democratic Path to Power*. Princeton, NJ: Princeton University Press.

Evans, Geoffrey (1999). 'Europe: A New Electoral Cleavage?' In Geoffrey Evans and Pippa Norris (eds), *Critical Elections: British Parties and Voters in Long-Term Perspective*. London: Sage, pp. 207–22.

Fiorina, Morris P. (1977). 'An Outline of a Model of Party Choice.' *American Journal of Political Science* 21: 601–25.

Gamble, Andrew (1985). *Britain in Decline*. London: Macmillan.

Gamble, Andrew (1988). *The Free Economy and the Strong State*. Basingstoke: Macmillan.

Garrett, Geoff (1994). 'Popular Capitalism: the Electoral Legacy of Thatcherism.' In Anthony Heath *et al.*, *Labour's Last Chance?* Aldershot: Dartmouth, pp.107–23.

Goldthorpe, John, David Lockwood, Frank Bechhofer, and Jennifer Platt (1968). *The Affluent Worker: Political Attitudes and Behaviour*. Cambridge: Cambridge University Press.

Gould, Philip, Peter Herd, and Chris Powell (1989). 'The Labour Party's Campaign Communications.' In Ivor Crewe and Martin Harrop (eds), *Political Communications: The General Election Campaign of 1997*. Cambridge: Cambridge University Press, pp. 72–86.

Heath, Anthony, John Curtice, Roger Jowell, Geoff Evans, Julia Field, and Sharon Witherspoon (1991), *Understanding Political Change*. Oxford: Pergamon Press.

Heath, Anthony, Roger Jowell, and John Curtice (1985). *How Britain Votes*. Oxford: Pergamon.

Heath, Anthony, Roger Jowell, and John Curtice (1987). 'Trendless Fluctuation: A Reply to Crewe.' *Political Studies* 35: 256–77.

Hewitt, Patricia and Peter Mandelson (1989). 'The Labour Campaign.' In Ivor Crewe and Martin Harrop (eds), *Political Communications: The General Election Campaign of 1997*. Cambridge: Cambridge University Press, pp. 49–54.

Heywood, Andrew (1994). 'Britain's Dominant Party System.' In Lynton Robins, Hilary Blackmore, and Richard Pyper (eds), *Britain's Changing Party System*. London: Leicester University Press, pp. 10–25.

Hobsbawm, Eric (1981). 'The Forward March of Labour Halted?' In Martin Jacques and Frances Mulhearn (eds), *The Forward March of Labour Halted?* London: New Left Books, pp. 1–19.

Hughes, Charles and Patrick Wintour (1990). *Labour Rebuilt: The New Model Party*. London: Fourth Estate.

Hutton, Will (1995). *The State We're In*. London: Jonathan Cape.

Jenkins, Simon (1995). *Accountable to None: The Tory Nationalization of Britain*. Harmondsworth: Penguin Books.

Katz, Richard and Peter Mair (1995). 'Changing Models of Party Organization and Party Democracy: The Emergence of the Cartel Party.' *Party Politics* 1: 5–28.

Kavanagh, Dennis (1995). *Election Campaigning: The New Marketing of Politics*. Oxford: Basil Blackwell.

Kelly, Richard (1989). *Conservative Party Conferences*. Manchester: Manchester University Press.

King, Anthony (1992). 'The Implications of One-Party Government.' In Anthony King *et al.*, *Britain at the Polls*. Chatham, NJ: Chatham House, pp. 223–48.

Kirchheimer, Otto (1966). 'The Transformation of Western European Party Systems.' In Joseph LaPalombara and Myron Weiner (eds), *Political Parties and Political Development*. Princeton, NJ: Princeton University Press, pp. 177–200.

Kitschelt, Herbert (1993). 'Class Structure and Social Democratic Party Strategy.' *British Journal of Political Science* 23: 299–337.

Kitschelt, Herbert (1994). *The Transformation of European Social Democracy*. Cambridge: Cambridge University Press.

Laakso, Markuu and Rein Taagepera (1979). '"Effective" Number of parties: A Measure with Applications to Western Europe.' *Comparative Political Studies* 12: 3–27.

Labour Party (1992). *It's Time to Get Britain Working Again*. London: Labour Party.

Labour Party (1997). *Labour into Power: a Framework for Partnership*. London: Labour Party.

Lees-Marshment, Jennifer (2001). *Political Marketing and British Political Parties: The Party's Just Begun*. Manchester: Manchester University Press.

Marshall, Gordon, Howard Newby, David Rose, and Carolyn Vogler (1988). *Social Class in Modern Britain*. London: Hutchinson.

McKenzie, Robert (1956). *British Political Parties*. London: Heinemann.

Miller, William (1983). 'The Denationalization of British Politics: the Reemergence of the Periphery.' *West European Politics* 6: 103–29.

Milne, Seamus and Patrick Wintour (2001). 'Union Fires Warning to Blair on Jobs.' *The Guardian*, 22 June.

Minkin, Lewis (1991). *The Contentious Alliance: The Trade Unions and the Labour Party*. Edinburgh: Edinburgh University Press.

Panebianco, Angelo (1988). *Political Parties: Organisation and Power*. Cambridge: Cambridge University Press.

Pedersen, Mogens (1979). 'The Dynamics of European Party Systems: Changing Patterns of Electoral Volatility.' *European Journal of Political Research* 7: 1–26.

Poguntke, Thomas and Paul Webb (eds) (2005, forthcoming). *The Presidentialization of Democracy: A Study in Comparative Politics*. Oxford: Oxford University Press.

Rae, Douglas W. (1971). *The Political Consequences of Electoral Laws*. New Haven, CT: Yale University Press.

Rallings, Colin and Michael Thrasher (2001). *British Electoral Facts 1832–1999*. Aldershot: Ashgate.

Rose, Richard and Ian McAllister (1983). *Voters Begin to Choose: From Closed-Class to Open Elections in Britain*. London: Sage.

Sanders, David (1993). 'Why the Conservatives Won – Again.' In Anthony King *et al., Britain at the Polls 1992*. Chatham, NJ: Chatham House, pp. 171–222.

Sanders, David (1996). 'Economic Performance, Management Competence and the Outcome of the Next General Election.' *Political Studies* 44: 203–31.

Sanders, David (1997). 'Conservative Incompetence, Labour Responsibility and the Feelgood Factor: Why the Economy Failed to Save the Conservatives in 1997.' Paper presented to the Assessing the 1997 General Election conference, University of Essex, September.

Sassoon, David (1993). 'The Union Link: the Case for Friendly Divorce.' *Renewal* 1: 28–35.

Scammell, Margaret (1995). *Designer Politics: How Elections Are Won*. Basingstoke: Macmillan.

Shaw, Eric (1994). *The Changing Labour Party since 1979: Crisis and Transformation*. Oxford: Clarendon Press.

Sked, Alan (1987). *Britain's Decline*. Oxford: Basil Blackwell.

Walters, Stephen (2001). *Tory Wars: Conservatives in Crisis*. London: Politico's.

Watt, Nicholas (2001). 'Parties May Face Ban on Multi-Million Gifts.' *The Guardian*, 13 February.

Webb, Paul D. (1992). 'Election Campaigning, Organisational Transformation and the Professionalisation of the British Labour Party.' *European Journal of Political Research* 21: 266–88.

Webb, Paul D. (1993). 'The Labour Party, the Market and the Electorate: A Study in Social Democratic Adaptation.' In John S. Sheldrake and Paul D. Webb (eds), *State and Market: Aspects of Modern European Development*. Aldershot: Dartmouth, pp. 107–25.

Webb, Paul D. (1994). 'Party Organizational Change in Britain: The Iron Law of Centralization?' In Richard Katz and Peter Mair (eds), *How Parties Organize: Change and Adaptation in Party Organizations in Western Democracies*. London: Sage, pp. 109–33.

Webb, Paul D. (1995). 'Reforming the Party–Union Link: an Assessment.' In David Broughton, David Farrell, David Denver, and Colin Rallings (eds), *British Parties and Elections Yearbook 1994*. London: Frank Cass, pp. 1–14.

Webb, Paul D. (1996). 'Anti-Party Sentiment in the UK: Correlates and Constraints.' *European Journal of Political Research* 29: 365–82.

Webb, Paul D. (2000). *The Modern British Party System*. London: Sage Publications.

Webb, Paul D. (2001). 'Parties and Party Systems: Modernization, Regulation and Diversity.' *Parliamentary Affairs* 54: 308–21.

Webb, Paul D. (2003). 'The Party System: Prospects for Realignment.' *Parliamentary Affairs* 56: 283–96.

Webb, Paul D. and Justin Fisher (2003). 'Professionalizing the Millbank Tendency: the Political Sociology of New Labour's Employees.' *Politics* 23: 10–20.

THREE Ephemeral Victories? France's Governing Parties, the Ecologists, and the Far Right

Andrew Knapp

Political markets, like any markets, can be rigged. Katz and Mair's model of the cartel party outlines how it can be done. Cartel parties, they argue, monopolize government office and use its perquisites to reinforce and perpetuate their ascendancy. Colluding with each other out of 'a mutual interest in collective organizational survival', they seek 'to place barriers in the path of new parties seeking to enter the system' (Katz and Mair 1995: 19–20, 23). And yet, admit Katz and Mair (1996: 532), 'there are no fully fledged cartel parties': messy empirical observation fails to live up to the clarity either of this archetype or of its predecessors, cadre, mass, or catch-all parties.

No country better illustrates this untidy reality than France. As early as the Fourth Republic (1946–58), France displayed some, but only some, precocious characteristics of a cartelized party system: the mainstream parties of government, from Socialists to conservatives, shared out the benefits of office among themselves, blurring distinctions between parties in and out of government, and cooperated in using institutional mechanisms – especially the electoral system – to penalize and even exclude outsiders like Communists, Gaullists, or Poujadists. Since the foundation of the Fifth Republic by General de Gaulle in 1958, French party politics has come closer to the cartel model in some respects, and has grown more distant in others. It is more cartel-like in the sense of being less ideologically charged (since the 1980s), more capital-intensive, more professionalized, and more dependent on the resources of the state than under the Fourth Republic. But it is also more bipolarized, with clearer distinctions between 'ins' and 'outs', and it engenders fiercer competition, even between the mainstream parties of government. The responses of mainstream governing parties to new entrants are correspondingly complex.

The simplest characterization of France's party system under the Fifth Republic is bipolar multipartism. The system should be seen as bipolar, first and foremost, because of the relationship of parties to government. Since 1958, governments have consisted of more or less coherent coalitions of Left and Right. From 1958 to 1981 the Right held power continuously, though its leadership passed from Gaullists to a president of the non-Gaullist Right, Valéry Giscard d'Estaing, from

1974 to 1981. Since 1981, however, France's voters have chosen alternation in power at every parliamentary election. The Socialist-dominated Left held office from 1981 to 1986 under the leadership of President François Mitterrand, also elected in 1981. The Gaullist-led Right governed from the parliamentary elections of 1986 until 1988, with the Gaullist Prime Minister Jacques Chirac uneasily 'cohabiting' with Mitterrand, whose seven-year term was two years longer than that of parliament. The Socialists were back in power from 1988, after Mitterrand's re-election to the presidency and immediate dissolution of parliament, until the parliamentary elections of 1993. The Gaullist-led Right succeeded them from 1993 to 1997 (with Prime Minister Balladur 'cohabiting' with the ailing Mitterrand from 1993 until 1995, when Chirac was elected to the presidency and appointed his lieutenant Alain Juppé to the premiership). The Socialist-led *gauche plurielle* or 'plural Left' won the snap elections called by Chirac in 1997, and the Socialist Prime Minister Lionel Jospin then cohabited for five whole years with Chirac. In 2002, when both parliamentary and presidential terms ended, Chirac was re-elected to the presidency, and the mainstream Right – most of which had merged into a new conservative party, the Union pour un Mouvement Populaire (UMP) regained power in parliament and in government. These coalitions commanded stable parliamentary majorities for all but nine of the Fifth Republic's first 45 years; even without such majorities, as from 1958 to 1962 and from 1988 to 1993, governments have been able to remain in office thanks to the 'rationalized parliamentarianism' that is a major element of the Fifth Republic Constitution. Alternation in power between Right and Left, contrary to the cartel model, has been regular and practically complete.

On the other hand France also possesses a clearly multi-party system. No fewer than sixteen candidates ran at the presidential elections of 2002, of whom seven each attracted the support of 5 percent or more of the voters. They included not only Chirac, backed by the neo-Gaullist Rassemblement pour la République (RPR) and Jospin, supported by the Socialists (PS), but also Jean-Marie Le Pen, the leader of the far-Right Front National (FN), who beat Jospin into second place and thus faced Chirac at the run-off ballot; a Eurosceptical left-winger, Jean-Pierre Chevènement; a Trotskyist, Arlette Laguiller; the candidate of the Greens (Les Verts), Noël Mamère; and François Bayrou, leader of the non-Gaullist (and non-*chiraquien*) moderate right-wing party, the Union pour la Démocratie Française (UDF). Similarly, in the parliamentary elections of 1997, six parties – the Communists (PCF) as well as the PS, Les Verts, the RPR, the UDF, and the FN – each achieved over 5 percent of the vote. While the parliamentary elections of 2002 signalled a significant concentration, with only three parties (PS, UMP, and FN) winning over 5 percent, it is too early to say if this is permanent. Moreover, some parties have remained outside the two big coalitions for greater or lesser periods of time. That was true of parts of the non-Gaullist moderate Right before 1974; of most of the various ecology movements before 1997; and of the FN since its foundation in 1972. Their isolation excluded these groupings from governmental office, and in the case of the last two from parliamentary representation, but did not prevent them from winning significant elected positions at local or regional level, nor from weighing significantly on national party strategies.

Bipolar multipartism has been shaped by a complex and varying balance of forces. The most powerful motors of bipolarization are institutional: above all, the two-ballot majority system used, with some variations, for elections to the National Assembly, to the presidency of the Republic (an office whose political role was greatly enhanced after 1958) and, at local level, to the councils of France's 96 *départements* and the larger municipalities (Schlesinger and Schlesinger 2000). These institutional arrangements have been reinforced by the behaviour of mainstream political parties, which have used them to maximize their own levels of representation through the electoral alliance strategies that form the basis of governmental coalitions. Bipolarity has also been underpinned by the willingness of most voters, confirmed in successive surveys, to position themselves within broad families of Left and Right (Duhamel 1997; SOFRES 2002d). At the same time, however, the broadly coherent bipolar edifice of the first two decades of the Fifth Republic was fissured, from the 1980s, by two nearly simultaneous developments. The first of these was institutional: the introduction of proportional representation for elections to the European Parliament from 1979, to the councils of France's 22 regions from 1986, to the National Assembly (once only, before the change in the electoral law was reversed) in 1986, and (within a mixed majority/ proportional list system), to larger municipalities from 1983. The second development has been described by one author as a full-scale electoral dealignment (Martin 2000): the collapse of the PCF vote, which fell from 20.6 percent at the parliamentary elections of 1978 to 11.2 percent at the European elections six years later, plus the breakthrough of the FN into national politics from 1983–84, followed by the rise of ecology as an electoral force from the late 1980s, and a more general unpredictability of electoral behaviour as voters crossed and re-crossed established boundaries within and (to a lesser extent) between Left and Right.

The impact on the party system of these two developments has been analysed by Parodi (1997) through the impeccably French image of the 'electoral accordion'. European and regional elections, he argues, are seen as of secondary importance, but offer a wide choice of electable candidates because they use the system of proportional representation. Voters are tempted to 'open' the accordion and spread their support across a range of lists. They thus ensure mediocre scores for the major parties. Presidential and parliamentary elections, on the other hand, are seen as mattering more, while the disciplines of the two-ballot majority system encourage 'useful' voting. Here, errant voters would return to the big mainstream parties, and the accordion would close. But it came to close less and less well, continued Parodi, because the habits engendered by proportional representation began to carry over into majority elections, leading to a drop in the vote for the larger parties here too.

Such habits were compounded by the behaviour of France's traditionally fissiparous parties and individualist politicians, notably under the periodic strain of European issues. All three of France's mainstream governing parties, as well as the FN, suffered splits between 1992 and 1999. The UDF lost its Eurosceptic wing, led by Philippe de Villiers, at the 1992 Maastricht referendum: a de Villiers list won 12.3 percent of the vote at the 1994 European elections, though de Villiers's score as a presidential candidate in 1995 was a mere 4.7 percent. After the regional elections of 1998 (see p. 76 below), the UDF suffered a more severe split when its conservatives and neo-liberals, grouped since the previous year under the Démocratie Libérale (DL) label, broke away from the broadly Christian Democratic rump of the party, which kept the UDF name. The RPR also saw Eurosceptics depart, under the leadership of Charles Pasqua: a joint Pasqua–de Villiers list at the 1999 European elections won 13.1 percent of the vote, slightly ahead of the 'official' RPR–DL list. The Socialists, too, lost a Eurosceptical group: Jean-Pierre Chevènement left the PS in 1993 and won 5.3 percent of the vote at the presidential election of 2002. These splits led neither to an Italian-style collapse of the party system, nor to the establishment on a lasting basis of any new players. The Pasqua-de Villiers party, the Rassemblement pour la France, fell apart within months of its creation in 1999; Chevènement's Pôle Républicain suffered a similar fate in 2002; DL was absorbed, together with a part of the UDF, into the UMP. But the 'accordion' dynamic, and the splits of the major parties, remain key to understanding the extreme fragmentation of the 2002 presidential vote, when electors who saw a Chirac–Jospin run-off as a foregone conclusion felt they could afford a first-ballot vote of dissent or protest (Parodi 2002).

France's party system therefore remains finely balanced between its bipolar, consolidating, centripetal dynamics and its multipolar, fragmenting, and centrifugal tendencies.[1] And patterns of party competition can be viewed in two ways. On the one hand, traditional Left/Right competition between the major parties – the PS and the parties of the Gaullist and non-Gaullist moderate Right – is still fierce and still makes a difference to government policy. On the other, the real stakes of this traditional Left/Right competition are less and less clear to voters. For over a decade, at least 55 percent of the French have considered the Left/Right distinction to be 'out of date' (SOFRES 2002d); only 37 percent of poll respondents discerned a substantial difference between Chirac's and Jospin's programmes in 2002, compared with 57 percent who did not (CSA 2002). And there is also a clear distinction between the mainstream 'parties of government' and the generally newer parties at the periphery of the political system – above all, the far Right (Cole 1998). Parties of government may, *in extremis*, resort to cartel-like behaviour. More frequently, and on a more individual basis, they have sought to co-opt, contain, or exclude new entrants, chiefly Les Verts and the FN. But they have also, especially in the 1980s, manipulated newer entrants to the system to gain an advantage over mainstream rivals, contributing thereby to the destabilization of the party system that could be clearly observed from the 1980s.

Changing electoral markets in France: the evidence

A general analysis of changes in electoral markets since 1980 presents two main difficulties. The first is that France was long characterized by a combination

Table 3.1 French electoral results, 1958–2002

	% of votes/ seats	Extreme left	Communists	Moderate left	Greens	Moderate right, including Gaullists	Extreme right	Other*	Total % of vote	Total no. of seats	Fractionalization	Effective number of parties	Total volatility	Votes cast as % of the electorate	Spoilt ballots as % of the electorate
1958	Votes	0	18.9	26.3	0	51.7	2.6	0.5	100	511	0.63	2.7		77.1	1.9
	Seats	0	10	84	0	384	1	32	100	511					
1962	Votes	2	21.9	19.9	0	55.4	0.8	0	100	482	0.6	2.5	8.8	68.7	2.1
	Seats	0	41	110	0	331	0	0	100	482					
1967	Votes	2.2	22.5	18.9	0	55.8	0.6	0	100	487	0.6	2.5	1.2	81.1	1.8
	Seats	0	73	123	0	291	0	0	100	487					
1968	Votes	4	20.1	16.5	0	58.9	0.1	0.5	100	487	0.58	2.4	5.3	80	1.4
	Seats	0	34	58	0	395	0	0	100	487					
1973	Votes	3.2	21.4	21.2	0	53.7	0.5	0	100	490	0.62	2.6	6.4	81.3	1.8
	Seats	0	73	105	0	312	0	0	100	490					
1978	Votes	3.3	20.6	26.3	2	46.7	0.8	0.2	100	491	0.67	3	7.7	83.2	1.6
	Seats	0	86	115	0	290	0	0	100	491					
1981	Votes	1.2	16.1	38.3	1.1	42.9	0.3	0	100	491	0.64	2.8	12	70.9	1
	Seats	0	44	289	0	158	0	0	100	491					
1986	Votes	1.5	9.7	32.8	1.2	44.6	10.1	0.1	100	577	0.67	3.1	12	78.5	3.4
	Seats	0	35	216	0	291	35	0	100	577					
1988	Votes	0.4	11.3	37.5	0.3	40.4	9.8	0.2	100	577	0.67	3.1	6.5	66.1	1.4
	Seats	0	27	276	0	273	1	0	100	577					
1993	Votes	1.7	9.1	19.9	10.9	44	12.8	1.5	100	577	0.73	3.7	19.8	69.8	3.7
	Seats	0	24	75	0	478	0	0	100	577					
1997	Votes	2.2	9.9	28.7	6.4	35.8	15.4	1.6	100	577	0.75	4	12.7	68.5	3.3
	Seats	0	37	275	8	256	1	0	100	577					
2002	Votes	2.8	4.8	27.9	4.5	43.4	12.7	3.9	100	577	0.71	3.5	9.3	64.4	2.8
	Seats	0	21	154	3	399	0	0	100	577					

*Others' seats for 1958 are chiefly overseas departments and territories. For later years, Deputies not registered with a parliamentary group have been distributed between Communists, Left, and Right according to political sympathy and campaign backers.

Sources: Lancelot 1998 (for 1958–97), Parodi 2002 (for 2002)

of stable voting behaviour for broad families of Right and Left, structured by religion and class (in that order), but unstable votes for individual parties within the two families. The second is the range of alliance options used by parties in France's two electoral systems: running or not running joint lists with partners at regional or European elections, and presenting joint first-round candidates or agreeing mutual withdrawals at the run-off in two-ballot elections. These two elements mean that measuring electoral change or volatility on the basis of party votes necessarily involves subjective choices about when two or more closely allied parties constitute a single political unit (Grunberg 1985; Bartolini and Mair 1990). Thus, for example, the representation of the Gaullists and other moderate Right as a single unit (Table 3.1) is justified by their habit of running single candidates in most constituencies at most parliamentary elections, and by their recent, if partial, merger (the UMP incorporated most of the moderate Right but the rump of the old UDF has chosen to remain independent); but it ignores the intense rivalries characteristic of presidential elections, and of parliamentary elections in 1978 and the 1960s. Similarly, measurement of vote-switching produces very different results according to whether two, three, or more units are taken into account.

With these caveats, French party politics since the early 1980s may almost be seen as a West European paradigm, with destabilization resulting both from a general loosening of old partisan ties and from the constitution of new political forces. This is borne out by data both at the aggregate and at the individual level.

Volatility and fractionalization (Table 3.1)

Across parliamentary elections since 1958 and counting six political forces (far Left; Communists; Socialists plus close allies; ecology parties; mainstream Right, including both Gaullists and non-Gaullists; and extreme Right), the three main indices yield broadly consistent results. A transitional period after 1958, with high volatility, indicated notably by a Pedersen index of 8.8 in 1962, was followed by stabilization in the later 1960s and 1970s. The period of disloca-tion beginning in 1978–81, however, saw higher levels of volatility, peaking at nearly 20 in 1993, a rising index of fractionalization, and an effective number of parties reaching four in 1997 for the first time in the Fifth Republic. The 1993 and 1997 elections are worth special notice; never has the Right achieved such a landslide (Jaffré 1993), and never has such a victory been so quickly reversed. Volatility in 2002, though less spectacular, was still higher than at any point in the pre-1978 period.

The enhanced vulnerability of
mainstream parties and candidates

Taken together, the four established forces of the Fifth Republic – Communists, Socialists, Gaullists, and non-Gaullist moderate Right – attracted over 90 percent of the first-round vote in 1978; that figure was below 75 percent in 1993 and 1997 and less than 77 percent in 2002. In relation to the total registered electorate, the vote for these parties was below 50 percent at each of the last three elections. Within this general perspective, the most consistent trend was the Communists' steep decline from 20 percent of the vote in 1978 to under 5 percent 24 years later. Their Socialist partners, though not showing a straight-line drop, have also been exposed. They lost over half their voters between 1988 and 1993, before starting a partial recovery from 1995 and stabilizing at slightly below 25 percent in the late 1990s, or 27–28 percent with smaller moderate left-wing groups and individuals. Their continuing vulnerability was well demonstrated at the 2002 presidential election, when Jospin, unsupported by any of the smaller groups, achieved a mere 16.2 percent of the vote and was beaten into third place (and thus denied a place on the run-off ballot) by Le Pen. Nor has the moderate Right been immune from danger: its 'landslide' of 1993 was achieved with 44 percent of the vote, a figure hardly greater than that which had sealed its defeat in the 1981 parliamentary elections; the comfortable victory of 2002 was achieved with a slightly lower vote share; and in 1997 the mainstream Right's share of the vote, at under 36 percent, was lower than at any time since the left-wing landslides of 1945.

The rise in the vote for 'marginal' parties and candidates

The 1980s and 1990s have been cluttered both with unprecedented numbers of candidates (up from an average of 5.4 per seat in 1981 to 11.2 in 1997 and 14 in 2002) and with high scores by players outside the mainstream governing parties. Some were ephemeral (the 12 percent achieved by Bernard Tapie's Radical list at the 1994 European elections), or largely confined to regional and European elections run on proportional representation (the 4–7 percent support attracted by Hunters' Rights (Chasse, Pêche, Nature et Tradition) lists since 1989, or the 12–13 percent won at European elections by the de Villiers/Pasqua Eurosceptic Right in 1994 and 1999). The record of the Trotskyist far Left appears potentially more lasting, with over 5 percent at presidential elections in 1995, regional elections in 1998, and European elections in 1999, and above all the 10 percent score, spread between three candidates, at the 2002 presidential election (though that had shrunk below 3 percent in the ensuing parliamentary elections).

The most important new forces, however, have been the ecology parties, of which Les Verts emerged from 1994 as the sole significant grouping, and the far Right. The record of ecology groupings has been erratic: 10.6 percent at the 1989 European poll, nearly 15 percent at the 1992 regional elections, and 10.7 percent at the 1993 parliamentary elections (albeit split into two or three different varieties in the latter two cases), 9.7 percent for Les Verts in 1999, but also a mere 3.3 percent for the presidential candidate Dominique Voynet in 1995, and 6.9 percent (some of this with the Socialists' help) at the 1997 parliamentary elections, 5.3 percent at the 2002 presidential elections and some 4.5 percent at the parliamentary elections six weeks later. The FN, on the other hand, quickly established a base line of 10 percent after its breakthrough in 1984: its score exceeded 15 percent at the presidential elections of 1995, at the 1997 parliamentary elections, and at the 1998 regional elections. This progression appeared to be halted by the FN's split of late 1998, which saw Le Pen's younger rival, Bruno Mégret, form his own Mouvement National Républicain (MNR) and take many of the FN's local and regional cadres with him. Appearances proved deceptive and the drop in the far Right's support at the 1999 European elections (a combined FN–MNR total of just 9 percent) proved temporary. Three years later, Le Pen's unprecedented score of 16.9 percent at the 2002 presidential election, though achieved in a particularly favourable context (Parodi 2002), underlined both the continued existence of a loyal far Right electorate and Le Pen's personal capacity to mobilize it even with a weakened party organization (Mayer 2002).

The rise of abstentions and spoilt ballots

Compared with the presidential and parliamentary elections of 1968–78, those of the 1988–2002 period showed a drop of over 5 points in the average level of valid votes cast. At the defining contest of French politics, the second ballot of the presidential election, the percentage of the electorate casting valid votes fell from 86 when Giscard won in 1974 to under 76 for Chirac's victories in 1995 and 2002; at the first ballot in 2002, for the first time in a direct presidential election, fewer than 70 percent of electors cast a valid vote. This was paralleled by low levels of valid votes at regional elections (55.3 percent in 1998), European elections (44 percent in 1999), municipal elections (66 percent in 2001, with under 60 percent among blue-collar workers, and barely 50 percent in major provinces and cities among the under-25s), and at a referendum (a mere 25.4 percent at the September 2000 referendum on shortening the presidential term to five years: the Yes 'won' with 18.6 percent of the electorate). At 64.7 percent of the electorate, the level of valid votes at the 1997 parliamentary elections was the second lowest in the history of the Fifth Republic – a striking total for an election the outcome of which was anything but certain; the parliamentary elections of June 2002, widely viewed as a shoo-in for the Right after Chirac's re-election to the presidency, produced an all-time record low level of valid votes for a National Assembly election of 61.6 percent. Change in the level of blank and spoilt ballots has been more erratic: at parliamentary elections, the figure of 2.8 percent of registered voters in 2002 was slightly down on the 3–4 percent observed in the 1990s; at presidential elections, on the other hand, the number of blank and spoilt ballots has risen steadily, tripling from 0.8 percent in 1974 to 2.4 percent in 2002.

Alternation in power

Not one of the five parliamentary elections of 1962, 1967, 1968, 1973 and 1978 led directly to a change of Prime Minister. By contrast *every* parliamentary and presidential election since 1981 has led to an *alternance* of one form or another. This was even true of 1995, when Chirac's election was partly inspired by public rejection both of his Gaullist rival Balladur (the incumbent premier) and of the disgraced Socialists (and their retiring President, Mitterrand), and of 2002, where Chirac's re-election precipitated the downfall of Jospin and his governing left-wing coalition.

The widening gap between the party system in the country and the system at parliamentary or governmental level

As the mainstream parties' share of the vote has shrunk, the distortions of the two-ballot electoral system, which rewards alliances and big parties and penalizes small, isolated, and unpopular parties, appear all the more flagrant. At the 1993 parliamentary elections, for example, the winning right-wing coalition took 85 percent of all National Assembly seats with the first-ballot support of 28.8 percent of the electorate; the FN and the ecology groupings, with the first-ballot votes of 15.6 percent of the electorate, won no seats at all. Chirac's argument that 'the gap is widening dangerously between the governing class and the man in the street' (Chirac 1995: 12) was confirmed when he was elected President with the first-ballot votes of just 15.9 percent of the registered electorate. In 2002, he was the first choice of fewer than 14 percent of registered voters (though the second choice, it is true, of 62 percent of them, when the alternative was Le Pen); the UMP's absolute majority of 64 percent of the National Assembly seats was built on the first-ballot votes of fewer than 22 percent of registered voters.

The changing importance of social cleavages

From 1978 onwards, left-wing parties lost ground among their core support groups such as men of working age, workers, teachers, the unemployed, and the young. Most strikingly, where the Left had won 77 percent of the vote of unskilled workers in 1978, it attracted 46 percent in 1997 – an election it won. Losses here were partly compensated for by gains among traditionally right-wing groups: women, the retired, managers, and even Catholics (Schweisguth 1994: 229–32). Similarly, the mainstream right-wing parties lost ground among women, managers, farmers, and the retired, but gained among men, wage-earners (especially in the private sector), and workers.

Part of this change may be seen as class dealignment: for example, managers and professionals forgetting earlier fears of Communism and being readier than in the 1970s to vote for 'responsible' left-wing candidates. Boy and Mayer (2000) on the other hand, noted a redefinition of the 'class' cleavage, which tends to run increasingly between the self-employed and wage- and salary-earners rather than between blue-collar and white-collar occupations. But perhaps the most striking change remained the gravitation of part of the Left's traditional social base to the FN. This was especially true of unskilled workers, 30 percent of whom voted FN in 1997 (similarly, Le Pen attracted 30 percent of the blue-collar vote at both ballots in 2002). In other words, a core section of FN support was constituted by people who would, during the long postwar boom, have been blue-collar Communist voters with stable if low-grade jobs (Schain, 2000), and who were now particularly exposed to the ravages of deindustrialization and unemployment. Referring to the political consequences of such upheavals, Flanagan and Dalton (1990: 239), argue that 'Cleavage theory predicts that the most virulent forms of conflict during this transitional period should emerge between the winners and losers in the social dislocations associated with post-industrial development.' It is hard to imagine a better illustration of this type of realignment than the rise of the FN. More generally, a large body of literature, both comparative (Kitschelt with McGann 1997; Perrineau 2001) and centred on France (Grunberg and Schweisguth 1997; Abrial *et al.* 2002; Chiche *et al.* 2002) has argued that the traditional Left–Right cleavage has now not only weakened, but has been partly replaced by a different cleavage based on opposition to, or support for, a society that is 'open', whether in relation to immigrants and ethnic minorities, to socially liberal ideas, or to Europe, or even to globalization; in other words, by a cleavage between moderate parties, especially the Socialists, and the far Right.

Vote switching

Jaffré and Chiche (1997: 292) have shown that total voter mobility between first rounds of elections rose from 21 percent in the decade from 1986 to 30 percent in 1995. It is true that the most dramatic form of mobility, between the main families of Left and Right, was fairly constant (11 percent for 1986, 12 percent for 1995). However, switching between Left and Right *between ballots of the same presidential election* roughly tripled in two decades, from 3.4 percent of voters in 1974 to 10 percent in 1995. An appreciable proportion of the latter figure was accounted for by '*gaucho-lepénistes*', voters (mostly working-class) who switched from the far Right at the first round to the Left at the second – for example, the estimated 27 percent of first-round Le Pen voters who backed Jospin at the run-off in 1995 (Perrineau 1995, 1997). The phenomenon of *gaucho-lepénisme*, however, had diminished by 2002, with under 10 percent of first-round FN voters switching to the Left at the parliamentary elections (Mayer 2002; IPSOS 2002).

The loosening of party attachments

The use of party membership as a means of analysing the relationship between citizens and politics is problematic in the case of France, because parties have historically tended to lack the strong organizational identities they possess elsewhere, and are prone to gross inflations of the official membership tally. Party identification should be treated with caution for the same reasons. These caveats aside, total party membership appears to have fallen by half, from over 900,000 in the late 1970s to under 450,000 in 2002.[2] The most fully comparable measure of party identification, the Eurobarometer figures, shows that the percentage of those who were 'closely attached' to a party in France fell from 28 percent in 1978 to 16 in 1992, and 'party sympathizers' (including the closely attached) from 69 percent to 52: both somewhat faster drops than the EU average (Schmitt and Holmberg 1995: 126–7; Schweisguth 2002: 57). At the same time, Chiche, Haegel, and Tiberj (2002: 231) have shown not only that party identification in France does not necessarily entail the adoption of a more or less homogeneous ideological package, but that ideological homogeneity has been *lowest* among supporters of France's two biggest parties of government, the Gaullists and the Socialists. Also noticeable, finally, has been the growing scepticism of the French – and especially younger voters – about the notions of Right and Left: nearly two-thirds of voters regarded the concepts as outdated in 1996, compared with barely one-third in 1981. That was reflected in the 2002 elections: the second round of the presidential election, which set the mainstream against the FN rather than Right versus Left, mobilized some 3 million more voters than the first ballot – and nearly 6 million more than either ballot of the parliamentary elections, which returned to a more orthodox Left–Right pattern. Of those who saw little use in voting where the stakes were defined by traditional politics, but who mobilized strongly, whether on the street or at the ballot box, against the FN, a disproportionate number were aged under 30 (Muxel 2002).

Disenchantment with politics and with parties

While the French have rarely been enthusiastic about politics and parties in general, their mistrust has deepened since the early 1980s. A series of political funding scandals involving the Socialists in the early 1990s and the Right later the same decade took their toll: by 1999, 61 percent of respondents to a regular SOFRES poll considered that politicians were 'generally corrupt', compared to 38 percent in 1977. Another SOFRES sample, asked for its feelings about politics in general, gave as leading responses 'mistrust' (57 percent) and 'boredom' (27 percent); 'respect' won 7 percent of responses and 'enthusiasm' 2 percent. The year 2000 saw 70 percent of respondents (against 50 percent a decade earlier) saying they 'did not feel well represented' by a party, and 74 percent (against 54 percent in 1989) expressed the same view about political leaders. In a 1998 survey, finally, 84 percent of respondents agreed with the statement that politics was 'in crisis', a 10 percent rise on the figure for 1989 (Corman 2001; Duhamel 2001).

Other arguments, it is true, indicate that French democracy is less crisis-ridden than the French think. The claim of a decline in votes for 'parties of government' rests on a subjective notion of what constitutes a party of government; Communists and Les Verts, after all, both had ministers in 1997. Arguments based on first-ballot voting figures ignore the fact that most first-round 'protest' voters turn to mainstream parties of Left and Right at the run-off. Abstentionism may have increased, but there is little to suggest that persistent, purposeful abstention has risen significantly (Appleton 2000: 219–20). The French may be dismissive or contemptuous of their parties and politicians in general, but average opinions of *individual* parties have shown no dramatic slump since the early 1980s. The survival of Le Pen, the protest candidate *par excellence*, to the second ballot of the 2002 presidential elections provoked a wave of hostile demonstrations and an overwhelming popular vote against him on 5 May 2002 (this result was due far more to a spontaneous reaction by voters than to any cartel-like arrangement between mainstream parties of Left and Right, which did not co-operate at all between ballots). Approval for the Fifth Republic's overall institutional record *rose* from 56 percent in 1976 to 71 percent in 2000; there is negligible hostility to democracy as such (Duhamel 2001). To some extent, too, it could be argued that focusing on voters' growing willingness to desert mainstream parties at *first ballots* misses the point. In the French system, the first ballot offers a safety-valve for voter discontent before wiser counsels prevail at the run-off – and the introduction of proportional representation allows new parties representation at levels where they can do relatively little harm, until such time as they are properly house-trained and become acceptable partners in second-ballot withdrawal agreements (Hanley 2002: 171–82).

In that context, the two main new entrants, the FN and Les Verts, presented very different challenges to the established parties, because one was clearly more fit to be house-trained. This is well illustrated by their respective positions in the regular SOFRES popularity ratings, which invited poll respondents to express 'good' or 'bad' opinions of individual parties. Les Verts are one of France's more popular parties. Over 125 months between September 1992, when SOFRES began giving them regular ratings, and January 2003, they enjoyed a positive balance of opinions during 66 months; the balance between good and bad opinions was exactly even for three months, and negative for 56 months, giving an average balance of –0.7 percent. Only the PS had a better record. The FN, on the other hand, repels most of the French. Over the 229 months between January 1984, when SOFRES first gave it a rating, and January 2003, the balance of opinions of the FN was negative *every* month, with an average balance of –66.8 percent: no party, not even the PCF, did worse (SOFRES 2002b). Since 1985, a clear majority of the French (averaging 66.5 percent across fourteen polls between October 1985 and May 2002) have believed that the FN is a danger to democracy. Such general opinions of parties are, of course, no guide to electoral support: the unpopular FN has almost always outpolled the relatively popular Verts. But they are a good indicator of the costs of alliance for the established parties: low for Les Verts, high for the FN. That in turn indicated the appropriateness of a strategy of integration into the mainstream for Les Verts, and of a strategy of exclusion for the FN.

Neither, though, was quite a foregone conclusion in the new context of instability and increased competition that characterized France's electoral market from the 1980s. Each of the four established parties experienced dramatic electoral setbacks in this new environment: the PCF almost continuously from

1981; the PS in 1983–4, in 1992–4, and in 2002; the mainstream Right in 1981, 1988, and 1997. Each disappointed voters, especially over the issue of unemployment, which rose from 1.7 million in 1981 to 3.2 million in 1996 and affected the young – new voters – disproportionately. Each saw elements of its core electorate shrink or defect as hitherto stable communities of class and religion lost their consistency. Each was forced by new competitors to address new issues – law and order, immigration, and the environment (Ignazi 1997). French politicians were in a position to be aware of all of this, being as sensitive as any others to lost votes, and probably even more obsessed by poll data; but the answers were far from obvious. The rest of this chapter considers two possible types of response by established parties. The first will be called structural, and covers changes both to the institutional framework of party competition and to the organization of the established parties themselves. It will be argued that while there have been changes in both of these areas since the mid-1980s, few may be seen as a direct response to changes in electoral markets. The second will be called strategic, and covers the established parties' direct responses to new competitors in their rhetoric, policies, and alliance strategies. These met with greater success, though not very quickly, not without qualification, and not necessarily very lastingly.

Structural responses: the institutional framework and party organization

Established parties in France have changed both the rules of the electoral game and their own organizations since the 1980s. According to the cartel model of party organization, we would expect them to have colluded in rigging the rules of the electoral game to their advantage (Katz and Mair 1995). We would also expect them to have professionalized their own organizations, and possibly also to have given their members more formal rights at the expense of substantive control over the leadership, and to have 'blurred' the distinction between members and non-members. Elements of such initiatives are indeed present in France, but they form part of a more complex, and less consistent, pattern than the cartel model suggests.

Electoral competition: the rules of the game

Institutional changes since the 1980s can be grouped in three categories. The first is diametrically opposed to the cartel model: it covers initiatives that were bound to open up competition rather than limit it. The second category covers a cartel-type initiative, but one which backfired. Only the third can be seen as corresponding to the cartel model, and then imperfectly.

In the first category we must place the introduction of proportional representation noted earlier in this chapter. The law of 1977 on direct European elections dates from a time when competition from new players was minimal; it can be seen as an attempt by the Giscardians of the UDF both to moderate the bipolarity of a political system that could still appear as 'civil war (between Left and Right) by other means', and to loosen the bipolar discipline that bound them to Chirac's turbulent neo-Gaullists. Subsequent European elections later, and unexpectedly, provided the opportunity for the FN's first national-level breakthrough (in 1984) and for record scores for Les Verts (in 1989 and 1999). The introduction of proportional representation for municipal elections (from 1983, partially) and regional elections (from 1986) also made life easier, not harder, for new entrants, allowing opposition members onto the councils of major towns for the first time since 1965 and placing severe difficulties in the way of the emergence of clear majorities on regional councils. The use of proportional representation for parliamentary elections in 1986, finally, flagrantly contradicts the cartel thesis. Introduced by one of the mainstream governing parties, the Socialists, against fierce attacks from the right-wing opposition (which tabled a motion of censure on the issue), it was seen, in part correctly, as a cynical attempt to head off an expected victory for the moderate Right by allowing a new entrant, the FN, to win seats in the National Assembly. The moderate Right still won in 1986, though with a narrow majority: its immediate restoration of the two-ballot system for parliamentary elections again provoked a motion of censure, one which mobilized the whole opposition, PS, PCF, and FN, and fell five votes short of a majority (Assemblée Nationale 1996: 141–3). Two other areas of legislation can also be seen as widening rather than narrowing the range of competition for office: the limitation of the very French practice of multiple elective office-holding, the *cumul des mandats*, by laws in 1985 and 2000, and the incentives, established in 2000, for male–female parity among party candidates at all elections.

In the second category of rule changes we may place the party finance laws of 1988, 1990, 1993, and 1995, which for the first time regulated political contributions and spending, and supplied public money for parties and campaigns. This may appear as a cartel-type initiative, both in its general thrust – public finance of parties being an essential component of the cartel thesis – and in the manner of its conception – an initiative taken by the Socialist President Mitterrand, and supported by the neo-Gaullist Prime Minister Chirac, in 1987, at a time of cohabitation (Favier and Martin-Rolland 1991: 703–4). In practice, however, the most important of the laws, that of 1990, and particularly the amnesty provisions linked to it, failed to rally a cross-party consensus, and was voted by a narrow majority of Socialist and centrist parliamentarians (Favier and Martin-Rolland 1996: 322–5). More important, France's Constitutional Council helped prevent the formation of a cartel of well-financed established parties by requiring that public finance be available to any party able to present 50 candidates at a parliamentary election (Uguen 1995: 102–5, 152–3). This again opened up competition to new entrants. Before the public finance laws, parties had been financed in part (for those in government) by 'special funds' at the disposal of the Prime Minister, and more generally by corrupt means, linked to the award of public works contracts and thus to the occupation of office at local or national level. After 1990, on the other hand, parties depended for their finance primarily on their ability to present candidates and win votes and seats. Though this gave an advantage to the larger parties, it was not an exclusive one – unlike the old corrupt system. In 2000, for example, the PS received 24.2 million euros of public subsidy and the RPR 16.8 million, but there was also over 6 million each for the PCF and the FN, 1.9 million for Les Verts, and even 700,000 euros for the Trotskyist Lutte Ouvrière (*Journal officiel* 2002). Public funding totalling over 80 million euros was distributed among no fewer than 41 parties, some of them almost certainly set up and maintained solely for that purpose (Dolez 1997). Public finance is the single most important reason behind the inflation in the number of parliamentary candidacies.

The third category of rule changes are those that have specifically targeted new players. Of relatively minor importance has been the 1990 'Gayssot law' on incitement to racial hatred, which has restrained some of Le Pen's more overtly racist outbursts without having a significant effect on the electoral market; it was voted by Socialist and Communist deputies but opposed even by the moderate Right. Of greater significance have been more recent changes to electoral systems. The first of these, passed in 1999, injected a significant but not overwhelming majority element, and a second ballot, into the system for electing regional councillors. Alone among institutional changes, it closely resembles a 'cartel' measure: it was proposed by President Chirac in the aftermath of the 1998 regional elections, which had rendered the emergence of clear majorities on regional councils particularly difficult because of the FN's strong performance, was backed by the Socialist premier Jospin, and was voted by the left-wing National Assembly majority (Levy 2001: 112–13). But this law was never applied. It was replaced in 2003 by altogether fiercer legislation which extended to European as well as regional elections. This incorporated tough thresholds into the regional electoral system (a list must obtain the votes of 10 percent of registered electors at the first ballot to take part in the second), and divided representation at European elections into eight regional constituencies, rather than a single constituency for the whole of France. The new law was anything but a consensual measure. Backed by Chirac's victorious UMP, it was opposed not only by its obvious victims – the FN, the PCF, and Les Verts, all of which stood to lose more or less drastically – but also by the junior partner in the right-wing coalition, the UDF, and by the Socialists, who probably stood to gain. Faced by a deluge of spurious opposition amendments, Jean-Pierre Raffarin's right-wing government used the biggest weapon in the government's legislative armoury, article 49–3, to pass the new law through the National Assembly in February 2003, provoking a censure motion from the Left. If its effect was likely to reinforce big established parties, then, the backing for the new legislation was very far from confirming a cartel pattern.

Party organization

The development of French party organization offers in some ways a more consistent picture, of professionalization and democratization, but without amounting to a purposeful attempt to reassert control over changing electoral markets. French parties have certainly enlarged their budgets (most recently thanks to public finance) and their professional staff: whereas before 1958, only the PCF had more than a dozen or so full-time headquarters officials (Williams 1964: 66), 40 years later the PS and the RPR (as well as the FN) each claimed over 100. This has been a slow, incremental process, shaped by the increasingly capital-intensive nature of political communication, and the growing number of elections to be fought (presidential from 1965, European from 1979, regional from 1986). Only the PCF has gone in the opposite direction, largely because of its dreadful electoral results: it announced plans to shed 44 of its 104 head-quarters staff after the 2002 defeats (*Le Monde*, 7–8 July 2002).

French parties – with the exception of the FN – have also democratized, usually in the wake of defeats. The most spectacular case is probably that of the PCF, which officially abandoned the Leninist model of democratic centralism in 1994, proceeded to go through a succession of somewhat unconvincing reorganizations, and in 2003 took the unprecedented step of accepting competition between three different motions for its 2003 congress (*Le Monde*, 4 March 2003). The Right's defeats of 1988 also led the RPR, dubbed by some of its own members 'the last Stalinist party in France', to liberalize and allow the organized expression of dis-senting views, within limits; ten years later, in the wake of the 1997 defeats, the RPR adopted the one member, one vote (OMOV) principle for the election of the party leader, and a genuinely competitive leadership election was held in December 1999 (Dolez and Laurent 2000). The UDF, with a smaller member-ship base, had already done the same when it reorganized in 1996 (Massart 1999: 358–9), and the principle was carried over for the election of the UMP leader (former Prime Minister Alain Juppé won the post without serious opposi-tion in November 2002). The Socialists have resisted OMOV for the leadership election, but used it to choose their presidential candidate in 1995, when Jospin's two-to-one support from PS activists, obtained against the party's first secretary, Henri Emmanuelli, greatly enhanced the legitimacy of his candidacy. Some parties have also sought to involve non-members in their activities, effectively blurring the distinction between members and non-members. Both the UDF and the UMP websites positively invite involvement, in forms such as fora on specific policy issues, from non-members. The PCF both launched grass-roots level 'thematic groups' including members and non-members and presented a European election list for 1999 with non-members running alongside card-carrying Communists (neither initiative was crowned with success).

Such changes have not, however, had great effect on the fundamental distri-bution of power within the parties, which continue to face a broadly consistent set of conflicting organizational pressures between central leaderships, rein-forced by the perspectives of presidential competition (and greatly complicated where a party has a president in the Élysée), and the demands of locally entrenched élites, reinforced by the 1982 decentralization reforms and sus-tained by the survival, however partial, of the *cumul des mandats*. The varying balance of these pressures on individual parties at particular moments in the electoral cycle has done more to affect their organization than changes in electoral markets.

Party leaderships and modes of candidate choice have shown similar resistance to change. French party leaders tend to be stayers. The departure of the Stalinist Georges Marchais from the PCF leadership in 1994 was due more to age and ill-health than to political discredit. In the UDF, the septuagenarian Giscard only left the leadership in 1996, fifteen years after his presidential defeat of 1981 (the party split just two years after). Chirac's effective leadership of the RPR dates from 1974, when he was already Prime Minister, and survived two presidential defeats. In the PS, Jospin became First Secretary in 1995, fourteen years after first holding the office; when he won the premiership in 1997, his own nominee François Hollande moved smoothly into the party post and stayed there after Jospin's defeat and (unusual) withdrawal from politics in 2002; the most likely Socialist candidate for the 2007 presidential race, Laurent Fabius, had been a young Prime Minister in 1984. The leadership teams of both the RPR and the PS in the late 1990s were already among the rising, or even the established, generation of party leaders in the early 1980s. Juppé, the first president of the new UMP in 2002, was already installed in Chirac's private office a quarter-century earlier; Hollande joined Mitterrand's Élysée staff in 1981. And the same *sort* of individuals, typically with a top civil service background, kept appearing at the heads of French parties: Juppé, and Fabius, and Hollande, and Jospin all attended the elite École Nationale d'Administration, as did Giscard and Chirac. In this context, the hypothesis of a replacement of old-style political hacks by new-style professionals was inapplicable to late twentieth-century France – or rather, it had already happened, in a peculiar French way, in the 1960s and 1970s (cf. Schonfeld 1980).

Nor does it appear that changing electoral markets have led to major changes in the choice of parliamentary candidates. In all cases, the possession of local office and of a post allowing significant amounts of time for politics (typically public employment for the Left, and self-employed business or the liberal professions for the Right), have been crucial qualifications for selection. The deputies elected in 1997 were little different from their predecessors in this respect, with a high proportion of incumbents, past candidates from 1993, and local elected officials in all four parties (Schlesinger and Schlesinger 2000: 140–3). Similarly, of the class of 2002, nearly 60 percent have a professional and managerial background, 60 percent had already sat in the Assembly (including about 40 losers from 1997 who returned to the Assembly in 2002), half are mayors, a third are councillors for a *département*, and nearly seven-eighths are men (Greffet and Andolfatto 2002). This last point deserves brief attention. The gender parity law of 2000 subjected parties to funding penalties if they failed to observe parity in parliamentary candidacies. Small parties, with few incumbent deputies, few candidates with a serious chance of election but a serious need for the money, observed the rule quite scrupulously: over 49 percent of candidates for the two main Trotskyist groups, for Les Verts, and for the FN, and 44 percent for the PCF, were women. Parity suffered, on the other hand, among parties with incumbents and serious constituency battles to fight: both the PS (where only 36 percent of candidates were women) and, even more, the moderate Right, where the figure barely reached 20 percent, chose to run their (male) incumbents and take the penalty (*Le Monde*, 11 June 2002).

In more general terms, two attempts at global reform can be discerned among France's established governing parties. One concerned the PCF. Robert Hue, Marchais's successor as leader from 1994, clearly saw the end of democratic centralism as the start of a larger process of shedding the party's Stalinist baggage and opening out to non-Communist forces in civil society. Hue's programme was set out in a work ambitiously entitled *Communisme: la mutation* (Hue 1995). Its genesis came at least two decades too late; its implementation too often lapsed into mere trendiness, as when the party headquarters, built in more prosperous days to a design by Oscar Niemeyer, was hired out for fashion shows; and Hue's critics attacked not only his *embourgeoisement* but also the continuing hold on the party of a sclerotic professional bureaucracy. Structural reform failed to prevent the PCF's progressive confinement to a handful of bastions, vulnerable to challenges from FN and Trotskyists alike. The other global reform was the merger of the RPR, DL, and most of the UDF in the new UMP. This involved the fusion of two distinct organizational cultures, that of the cadre party for the UDF and DL, and something closer to the catch-all party for the RPR, into what was intended by its first leader, Alain Juppé, to be a big modern conservative party on the pattern of the German CDU-CSU or the Spanish PPE (Knapp 2003; *Le Monde*, 22 June 2002). Nearly a year after its launch in April 2002, however, the UMP grass-roots organization was still 'virtual' and marked by squabbles between its former components, while its popularity ratings had gone negative from late 2002 (*Le Monde*, 11 March 2003). There was little sign, therefore, that Chirac's second victory had created a dynamic commensurate with Juppé's ambition.

French parties have succeeded neither in remodelling the rules of political competition to shut out new entrants (though the most recent electoral reform, backed by the UMP alone, could point in that direction), nor in reinventing their organizations to improve links with civil society. They still affect to value organizational strength on something resembling a mass party model: after a brief influx of new members during and after the 2002 elections, both the UMP and the PS launched new membership drives late in 2002 (*Le Monde*, 17 December 2002). But the likelihood of their organizations being able to reach into the working-class communities where the Left (and especially the PCF) had often been strong before 1981, and where alienation from the political system is now at its greatest, is slight. Capable neither of reinventing themselves nor of redefining the institutional framework, the established parties met new challenges chiefly by tactical methods, which progressively solidified into long-term strategic choices. Without being wholly ineffective, these achieved patchy results.

Strategic responses I: the Socialists' war on two fronts

The essential characteristics of party competition in France – many parties, and varied dynamics arising from equally varied electoral systems – impose an almost inexhaustible series of choices on the major parties. The impact of such choices, even the smaller ones, on the electoral market is highly unpredictable. This is well demonstrated by the Socialists' behaviour before the 2002 presidential election. Mainstream parties have an opportunity to shape the configuration of presidential competition because all presidential candidates must be sponsored by at least 500 out of France's 36,000 or so mayors. Major parties may therefore encourage their mayors to sign for minor candidates who they believe will indirectly serve their own interests. In 2002, Socialist mayors, with party approval, provided signatures for the young Trotskyist candidate Olivier Besancenot, because he was expected to take votes from Arlette Laguiller of Lutte Ouvrière, who was considered more dangerous. They also backed Christine Taubira, the West Indian candidate for the small (and moderate) Left Radical party, in the hope that Taubira would attract black voters, who might otherwise have abstained, but who might go on to back Jospin at a second ballot; indeed, the Socialists even refused Taubira's offer to withdraw in mid-campaign if they would cover her election expenses.[3] The PS therefore contributed to the fragmentation of the electoral market – and thus to the first-ballot elimination of its own candidate Jospin, who would have beaten Le Pen into third place had he benefited from a quarter of Besancenot's vote or a half of Taubira's. This is perhaps an extreme instance of relatively minor decisions having a disproportionate impact, but it does illustrate the range of choices confronting mainstream parties, at local as well as at national levels. The rest of this chapter, however, will be limited to the tactics and strategy followed by the major French parties towards the two most consistent of the new entrants.

The Socialists faced challenges both from the FN and from the ecology movement. As a mainstream governing party they should, on the cartel model, have moved to exclude the one and to incorporate the other. In fact they were slow to react to either. The FN was long seen solely as a problem for the Right. As late as 1995, some Socialist elected officials refused to acknowledge its attractiveness to their voters. For some Socialists, indeed, the FN was for a long time not a threat, but an opportunity to sow confusion within the mainstream Right. The ecology movement, on the other hand, was seen by many Socialists as a single-interest group rather than a political movement; its weak organization and seeming inability to fix a loyal electorate militated against its being taken seriously. That only began to change after the ecologists had proved their attractiveness to Socialist voters in the elections of 1992–3. At the same time, the Socialists' perceptions of challenges were complicated by three elements: by their own factionalism and culture of debate; by the widening gap, especially after 1988, between the Socialist President Mitterrand and his party; and by the differing views of activists, broadly liberal on questions such as immigration, and voters, many of whom were less so.

The Socialists and the FN

President Mitterrand can reasonably be accused of assisting the FN's early breakthrough. It was Mitterrand who instructed heads of public television networks to give Le Pen the television coverage he had hitherto lacked, and which he had requested in a letter to the President (Faux *et al.* 1994: 19–29) – Le Pen's first major television appearance, on the *Heure de vérité* interview programme in February 1984, was a key step in raising his media profile. It was also Mitterrand who pressed the government to adopt proportional representation for the 1986 parliamentary elections, giving the FN the respectability of a parliamentary group. On both of these counts the Socialists – or at least Mitterrand – may justly be accused of assisting the FN. More debatable is the claim of the Right that Mitterrand's periodic proposal that immigrants should be allowed to vote at local elections was designed to provoke a debate on immigration that would embarrass the Right and benefit the FN.

In public, Mitterrand and the Socialists frequently appeared less inclined to confront the FN itself than to accuse the mainstream Right of complicity with it. Jospin compared the mainstream Right's attitude to Le Pen with that of German conservatives towards Hitler in 1983; Prime Minister Édith Cresson asserted in 1992 that 'the [mainstream] Right isn't a barrier against the FN, it's a trampoline' (Favier and Martin-Rolland 1991: 76; 1999: 137). Indeed, for much of the period after the FN's breakthrough, the Socialists appeared to 'sub-contract' opposition to the FN to specialized associations, notably SOS-Racisme (from 1984) and the Manifeste contre le Front National (from 1990). SOS-Racisme – a notionally independent movement, though launched with support and money from the Élysée – focused chiefly on mobilizing the young against the FN. Its early leaders, such as Harlem Désir and Julien Dray (initially an activist in the Trotskyist Ligue Communiste Révolutionnaire), reached senior positions within the PS inside a decade. The Manifeste was launched by the Socialist Deputy Jean-Christophe Cambadélis (who had joined the PS from another Trotskyist group in 1986) in the wake of the desecration of the Carpentras Jewish cemetery by skinheads in May 1990. More pedagogical than SOS-Racisme, it has been primarily committed to helping cadres of left-wing parties mount an effectively argued opposition to the FN; interestingly, the then First Secretary of the PS, Pierre Mauroy, only signed its manifesto eighteen months after its first appearance.

However, the Socialists also made rhetorical concessions to Le Pen's agenda. Thus Prime Minister Laurent Fabius, facing Chirac in a television debate in 1985, vaunted his government's record in expelling illegal immigrants, and added that 'on these issues [law and order and immigration], with one or two exceptions, I don't think there are any major disagreements' between the Socialists and the mainstream Right (Favier and Martin-Rolland 1991: 360); Cresson warmly endorsed the use of charter aircraft to deport illegal immigrants, a technique introduced by the hardline Gaullist Interior Minister Charles Pasqua; Mitterrand himself shocked many Socialists in 1989 by claiming that France's 'threshold of tolerance' in relation to immigrants had been crossed in the 1970s (Favier and Martin-Rolland 1996: 299). In policy terms, the Socialists were reluctant to appear as liberals: in 1989, for example, the tough restrictions passed under the Chirac government on conditions of aliens' entry into and residence in France, and on police identity controls, were moderated but not repealed (though the Socialists did back the Gayssot bill on incitement to racial hatred the following year).

Following the defeat of 1993, and especially after the presidential election of 1995, the PS adopted a more coherent attitude to the FN. The inclusion of Cambadélis in the PS leadership from 1993 indicated greater readiness to view the FN as a direct threat; after 1995, Jospin also made Ahmed Ghayet a delegate responsible for problems of integration, while Gérard Le Gall was commissioned to produce a report on fighting the FN. There have been no verbal concessions to the FN agenda by a senior PS leader since 1995; nor has the FN been used against the moderate Right. The treatment of the *sans-papiers* – the 150,000 or so immigrants left in an administrative limbo by the immigration legislation of the 1993–7 right-wing governments – was cautious (the question was initially handed over for a report by the sociologist Patrick Weil), but clearly more liberal than that of the Right: by January 2001, some 80,000–100,000 of the *sans-papiers* had residence permits. Where they had the necessary activists, the Socialists also took to noisy demonstrations against the FN during the 1997 campaign. One of these provoked Le Pen into punching a Socialist candidate, Annette Peulvast-Bergeal (Darmon and Rousso 1998: 142–4), and so set in motion the train of events that would lead, indirectly, to the split of the FN (see p. 77 below). Finally, the Jospin government attempted to reach out to the Left's lost bases in working-class France through the 35-hour week, which was expected both to create jobs and give wage-earners more leisure. Although the 35-hour week was, ironically, most favourably received by professionals and managers, and entailed low wage growth and newly flexible working patterns, the initiative was nevertheless intended to offer some of the benefits of growth to ordinary wage-earners, for the first time since the early 1980s.

In general, however, the Socialists' record on containing or reversing the FN's rise has been mediocre. The FN initially appeared as an opportunity to some (including Mitterrand), and an embarrassment to others – hence the habit of 'subcontracting' anti-FN activities. Nearly a decade elapsed between the FN's national breakthrough and the development of a coherent PS policy. Even after the FN's break-up in 1998–9, the Socialists' potential for disunity and indecision was demonstrated by their failure to defeat far-right mayors in the towns of Orange, Marignane, and Vitrolles at the 2001 municipal elections. And the dismissive reaction in the Jospin campaign headquarters to Gérard Le Gall's warning, made days before the first ballot of the 2002 presidential election, that Le Pen could overtake Jospin testifies to a continuing failure among Socialists to consider the FN as a danger to themselves.[4]

The Socialists and the ecology movement

The other new entrant, the ecology movement, posed almost diametrically opposite difficulties for the Socialists. The values of France's ecologists were far less of an affront than those of the FN to the Republic or the Left. Ecologists were also rather obviously both a useful reserve of marginal second-ballot votes and attractive to at least a fringe of Socialists. But they were electorally unstable, as Table 3.1 shows, and organizationally fragmented. The 10.9 percent of the vote achieved in 1993 was divided between three different groupings, one of them serving solely to attract public finance (Dolez 1997); indeed, Sainteny (2000: 400–4) lists over half a dozen ecology 'parties' operating in the 1993–5 period, and as many different ones in 1998. This combination almost invited the tactical, instrumental character of the Socialists' initial response, which sought to prove their own Green credentials, to discredit political ecology groupings, and to establish their own Green satellites.

Attempts to 'green' the PS itself and Socialist-led governments have included appointments as well as concessions of policy and (more often) of rhetoric. The PS leadership has included a spokesman on environmental questions since the Pau congress in 1975 (Jospin's first Education Minister, Claude Allègre, began his political career as Jospin's adviser on the environment). After each of his presidential victories, Mitterrand appointed a Green minister (Alain Bombard in 1981, and the former French Friends of the Earth leader and former presidential candidate from 1981, Brice Lalonde, in 1988) with a view to attracting ecology votes at the ensuing parliamentary elections. Policy concessions were rather limited: Mitterrand's 1981 electoral promise to 'review' France's nuclear programme had little impact on energy policy after his election, while the 1990 national plan for the environment, projecting a doubling of environmental spending in ten years, later fell foul of government spending constraints. These nods to the Green agenda were closely linked to electoral concerns. Indeed, Sainteny (2000: 158–96) has argued that the ecology movement's electoral strength, and the proximity of elections, have had a determining effect on the number of references to environmental questions by all the mainstream parties, on the number and range of environmental measures taken by governments, and even on the status of the Environment Ministry in official protocol.

At the same time the ecology movement, and especially Les Verts, the leading but not the only group from 1984, was the object of deliberate attacks which sought to present it as negative, single-issue groups, lacking both the broad programme of a real party and the competence to govern. Fabius, for example, claimed that ecology groups were full of 'reactionaries nostalgic for a pre-industrial past', while his associate Henri Weber asserted that ecology was 'not a policy, nor even an ideology, but a preoccupation' (Sainteny 2000: 205–8). The Socialists also tried to create tame ecology groups from 1983. The most substantial was Génération Écologie (GE), launched in 1990 by the environment minister Lalonde. GE was at least as much a Mitterrand initiative, aimed at broadening the presidential coalition beyond the faction-ridden PS (comparable initiatives were aimed at the centrists and the centre-left Radicals) as it was a Socialist one. In the short term it was successful, winning comparable levels of support to those of Les Verts in both the 1992 regional elections and the 1993 parliamentary elections. But GE rapidly fell victim to a dearth of patronage (Lalonde left the government in 1992, and 1993 saw no ecologist deputies elected) and to its leader's own political promiscuity: his gravitation, after 1993, to the new right-wing majority won little support.

The electoral disaster of 1993 transformed Socialist policy on the ecology movement. Staring defeat in the face, the Socialist First Secretary Laurent Fabius had tried unsuccessfully to negotiate with Les Verts, in the summer of 1992; in February 1993, former Prime Minister Michel Rocard had called for a 'big bang' that would produce a broad centre-Left alliance of Socialists, 'critical' Communists, ecologists, 'social' centrists, as well as groups from civil society (Favier and Martin-Rolland 1999: 365, 377). The Rocard speech was the first public declaration of a Socialist readiness to accept ecologists as partners, rather than try to patronize them, dismiss them, attack them, or incorporate them into a satellite group. After Rocard succeeded Fabius in April, he sought to implement the 'big bang' idea, to reach into civil society and win new partners for the PS, with a series of meetings called the *Assises de la transformation sociale*. Yet the two men Rocard delegated to run the *Assises*, Jospin and Cambadélis, had a much more classical vision of their party's alliance strategy: a straightforward alliance of left-wing parties including ecologists and the PCF – what was to become the *gauche plurielle* (Clift 2000; Amar and Chemin 2002). This orthodox strategy prevailed for three reasons. First, Rocard resigned from the Socialist leadership after a crushing defeat at the 1994 European elections; seven months later Jospin was the party's presidential candidate and the *de facto* (and soon *de jure*) socialist leader. Secondly, the PCF became a more amenable partner after Hue succeeded Marchais in January 1994. Thirdly, the ecologists possessed, in Les Verts and in their 1995 presidential candidate Dominique Voynet, elements available to cooperate with the Socialists. As Hanley (2003) remarks, the Socialists' 'gamble on the Greens' involved restoring the fractured bipolarity of the party system by giving solidity to a new political entrant, 'decanting' those among the ecologists who were interested in winning power in harness with the Left.

It also involved the restoration of the Socialists' old hegemony on the Left. That was achieved at the 1995 presidential elections, thanks to Jospin's first-ballot score of 23.3 percent, against Hue's 8.6 – and Voynet's 3.3. The January 1997 agreement between the Socialists and Les Verts (who ratified it by a narrow majority) provided for a clear first-ballot run for Les Verts candidates in 29 constituencies at the next parliamentary elections, and for the PS candidate in 77 others, as well as mutual support at the run-off. Common policy commitments included more liberal immigration legislation, the 35-hour week, gender parity, the five-year presidential term, and limitations on the *cumul des mandats*, as well as a limited range of environmental measures including the closure of the Superphénix nuclear reactor, a moratorium on new reactors till 2010, and the abandonment of the Rhine–Rhône canal project. The Left's victory five months later led to Voynet's appointment as France's First Minister from Les Verts, charged with the rather obvious portfolio of environment and regional planning.

The Socialist strategy had apparently led to the harmonious incorporation of a new political force within the old bipolar framework. But the alliance was subjected to severe strains over the next five years and was left in tatters by the 2002 defeats. Les Verts complained that the Socialists were as overbearing as ever. Voynet's one middle-ranking ministry represented barely one-thirtieth of the government in return for one-seventh of the *gauche plurielle* vote, and the appointment of Guy Hascoët to a very junior position in the summer of 2000 was scant compensation. The Jospin government showed slight interest in environmental policy, failing to find parliamentary time before 2002 for Voynet's long-awaited bill on water pollution and making no haste to back her efforts to implement European directives on bird conservation against a vociferous hunting lobby. Voynet's periodic expressions of dissatisfaction were ignored or slapped down by Jospin. For the Socialists, on the other hand, the experience was equally problematic. Voynet was seen as too quick to follow her party's concerns, rather than government policy, over issues such as the *sans-papiers*, and too slow at her ministerial job (her reaction to the 2000 *Erika* oil slick disaster was especially lamentable). That Les Verts gained votes – 9.7 percent at the 1999 European elections, 12.4 percent at the municipal and cantonal elections of 2001 in seats they contested independently – was not necessarily to be regretted, except that they still took some of their votes from the Socialists, and proved more unreliable than the Communists at delivering second-ballot support to Socialist candidates. Les Verts are also more faction-ridden than the Communists, making the organization as unreliable as the voters. That became clear during and after the 2002 elections. Les Verts first dithered – democratically – over their choice of presidential candidate, actually dropping their first choice Alain Lipietz in favour of Noël Mamère. Then, after a defeat at the legislative elections which left them with just three National Assembly seats, they marginalized the main advocates of the *gauche plurielle* alliance, Mamère and Voynet, at their December 2002 congress. Finally, after a month without any leadership at all, they chose the unknown Gilles Lemaire, a former Trotskyist who had only joined Les Verts in 1999, as national secretary. Lemaire was highly critical of the *gauche plurielle* record and reluctant to commit to any further alliance with the PS, although such a link was rendered more necessary than ever for Les Verts by the 2003 electoral reform. Relations between the two parties were effectively rolled back a decade, to the period of the 1993 defeat, but with the pro-alliance group in Les Verts much weakened.

Of the two obvious strategies available to an established party like the PS in dealing with new entrants, one, the incorporation of Les Verts into an alliance that responded to the party system's bipolar constraints, was attempted systematically after 1993, but was not consolidated sufficiently to resist the inevitable strains of the 2002 defeats. The other, the exclusion of the FN, was undertaken in the most erratic of manners and never in conjunction with the mainstream

Right. The mainstream Right's own exclusion strategy was late and slow, of limited success, but ultimately vital in containing the FN.

Strategic responses II: the Right and the *Front National*

For the RPR and the UDF, the ecology groups were a largely secondary concern. President Giscard d'Estaing had, it is true, engaged a substantial series of environmental measures after their initial successes (Sainteny 2000: 181). The early 1990s also saw a brief flurry of interest in the Green vote, during which a dose of proportional representation and a new offence of damage to the environment were included in right-wing programmes. But neither proposal was implemented, and no ecology group, not even Lalonde's Génération Écologie, was considered as of serious interest as a potential partner. The presidential candidacy of Corinne Lepage, environment minister of the first Juppé government of 1995, was consented to rather than backed by the Chirac camp in 2002.

The challenge from the FN, by contrast, was one of direct and obvious concern to the mainstream right-wing parties. It was first posed at a municipal by-election at Dreux in September 1983, at which the FN list did well enough at the first round to be a necessary partner for any victory by the RPR–UDF candidates against the incumbent Socialist mayor. The RPR–UDF list duly opened up to FN candidates; the RPR Secretary-General Bernard Pons campaigned for the merged list; Dreux was won for the Right; but Chirac promised that the experience would not be repeated nationally (Favier and Martin-Rolland 1991: 77–9). It was to take the Right five years to develop a more consistent strategy towards the FN.

The FN conundrum for the RPR and the UDF had three main elements. First, Le Pen and his party articulated issues which the mainstream Right could not be seen to ignore once a competitor expressed them. A clear majority of the French – 58 percent, for example, in 1993, 59 percent in 2002 – agreed with the proposition that there were 'too many immigrants' in France (Martin 2000: 256; SOFRES 2002a). Between one-sixth and one-third of poll respondents, but between a quarter and a half of RPR–UDF sympathizers, have expressed their 'agreement with Le Pen's ideas', notably on the immigration and law and order issues (Mayer and Perrineau 1993: 65; SOFRES 2002a). Although the proportion tended to fall slowly over time, and although a majority (over 80 percent in 2002) found Le Pen's views 'excessive' or 'unacceptable', these were questions that the mainstream Right was bound to address. Secondly, what Dreux appeared to demonstrate was that the FN, by supplying or withholding its support, could make the difference between victory and defeat for the Right. This was most plausibly the case when the mainstream Right's forces were evenly balanced with those of the Left, as in 1988 (when it was argued that Le Pen had lost Chirac the presidential election) and in 1997 (when the FN maintained its candidates at the run-off ballot against the mainstream Right in 76 constituencies, and the Right lost in 47 of them – enough to lose it an absolute majority in the Assembly). Conversely, the FN's leverage was much reduced in periods like the early to mid-1990s, or at the parliamentary elections of 2002, when the Left's weakness ensured a comfortable overall advantage for the moderate Right. And even in 1988 and 1997, the FN's capacity to seal the Right's fate was probably overstated (cf. Ysmal 1998: 299). But the perception remained partly true and highly important. Thirdly, however, no alliance with the FN would be cost-free because the FN, as noted above, is France's most repulsive party. Alliances with the far Right cost votes, especially from within the moderate Christian Democratic wing of the UDF.

Three further factors complicated the debate within the RPR and the UDF. First, although clear majorities of moderate right-wing voters have tended, in opinion polls, to oppose an alliance with the far Right (Mayer and Perrineau 1993: 74), these positions have been much less solid at times, and especially in localities, where victory was in the balance; in 1998, indeed, little more than a third of RPR–UDF supporters rejected the idea of an alliance under all circumstances (Buisson 1999: 33). Secondly, the elites of both parties have been divided on the issue. Both included a minority of anti-Fascists, such as the RPR's Michel Noir, who embarrassed Chirac in 1987 by declaring that the Right would do better to lose the (1988) elections than to lose its soul, or the UDF's Bernard Stasi, whose views earned him the FN's targeted enmity and the loss of his Épernay constituency. Both parties have also included FN sympathizers like Claude Labbé, president of the RPR parliamentary group before 1986, or the UDF's veteran reactionaries Alain Griotteray or Michel Poniatowski. Both have also had their opportunists, like Jean-Claude Gaudin, the UDF's Marseilles boss who was ready to do deals with the FN to save seats for the Right in his region in 1988. Finally, the two parties also brought different ideological and organizational perspectives to the problem. The RPR's electorate was slightly more open to FN ideas (Buisson 1999: 33), but the organization was more tightly controlled from the centre. The UDF electorate, on the other hand, or rather its Christian Democratic wing, was more resistant to the FN's ideas, but the party was more dependent on local office than the RPR and less amenable to central direction. At the same time the two parties' close alliance more or less dictated a common policy; one of them could not join an alliance with the FN while the other held it in quarantine.

The mainstream Right has rarely hesitated to address the issues raised by the FN, immigration and law and order, both in rhetoric and, more importantly, in law. Chirac's notorious speech of 1991 referring to the 'smells' of immigrant households and the polygamy that prevailed there was unusual for him but has been matched by other politicians of the Right (Mayer and Perrineau 1993: 64–6). Ten years later, Chirac placed law and order at the centre of his 2002 campaign, initially during a calculated manœuvre to sidestep questions about corrupt practices during his stewardship of the Paris Town Hall during a television interview on 14 July 2001. Each of the mainstream Right's election victories, in 1986, 1993, and 2002, has been followed by a reinforcement of measures to expel illegal immigrants and of police powers – the latter in a draconian manner in 2002–3. This did not, of course, amount to applying the FN's programme: the mainstream Right has never sought the systematic expulsion of *all* immigrants, as the FN has, or planned to restore the death penalty (Chirac, indeed, had voted for its abolition in 1981) or to strip naturalized immigrants of citizenship. For that reason, Le Pen has claimed that voters will always 'prefer the genuine article' to imitations, and critics of the moderate Right have suggested that mainstream politicians who give a high profile to immigration and law and order merely enhance the FN's appeal (Mayer and Perrineau 1993: 66–8). Support for the mainstream Right's policies, however, can be found in the polling evidence, which suggests that most voters care *about* the issues but not *for* the FN's treatment of them (SOFRES 2002a).

By contrast, the FN itself, as opposed to its agenda, has been the object of regular attacks from the mainstream Right. Chirac has referred to the FN as 'people who tried several times to murder General de Gaulle, who have always been in the other camp, never on the side of the democrats, or of the Gaullists' (*Libération*, 7 May 1990), and both he and Juppé have attacked Le Pen and his party as 'racist, anti-semitic, and xenophobic' (*Le Monde*, 22–23 September 1996, 25 March 1998). These attacks have been reciprocated by Le Pen himself, who referred to Chirac in 1995 as 'like Jospin only worse' (Dély 1999: 73).

The most controversial aspect of the Right's response to the FN, however, was the question of alliances. For five years after the Dreux by-election, the RPR–UDF leaderships refused any form of national negotiation with the FN but tolerated local agreements. As Bernard Pons, the RPR's secretary-general at the time of the Dreux by-election, admitted later, 'We managed it badly. We didn't have a clear answer. We were torn between our decision not to accept a national-level alliance, and local exigencies which often pointed in the opposite direction' (Knapp 1994: 84). The most notorious agreements, dating from 1986, involved the inclusion of FN councillors in right-wing majorities – and executives – on five regional councils (including Aquitaine, headed by the former Prime Minister and Resistance hero Jacques Chaban-Delmas). This ambiguous position won little credit from the FN electorate, and offered the Left an opportunity to take the moral high ground. The policy changed, in the RPR, after the 1988 defeats and a lengthy debate within the party leadership. In September 1988, following one of Le Pen's more grotesque verbal outbursts, Alain Juppé, as RPR secretary-general, announced a ban, soon replicated by the UDF, on all national and local alliances with the FN (Juppé 1993: 31–3).

Imposed by Parisian leaderships on the parties' sometimes reluctant grass roots, the ban was never watertight; there were local infringements, some of which (for example, the agreement with the FN that secured election for the RPR mayor of Béziers in 1989) provoked disciplinary measures. Such measures were also applied to RPR figures like Alain Carignon who proposed a 'republican front' with the PS against the FN. The ban on alliances provoked open criticism within both parties, especially after the defeat of 1997, when right-wing leaders like Alain Peyrefitte and Charles Pasqua for the RPR, or

Alain Griotteray for the UDF, wondered aloud about the possibility of an alliance (*Le Monde*, 11, 15–16, 17 and 24 June, 1 July 1997). Broadly speaking, though, the quarantine held, and after a decade it helped split the FN. This can be seen from consideration of the crisis of spring 1998, when it was most nearly broken for good.

The regional and cantonal elections of March 1998 concerned councils elected in exceptionally prosperous years for the mainstream Right (1992 and 1994); left-wing gains were therefore inevitable. That tempted local and regional councillors of both RPR and UDF, anxious to keep their seats or their majorities, and encouraged by opinion polls showing as many as 40 percent of moderate right-wing sympathizers backing alliances with the FN, to rail against the *'diktat* from Paris' banning such deals (*Paris-Match*, 25 March 1998). In the RPR, a high-profile example was made of a former party secretary-general, Jean-François Mancel, who was expelled for accepting FN votes to secure re-election as councillor for his *département*. In the UDF, a weaker party more dependent on its regional positions, the damage was more extensive. Three incumbent UDF regional presidents (Charles Millon in Rhône-Alpes, Charles Baur in Picardie, Jacques Blanc in Languedoc-Roussillon), as well as the non-aligned right-winger Jean-Pierre Soisson in Burgundy, flouted the official RPR–UDF line by accepting support from FN regional councillors so as to hang onto their presidencies. This threw the Right into open crisis (Ysmal 1999). Chirac solemnly condemned the alliances in a special presidential broadcast; right-wing RPR and UDF supporters tore up their membership cards in disgust; left-wing and centrist voters, on the other hand, punished the mainstream Right at the second round of the cantonal elections, especially in those regions where the alliances had been concluded three days before. Less than two months later, the UDF broke up. Its formerly Christian Democratic wing, led by François Bayrou, kept the UDF name, and was resolved to keep Millon and his friends in quarantine along with the FN, while Alain Madelin's right-wing DL was more conciliatory towards the rebels. Millon, meanwhile, went on to form his own micro-party, simply called 'La Droite', which openly accepted the principle of alliances with the FN. The episode prolonged the dislocation of the mainstream Right that had started with the 1997 defeat.

From the point of view of the far Right, though, the episode was even more disastrous. The FN had become increasingly divided between Le Pen's supporters and those of the party's delegate-general, Bruno Mégret, widely seen as Le Pen's heir. The two men differed less on policy – Mégret's line on immigration has never been any more 'moderate' than Le Pen's – than on strategy. Le Pen, an outsider for all of his political life, sought to provoke the collapse of the mainstream Right by repeated attacks from outside; once that had happened, the FN could offer them an alliance on its own terms. Mégret, on the other hand, was a political insider, a civil servant, former chief of staff to a Gaullist minister before 1981, one of a younger generation who had gravitated to the FN from the mainstream Right in the mid-1980s. Since then, he had played a crucial role in professionalizing the FN's organization and in building satellite groups to improve its reach into civil society – in the expectation of winning power, or a share of it, within a decade. Instead, Mégret and the FN's other 'modernists' saw their party reach a peak of 15 percent in the mid-1990s, just 0.6 percent higher than Le Pen's presidential result of 1988, and then stay there, no closer to government than ten years earlier. Increasingly, they blamed the ageing, coarse, unpredictable, truculent and too obviously racist Le Pen for the FN's continued pariah status. The Mégret strategy was to seek an alliance with the mainstream Right as quickly as possible and on virtually any terms, and thereafter to become indispensable allies to the RPR–UDF and dictate to the whole Right. Le Pen rightly saw the Mégret strategy as a threat, since its fulfilment would be facilitated by his own removal (Buisson 1999: 33; Darmon and Rousso 1998: 245–55). But he was obliged to back it in 1998 because of Mégret's ascendancy in the party and because he could offer no obvious alternative perspective. Applied to the regional elections, the Mégret strategy meant offering the mainstream Right a minimal contract for administering regions together, including tax cuts, rigorous management, but none of the more objectionable FN themes. The outcome of the offer, however – acceptance by four right-wing regional presidents out of twenty, each of whom faced near-ostracism by respectable politicians – was disappointing: the FN failed to break through into mainstream politics and Mégret was personally weakened, a ripe target for Le Pen's fight-back. Within less than a year, a dispute over the composition of the FN's list for the 1999 European elections (itself provoked, indirectly, by Le Pen's conviction for punching Peulvast-Bergeal in 1997, and his resulting temporary ban from holding elective office) had led to Mégret's departure and the FN's split into two parties, the old FN and Mégret's Mouvement National Républicain, commanding no more than 10 percent of the vote between them. Le Pen had had many previous disputes with his close lieutenants without breaking up his party. What made the quarrel with Mégret so destructive was that the FN of the 1990s contained two cultures, a culture of protest and a culture of integration into mainstream politics, and that each commanded a comparable level of support. When the FN split, it split down the middle (Hainsworth and Mitchell 2000: 452). But nothing could have been better calculated than the effects of the mainstream Right's ban on alliances to generate long-term frustration within the Mégret camp and ultimately to provoke the break-up.

From the perspective of 1999, or even of 2001, it could therefore have been assumed that the mainstream Right had pursued a successful strategy of exclusion – late, and imperfectly, but successfully because of the FN's split. At the 1999 European elections, the far Right won just 9 percent of the vote, divided between 3.3 percent for the MNR, kept out of Strasbourg by the 5 percent threshold, and the 5.7 percent which just allowed the FN to keep five MEPs. At the 2001 municipal elections, the far Right presented lists in 297 towns, where the FN had run in 456 in 1995. At that year's cantonal elections, only 26 far-Right candidates (24 FN and 2 MNR) reached the run-off ballot compared with 306 FN candidates in 1998. The manner of the split – the departure of most of the FN's cadres in *départements* for the MNR, which then proved to be the electorally weaker party – was especially damaging to the organization of the far Right. Even then, though, the far Right was more contained than excluded, as Le Pen's result in 2002 illustrated. Certainly, it was more a personal victory for Le Pen, achieved in remarkably favourable external circumstances but with minimal organizational support, than a party victory; this organizational weakness was reflected in the FN's relatively poor performance at the June 2002 parliamentary elections (Mayer 2002). The FN remained as isolated from mainstream politics as ever at the end of 2002 (Ivaldi 2002). Yet there remained a substantial and largely loyal far Right electorate, contained in a near-ghetto by France's institutions and by the mainstream Right's refusal to join an alliance – but not dispersed.

Conclusion

This chapter has attempted to answer two sets of questions. First, how far does the French case confirm the 'cartel' thesis, which suggests that established parties will collude in a variety of ways to exclude, or failing that to co-opt, new entrants? Secondly, and independently of the cartel model, what techniques have established parties used to respond to changes in the electoral market, and particularly to new entrants, and how successful have they been?

France supplies rather little evidence of parties behaving according to the cartel model. The two-ballot majority system, established for parliamentary and presidential elections in the founding years of the Fifth Republic (some 30 years before cartel parties were thought of), has served as a highly effective airlock because the *de facto* requirement of alliances to win seats and office has kept undesirable parties at a safe distance from France's core institutions. The system has also, however, encouraged stiff bipolar competition among established parties, not multi-polar collusion. While such parties have frequently manipulated the rules of political competition, therefore, they have often done so in order to embarrass mainstream adversaries rather than to penalize new entrants, and they have only rarely acted in concert. The 1999 law reforming the regional electoral system was perhaps the only example of established parties colluding in a manner clearly directed against a new entrant; and it will never be applied. Other institutional changes have either tended to favour new entrants (the early introduction of proportional representation, or the introduction of public finance for parties) or have failed to win a consensus among established parties (the reintroduction of the two-ballot system in 1986, or the electoral reform of 2003, both carried by the Right against strong left-wing opposition).

Parties have thus responded to changes in electoral markets on a largely individual basis. Part of this response has been organizational. They have slowly professionalized their organizations, using public funding to expand the payroll at central offices (with the exception of the declining PCF). They have sought to involve non-members in their activities, in rather cosmetic ways for the right-wing parties, more spectacularly in that of the PCF at the 1999 European elections. They have democratized, adopting OMOV for choosing the party leader (in the case of the moderate right-wing parties) or presidential candidate (in that of the PS), and allowing more organized expression of dissent (in the RPR and the PCF). More global reorganization has affected the PCF, in a state since 1994 of almost permanent organizational change (but also permanent decline), and the moderate Right (largely regrouped as the UMP, which had still not resolved the characteristic problems of merger in the first year of its existence). Some of these initiatives are reminiscent of the cartel model, in which parties professionalize even as they lose members, and engage in democratic window-dressing to conceal an increasingly top-down organizational reality. That said, the party that has experienced the sharpest membership decline, the PCF, has also had to cut its staff. The measures of democratization have, on occasion, placed real power in the hands of members, rather than enrolling them as 'cheerleaders' (Katz and Mair 1995: 20). Most importantly, perhaps, the basic Fifth Republic model of a mainstream party of government, in which a complex pattern of collusion and competition between local-level *notables* and national-level *présidentiables*, discernible since the 1970s, has not been radically altered by recent reorganizations.

At the heart of French parties' responses to changing markets, however, have been their efforts to grapple with the tactical and strategic problems posed by the arrival of new players, most importantly though far from solely the ecology groupings and the far Right. Established parties undertook these on a largely individual basis (or in tandem in the case of the RPR and UDF), and slowly: if the point of departure is set at 1983–4, which saw both the breakthrough of the FN and the formation of Les Verts, then it took the Right five years to fix a coherent strategy in relation to the former, and the PS a decade to engage with the latter. The intervening period saw attempts to manipulate new entrants for the purposes of bipolar competition between established parties, most notably by the Socialists in relation to the FN.

At the same time the two cases present obvious and radical differences. While each new entrant mobilized on values commanding widespread support – tougher measures on law and order and tighter restrictions on immigration for the FN, better environmental protection for Les Verts – the public perception of the two *parties* is radically different: the FN remains repulsive, Les Verts (relatively) popular. While the FN's integration into the political mainstream is not unthinkable – it has clearly tempted politicians of the moderate Right – it would entail substantial costs which the parties of the moderate Right, out of interest or principle or both, have not been prepared to pay. The costs of integrating ecology groupings into a left-wing alliance, on the other hand, while not insignificant (alliances are more unmanageable the more partners they include) are almost certainly lower than those of leaving them outside the system.

These distinctions inevitably shape the aspect that 'success' takes on in each case: incorporation for the ecologists, exclusion for the far Right. More precisely, success in relation to ecology groupings would involve, first, their 'decanting' into a single party; secondly, the consolidation of such a party into a reliable political force, organizationally strong and capable of making negotiated agreements stick; thirdly, the lasting commitment of such a party to alliance with mainstream partners; and fourthly, the management of electoral competition to ensure that the ecology party attracts voters who would otherwise have remained out of reach of the political mainstream, without eating too far into the electoral base of the mainstream parties. By contrast, success in relation to the far Right would consist in keeping it as fragmented as possible, as weak as possible, and as marginal as possible.

The achievements of the established parties in relation to these criteria may appear partial, even ephemeral. Among ecology groupings, Les Verts have become the only serious organization, thanks in part to their alliance with the PS. Between 1997 and 2002 they gained the experience of a 'party of government' (Bozonnet 2002: 160), ensuring unprecedented integration into the political system. Yet their integration has not lasted, or not fully. At the outset of 2003 they appeared distinctly unpromising partners for any future left-wing return to power: weak, fragmented, and – as the choice of Lemaire as national secretary showed – sceptical about the whole idea of an alliance with the mainstream. Les Verts and the wider ecology movement remain somewhere between a culture of government, a culture of grass-roots activism and protest, and a belief that they are destined to supersede the Socialists (Lipietz 1993). When electorally strong, as between 1999 and 2001, they have taken votes from the PS as well as adding to the overall left-wing total; when weak, their electoral usefulness has been marginal; and their voters have been less inclined than the Communists to switch to other left-wing candidates at second ballots. The Socialists, on the other hand, have oscillated between serious attempts to transform Les Verts into a consistent, reliable partner, and their more traditional hegemonic habits and disinclination to take ecology seriously. By failing to incorporate environmental concerns into a wider left-wing project, by limiting their impact in the Jospin government's public policy, by at times encouraging factional struggle within Les Verts (Hanley 2003), the Socialists probably helped to maintain their partners' semi-detached relationship to mainstream politics.

The far Right, on the other hand, has been successfully confined to the margins of the French political system, at least nationally. But none of the established parties was able to prevent the main achievement of the FN under Le Pen: the constitution of an electorate amounting to more than one voter in ten which, however composite in terms of social origins and political itineraries, was remarkably consistent in its authoritarian, ethnocentric values (Perrineau 1997; Mayer 1999). It was that, above all, which allowed the FN to survive the split of 1998–99, and the considerable organizational damage that resulted, and to re-emerge in strength in 2002. Despite the Raffarin government's energetic attempts to address the law and order issue by an exorbitant increase in police powers, the FN is likely to remain strong, but within a ghetto – unless, that is, its localized strength enables it to turn the majority bias of the 2003 election law to its advantage. That the main hope for a significant reduction in the FN's support lies in the approaching struggle for the succession to Le Pen, aged

75 in 2003, is the measure of the limitations to the success of mainstream parties in facing the challenge.

A further failure of the mainstream parties has been their inability to address the wider malaise in French politics. The aspiration to 'rehabilitate' politics expressed by the Jospin government as it took office in 1997 was barely fulfilled – despite a favourable judgement of its record by 54 percent of poll respondents as late as February 2002 (SOFRES 2002c). The spurning, by a majority of the electorate at the first round of the 2002 presidential election, of mainstream candidates in favour of abstention or of anti-system players testified to the extent of the malaise. What followed, though, demonstrated its limits. At the second round, after a large-scale mobilization on the streets against the perceived threat to democracy represented by Le Pen's presence at the run-off, Chirac won an overwhelming popular vote of confidence from 62 percent of the registered electorate, and 82 percent of the voters, including many who would have written him off as irredeemably corrupt just two weeks earlier. At the parliamentary elections, 80 percent of the voters (though barely half of the electorate) turned out to back the mainstream parties, ensuring a comfortable majority for the dull but reassuring Raffarin. The sudden rejection of established parties and politicians, combined with a susceptibility to the temptations of multiple populisms; an outburst of support for 'the Republic' against a perceived threat; and more or less resigned and conditional return to the muddy waters of the political mainstream. These are signs not so much of a new and more dangerous relationship of the French to political parties, as of a well-worn pattern played out, periodically, in French politics for as long as the Republic has existed.

Notes

1 For a fuller discussion of bipolar multipartism, cf. Knapp and Wright 2001: ch. 9.

2 The UMP claimed a highly improbable 164,000 members at its first congress in November 2002, but some of its own senior members put the true figure closer to 90,000 (*Le Monde*, 20 November 2002). The PS claimed 147,000 in December 2002 (*Le Monde*, 17 December 2002), and the PCF 133,000 in February 2003 (*Le Monde*, 4 March 2003 and http://www.pcf.fr). The FN claimed 60,000 members in 2003 (http://www.frontnational.com). Les Verts have never claimed more than 10,000 members, the UDF is always reticent about membership but probably has no more than 20,000, while the Eurosceptic right-wing breakaway party, the RPF, claimed 33,000 in 2000 (22 February 2000) but broke up almost immediately.

3 I am grateful to private sources in the PS for this information, supplied in May 2002 and public knowledge since.

4 This episode was recorded in a fly-on-the-wall documentary on the Jospin campaign, 'Comme un coup de tonnerre', broadcast on France 2 (20 June 2002).

References

Abrial, Stéphane, Bruno Cautrès, and Jocelyn Evans (2002). 'Stabilité et recomposition du système de partis français.' *Revue politique et parlementaire* 1020–21, September–December, pp. 228–43.

Amar, Cécile and Ariane Chemin (2002). *Jospin & Cie. Histoire de la gauche plurielle, 1993–2002.* Paris: Seuil.

Appleton, Andrew (2000). 'The France that Doesn't Vote: Nonconsumption in the Electoral Market.' In Michael Lewis-Beck (ed.), *How France Votes.* New York, NY: Chatham House, pp. 206–26.

Assemblée Nationale (1996). *Les Gouvernements et les assemblées parlementaires sous la Ve République.* Paris: Assemblée Nationale.

Bartolini, Stefano and Peter Mair (1990). *Identity, Competition and Electoral Availability: the Stabilization of European Electorates, 1885–1985.* Cambridge: Cambridge University Press.

Boy, Daniel and Nonna Mayer (2000). 'Cleavage Voting and Issue Voting in France.' In Michael Lewis-Beck (ed.), *How France Votes.* New York, NY: Chatham House, pp. 153–75.

Bozonnet, Jean-Paul (2002). 'Les Verts: échec et résistance.' *Revue politique et parlementaire* 1020–21, September–December, pp. 150–61.

Buisson, Patrick (1999). 'La Droite dans tous ses états.' In SOFRES, *L'État de l'opinion 1999.* Paris: Seuil, pp. 11–48.

Chiche, Jean, Florence Haegel, and Vincent Tiberj (2002). 'La Fragmentation partisane.' In Gérard Grunberg, Nonna Mayer, and Paul M. Sniderman (eds), *La Démocratie à l'épreuve: une nouvelle approche de l'opinion des Français.* Paris: Presses de Sciences Po, pp. 203–37.

Chirac, Jacques (1995). *La France pour tous.* Paris: Éditions du Nil.

Clift, Ben (2000). 'PS Factionalism and Electoral Strategy: the Interaction of Intra-Party Politics and Party System Change.' Paper presented to the conference on Changes in the Contemporary French Party System: Internal Dynamics and External Context, University of Salford, 30 September. In Jocelyn Evans (ed.), *The French Party System.* Manchester: Manchester University Press, 2003.

Cole, Alistair (1998). *French Politics and Society.* New York, NY: Prentice Hall.

Corman, Gilles (2001). 'L'Image de la politique dans le contexte de l'affaire Méry, ou les ravages de l'accoutumance.' In SOFRES, *L'État de l'opinion 2001.* Paris: Seuil, pp. 217–24.

CSA (2002). 'Les Français et les programmes de Lionel Jospin et de Jacques Chirac.' http://www.csa-tmo.fr/fra/dataset/data2002/opi20020321a.htm

Darmon, Michaël and Romain Rousso (1998). *L'après Le Pen.* Paris: Seuil.

Dély, Renaud (1999). *Histoire secrète du Front national.* Paris: Grasset.

Dolez, Bernard (1997). 'Les "petits" partis au regard de la réglementation du financement de la vie politique.' In Annie Laurent and Bruno Villalba (eds), *Les petits partis: De la petitesse en politique.* Paris: L'Harmattan, pp. 91–107.

Dolez, Bernard and Annie Laurent (2000). 'Quand les militants RPR élisent leur président.' *Revue Française de science politique* 50: 125–46.

Duhamel, Olivier (1997). 'Derrière le brouillard, le bipartisme?'. In SOFRES, *L'État de l'opinion 1997.* Paris: Seuil, pp. 81–98.

Duhamel, Olivier (2001). 'Confiance institutionnelle et défiance politique: l'a-démocratie française.' In SOFRES, *L'État de l'opinion 2001.* Paris: Seuil, pp. 67–78.

Faux, Emmanuel, Thomas Legrand, and Gilles Perez (1994). *La Main droite de Dieu: enquête sur François Mitterrand et l'extrême droite.* Paris: Seuil.

Favier, Pierre and Michel Martin-Rolland (1991). *La Décennie Mitterrand.* Volume II: *Les Épreuves.* Paris: Seuil.

Favier, Pierre and Michel Martin-Rolland (1996). *La Décennie Mitterrand.* Volume III: *Les Défis.* Paris: Seuil.

Favier, Pierre and Michel Martin-Rolland (1999). *La Décennie Mitterrand.* Volume IV: *Les Déchirements.* Paris: Seuil.

Flanagan, Scott C. and Russell J. Dalton (1990). 'Models of Change.' In Peter Mair (ed.), *The West European Party System.* Oxford: Oxford University Press, pp. 232–46 (reprinted from *West European Politics* 2 (3), 1979).

Greffet, Fabienne and Dominique Andolfatto (2002). 'Les Députés de 2002: la "maison sans fenêtres" s'ouvre-t-elle?' *Revue politique et parlementaire* 1020–1, September–December, pp. 219–27.

Grunberg, Gérard (1985). 'France.' In Ivor Crewe (ed.), *Electoral Change in Western Democracies*. London: Croom Helm, pp. 202–29.

Grunberg, Gérard and Étienne Schweisguth (1997). 'Vers une tripartition de l'espace politique.' In Daniel Boy and Nonna Mayer (eds), *L'Électeur a ses raisons*. Paris: Presses de Sciences Po, pp. 179–218.

Hainsworth, Paul and Paul Mitchell (2000). 'France: the Front National from Crossroads to Crossroads?' *Parliamentary Affairs* 53: 443–56.

Hanley, David (2002). *Party, Society, Government: Republican Democracy in France*. Oxford: Berghahn.

Hanley, David (2003). 'Managing the Plural Left: Implications for the Party System.' In Jocelyn Evans (ed.), *The French Party System*. Manchester: Manchester University Press pp. 76–90.

Hue, Robert (1995). *Communisme: la mutation*. Paris: Grasset.

Ignazi, Pierro (1997). 'New Challenges: Postmaterialism and the Extreme Right.' In Martin Rhodes, Paul Heywood, and Vincent Wright (eds), *Developments in West European Politics*. Basingstoke: Macmillan, pp. 300–19.

IPSOS (2002). 'Premier tour législatives 2002', telephone poll, 9 June 2002, 2,925 respondents, on http://www.ipsos.fr/CanalIpsos/poll/7571.asp

Ivaldi, Gilles (2002). 'L'Extrême-droite renforcée mais toujours isolée.' *Revue politique et parlementaire*, 1020–1, pp. 133–49.

Jaffré, Jérôme (1993). 'Les grandes vagues électorales sous la Cinquième République: le raz de marée de 1993.' In Pascal Perrineau and Colette Ysmal (eds), *Le Vote sanction: les élections législatives des 21 et 28 mars 1993*. Paris: Presses de la Fondation Nationale des Sciences Politiques, pp. 251–67.

Jaffré, Jérôme (2001). 'Le retournement electoral.' *Le Monde*, 29 March.

Jaffré, Jérôme and Jean Chiche (1997). 'Mobilité, volatilité, perplexité.' In Daniel Boy and Nonna Mayer (eds), *L'Électeur a ses raisons*. Paris: Presses de Sciences Po, pp. 285–325.

Journal officiel (2002). Commission Nationale de Comptes de Campagne et des Financements Politiques, 2002, *Publication générale des comptes des partis et groupements politiques au titre de l'exercice 2000*, annexe au *Journal officiel* du 4 avril 2002.

Juppé, Alain (1993). *La tentation de Venise*. Paris: Grasset.

Katz, Richard S. and Peter Mair (1995). 'Changing Models of Party Organization and Party Democracy: the Emergence of the Cartel Party.' *Party Politics* 1: 5–28.

Katz, Richard S. and Peter Mair (1996). 'Cadre, Catch-All, or Cartel? A Rejoinder.' *Party Politics* 2: 525–34.

Kitschelt, Herbert with Anthony J. McGann (1997). *The Radical Right in Western Europe: a Comparative Analysis*. Ann Arbor, MI: University of Michigan Press.

Knapp, Andrew (1994). *Gaullism since de Gaulle*. Aldershot: Dartmouth.

Knapp, Andrew (2003). 'From the Gaullist Movement to the President's Party.' In Jocelyn Evans (ed.), *The French Party System*. Manchester: Manchester University Press pp. 121–36.

Knapp, Andrew and Vincent Wright (2001). *The Government and Politics of France*, 4th edn. London: Routledge.

Lancelot, Alain (1998). *Les Élections nationales sous la Ve République*, 3rd edn. Paris: Presses Universitaires de France.

Levy, Jonah (2001). 'Territorial Politics after Decentralization.' In Alain Guyomarch, Howard Machin, Peter Hall, and Jack Hayward (eds), *Developments in French Politics 2*. Basingstoke: Palgrave, pp. 92–115.

Lipietz, Alain (1993). *Vert espérance. L'avenir de l'écologie politique*. Paris: Éditions de la Découverte.

Martin, Pierre (2000). *Comprendre les évolutions électorales*. Paris: Presses de Sciences Po.

Massart, Alexis (1999). *L'Union pour la Démocratie Française (UDF)*. Paris: L'Harmattan.

Mayer, Nonna (1999). *Ces Français qui votent Le Pen*. Paris: Flammarion.

Mayer, Nonna (2002). 'Les hauts et les bas du vote Le Pen 2002.' *Revue Française de science politique* 52: 505–20.

Mayer, Nonna and Pascal Perrineau (1993). 'La Puissance et le rejet ou le lepénisme dans l'opinion.' In SOFRES, *L'État de l'opinion 1993*. Paris: Seuil, pp. 63–76.

Muxel, Anne (2002). 'La Participation politique des jeunes: soubresauts, fractures et ajustements.' *Revue Française de science politique* 52: 521–44.

Parodi, Jean-Luc (1997). 'Proportionnalisation périodique, cohabitation, atomisation partisane: un triple défi pour le régime semi présidentiel de la Cinquième République.' *Revue Française de science politique* 47: 292–312.

Parodi, Jean-Luc (2002). 'L'Énigme de la cohabitation, ou les effets pervers d'une pré-sélection annoncée.' *Revue Française de science politique* 52: 485–504.

Perrineau, Pascal (1995). 'La Dynamique du vote Le Pen: le poids du gaucho-lepénisme.' In Pascal Perrineau and Colette Ysmal (eds), *Le Vote de crise: l'élection présidentielle de 1995*. Paris: Presses de Sciences Po, pp. 243–62.

Perrineau, Pascal (1997). *Le Symptôme Le Pen: radiographie des electeurs du Front National*. Paris: Fayard.

Perrineau, Pascal (2001). 'L'Extrême droite en Europe: des crispations face à la "société ouverte"'. In Pascal Perrineau (ed.), *Les Croisés de la société fermée: l'Europe des extrêmes droites*. Paris: L'Aube, pp. 5–10.

Sainteny, Guillaume (2000). *L'Introuvable écologisme français?* Paris: PUF.

Schain, Martin (2000). 'The National Front and the Legislative Elections of 1997.' In Michael Lewis-Beck (ed.), *How France Votes*. New York, NY: Chatham House, pp. 69–86.

Schlesinger, Joseph A. and Mildred S. Schlesinger (2000). 'The Stability of the French Party System: The Enduring Impact of the Two-Ballot Electoral Rules.' In Michael Lewis-Beck (ed.), *How France Votes*. New York, NY: Chatham House, pp. 130–52.

Schmitt, Hermann and Sören Holmberg (1995). 'Political Parties in Decline?' In Hans-Dieter Klingemann and Dieter Fuchs (eds), *Citizens and the State*. Oxford: Oxford University Press, pp. 95–133.

Schonfeld, William R. (1980). 'La Stabilité des dirigeants des partis politiques: le personnel des directions nationales du Parti socialiste et du mouvement gaulliste.' *Revue Française de science politique* 30: 477–505.

Schweisguth, Étienne (1994). 'L'Affaiblissement du clivage gauche-droite.' In Pascal Perrineau (ed.), *L'Engagement politique: déclin ou mutation?* Paris: Presses de la Fondation Nationale des Sciences Politiques, pp. 215–37.

Schweisguth, Étienne (2002). 'La Dépolitisation en questions.' In Gérard Grunberg, Nonna Mayer, and Paul M. Sniderman (eds), *La Démocratie à l'épreuve: une nouvelle approche de l'opinion des Français*. Paris: Presses de Sciences Po, pp. 51–86.

SOFRES (2002a). 'L'Image du Front National.' http://www.sofres.com/études/pol/280502_frontnationa_r.htm

SOFRES (2002b). 'Les Popularités des partis politiques.' Derived from http://www.2002.sofres.com/partis.htm

SOFRES (2002c): 'L'Image de Lionel Jospin.' http://www.2002.sofres.com/pol/060202_chron_r.htm

SOFRES (2002d). 'Évolution du clivage droite–gauche depuis 10 ans.' http://www.sofres.com/études/pol/140202_clivage_n.htm

SOFRES, various dates, *L'État de l'opinion*. Paris: Seuil.

Teinturier, Bruno (2001). 'La Gauche tranquille au pouvoir.' In SOFRES, *L'État de l'opinion 2001*. Paris: Seuil, pp. 47–66.

Uguen, Jean-Luc (1995). *Les Élus et l'argent*. Paris: Syros.

Williams, Philip (1964). *Crisis and Compromise: Politics in the Fourth Republic*. London: Longmans.

Ysmal, Colette (1998). 'Le Second tour: le prix de l'isolement de la droite modérée.' In Pascal Perrineau and Colette Ysmal (eds), *Le Vote surprise: les élections législatives des 25 mai et 1er juin 1997*. Paris: Presses de Sciences Po, pp. 285–301.

Ysmal, Colette (1999). 'Domination des droites et crépuscule de la droite modérée.' In Pascal Perrineau and Dominique Reynié (eds), *Le Vote incertain: les élections régionales de 1998*. Paris: Presses de Sciences Po, pp. 163–84.

Zemmour, Eric (1998). *Le Livre noir de la droite*. Paris: Grasset.

FOUR   Embracing Dealignment, Combating Realigment: German Parties Respond

Susan E. Scarrow

A quarter-century ago the German Federal Republic was a model of party system consolidation. Between 1949 and 1961 the number of parties winning Bundestag seats dropped from eleven to four, and by 1972 a remarkable 99 percent of voters cast their ballots for one of these four parties. This pattern persisted throughout the 1970s, but soon new pressures began rearranging the German political landscape. The ensuing changes were associated with three inter-related developments: the declining reach of traditional cleavage-based politics, the weakening of partisan loyalties, and the advent of new party competitors. In the 1990s German unification exacerbated all three trends, and brought new challenges of its own.

This chapter focuses on the two parties which most benefited from (West) Germany's original electoral alignments, the Christian Democratic Union (CDU) and the Social Democratic Party (SPD), and shows how they responded to their increasingly unpredictable electoral environment. As will become clear, strategists in both parties initially welcomed and even promoted dealignment, treating it as an opportunity to win new voters for their party. However, the large parties subsequently have struggled to find political issues which simul-taneously can combat realignment and mobilize the politically unattached.

The basic contours of the Federal Republic's cleavage politics emerged during the 1950s. The Christian Democratic Union was the dominant force on the centre-right, sitting as a single group in the Bundestag with its Bavarian counterpart, the Christian Social Union (CSU). The SPD was the leading party of the Left. In between was the much smaller Free Democratic Party (FDP), which frequently served as coalition-maker at both the state and federal level. This system was anchored by strong ties between the big parties and specific social sectors. The CDU was founded as a cross-denominational, moderate con-servative party which drew strongest support from the church-going public. The SPD drew strongest support from unionized blue-collar workers.

These patterns of group support have endured. However, in recent years their importance has faded, both because the relevant groups are shrinking, and because the parties have wooed support beyond their traditional sectoral bases. From the 1950s onward the SPD actively and successfully courted white-collar workers and public employees. In the 1970s, when the CDU was first in opposition at the federal level, it also pursued a centrist strategy to broaden its appeal. Thus, in the 1960s and 1970s Germany's two big parties pursued policy-convergent strategies which reflected, and reinforced, social trends which were eroding traditional cleavage politics. Partly as a result, by the 1980s both of these self-proclaimed 'people's parties' found themselves facing an electorate that was increasingly disengaged from traditional political alternatives.

The emergence of the Green Party in the late 1970s was a further sign of change. The Greens drew much of their initial support from those on the Left who were dissatisfied with the way the SPD-led government dealt with issues such as environmental protection and disarmament. Support for the Greens grew rapidly, and in 1983 they became the first new party to enter the Bundestag since the 1950s. Meanwhile, in 1982 the then thirteen-year-old centre Left coalition collapsed when the FDP switched its support to the CDU/CSU. The new centre Right coalition, led by Helmut Kohl, was to govern for the next sixteen years. Despite the longevity of these coalitions, the waning years of the twentieth century saw important changes in German electoral behaviour, including declining electoral turnout and increasing support for parties of the far Right.

German political calculations were disrupted by the unexpected events of 1989 and 1990, which culminated in the unification of West and East Germany. Unification clearly inaugurated a new political era, although given the magnitude of the social and economic tasks, it can also be said that the integration of approximately 15 million East Germans with 60 million West Germans produced surprisingly small shifts in the roster of political parties. In 1990 the newly founded or re-founded East German parties rapidly oriented themselves to western party counterparts, and most of these alliances became formal mergers immediately before or after the 1990 'Unification Election'. The one eastern party to survive this consolidation wave was the Party of Democratic Socialism (PDS), the democratic successor to East Germany's ruling Socialist Unity Party (SED).[1]

The 1990 state and federal elections provided the first indications of the new contours of the expanded political system. Though some analysts assumed that the eastern Social Democrats would fare well in an area that was once a socialist stronghold, eastern voters overwhelmingly endorsed the CDU and FDP, the parties which advocated rapid unification (von Winter 1996: 299–301). Eastern support helped the CDU/CSU/FDP coalition retain national office in 1990 – an event that had seemed highly unlikely only eighteen months earlier, before unification had altered political priorities and changed the electoral base. In contrast the SPD, led by a very reluctant supporter of unification (Oskar Lafontaine), received the party's lowest vote share since 1957. However, the CDU's unification bonus soon faded and electoral patterns shifted during the 1990s as the post-unification economic boom collapsed. In 1994 the centre Right government only

Table 4.1 German electoral results, 1949–2002

Elections % votes (seats)	1949	1953[1]	1957[1]	1961	1965	1969	1972	1976	1980	1983	1987	1990[1,2]	1994	1998	2002
CDU/CSU	31.0	45.2	50.2	45.3	47.6	46.1	44.9	48.6	44.5	48.8	44.3	43.8	41.4	35.2	38.5
	(139)	(243)	(270)	(242)	(245)	(242)	(225)	(243)	(226)	(244)	(223)	(319)	(302)	(245)	(248)
FDP	11.9	9.5	7.7	12.8	9.5	5.8	8.4	7.9	10.6	7.0	9.1	11.0	6.9	6.2	7.4
	(52)	(48)	(41)	(67)	(49)	(30)	(41)	(39)	(53)	(34)	(46)	(79)	(47)	(43)	(47)
Greens[3]	–	–	–	–	–	–	–	–	1.5	5.6	8.3	5.0	7.3	6.7	8.6
									(0)	(27)	(42)	(8)	(49)	(47)	(55)
PDS	–	–	–	–	–	–	–	–	–	–	–	2.4	4.4	5.1	4.0
												(17)	(30)	(36)	(2)
SPD	29.2	28.8	31.8	36.2	39.3	42.7	45.8	42.6	42.9	38.2	37.0	33.5	36.4	40.9	38.5
	(131)	(151)	(169)	(190)	(202)	(227)	(230)	(214)	(218)	(193)	(186)	(239)	(252)	(298)	(251)
Others	27.9	16.7	10.5	5.7	3.6	5.4	1.0	0.9	0.4	0.4	1.5	4.1	3.6	5.9	3.0
	(77)	(45)	(17)	(0)	(0)	(0)	(0)	(0)	(0)	(0)	(0)	(0)	(0)	(0)	(0)
Total	100.0	100.0	100.2	100.0	100.0	100.0	100.1	100.0	99.9	100.0	100.2	99.8	100.0	100	100
	(399)	(487)	(497)	(499)	(496)	(499)	(496)	(496)	(497)	(498)	(497)	(662)	(680)	(669)	(603)
Turnout (%)	78.5	86.0	87.8	87.7	86.8	86.7	91.9	90.7	88.6	89.1	84.3	77.8[4]	79.0[5]	82.2[6]	79.1
Electorate (000s)	31,208	33,202	35,401	37,441	38,510	38,677	41,446	42,058	43,232	44,089	45,328	60,437	60,452	60,710	61,433
Fractionalization index	0.80	0.70	0.64	0.65	0.61	0.60	0.58	0.58	0.61	0.61	0.65	0.68	0.68	0.70	0.69
Effective no. of parties	5.0	3.33	2.78	2.86	2.56	2.5	2.38	2.38	2.56	2.56	2.94	3.13	3.13	3.33	3.34
Total volatility		19.0	8.3	11.5	6.8	6.2	5.7	4.1	4.5	8.4	6.0	7.8	7.8	8.3	7.8

[1] Major electoral system changes these years.
[2] Results for unified Germany from 1990 onwards.
[3] Bündnis '90/Greens after 1990.
[4] West: 78.6%; East: 74.5%
[5] West: 82.2%; East: 72.6%
[6] West: 82.8%; East: 80.1%

Sources: Schindler 1984, 1986, 1988, 1994; Bundeswahlleiter 1998, 2002

Table 4.2 Government composition in Germany,
1949–2003

Years in office	Governing coalition
1949–53	CDU/CSU, FDP, DP
1953–55	CDU/CSU, FDP, DP, GB/BHE
1955–56	CDU/CSU, FDP, DP
1956–61	CDU/CSU, DP
1961–66	CDU/CSU, FDP
1966–69	CDU/CSU, SPD
1969–82	SPD,FDP
1982–98	CDU/CSU, FDP
1998–present	SPD, B'90/Greens

Source: Schindler 1986: 356–64; Dalton and Burklin, 2003

CDU/CSU	Christian Democratic Union/Christian Social Union
FDP	Free Democratic Party
DP	German Party
GB/BHE	Pan-German Block/Block of Expellees
SPD	Social Democratic Party of Germany
B'90/Greens	Federation '90/Greens

narrowly retained its Bundestag majority. Meanwhile the SPD increased its support in both east and west, and the PDS benefited from eastern dissatisfaction with slow economic development. The 1998 election brought a new era in German politics, as the SPD returned to office for the first time in sixteen years, this time with the Greens as their coalition partner (Table 4.2).

Thus, if we look only at the list of viable party competitors, we can say that unification only marginally altered the political balances established during 40 years of party competition in West Germany. But that did not make it politically inconsequential. During the 1990s it became clear that unification had accelerated several trends which were already evident in West Germany, including the decline of social cleavage politics, and the increasing unpredictability of electoral outcomes and coalition calculations.

Signs of change in German electoral markets

In the 1980s and 1990s both aggregate and individual-level data attested to important shifts in established patterns of German electoral competition. One aspect of this was the shrinking size of the social groups which had sustained West Germany's cleavage politics. Secularization eroded the CDU's base, while labour market changes forced the SPD to reduce its reliance on blue-collar support.

Unification further undermined traditional cleavage politics. Researchers quickly refuted initial depictions of eastern voters as motivated by issues alone, without socio-structural predispositions (von Winter 1996: 301–4). However,

Table 4.3   Voter loyalties in Germany, 1972–2002

	1972	1976	1980	1983	1987	1990	1994	1998	2002
Party identifiers as % of total electorate (West/Western Germany)[1]	75	81	75	74	72	71	67	62	65
Very strong identifiers	17	12	13	10	10	11	12	9	12
Strong identifiers	38	35	33	29	31	29	24	22	25
Weak identifiers	20	35	29	35	31	31	31	31	27
Non-identifiers (none, don't know)	20	16	19	22	25	27	31	36	32
Party shifters (from preceding election)[2]			16	24	21	23	24	25	23

[1]Dalton 1996: 47; Dalton and Bürklin 2003.
[2]1980–94 Conradt 1996: 169; Dalton and Bürklin 2003.

socio-political trends in the east did not duplicate traditional western patterns. The CDU's character as a party of church-goers was further diluted by its support in the secular east. Its identity as a middle-class party also was weakened, because the CDU received comparatively low support among the eastern middle class, while it initially drew strong support from eastern blue-collar voters. In 1998 blue-collar support for the SPD increased markedly in the east, but even so remained well below support levels in the west. These levels further converged in 2002, not so much because of changes in the east, but because the SPD lost support among blue-collar workers in the west. Thus, both the eastward expansion of the German electorate, and long-term shifts in western German demographics, helped further weaken the sway of traditional cleavage politics (Dalton and Bürklin 1996: 187; Gluchowski and Wilamowitz-Moellendorff 1997; Jung and Roth 1994: 11; Roth 2003; Weins 2000) (Table 4.3).

There were other indications that the old electoral order was becoming less stable. Electoral volatility almost doubled between 1976, its postwar low, and 2002 (see Table 4.1). Individual-level data also indicated that citizens were becoming less attached to particular parties, and were more likely to switch preferences between elections. Moreover, participation in federal elections dropped by over 10 percent between the 1970s and the 1990s, remaining under 80 percent in 2002 despite the expected closeness of the contest. A net result of all this change was a drop in support for the two big party blocks (CDU/CSU and SPD). Whereas about 80 percent of eligible voters had supported these three parties in the 1970s, by the 1990s this had fallen to around 60 percent.

In short, from the mid-1980s onwards electoral outcomes and citizen attitudes reinforced the impression that patterns of German politics were on the verge of rapid and possibly far-reaching changes. However, academic analysts and partisan strategists often disagreed about the extent, the causes, and the implications of these developments.

Perceptions of change

Ongoing disagreements about the extent of changes in German electoral politics demonstrate clearly that the evidence supports a range of conclusions. For instance, some scholars have emphasized the persistence of social group voting (Gabriel and Brettschneider 1994), while others have highlighted the shrinking size of these traditional social groups (Berger *et al.* 1983; Oberreuter 1996; Veen 1991b; Veen and Gluchowski 1994). Equally, some have pointed to declining turnout and declining party enrolments as symptoms of increasing hostility to partisan politics and/or decreasing party loyalty (Eilfort 1994, 1996; Falter and Schumann 1993; Feist 1992, 1994; Kleinhenz 1995; Rattinger 1993; Wiesendahl 1998), whereas others have interpreted these as indicators of the 'normalization' of German politics (Lösche 1995: 9; Rieger 1994; Roth 1992). Finally, some have focused on increasing vote switching and weakening party attachments as evidence of the impact of declining party loyalty (Dalton and Rohrschneider 1990; Falter and Rattinger 1997; Veen 1994). However, others downplay the importance of these changes, arguing that most 'floating voters' merely switch between voting and non-voting, or between coalition partners (Zelle 1994; Schultze 1995). They also argue that declining intensity of party identification is less important than stability in the levels of those reporting any partisan attachment (Schmitt and Holmberg 1994: 116; Zelle 1994).

Although the scholarly debate continues, strategists within the German political parties seem to have been most influenced by the accounts that highlight electoral change. While some scholars may downplay the significance of voters switching between voting and non-voting, or between traditional coalition partners, individual parties are obviously affected by such fluctuations. Similarly, whether or not declining turnouts signal crisis or normality for the system as a whole, they certainly increase the potential payoff of parties' mobilization efforts. As a result, strategists in both the SPD and CDU have explored various ways for the parties to succeed in what they regard as a changed environment.

Their decisions have been supported by an impressive awareness of social scientific research. In addition to following academic debates, the well-funded German parties have commissioned their own surveys to assess electoral change. Since the 1980s and early 1990s, studies prepared for the SPD have highlighted the growing importance of floating voters. They also focused attention on the erosion of traditional socio-political linkages, and on the parallel growth of lifestyle-defined milieus which transmit only weak political cues (SPD 1984, 1987; SINUS-Institut 1992). Researchers close to the CDU drew similar pictures (Radunski 1985; Gluchowski 1989, 1992; Veen 1995; Müller-Rommel and Poguntke 1990).

These and other studies helped convince party organizers that new challenges were at hand. As early as 1985 one of the CDU's top strategists proclaimed a new era in German electoral politics:

What seems to be occurring here in the German Federal Republic is something that we have seen in other western democracies – particularly in America – over the past decade. Voters' decisions are less predictable, more differentiated, more changeable, more likely to be withheld, but they are also more emotional and less tied down. As a result, politics is becoming less settled and more short-term, and there is more support for quicker, and more abrupt, developments. (Radunski 1985: 3)

Ahead of the 1990 election he repeated his warning that the CDU faced new challenges because Germany had become a '*Stimmungsdemokratie*' (a democracy governed by the public mood), where up to 40 percent of the electorate were floating voters, where new social movements competed with traditional parties, and where citizens were disengaged from the public sphere (Radunski 1989). Similarly, the SPD's top party manager proclaimed that the strategically decisive group in the 1994 elections would be 'the approximately 40 percent of the electorate who are no longer affiliated, who feel that no one really represents them any more, and who, when asked which party they find most sympathetic, simply answer, "none at all"' (SPD 1993: 364).

Thus, from the 1980s onward strategists for both the SPD and the CDU identified the waning of traditional cleavage politics as an increasing threat. They also expressed fears about losing votes to new parties on the Left or Right in a possible electoral realignment. Both parties thus confronted the double task of mobilizing those with low political interest while trying to prevent the consolidation of support for new competitors. Both turned to programmatic adjustments and organizational reforms to meet the twin challenges of probable dealignment and possible realignment.

Programmatic responses to electoral change

Both the SPD and CDU re-examined their political positions in response to perceived electoral vulnerabilities. However, these 'catch-all' parties found it difficult to attract the disengaged even though – or perhaps because – they were willing to abandon previous programmatic emphases.

The SPD

In the 1980s and 1990s the SPD reacted more strongly to signs of electoral change than did the CDU. This was partly because the SPD was in opposition for most of this period, but also because it was the SPD's support base which was more immediately affected by increasing electoral volatility. The biggest beneficiary of this volatility was the Greens. The question of how to react to the Greens perplexed SPD strategists. Initially, the issue was whether the SPD should even bother to react to this new party: was Green support just an ephemeral phenomenon, or was this new competitor a permanent political rival? Even in the early 1980s the party chair and others subscribed to the latter view. They linked Green success with underlying value changes, and pointed to surveys suggesting that the Greens threatened the SPD's dominance on the Left. According to this interpretation, the SPD's future success depended on whether it could integrate post-materialist concerns with the party's traditional appeals (Glotz 1981; *Der Spiegel* 1981). In contrast, others saw Green support as less of a threat, and argued that the SPD would drive away its blue-collar constituents if it de-emphasized social welfare commitments in order to accommodate New Left demands (Löwenthal 1981; *Der Spiegel* 1981).

The SPD's 1983 campaign finessed the issue of choosing between a centrist or new left strategy by pursuing the double goal of excluding *both* the FDP and the Greens from the Bundestag (INFAS 1983: 11–19). This approach proved notably unsuccessful. In 1983 the SPD received its lowest vote share in twenty years, the Greens entered the Bundestag for the first time, and the FDP returned with a reduced, but still healthy, vote. The SPD's internal debate on the merits of various approaches continued throughout the 1980s, but over time the Greens' continuing electoral success persuaded most in the SPD that the party needed to highlight ideas designed to unite both the 'Old' and the 'New' Left. Recognizing this as an appropriate strategy proved to be much easier than implementing it.

In the wake of its 1983 defeat, the SPD leadership commissioned an analysis of how different strategies might affect the party's electoral prospects. The report concluded that the SPD could not hope to return to government merely by winning over the less attached Green supporters; it also needed to win votes from the much larger group of weak CDU/CSU supporters. Yet the report also warned that the SPD was likely to lose votes on either the Left or the Right whenever it gave pre-election signals about its preferred coalition partner (SPD 1984). Buttressed by this analysis, as well as by favourable opinion polls and propitious state election victories, the SPD's 1987 campaign team attempted to finesse the coalition issue by proclaiming that the SPD's goal was to win an absolute majority at the federal level. Such an optimistic aim seemed increasingly implausible as the campaign progressed, and party leaders eventually undermined their own credibility when they refused to discuss coalition scenarios (Fogt 1991). In subsequent elections the SPD has not been so bold as to assert that speculation about coalitions is irrelevant, but party leaders have nevertheless tried to maintain tactical ambiguity on this issue whenever possible. Only in 2002, when the SPD was already in office, did the party proclaim ahead of the election that its preferred outcome was a continuation of its coalition with the B '90/Greens.

Related to questions about the SPD's governing partners were questions about its own changing support base. Studies prepared for the party during the 1980s highlighted the SPD's need to draw a more heterogeneous electoral support, given the shrinking size in the workforce of the party's traditional core supporters, unionized manual workers. Analysts argued that the SPD needed to attract more support from two politically unaligned and growing groups: the 'technocratic-liberal' and 'upwardly mobile' milieu (SPD 1984, 1987). A report issued after the 1987 election strongly warned against the 'false alternative' of choosing between the party's traditional electorate and these new sectors. Instead, the SPD should strive to bridge the gap between unionized manual workers, who valued the party's traditional message of solidarity, and those employed in growth industries, who especially valued individualism, technological progress, and environmental protection (SPD 1987: 49). After the SPD's defeat in 1990, a new study for the party Executive reiterated this message. This new report once again urged the SPD to court voters from the growing segments whose political preferences grew out of their lifestyle more than their occupational or organizational attachments (SINUS-Institut 1992).

In the 1980s and 1990s the SPD's publicity, programmes, and organization reflected analysts' advice to pursue both the new and old Left by projecting an image of modernity and individualism alongside its traditional support for social solidarity and economic security. On the programmatic level, the effort to form an electoral coalition between the new and old Left dominated the years preceding the party's 1989 approval of an updated party manifesto. This document sought to reconcile the interests of the party's diverse constituencies by emphasizing such themes as ecologically sustainable economic growth, democracy in state and society, and social justice (Lösche and Walter 1992: 125–31; Braunthal 1994: ch. 9; SPD 1989).

Whatever the manifesto's success in bridging gaps within the party, it failed to achieve its main goal – helping the SPD win the 1990 election. Its themes of ecological renewal and social justice proved to be difficult to translate into good campaign slogans, and, in any case, they were at least temporarily marginalized as the events leading up to unification abruptly shifted the focus of German concerns. Despite this, both the SPD's 1992 short-term programme (*Sofortprogramm*) and its 1994 campaign manifesto retained a similar focus on themes chosen to unite the old and new Left. In 1994 this again seemed a promising strategy, as the SPD started the long campaign season with a strong lead in opinion polls. Once again, however, the party's efforts to broaden its constituency proved insufficient.

After the 1994 election German political debates shifted once again, as unemployment and public indebtedness rose to postwar highs. The new circumstances encouraged some SPD leaders to focus on more traditional economic concerns, such as defending welfare state programmes and protecting employment. This renewed focus on 'Old Left' themes reflected the SPD's diminished concern about the Green challenge. By the 1990s the Greens' national electoral support had stabilized well below the highest levels that SPD planners once feared. At the same time, the Greens had become a more pragmatic party, making them more attractive to the SPD as a potential coalition partner. These changes encouraged SPD campaigners to shift their efforts away from the conversion of Green voters, towards the mobilization of unaligned centrists. By the mid-1990s the SPD's drift away from new Left issues had become so pronounced that some party leaders began to warn that the SPD could not win elections if it neglected post-materialist issues (Schoppe 1995; Rau 1996).

In the run-up to the 1998 elections the old strategic dilemmas crystallized once again, this time in debates about the choice of candidate for Chancellor: should the party choose Gerhard Schröder, the self-proclaimed candidate of the 'new centre' ('*die neue Mitte*'), or Oskar Lafontaine, the champion of the party left? Once again, the SPD sought to finesse the problem of a divided and volatile electorate, this time by postponing its nomination for as long as possible. In the event, Schröder secured the post because of his popularity in opinion polls and his convincing showing in state elections. Yet even after it picked a centrist Chancellor candidate the SPD did not commit to a preferred coalition strategy, trying to keep its options open even in the final weeks of the 1998 campaign by hinting that a grand coalition with the CDU might be at least as desirable as an alliance with the B '90/Greens. However, when the election brought the CDU its worst results in years, the SPD chose to return to government at the head of the first federal-level Red–Green coalition.

The new government's initial problems were due at least as much to unresolved tensions within the SPD as to any differences between the coalition partners. With the Left-leaning Lafontaine still ensconced as party chair and finance minister, and with strong SPD minister-presidents in many of the German states, Schröder's SPD remained an ideologically diverse and potentially undisciplined party. However, the party's left wing weakened with Lafontaine's sudden departure from politics in the spring of 1999. Subsequently, Schröder's government started looking more successful as it took on such centrist projects as tax reform, and as it managed to navigate new left issues, such as the future of nuclear energy, without ceding too much to the Greens. The SPD's hold on the centre was strengthened by the party finance scandals which rocked the CDU from the autumn of 1999 (see p. 97 below). Under Schröder's initiative the SPD embarked on a new round of programme writing in anticipation of the elections of 2002, this time aiming to firm up the party's position in the centre of 'civil society' (see also Blair and Schröder 2000). However, as the country's economic problems worsened ahead of the 2002 election, the SPD found it increasingly difficult to project its preferred centrist image of economic competence. In this period, government economic reform initiatives that reflected the SPD's would-be position in the 'new middle' were stymied by the party's unwillingness to offend the union-dominated 'Old Left', the party's traditional core constituency.

Thus, by 1998 SPD goals had clearly shifted from trying to exclude the Greens from the legislature to trying to maximize its own position in relation to that of its presumed New Left coalition partner. At least as long as the CDU remained a weak competitor for the centre ground, the SPD found that working with the Greens, rather than against them, was a very successful strategy. However, one result of the SPD's shifting strategies of the 1980s and 1990s was a progressive blurring of the party profile.

The CDU

In the 1970s the CDU found itself out of national office for the first time in the history of the Federal Republic, apparently on the wrong side of demographic and social trends. Under Helmut Kohl's leadership the party adjusted its policies to this new environment, adopting a new programme in 1978 which emphasized themes such as promoting economic growth and a sustainable welfare state through cooperation between labour and capital (Hofmann 1993: 211–15). The party's programmatic introspection ended as it gained ground in state elections towards the end of the 1970s. In following years the CDU's programmatic debates were much less intense than those on the Left, not least because the party won four consecutive federal elections after 1980. Yet between these victories the party repeatedly fared badly in state elections, which kept CDU strategists from becoming complacent about the changing electoral market.

CDU analysts, like their SPD counterparts, first identified declining voter loyalty as a potential problem in the 1980s. After the CDU saw its vote share decline in 1987, the party's general secretary, Heiner Geißler, warned about the risks and opportunities presented by increasing electoral volatility. As Geißler explained, the election showed that something had changed – 'the number of loyal partisans has declined, the number of floating voters has grown. This constitutes a danger, but also an opportunity, because the SPD also has fewer loyalists' (CDU 1987: 45).[2] Throughout the next decade Geißler and others returned to this theme, urging the CDU to respond to the twin threats of increasing individualism and decreasing voter loyalty (for instance, Feldmeyer 1987; Gluchowski 1989; Veen 1991a, 1995).

These strategists argued that the CDU should respond to societal changes by competing for the centre, because most of the party's less attached supporters were centrists who might support the SPD if the CDU ignored their concerns. This vision of the CDU as 'the people's party of the centre' ('*Volkspartei der Mitte*') became more controversial as the party suffered a string of state and local election losses in 1988 and 1989. Far-right parties did unexpectedly well in these contests, and the party system seemed about to produce a right-wing counterpart to the newly established Greens. In response, some party leaders pushed the CDU to take more conservative positions to protect the party from being outflanked. The dispute over strategy came to a head in the summer of 1989, when centrists mounted an unsuccessful challenge to Chancellor Kohl's right-leaning party leadership. Kohl easily won this confrontation, and his challengers soon lost power within the party.

The threat of a rightward expansion of the party system receded as German unification robbed right-wing parties of a key nationalist issue. Internal rivalries also hindered the small right-wing competitors from consolidating their initial electoral success (Backes 1998). Equally important, in the early 1990s the CDU acted to limit the far Right's appeal by steering a rightward course on such issues as (restricting) abortion, (reducing) asylum guarantees, and (expanding) German military participation in international peacekeeping missions. Yet even though the far-right threat seemed to have subsided by the mid-1990s, these parties continued to score enough successes in state elections to keep the CDU on notice that any shift to the centre could cost it votes on the Right.

In the 1990 'Unification Election' the CDU scored a victory of a size that would have seemed unimaginable only eighteen months earlier. In 1994, as the post-unification boom turned into a recession, the CDU retained barely enough seats to maintain the centre-right coalition, and the party's prospects did not improve in the run-up to the 1998 election. In 1998 the CDU received its second-lowest vote share ever, and immediately thereafter Helmut Kohl stepped aside as party leader in favour of his long-time lieutenant and heir apparent, Wolfgang Schäuble. For a while, the new leadership seemed to do well, and the party recovered ground as the new Red–Green coalition struggled. In early 1999 the party launched a nationwide petition drive against proposed changes in Germany's restrictive citizenship laws, a strategy which helped the CDU win a string of state elections in 1999. However, by the end of that year the party was overwhelmed by revelations about funding scandals, and its popularity plummeted. These scandals involved millions of Deutschmarks in contributions which the CDU had illegally failed to report, and the gravity of the affair was aggravated by the former Chancellor's persistent refusal to name the source of some of the funds (Scarrow 2003). As the CDU struggled to put these scandals behind it, the party leadership was rapidly handed over to a new generation, with the easterner Angela Merkel taking over as party chair, and Friedrich Merz taking over as head of the party's parliamentary group. But under this new leadership, as under Kohl and Schäuble, the CDU's main themes remained the same, with the party stressing economic competence and the protection of German identity. For a couple of years after this leadership turnover, the CDU struggled to regain ground, temporarily frustrated by the SPD's success in positioning itself as the party of economic competence. Nevertheless, the CDU did not drastically revise its political agenda in the wake of the party finance affair, and its economic emphasis and anti-immigrant rhetoric once again attracted support as the SPD-led government proved unable to deal with the country's economic problems.

Thus, for both the CDU and SPD the threats of party system *realignment* were largely contained by the mid-1990s. By this point the SPD could antici-pate enduring but limited competition from one or two parties on its left (the B '90/Greens in the West, the PDS in the east). Meanwhile, no single party had established itself as a viable national electoral option to the right of the CDU, though far-right parties continued to claim single-digit support in a few state elections. In contrast, *dealignment* remained a growing challenge to both parties, and both continued to experiment with ways to court a more volatile electorate. Their search led them not only to the programmatic responses discussed above, but also to organizational reforms and new campaign strategies designed to appeal to broader, and more fickle, electorates.

Projecting the party image: organizational reform

In recent years the SPD and CDU have adopted similar organizational approaches to combat weakening voter loyalties and rising apathy (and antipathy) towards partisan politics. In the late 1980s and early 1990s both parties initiated internal reforms intended to project a more diverse and dynamic image, and to attract new party members. At the same time, both parties continued centralizing and professionalizing their campaign operations.

The professionalization of the German party organizations began in the late 1960s and early 1970s, long before signs of dealignment appeared. These changes were fuelled by a sharp rise in public subsidies for state and national parties. Initial professionalization also coincided with rapid growth in the parties' voluntary organizations. In the 1970s organizers in both parties pointed to membership growth as evidence of strong popular support, and their campaign strategies emphasized the need to mobilize members before elections. Because party leaders viewed formally enrolled supporters as electorally useful, when memberships began to shrink in the 1980s they backed organizational reforms intended to revitalize the membership organizations.

The SPD turned to organizational reform after its disappointing performance in 1990, when key party strategists began to promote organizational 'modernization' as an electorally necessary complement to programmatic efforts (Thierse 1992; Blessing 1992). In this spirit the SPD Executive called for organizational self-study and reform, arguing that 'the only kind of SPD which will win elections is one that brings together so-called loyal partisans and floating voters' (SPD 1991: 712). The subsequent report highlighted organizational changes designed to appeal to key groups, including women and younger citizens, as well as all those attracted by 'modernity' themes. According to reformers, the right organizational changes could produce electoral dividends: 'What is needed is to develop our working structures and our communication capacities so that in the future the SPD can win and motivate members, and so that it can win elections' (Projektgruppe SPD 1993: 17). In 1995 a new report reiterated the call to stabilize membership levels and win members from groups under-represented in the party (SPD 1995: 3).

Even before the 1993 report was debated by the party conference the SPD experimented with one of its recommendations when the post of party leader unexpectedly became vacant. The SPD used a hastily arranged membership ballot to select its next leader. This *ad hoc* procedure mobilized many members and generated favourable publicity. In its wake, the party conference adopted a slate of plebiscitary reforms, including authorizing the use of membership ballots to select party office-holders and to determine party policies. Leaders hoped these well-publicized amendments would improve the party image. Given their origins, it is perhaps not surprising that in practice little power has devolved to members as a result of these changes, not least because the new procedures are optional, and because so far they have not produced clear electoral dividends (for details, see Scarrow 1999).

The CDU pursued a similar programme of organizational reforms. It actually began its reform discussions in the late 1980s – ahead of the SPD – when party managers became worried about the party's declining popularity and stagnating membership. But the immediate impact of these debates was limited, because reformers were tainted by association with the unsuccessful challenge to Helmut Kohl's leadership in 1989, and because German unification temporarily boosted CDU popularity. However, within a few years new party managers were echoing the would-be reformers of 1989, who had argued that the CDU must change its organizational practices in order to adapt to increasing indivi-dualism, the growing number of floating voters, and the competition of new social movements (Radunski 1989: 22–3; Hintze 1993; Reck 1995).

As in the SPD, organizational reformers in the CDU were motivated largely by worry about the party's membership demographics. They assumed that voters would equate who the party was with what the party stood for. One report noted with concern that party membership was disproportionately old and disproportionately male, and that employees in new service industries and new technical fields were under-represented. The authors urged local parties to experiment with ways to appeal to these groups, for instance by sponsoring more informal meetings and project-oriented events, and by nominating more women and young people as party candidates (CDU 1989: 456ff).

Like their SPD counterparts, CDU reformers also advocated giving members a greater role in party decision-making. Such changes were supposed to help retain members, because 'Members don't want to just carry out the decisions of party committees; they want to participate in the political decision-making process' (CDU 1989: 460). In 1995, after the party gained experience with plebiscitary reforms in some of its state organizations, the CDU national party Executive endorsed the use of membership ballots to select party office-holders and candidates, and to decide policy positions. As in the SPD, the party conference was suspicious of leaders' proposals, fearing that plebiscitary arrangements would shift power to leaders by empowering inactive and easily manipulated 'ordinary' members at the expense of party activists. Because of these concerns, the CDU conference approved the idea of internal 'primaries', but rejected calls for intra-party votes on party policies.

Thus, in the late 1980s and early 1990s both the SPD and CDU attempted to cater to voters' changing political preferences, and to modernize their own organizational images, by increasing the rights of individual members. Despite the great fanfare accorded to some of the reforms, their immediate electoral benefits were limited. Most concretely, in the 1990s none of the state or federal party leaders picked by membership ballots won the subsequent election. In addition, the organizational reforms failed to halt declines in party member-ships, or to boost the proportion of younger members (Scarrow 1999). Such a track record understandably dampened electorally oriented leaders' interest in these 'democratizing' reforms.

The reforms described above had their roots in organizational debates that pre-dated unification, and were mainly spurred by perceived dealignment. In the 1990s the parties also acquired the new problem of building eastern organizations capable of consolidating, and extending, their initial support. The CDU started this task with the advantage – but also potential liability – of property, money, and members inherited from its namesake eastern 'block party', a party which had survived for 40 years by supporting the East German regime. In contrast, Social Democrats in the east had to start from scratch in late 1989. With or without pre-existing resources, neither party was able to build strong organizations in the eastern states. Indeed, in many parts of the region the shortage of active partisans became so acute by the end of the 1990s that all the eastern parties – even the PDS – were finding it difficult to locate sufficient local government candidates. It is clear that eastern organizations are never going to be the membership parties that their western counterparts historically aspired to be. Instead, they will be what Germans often refer to as 'Americanized' associations, centred around office-holders and professional organizers, dependent on public subsidies, and forced to recruit candidates outside the party (Schmidt 1998). Such bare-bones organizations are not able to combat dealignment by developing year-round bonds with social groups or by cultivating community contacts. The most they can hope for is to mount election campaigns which successfully appeal to a weakly aligned electorate.

Projecting the party image: candidates and campaigning

The professionalization of German campaigns has been driven by increases in party funding and the availability of new communications technologies. It has also been propelled by party analysts' conviction that media images are increasingly decisive in the current political climate.

Because the big parties cooperated in raising public campaign subsidies from the late 1960s onwards, they have had funds to take advantage of new technologies. During this period the parties also increased their reliance on marketing professionals, and boosted central party control over campaigns at all levels. As political advertising became more professional and more centralized, party messages became more focused and, some said, more candidate-oriented. This was especially visible in the CDU campaigns in 1990 and 1994, which made Chancellor Kohl the major selling point, and in the SPD's 1998 and 2002 campaigns, when the Chancellor candidate and his designated team, not the party headquarters, ran the national campaign (Boll 1996; Semetko and Schoenbach 1995). The focus on candidates reached its logical apex in 2002 when, for the first time, the leading candidates of the two largest parties participated in one-on-one debates, much-hyped 'duels' in the final weeks of the campaign.

Such 'personalization' of politics was not new in the Federal Republic. Indeed, the CDU of the 1950s and early 1960s was so closely identified with Konrad Adenauer that it was commonly designated 'the Chancellor's election club' (*Kanzlerwahlverein*). The party shook off this image in the 1970s, in part because it was harder to personalize the party image while in opposition. That changed after the CDU returned to federal office in 1982, when Helmut Kohl gradually reasserted the Chancellor's predominance within the party. The personalization of the CDU campaigns increased in the 1990s to take advantage of Kohl's newfound popularity as the 'Chancellor of Unity'. By 1998, with Kohl looking less popular and more vulnerable, a personalized campaign no longer offered the CDU such a clear advantage; nevertheless, party publicity continued to prominently feature the party's long-serving leader (Clemens 2000).

After its loss in 1998, the CDU once again faced the problem common to all German parties when they are in opposition: the difficulty of using candidate-focused publicity when there are several rival leadership claimants. A similar problem partly explains why the SPD in opposition did not move as far as the CDU towards candidate-centred campaigning. Thus, even in 1994 and 1998, when the SPD campaigns ran unusually personal advertisements featuring the party's candidate for Chancellor, they also gave prominent billing to the leadership 'teams' in order to counter unease about the known rivalries within party's the top ranks (Boll 1996; Braunthal 2000).

For both the CDU and the SPD the great attraction of candidate-centred campaigns was that they distracted attention from potentially divisive issues. In the case of the CDU in the 1990s, this meant deflecting blame in a period when government action was constrained by growing budget deficits, and by a political situation which made the CDU reliant on SPD cooperation to pass important legislation. In the SPD's case, candidate-centred campaigning diverted attention from issues that might aggravate divisions in the party's broad electoral coalition. In the mid-1990s at least it seemed as if one ironic effect of the parties' personalized campaigns may have been to increase candidate-oriented voting, thus contributing to the very trends of dealignment and volatility with which the parties were already contending, though some of this effect may have faded in subsequent elections. Even so, candidate images remained important to the vote choice of unaligned voters, and hence remained a prime concern of the party's campaign planners (Anderson and Brettschneider 2003; Rohrschneider and Fuchs 2003; Zelle 1996: 62).

The big German parties also reached out to the politically unattached by assembling more demographically balanced candidate lists. Since the mid-1980s strategists in both parties have argued that parties must have young and female candidates to reinforce their efforts to reach these critical groups. These strategic arguments, paired with arguments about equity, prompted the SPD to adopt quotas for female candidates as early as 1986. The CDU followed suit a decade later. In explaining his new support for this reform, the CDU general secretary made clear his electoral calculations: he noted that the CDU was losing its traditional advantage with female voters, and he linked this change to surveys showing that female voters wanted more women in political leadership positions (CDU 1995: 197–203).

SPD strategists were also concerned to get younger candidates in order to make the party more attractive to younger voters. The SPD's 1992 reform report urged local parties to reserve at least 10 percent of winnable places on local government slates for people under 31 years old. In 1996 the SPD's youth congress reaffirmed the party's commitment to elect a greater number of under-40s to the Bundestag. Though these efforts have not been entirely successful, strategists' concern to diversify the party's public face is consistent with other facets of contemporary campaign efforts, which are as much about projecting images at target groups as they are about specific policies (Boll 1996).

Relations with other parties

In recent decades German parties have rethought their coalition calculations as new challengers emerged and as state-level party systems became less homogeneous. During the 1990s most of the eastern states developed three-party systems based on the SPD, CDU, and PDS, whereas western states evolved into three- or four-party systems with Green parties and sometimes the FDP, but without the PDS. Of course, all five parties (plus the Bavarian CSU) held seats at the national level. These state- and federal-level differences aggravated disagreements within parties about how best to deal with competitors.

For the SPD, dealing with the Greens presented the biggest challenge. At stake were two questions: could state-level SPD/Green coalitions govern effectively, and, even if they did, would they scare off the SPD's centrist voters and undermine chances of national victory? The first such coalition, in Hesse from 1983 to 1987, ended abruptly and with some rancour. However, the Greens became more committed to making such coalitions work after their losses in the 1990 federal election. This pragmatic strategy paid electoral dividends for the Greens (now merged with their eastern counterparts and renamed Federation [*Bundnis* – B] '90/Greens). As support for the FDP dropped, the SPD often had little choice but to gamble on alliances with the Greens. By 1998 a majority of the states in western Germany had been governed at some point by a Red-Green or 'traffic light' (SPD–FDP–Green) coalition. While these partnerships were not trouble-free, both parties increasingly recognized their shared interest in demonstrating that Red-Green coalitions could govern responsibly. Though they shied away from a formal pre-election pact ahead of the 1998 election, such an outcome seemed increasingly favoured by both sides. The Greens tested the limits of such togetherness before the election, when the more 'fundamentalist' party conference adopted a platform containing elements (including a steep rise in gasoline tax) that were unacceptable to the SPD. Even though SPD leaders strongly repudiated such unpopular proposals, they did not disown cooperation with the Greens, and a Red-Green coalition was quickly formed after the 1998 election. The first year of the collaboration got off to an unpromising start, but by 2002 the leaders of the two parties were working well together, even going so far as to stage an unprecedented joint campaign rally immediately before the 2002 election.

The political division into left and right blocks was deepened by the CDU's steadfast refusal to cooperate with the Greens. In the mid-1990s CDU pronouncements often grouped the Greens with the PDS and far-right parties, and denounced all as unacceptable government partners. This line began to soften later in the decade, with a few voices on both sides questioning the taboos which divided B'90/Greens and the CDU. There were even a few local-level experiments in cooperation between the two parties, but these had no immediate implications for federal politics.

The CDU's coalition calculations were affected much more by the declining fortunes of the FDP, its long-time partner. Although the FDP did relatively well in the east in the first post-unification elections, it was unable to consolidate this support. Meanwhile, internal disputes helped to erode its appeal in the west. As a result, by the end of the 1990s the FDP was represented in only three state parliaments (all in western states). Wherever the FDP failed to win seats, the CDU's best hope for getting into government was either to win an absolute majority, or to participate in a grand coalition. The CDU tried both options in a few state legislatures, but in many states was driven into opposition because it lacked an obvious partner.

Unification brought one other major strategic complication for the big parties, particularly the SPD: the establishment of the PDS in the federal and eastern state party systems. Since western party leaders initially assumed that the PDS would fade away rapidly, they only began focusing on relations with this party after it became apparent that the PDS would do well in 1994 state and federal elections. In the national arena the SPD did little to accommodate this new rival. The SPD Executive strongly rejected proposals for formal coalitions with the PDS, and warned that efforts to court former PDS supporters could drive away centrist voters in the west (*Vorwärts* 1995). There were vocal dissenters to this strategy of non-cooperation with the PDS, above all within the eastern SPD. Some argued that the party should work with reformed Communists at municipal and state levels, especially where the only other viable option was a grand coalition with the CDU (*Frankfurter Allgemeine Zeitung* 1996; Günsche 1997).

In 1994, several months ahead of federal elections, the SPD in Saxony-Anhalt dismayed national party leaders by forming a minority government which depended on PDS support. The CDU attacked this arrangement, equating a vote for the SPD with a vote to put the PDS in office. Some in the CDU sought to campaign on a similar issue of state coalitions in the elections of

1998. However, by then many CDU politicians, particularly those in the east, were arguing for a more tolerant approach, noting that in the long term the eastern CDU could use the support of ex-PDS voters (Schmidt 1996, 1998). The waning of the CDU attacks made it easier for the SPD to take a more conciliatory approach to the PDS, and even led to the establishment of SPD–PDS coalitions in Mecklenburg-Western Pomerania and Berlin. Dealing with the PDS at the national level became less of a concern for the SPD after the 2002 election, when the PDS gained only two seats in the Bundestag, but the question of whether the PDS was a desirable or reliable coalition partner remained a problem for the SPD at the state level.

In short, the big parties' responses to an already fluid electoral environment were complicated by the expansion of the German party system, and by the electoral volatility which particularly threatened the smallest parties. The result was a period of shifting electoral alliances and experiments with new coalition patterns at the state level. These diverse coalitions further blurred distinctions between the parties, and thus undermined party efforts to combat eroding political loyalties.

Institutional responses

Despite their long-standing rivalry, the large German parties have occasionally collaborated to reshape the rules of competition, most notably in the area of party subsidies. In the 1980s the big parties cooperated several times to expand these subsidies to combat their increasing debts (a practice the Constitutional Court ended in 1992 when it capped overall subsidies to parties). The parties have shown much less interest in manipulating election rules to shield themselves from electoral change. Above all, the biggest parties have not made the one institutional change that might best insulate them from more volatile voting preferences: they have not introduced a majoritarian electoral system. Both parties endorsed this reform in the 1960s, but failed to implement it during the Grand Coalition period. The proposal has never again received sustained attention. Since then the parties have only tinkered with electoral rules. As a result, the consequences of changing electoral behaviour are being played out under existing rules.

Conclusion

The preceding sections have shown how difficult it has been for the SPD and CDU to devise strategies to cope with the combined effects of demobilization and possible realignment. Both parties have turned to programmatic shifts, organizational reform, and new campaign styles to combat weakening political loyalties. Because German party strategists have been well armed with information about voters' preferences, they should have been able to steer their parties in classic Downsian fashion. Yet both parties struggled to adopt vote-maximizing strategies. These problems have been particularly evident for the SPD, which lost a string of federal elections while wavering between new Left and centrist appeals.

Why did the SPD find it so difficult to implement a winning strategy? Herbert Kitschelt has blamed the party organization, especially the blocking position of the 'Old Left' within it, for the party's slowness in adjusting to the increasing appeal of new Left themes (Kitschelt 1994: 247–9). While the relative strength of party factions clearly shaped party policies, and hindered opportunistic policy shifts, organizational in-fighting was not the sole reason for the SPD's strategic hesitation. SPD leaders might have reacted similarly even had they enjoyed complete freedom, because there were conflicting signals about popular preferences. At various points during the past two decades estimates of Green voting potential have ranged between 5 percent and 20 percent. In the 1980s and 1990s the SPD's electoral prospects repeatedly fluctuated between mid-term highs, when the party seemed poised to win the next federal election, and post-election lows, after voters failed to deliver on earlier expressions of support. Such shifting landscapes clearly contributed to the SPD's apparent indecisiveness.

The CDU also showed some initial uncertainty about how best to react to changing electoral markets. However, since the end of the 1980s it has consistently given high priority to preventing the establishment of a new party to its right. Though this response seemed validated by the failure of the far Right to enter the national legislature – in contrast to the experience in neighbouring countries – it was not an unqualified success. At the end of the 1990s average support for far Right parties in state and local elections was still higher than at the beginning of the 1980s. Thus, while CDU determination to shut out the Far Right may have prevented a large-scale realignment, it by no means erased the threat from the Far Right. Moreover, despite the CDU's string of federal election victories, the party weakened throughout the 1990s. In 1994 it received its lowest vote share since 1949, and by the time the CDU lost the 1998 federal election it remained in government in only four of Germany's sixteen states. After this it slowly regained ground, but it was almost five years later, and five months after the 2002 federal election, before the CDU/CSU regained control of governments in a majority of Germany's states. Moreover, the victories it achieved in state elections in 2003 might be seen more as a repudiation of the SPD's national governance than as a validation of the CDU's political strategy.

Conversely, the SPD's strategic indecisiveness was not a complete failure. In the 1980s and 1990s the SPD's political flexibility contributed to its success in increasingly heterogeneous state legislatures. The party assumed a growing national role as SPD-led coalitions gained the majority in the country's upper chamber, the Bundesrat. By the mid-1990s the SPD occupied a pivotal position as the sole party which could form coalitions with all other parties.

For both parties, finding an ideal vote-maximizing position in a shifting electoral market-place was complicated by the fact that dealignment was as much of a threat as realignment. Dealignment makes it difficult for large parties to respond to an emerging competitor by co-opting its issues (Kitschelt's oligopolistic response), because voters with weak party attachments are more likely to defect if 'their' parties de-emphasize traditional commitments. This is a particular problem under proportional representation, where parties are most vulnerable to abstention or protest voting. In this environment German parties needed to mobilize existing supporters even as they sought to capture new ones.

The German parties' responses to realignment contained, but did not eliminate, the threat of a far-reaching shift in voters' loyalties. However, their responsiveness to electoral market cues may have compounded the effects of weakening party attachments. As the number of non-voters and vote-switchers has grown, the parties have taken programmatic and organizational steps to mobilize the weakly aligned. Paradoxically, such strategies may contribute to parties' strategic challenges by promoting the erosion of electoral loyalties. In the current climate of candidate-centred campaigning and issue-oriented politics, such erosion seems likely to continue.

Notes

1 In 1990 the PDS won seats under a one-time regional application of the 5 percent electoral threshold. In 1994 it entered parliament under a provision of the electoral law which awards a fully proportional quotient of seats to parties which win at least three single-member district races. (The PDS won four direct seats in 1994.) In 1998 the PDS received 5.1 percent of the popular vote and won four direct seats, and in 2002 4 percent and just two direct seats.

2 This and other translations by the author.

References

Anderson, Christopher J. and Frank Brettschneider (2003). 'The Likeable Winner v. the Competent Loser: Candidate Images and the German Election of 2002.' *German Politics and Society* 21: 95–118.

Backes, Uwe (1998). 'Rechtsextremismus in Deutschland: Ideologien, Organization und Strategien.' *Aus Politik und Zeitgeschichte* 9–10: 27–35.

Berger, Manfred *et al.* (1983). 'Stabilität und Wechsel. Eine Analyse der Bundestagswahl 1980.' In Max Kaase and Hans-Dieter Klingemann (eds), *Wahlen und politisches System*. Opladen: Westdeutscher Verlag, pp. 12–57.

Blair, Tony and Gerhard Schröder (2000). 'The Third Way/Die Neue Mitte.' In Bodo Hombach (ed.), *The Politics of the New Centre*. Cambridge: Polity Press, pp. 157–77.

Blessing, Karlheinz (1992). *SPD 2000: Die Modernisierung der SPD*. Marburg: Schüren Presseverlag.

Boll, Bernhard (1996). 'Media Communication and Personality Marketing: the 1994 German National Election Campaign.' In Geoffrey Roberts (ed.), *Superwahljahr: The German Elections of 1994*. London: Frank Cass, pp. 120–40.

Braunthal, Gerard (1994). *The German Social Democrats since 1969.* Boulder, CO: Westview Press.

Braunthal, Gerard (2000). 'The SPD: From Opposition to Governing Party.' In David Conradt, Gerald Kleinfeld, and Christian Søe (eds), *Power Shift in Germany.* New York: Berghahn Books, pp. 18–37.

Bundestagswahlleiter (1998). www.bundeswahlleiter.de/btw98/btwahl_btw98.htm

Bundestagswahlleiter (2002). www.bundeswahlleiter.de/btw2002/btwahl_btw2002.htm

CDU (1987). *Protokoll CDU Bundesparteitag 1987.* Bonn: CDU.

CDU (1989). 'Moderne Parteiarbeit in den 90er Jahren.' In *Protokoll CDU Bundesparteitag 1989.* Bonn: CDU.

CDU (1995). *Protokoll CDU Bundesparteitag 1995.* Bonn: CDU.

Clemens, Clay (2000). 'The Last Hurrah: Helmut Kohl's CDU/CSU and the 1998 Election.' In David Conradt, Gerald Kleinfeld, and Christian Søe (eds), *Power Shift in Germany.* New York: Berghahn Books, pp. 38–58.

Conradt. David (1996). *The German Polity, 5th edn* White Plains, N.Y.: Longman.

Dalton, Russell (1996). 'A Divided Electorate.' In Gordon Smith, William Paterson and Stephen Padgett (eds), *Development in German Politics, 2.* Durham, N. C.: Duke University Press, pp. 35–54.

Dalton, Russell J. and Wilhelm Bürklin (1996). 'The Two German Electorates.' In Russell J. Dalton (ed.), *Germans Divided: the 1994 Bundestag Elections and the Evolution of the German Party System.* Oxford: Berg, pp. 183–208.

Dalton, Russell J. and Wilhelm Bürklin (2003). 'Wähler als Wandervogel: Dealignment and the German Voter.' *German Politics and Society* 1: 57–75.

Dalton, Russell J. and Robert Rohrschneider (1990). 'Wählerwandel und die Abschwächung der Parteineigungen von 1972 bis 1987.' In Max Kaase und Hans-Dieter Klingemann (eds), *Wahlen und Wähler: Analysen aus Anlaß der Bundestagswahl 1987.* Opladen: Westdeutscher Verlag, pp. 297–324.

Eilfort, Michael (1994). *Die Nichtwähler.* Paderborn: Ferdinand Schöningh.

Eilfort, Michael (1996). 'Auch ein "Super-Nichtwahljahr".' In Heinrich Oberreuter (ed.), *Parteiensystem am Wendepunkt?* Munich: Olzog Verlag, pp. 72–92.

Falter, Jürgen W. and Hans Rattinger (1997). 'Die deutschen Parteien im Urteil der öffentlichen Meinung 1977–1994.' In Oscar W. Gabriel, Oskar Niedermayer, and Richard Stöss (eds), *Parteiendemokratie in Deutschland.* Bonn: Bundeszentrale für politische Bildung, pp. 495–513.

Falter, Jürgen W. and Siegfried Schumann (1993). 'Nichtwahl und Protestwahl: Zwei Seiten einer Medaille.' *Aus Politik und Zeitgeschichte* 11: 36–49.

Feist, Ursula (1992). 'Niedrige Wahlbeteiligung – Normalisierung oder Krisensymptom der Demokratie in Deutschland?' In Karl Starzacher *et al.* (eds), *Protestwähler und Wahlverweigerer: Krise der Demokratie?* Cologne: Bund Verlag, pp. 40–57.

—— (1994). 'Nichtwähler 1994.' *Aus Politik und Zeitgeschichte* 51–2: 35–46.

Feldmeyer, Karl (1987). 'Schein oder Wirklichkeit.' *Frankfurter Allgemeine Zeitung* 8 August, p. 10.

Fogt, Helmut (1991). 'Politische Entwicklung und Wahlkampf der Parteien 1983–1987.' In Hans-Joachim Veen and Elisabeth Noelle-Neumann (eds), *Wählerverhalten im Wandel.* Paderborn: Ferdinand Schöningh, pp. 21–84.

Frankfurter Allgemeine Zeitung (1996). 'Thierses Thesenpapier wird beschwiegen.' 20 December, p. 5.

Gabriel, Oscar W. and Frank Brettschneider (1994). 'Soziale Konflikte und Wählerverhalten.' In Hans Rattinger, Oscar W. Gabriel, and Wolfgang Jagodzinski (eds), *Wahlen und politische Einstellungen im vereinigten Deutschland.* Frankfurt am Main: Peter Lang, pp. 7–45.

Glotz, Peter (1981). 'Partei oder Kreuzzug?' *Der Spiegel* 50: 106–7.

Gluchowski, Peter (1989). 'Vom Milieu zum Lebensstil – Wandel der Wählerschaft.' *Eichholz-Brief* 4: 66–76.

Gluchowski, Peter (1992). 'Wähler und Parteien in den 80er Jahren – ein Verhältnis im Wandel.' In Erich Hübner and Heinrich Oberreuter (eds), *Parteien in Deutschland zwischen*

Kontinuität und Wandel. Munich: Bayerische Landeszentrale für politische Bildungsarbeit, pp. 89–123.

Gluchowski, Peter and Ulrich von Wilamowitz-Moellendorff (1997). 'Sozialstrukturelle Grundlagen des Parteienwettbewerbs in der Bundesrepublik.' In Oscar W. Gabriel, Oskar Niedermayer, and Richard Stöss (eds), *Parteiendemokratie in Deutschland*. Bonn: Bundeszentrale für politische Bildung, pp. 179–208.

Günsche, Karl-Ludwig (1997). 'Die SPD-Qual der Wahl mit der PDS.' *Die Welt* 7 January, p. 2.

Hintze, Peter (1993). 'Die Volkspartei ist unentbehrlich.' *Union* 1: 6–7.

Hofmann, Robert (1993). *Geschichte der deutschen Parteien*. Munich: Piper Verlag.

INFAS (1983). *INFAS-Report Wahlen: Bundestagswahl 1983*. Bonn: photocopy.

Jung, Matthias and Dieter Roth (1994). 'Kohls knappster Sieg.' *Aus Politik und Zeitgeschichte* 51–52: 3–15.

Kitschelt, Herbert (1994). *The Transformation of European Social Democracy*. Cambridge: Cambridge University Press.

Kleinhenz, Thomas (1995). *Die Nichtwähler*. Opladen: Westdeutscher Verlag.

Lösche, Peter (1995). 'Parteienverdrossenheit ohne Ende?' In *Die Zukunft der Volksparteien*. St Augustin: Konrad-Adenauer-Stiftung, pp. 1–21.

Lösche, Peter and Franz Walter (1992). *Die SPD: Klassenpartei, Volkspartei, Quotenpartei*. Darmstadt: Wissenschaftliche Buchgesellschaft.

Löwenthal, Richard (1981). 'Identität und Zukunft der SPD.' *Neue Gesellschaft* 28: 1085–9.

Müller-Rommel, Ferdinand and Thomas Poguntke (1990). 'Lebensstile und Wahlverhalten.' *Bürger im Staat* 171–8.

Oberreuter, Heinrich (1996). 'Zwischen Erlebnisgesellschaft und Medieneinfluß.' In Heinrich Oberreuter (ed.), *Parteiensystem am Wendepunkt?* Munich: Olzog, 9–22.

Projektgruppe SPD 2000 des Parteivorstands (1993). 'Ziele und Wege der Parteireform.' In Karlheinz Blessing, *SPD 2000: Die Modernisierung der SPD*. Marburg: Schüren Presseverlag, pp. 16–45.

Radunski, Peter (1985). 'Die Wähler in der Stimmungsdemokratie.' *Sonde* 2: 3–13.

Radunski, Peter (1989). 'Volkspartei in den 90er Jahren – Die Union vor neuen Herausforderungen.' *Sonde* 3: 21–9.

Rattinger, Hans (1993). 'Abkehr von den Parteien? Dimensionen der Parteiverdrossenheit.' *Aus Politik und Zeitgeschichte* 11: 24–35.

Rau, Johannes (1996). 'Die SPD: Links und Frei.' *Vorwärts* 1: 18.

Reck, Hans-Joachim (1995). 'Fähig für die Zukunft bleiben.' *Union* 1: 20–1.

Rieger, Günther (1994). 'Parteienverdrossenheit: Kritische Anmerkungen zur Empirie, Wahrnehmung und Interpretation abnehmender politische Partizipation.' *Zeitschrift für Parlamentsfragen* 25: 441–58.

Rohrschneider, Robert and Dieter Fuchs (2003). 'It Used To Be the Economy: Issues and Party Support in the 2003 Election.' *German Politics and Society* 21: 76–94.

Roth, Dieter (1992). 'Sinkende Wahlbeteiligung – eher Normalisierung als Krisensymptom.' In Karl Starzacher, Konrad Schacht *et al.* (eds), *Protestwähler und Wahlverweigerer: Krise der Demokratie?* Cologne: Bund Verlag, pp. 58–76.

Roth, Dieter (2003). 'A Last Minute Success of the Red–Green Coalition.' *German Politics and Society* 21: 35–56.

Scarrow, Susan (1999). 'Parties and the Expansion of Participation Opportunities: Who Benefits?' *Party Politics* 5: 275–82.

Scarrow, Susan (2003). 'Party Finance Scandals and their Consequences in the 2002 Election: Paying for Mistakes?' *German Politics and Society* 21: 119–37.

Schindler, Peter (ed.) (1983). *Datenhandbuch zur Geschichte des deutschen Bundestages 1949 bis 1982*. Baden-Baden: Nomos.

Schindler, Peter (1986). *Datenhandbuch zur Geschichte des deutschen Bundestages 1980 bis 1984*. Baden-Baden: Nomos.

Schindler, Peter (1988). *Datenhandbuch zur Geschichte des deutschen Bundestages 1980 bis 1988*. Baden-Baden: Nomos.

Schindler, Peter (1994). *Datenhandbuch zur Geschichte des deutschen Bundestages 1983 bis 1991*. Baden-Baden: Nomos.

Schmidt, Ute (1996). 'Risse im Gefüge der vereinigten CDU.' *Die neue Gesellschaft/Frankfurter Hefte* 43: 303-308.

Schmidt, Ute (1998). 'Sieben Jahre nach der Einheit: Die ostdeutsche Parteienlandschaft im Vorfeld der Bundestagswahl 1998.' *Aus Politik und Zeitgeschichte* 1–2: 37–53.

Schmitt, Hermann and Sören Holmberg (1994). 'Political Parties in Decline?' In Hans-Dieter Klingemann and Dieter Fuchs (eds), *Citizens and the State*. Oxford: Oxford University Press, pp. 95–133.

Schoppe, Bernd (1995). 'Die Partei, die nur soziale Gerechtigkeit eintritt, ist nicht Mehrheitsfähig.' *Vorwärts* 7: 18–19.

Schultze, Rainer-Olaf (1995). 'Widerspüchliches, Ungleichseitiges und kein Ende in Sicht: Die Bundestagswahl vom 16. Oktober 1994.' *Zeitschrift für Parlamentsfragen* 26: 325–52.

Semetko, Holli A. and Klaus Schoenbach (1995). 'The Media and the Campaign in the New Germany.' In David P. Conradt *et al.* (eds), *Germany's New Politics*. Tempe, AZ: German Studies Review, pp. 51–68.

SINUS-Institut (1992). *Lebensweltforschung und soziale Milieus in West- und Ostdeutschland*. Heidelberg: photocopy.

SPD (Parteivorstand) (1984). *Planungsdaten für die Mehrheitsfähigkeit der SPD – Zusammendfassender Bericht*. Bonn: photocopy.

SPD (1987). *Die Bundestagswahl vom 27.1.1987 – Analyse und Konsequenzen*. Bonn: photocopy.

SPD (1989). *Basic Policy Programme of the Social Democratic Party of Germany*. Bonn: SPD.

SPD (1991). *Protokoll: SPD Parteitag 1991*. Bonn: SPD.

SPD (1993). *Protokoll: SPD Parteitag 1993*. Bonn: SPD.

SPD (1995). *Materialien: Abschlußbericht der Arbeitsgruppe 'Mitgliederentwicklung'*. Bonn: SPD.

Der Spiegel (1981). 'Dann ist die Regierung schon 1982 am Ende.' 51: 24–30.

Thierse, Wolfgang (1992). 'SPD 2000 – Worum geht es bei der Parteireform?' in Malte Ristau, Michael Scholing, and Johannes Wien (eds), *Tanker im Nebel: Zur Organization und Programmatik der SPD*. Marburg: Schüren Presseverlag, pp. 83–93.

Veen, Hans-Joachim (1991a). *Abschluß, Neubeginn und Übergang*. St Augustin: Konrad-Adenauer-Stiftung.

Veen, Hans-Joachim (1991b). 'Einführung – Wählergesellschaft im Umbruch.' In Hans-Joachim Veen and Elisabeth Noelle-Neumann (eds), *Wählerverhalten im Wandel*. Paderborn: Ferdinand Schöningh, pp. 9–20.

Veen, Hans-Joachim (1994). 'Zukunft und Gefährdung der Volksparteien.' In Günther Rüther (ed.), *Politik und Gesellschaft in Deutschland*. Cologne: Verlag Wissenschaft und Politik, pp. 129–37.

Veen, Hans-Joachim (1995). 'Illusionen der Bürgergesellschaft.' In Peter Lösche and Hans-Joachim Veen (eds), *Die Zukunft der Volksparteien*. St Augustin: Konrad-Adenauer-Stiftung, pp. 21–35.

Veen, Hans-Joachim and Peter Gluchowski (1994). 'Die Anhängerschaft der Parteien vor und nach der Einheit – eine Langfristbetrachtung von 1953 bis 1993.' *Zeitschrift für Parlamentsfragen* 25: 165–85.

von Winter, Thomas (1996). 'Wählerverhalten in den östlichen Bundesländern.' *Zeitschrift für Parlamentsfragen* 27: 298–316.

Vorwärts (1995). 'SPD muß PDS-Wähler auf ihre Seite ziehen: Vorstandsbeschluß.' 1: 26–7.

Weins, Cornelia (2000). 'The East German Vote in the 1998 General Election.' In Stephen Padgett and Thomas Saalfeld (eds), *Bundestagswahl '98: End of an Era?* London: Frank Cass, pp. 48–71.

Wiesendahl, Elmar (1998). 'Wie geht es weiter mit den Großparteien in Deutschland?' *Aus Politik und Zeitgeschichte* 1–2: 13–28.

Zelle, Carsten (1994). 'Steigt die Zahl der Wechselwähler? Trends des Wahlverhaltens und der Parteiidentifikation.' In Hans Rattinger, Oscar W. Gabriel, and Wolfgang Jagodzinski (eds), *Wahlen und politische Einstellungen im vereinigten Deutschland*. Frankfurt am Main: Peter Lang, pp. 47–91.

Zelle, Carsten (1996). 'Candidates, Issues and Party Choice in the Federal Election of 1994.' In Geoffrey Roberts (ed.), *Superwahljahr: The German Elections of 1994*. London: Frank Cass, pp. 54–74.

FIVE   Party Responses to Electoral
        Dealignment in Italy

Luciano Bardi

The Italian electoral market

Italy's electoral market has changed dramatically in recent years. Up to the late
1970s, Italian parties had very little to worry about in terms of the erosion of
voter loyalties. In fact, although some ecological realignment (i.e. a decline
in agrarian/traditional/religious groups paralleled by an increase in their
urban/secular counterparts) undoubtedly took place in the postwar period, the
major parties scarcely seemed to notice it. But by the beginning of the 1990s,
however, volatility had reached levels seldom seen in western electoral history
and once-mighty political parties had seen their electorates shrink dramatically
or all but disappear. Besides those factors that are common to many western
democracies, two specific and interrelated parts of this change need to be discussed: first, the momentous party system transformation; and secondly, the
radical electoral law reform. Although these changes can themselves be seen as
partial responses to changes in the electoral market, they have enormously contributed to changing voter attitudes and behaviour, as well as party responses.

Party system change

Prior to 1994, the Italian party system was very fragmented, with at least eight
national parliamentary parties at any given time. Only four parties, however,
had consistently relevant electoral support: the DC,[1] for many years the
system's dominant party; the PCI, the strongest opposition party; the PSI, and
the neo-Fascist MSI. All the other parties usually obtained less than 5 percent
of the vote, until in 1992 the recently created LN polled more than 8 percent.
The full extent of the change and the birth of the 'new' party system only
became manifest with the 1994 elections and was confirmed in 1996 and 2001
(Table 5.1). These events, however, did nothing but formalize changes that had
been unfolding since the beginning of the 1990s. The 'clean hands' investigations, which annihilated a host of traditional parties (PLI, PSDI, PRI, and, for
all practical purposes, the PSI and the once-mighty DC), and a new, mostly

plurality, electoral law were the catalysts for the change in the party system and in individual parties. But the LN had already become a force to be reckoned with in the regional elections of May 1990, and in February 1991 the PCI had already dissolved itself and formed the PDS. The general election of March 1994 appeared to have made the change irreversible, however.

With respect to the pre-1992 period there is now one completely new party and one new confederation of parties: FI and the Margherita (Daisy). Silvio Berlusconi's creation, FI, consistently close to the 30 percent mark in all recent elections, is now the largest party in Italy. The Margherita is the name chosen by four centre Left parties (Romano Prodi's Democratici, PPI, UDEUR, and RI) for the pre-electoral confederation they formed to contest from a position of greater potential strength the 2001 elections. The confederation is being maintained after the formation of a common parliamentary party and might yet become a permanent feature in the Italian party system. The LN, dropping to less than 4 percent of the vote, has lost its position as the fourth largest party but remains an important actor in at least the north-east. The PCI's transformation resulted in the formation of two separate parties, the PDS and RC, which for three general elections jointly exhibited roughly the same electoral strength as their predecessor. The RC's decision in 1998 to withdraw its support for the centre Left government led by Romano Prodi caused a further split and gave birth to the PDCI, a party still loyal to the Communist tradition but more willing to accept the compromises that are necessary for the maintenance of governmental majorities and even particular prime ministers.[2] Similarly the evolution of the MSI produced two offspring, the die-hard and small MSI-FT, and the much more mainstream and ostensibly respectable AN, now the third largest party in the system. The most important change, however, is the disappearance of the DC, whose political heritage was divided between the already mentioned PPI and the CCD-CDU, two parties that joined respectively the centre Left (now as part of the Margherita) and the centre Right.[3] The CCD-CDU, now officially fused in the UDC, had a very poor result in 2001, failing to pass the 4 percent threshold in the proportional part of the Chamber of Deputies election. Like the LN, the party has sizeable parliamentary parties in both chambers because of its success in the plurality part of the elections. The only parties that did not change very much between the two periods were regional parties, such as the PSdA and the PPST/SVP, and the Greens. All of these parties, however, were forced to support explicitly the centre Left coalition. Finally, the PR is constantly declining in importance and electoral support.

The new electoral law

The other important factor was Italy's new electoral law. Electoral reform, besides being itself a factor of party system transformation, produced changes in election competition rules. Three-quarters of the seats are now won in

Table 5.1 National level election results and seat distribution (Camera dei Deputati) in Italy, 1948–2001

Year		PSIUP RC[a]	PCI DS	PSI	PSDI	PRI	PR	VER	RI	DC PPI	IdV	DE	CCD/ CDU	FI	PLI	MSI AN	PNM[9] PDIUM	LN	PPST	Oth.	Total
1948	%		31.0[b]		7.1	2.5				48.5					3.8	2.0	2.8		0.5	1.8	100
	s		183		33	9				305					19	6	14		3	2	574
1953	%		22.6	12.7	4.5	1.6				40.1					3.0	5.8	6.9		0.5	2.3	100
	s		143	75	19	5				263					13	29	40		3	0	590
1958	%		22.7	14.2	4.6	1.4				42.3					3.5	4.8	4.8		0.5	1.2	100
	s		140	84	22	6				273					17	24	25		3	2	596
1963	%		25.3	13.8	6.1	1.4				38.3					7.0	5.1	1.7		0.4	0.9	100
	s		166	87	33	6				260					39	27	8		3	1	630
1968	%	4.4	26.9	14.5[d]		2.0				39.1					5.8	4.5	1.3		0.5	1.0	100
	s	23	177	91		9				266					31	24	6		3		630
1972	%	1.9	27.1	9.6	5.1	2.9				38.7					3.9	8.7			0.5	1.6	100
	s	0	179	61	29	15				266					20	56			3	1	630
1976	%	1.5	34.4	9.6	3.4	3.1	1.1			38.7					1.3	6.1			0.5	0.3	100
	s	6	227	57	15	14	4			263					5	35			3	1	630
1979	%	1.4	30.4	9.8	3.8	3.0	3.5			38.3					1.9	5.3			0.6	2.0	100
	s	6	201	62	20	16	18			262					9	30			4	2[b]	630
1983	%	1.5	29.9	11.4	4.1	5.1	2.2			32.9					2.9	6.8		0.3	0.5	2.4	100
	s	7	198	73	23	29	11			225					16	42		1[h]	3	2	630
1987	%	1.7	26.6	14.3	2.9	3.7	2.6	2.5		34.3					2.1	5.9		1.3	0.5	1.4	100
	s	8	177	94	17	21	13	13		234					11	35		1[i]	3	3	630
1992	%	5.6	16.1	13.6	2.7	4.4	1.2	2.8		29.7					2.9	5.4		8.6	0.5	6.5	100
	s	35	107	92	16	27	7	16		206					17	34		55	3	15	630
1994	%	6.0	20.4	2.2			3.5	2.7		15.7[e]				21.0		13.5		8.4	0.6	6.0	100
	s	39	164[c]							33			27[f]	113		109		117		15	630

(Continued)

Table 5.1 Continued

	PSIUP RC[a]	PCI DS	PSI	PSDI	PRI	PR	VER	RI	DC PPI	IdV	DE	CCD/ CDU	FI	PLI	MSI AN	PNM[g] PDIUM	LN	PPST	Oth.	Total
1996 %	8.6	21.1	0.4			1.9	2.5	4.3	6.8			5.8	20.6		15.7		10.1		2.2	100
s	35	167					14	27	80			30	123		93		59		2	630
2001 %	5.0 1.7	16.6	1.0			2.3	2.2		14.5[j]	3.9	2.4	3.2	29.4		12.0		3.9	0.5	2.4	100
s	21	136	6				7		76[j]			38	178		97		29	3	28	619[k]

[a]PSIUP: 1968, 1972; PDUP: 1979; DP: 1976, 1983, 1987; RC: 1992, 1994, 1996; RC + PBCI: 2001.
[b]Fronte Popolare/People's Front (electoral alliance between PCI and PSI).
[c]Includes seats assigned to La Rete, Verdi, and PSI candidates endorsed by the Progressisti, the PDS-led electoral alliance.
[d]PSU (Partito Socialista Unificato).
[e]PPI + Patto Segni.
[f]The CCD did not present its own candidate lists in the PR part of the election and consequently CCD vote percentages are not available for 1994. 27 CCD deputies were however elected in either the PR or the plurality parts of the election as FI candidates and went on to form a separate parliamentary group.
[g]PNM: 1948, 1953; PNM + PMP: 1958; PDIUM: 1963, 1968.
[h]Liga Veneta/Venetian League.
[i]Lega Lombarda/Lombard League.
[j]Margherita.
[k]The total is 619 instead of 630 because 11 seats could not be assigned in the PR part of the election owing to an insufficient number of F1 candidates.

Source: Official Ministry of Internal Affairs data

single-member plurality districts, inducing parties to form electoral coalitions to contest elections nationwide. The remaining 25 percent of the seats are assigned through proportional representation. Consequently, the direction of competition is now prevalently centripetal where it used be centrifugal. These changes have produced additional results in the structuring of coalitions in the electoral and, broadly speaking, political arenas. As sweeping as the transformation of the Italian party system may have been, its structural impact was contradictory. In the electoral arena the number of parties has gone down dramatically, as demonstrated by the relevant scores reported in Table 5.1. On the other hand, in the legislative arena we are confronted with an increase in the number of parties and fractionalization. After the 2001 election, respectively 15 and 19 parties were still represented in the Chamber of Deputies and in the Senate (Verzichelli 2002). Whereas the effects in the electoral arena can appear obvious consequences of the majoritarian impact of electoral reform, those in the legislative arena can be seen as responses dictated, at least in part, by an increasingly complex electoral market.

Electoral dealignment

The change in the party system was preceded by a period of electoral dealignment. Table 5.2 lists scores for aggregate indicators of voter mobility between 1948 and 2001. Indices of total volatility (TV) and bloc volatility (BV) are used for comparative purposes. They are not very accurate indices of mobility as they do not account for compensations resulting from identical numbers of electors switching from one party to another and vice versa. This problem is more severe in multi-party systems such as that in Italy. In multi-party systems compensations can also follow a circular pattern (from A to B to C to A) and not necessarily only a bi-directional one (from A to B and from B to A). The electoral mobility index (EM), based on estimated electoral flows, instead addresses exactly the issue of how many electors switch electoral allegiances between elections, including flows to and from abstentionism.[4]

The data reported in Table 5.2 show that electoral behaviour patterns have indeed undergone a very important transformation. After the initial consolidation phase, TV, BV and fractionalization (F) scores remained fairly stable between 1958 and 1987, but changed dramatically in 1992. The transformation was the result of three sets of direct causes: (1) change in political demand towards specific parties or even parties in general, resulting from greater potential voter mobility; (2) change in the political supply provided by the parties (a) as a result of the scandals and judicial actions that followed *tangentopoli* (literally 'bribe city'); (b) as a consequence of their need to make new and different strategic choices in response to the new electoral law; and (c) as a response to the changing structure of political/electoral demand; (3) direct effects of the electoral law on individual parties' parliamentary delegations (Bardi 1996b). Certainly it can be surmised that the change produced by the 1992 elections was the exclusive consequence of changes in electors' party

Table 5.2   Dealignment and party system change in Italy, 1948–2001 (indices based on Chamber of Deputies results)

	TV	BV	EM	N	F
1948	22.8	2.1		2.9	0.66
1953	13.3	2.4		4.2	0.76
1958	4.5	0.7		3.8	0.74
1963	7.9	4.0		4.2	0.76
1968	3.4	0.6		3.6	0.75
1972	4.9	1.3		3.6	0.76
1976	8.2	4.0		3.1	0.72
1979	5.3	2.6	20[a]	3.4	0.74
1983	8.5	1.6	20[a]	4.0	0.78
1987	8.4	1.3	21	4.1	0.78
1992	14.2	7.5	30	5.7	0.85
1994	36.2	8.9	58[b]	5.7[c] 3.6[d]	0.87[e] 0.78[f]
1996	18.2	8.9	41	6.2[c] 2.7[d]	0.86[e] 0.67[f]
2001	22.0	2.6	44	5.2[c] 2.0[d]	0.84[e] 0.60[f]

TV = total volatility; BV = bloc volatility; EM = electoral mobility; N = number of effective parties;
   F = fractionalization;
TV and BV indicators calculated according to criteria used by Bartolini and Mair (1990); F (Rae
   1971); N (Laakso and Taagepera 1979); EM (Biorcio and Natale 1989).
1948–83: F and N scores were kindly provided by Leonardo Morlino; 1948–83: TV and BV scores
   are from Bartolini and Mair (1990); 1987–96 scores are based on my own calculations on
   official data; all EM scores were kindly provided by Paolo Natale.

[a]Estimate.
[b]According to Paolo Natale this score is to be considered with great caution or at least with
approximation due to the many changes in party identities between 1992 and 1994 which make
the identification of electoral flows very difficult.
[c]Based on seat distribution among parliamentary parties formed in the Italian Chamber of
Deputies after the election.
[d]Based on total seats obtained in the election by coalitions and individual parties not included in
coalitions.
[e]Based on vote percentages obtained by individual parties in the proportional part of the election.
[f]Based on vote percentages obtained by coalitions and individual parties not included in coalitions
in the plurality part of the election.

choices; in 1994, when elections were held for the first time under the new electoral rules and after the beginning of the *tangentopoli* investigations, all three sets of factors were most likely at work; in 1996 and even more so in 2001, the impact of *tangentopoli* on the shaping of electoral supply was probably exhausted. For all four post-1987 elections TV values are much higher than in the past. The 1992 value, the only one exclusively determined by electors' voting decisions, is particularly important: at 14.2 it was the highest registered up to that point between two parliamentary elections and almost double the average (7.2) of all previous elections. The BV value (7.5) was even more impressive, considering the average (2.1) for the 1953–87 period (Bardi 1996a, 1996b). The EM score is almost 50 percent higher than all the previous ones and confirms the trend revealed by the other indicators.

Analysis of the 1994 values is somewhat more complicated. While the 1994 BV value is only slightly higher than the 1992 one, the TV value of 36.2 is perhaps the highest ever observed in western democratic elections (Bartolini and Mair 1990: 69). But this time the change cannot be entirely imputed to increases in electoral availability. Volatility and mobility are measures very much affected by changes in the composition of the field of parties contesting the election, and it is probable that a relevant number of electors were forced to alter their habitual choices because of differences in the electoral supply.

The 1996 TV and EM scores (18.2 and 41 respectively) were the second highest ever observed between two postwar parliamentary elections. They resulted from the diminished importance of changes in electoral supply. At least one important change, the CDU exit from the PPI, had taken place since the previous elections, probably as a response to the prevalent majoritarian logic in electoral competition.[5] This direct cause of party system change could also be on the point of losing most of its importance. The 2001 scores confirm that there is a tendency towards stabilization of the electorate. The only scores that remain high (TV and F in the PR part of the election) are influenced by the continuing changes on the supply side of the electoral market, suggesting that parties have not yet adjusted their response to changing market conditions.

This impression is confirmed by party identification and voter turnout data. Party identification time-series data is practically non-existent in Italy and party identification trends can only be inferred on the basis of rather heterogeneous sources. The combined impression one may get from Eurobarometer data and a number of studies is that party identification declined, and fairly significantly, between 1985 and 1991, and then stabilized in the 1990s (Mannheimer 1989, 1994; Mannheimer and Sani 1987; Schmitt and Holmberg 1995). Other recent surveys (Maraffi 2002) show substantial stability between 1990 (55 percent) and 2001 (57 percent), consistent with the Eurobarometer data (Table 5.3).

In Italy, voter turnout has always been considered an important manifestation of political participation. As elections hardly ever created significant change, high turnout was taken to indicate the existence of some form of popular 'permissive consensus' by the centrist majority parties and to reveal a commitment to the values of the Resistance-inspired Constitution by the leftist opposition. Most Italian citizens perceived voting as a civic duty more than as a right, and Italy's average turnout in parliamentary elections between 1946 and 1976 was second only to that of Austria. Thus the noticeable decline in turnout percentages along with an increase in spoiled and blank ballots from 1979 onwards was viewed with concern by all major Italian parties (Table 5.4). Conversely, the PR and other non-cartel parties greeted the trend as revealing popular dissatisfaction with the traditional alternatives.

Given the almost complete disarray of the traditional parties at the time of the 1994 elections, a further, and sharper, drop in voter turnout was expected by many. The 86.2 percent turnout was indeed the lowest ever in parliamentary elections, but the difference from 1992 (−1.1 percent) was smaller than expected. But the downward trend continued in 1996 and 2001. Considering spoiled and blank ballots, only 75 percent of the electorate cast valid votes in 2001.

Table 5.3   Voter loyalties in Italy,
1978–96

	Strong identifiers	All identifiers
1978	46	77
1979	45	78
1980	39	69
1981	44	73
1982	38	67
1983	41	71
1984	37	71
1985	37	67
1986	38	66
1987	36	64
1988	39	69
1989	35	62
1990	31	58
1991	29	51
1992	31	56
1993	26	51
1994	34	60
1996	30	56

Source: Eurobarometer

Table 5.4   Voters, Turnout, Valid Votes, Spoiled, and Blank Ballots in Elections to the Chamber of Deputies, 1968–2001

		Turnout		Spoiled ballots		Blank ballots		Valid votes	
	Voters	N	%	N	%	N	%	N	%
1968	35,567	33,014	92.8	560	1.6	640	1.8	31,814	89.6
1972	37,050	34,524	93.2	508	1.4	601	1.6	33,415	90.2
1976	40,423	37,761	93.4	436	1.1	597	1.5	36,727	90.8
1979	42,203	38,253	90.6	744	1.7	838	2.0	36,797	86.9
1983	44,047	39,188	89.0	1,340	3.1	942	2.1	36,906	83.8
1987	45,690	40,599	88.9	1,232	2.7	775	1.7	38,592	84.5
1992	47,436	41,439	87.3	1,319	2.8	876	1.8	39,244	82.7
1994	48,225	41,554	86.2	1,411	2.9	1,422	2.9	38,721	80.3
1996	48,846	40,402	82.9	1,660	4.1	1,242	3.1	37,500	76.9
2001	49,257	40,100	81.4	1,363	3.4	1,514	3.8	37,101	75.3

PR part of the election for 1994–2001, Ns (in thousands) and percentages of total electorate.

Sources: 1968–87: Nuvoli and Spreafico (1990); 1992–2001: Electoral Service of the Italian Ministry for Internal Affairs

Summing up, the dealignment of the 1980s was coupled with a major realignment. The LN's ability to channel long-repressed popular dissatisfaction against the established parties was reflected, by Italian standards, in quasi-revolutionary results. It would be a mistake, however, to attribute to this factor the much greater changes that occurred in 1994 and even 1996. These were caused by exogenous factors (scandals and institutional reform) that operated on the supply side and totally transformed the range of choices offered to the electorate. It is very unlikely that without the scandals parties such as the DC or even the PSI would have collapsed as a result of just one unfavourable election.

Party perceptions of electoral dealignment

We have seen that dealignment cannot be considered a widely noticeable phenomenon until the mid-1970s. Coherent with the data, a generalized party preoccupation with dealignment is not noticeable until the early 1980s, mostly as a reaction to declining electoral turnout. But individual parties' electoral trends were much more discernible throughout the whole period. Consequently, for most of the postwar period parties reacted individually to the ups and downs in their own electoral fortunes rather than to any wider manifestations of dealignment in general. In some cases party strategies were deeply affected by such concerns. This is certainly true of Italy's two major parties, the DC and the PCI and, to a lesser extent, of the PSI.

Two major departures from the past characterize perceptions of dealignment in the 1990s: first, coalitions compete for the same available electorate, which now seems to be mainly concentrated near the centre of the political spectrum; in the past dealignment mostly concerned contiguous parties competing in pairs for limited and selected portions of the electorate situated along the whole political spectrum; secondly, individual parties are now more concerned with within-bloc dealignment than in the past, in that their relative strengths are important for their position within the coalition as well as for their influence on coalition leadership selection.

The post-1992 transformation left all political parties, old and new, with perceptions of persistent high voter mobility. These impressions are reinforced by the continuing realignment in the party system. The disappearance or transformation of political parties continues to make sizeable portions of the electorate potentially available irrespective of their propensity to switch parties. At any rate, parties are still in the process of getting adjusted to the new party system and to the competition rules of the current electoral law; they all seem to be very aware of dealignment and to perceive it more as an opportunity than as a threat. In other words, the political system's continuing fluidity, something that will continue at least until the final approval of widely advocated but never agreed upon constitutional reforms, prompts dynamic rather than static postures by Italian political parties. The most important consequence of this situation is that the border between the two coalitions is still blurred, as individual parties and electoral alliances try to occupy what is still a relatively available political space.

At least for the larger parties, within-bloc dealignment now appears to be more relevant than in the past. This is also partially due to the new significance of electoral alliances' internal dynamics, with special regard to leadership selection. In the pre-1992 system, the identity and qualities of coalition leaders were relatively unimportant and within-bloc equilibria were extremely stable.

The governmental coalition make-up and strength were the sum of the electoral results of the individual parties that would eventually be included after the election. In fact the actual selection of the Prime Minister, the closest thing to a coalition leader, only took place after the election itself. The governmental coalition leadership was never determined by inter-party electoral equilibria, so evident and unquestionable was the DC electoral superiority. In 1992, after 40 years of almost continuous decline, the DC's share of the vote (29.7 percent) was still more than double that (13.6 percent) of its strongest ally (the PSI) and accounted for more than half of the coalition's total (53.8 percent). The party's internal balance, in its turn depending on an intricate web of personal relationships, ties with external interest groups and civil society in general, but most of all involving links with and control over sectors of the state apparatus, was in reality the most important factor in determining the coalition's overall leadership, even when it was held by PRI or PSI exponents.[6] Inter-party balance was even less relevant for the pre-1992 opposition, not only because opposition parties pursued separate strategies before and after elections, but also because of evident PCI superiority over the small leftist parties and the PSI, before it entered the centre Left governmental coalition. Indeed, Bettino Craxi's hope to make the PSI the hegemonic party of the Left ultimately relied on inter-bloc (from Left proper to centre Left) rather than within-bloc dealignment. As for the right, the MSI was the only party left after 1968.

In the present party system coalitions have recognized leaders before and sometimes even between elections. Leaders must have personal and political qualities but their status also depends on their party's strength and electoral performance. The two coalitions' most important party leaders have been considered for most practical purposes coalition leaders as well, although this is more true of the centre Right Polo than of the centre Left Ulivo. In the Polo, Silvio Berlusconi's leadership has been recognized formally since the formation of the alliance. In that case several factors contributed to the choice even before FI could reveal its electoral appeal; later on it was clear that the latter was to a large extent reflective of the fact that FI was 'Berlusconi's party'. Without the party's unprecedented success, Berlusconi's leadership in the coalition would be open to question. In other words, Berlusconi's ascent to coalition leadership was due to his personal qualities, but his ability to maintain that leadership would be seriously impaired if not for FI primacy within the coalition.

The situation is more complex in the Ulivo. The PDS secretary, Massimo D'Alema, was the coalition's leading figure even before its various components formally coalesced. The overwhelming electoral and organizational superiority of the PDS over the other parties making up the centre Left was the decisive factor. Nor was D'Alema's *de facto* leadership imperilled in 1996 by the appointment of Romano Prodi as a prime ministerial candidate more acceptable to the moderate components of the centre Left electorate. Even after the Ulivo victory and Prodi's actual ascent to the head of the Executive, D'Alema's political leadership was clearly maintained. In 1998, Prodi's own downfall and D'Alema's takeover as Prime Minister seemed to have finally settled the issue.

But the defeat of the Ulivo in the 2000 regional elections forced D'Alema's resignation and marked the end of his leadership.[7] Neither his successor as Prime Minister, Giuliano Amato, nor the leader of the coalition in the 2001 electoral campaign, Margherita exponent Francesco Rutelli, was able to establish a firm leadership position.

Coalition leadership thus seems to rest on the relative within-coalition strength of the leader's party and its appeal to the moderate electorate. It can be affected by within-bloc electoral flows, especially if favouring parties closer to the centre. For the time being Berlusconi's leadership is secured by the sheer electoral size of FI and by the second largest party in the coalition, AN, being situated further to the right. In contrast, the primacy of the DS (formerly PDS) could be challenged by the Margherita, now only a few percentage points behind (18.3 percent vs. 14.5 percent in 2001) and part of the political centre.

Things are very different for the smaller parties. In their case the fundamental issue is to demonstrate that they can maintain exclusive control over select, albeit small, portions of the electorate. This can be done through the encapsulation of specific ideological constituencies, as is the case with the Greens, and, to a certain extent, with the UDC; or through the acquisition of special positional advantages, mostly by attracting portions of the moderate centre (RI, CDU and then UDR), but also of the extremes (RC). Usually it is sufficient for such parties to guarantee to their potential coalition partners control of a part of the electorate that may be as small as 1.5 or 2 percent. Such are in fact the margins by which many seats are won in the plurality part of the election. This can make several small parties *indispensable* for the electoral success of the coalition and sometimes allows them to bargain for a higher number of safe constituency candidatures than their sheer electoral appeal would grant.[8]

Party responses to electoral dealignment, 1948–92

As we have seen, the term dealignment can be used to describe changes in electoral market conditions in Italy to a limited extent prior to 1992. What took place after that was termed with varying degrees of emphasis a major realignment, a fully-fledged transformation of the party system, or even a French-style transition between different republics – that is, a fundamental change in the political system and in its relationship with civil society. To be sure, this last position takes for granted fundamental changes yet to come, even if this prospect was made less likely after parliament failed to discuss, let alone approve, institutional reform proposals already drafted by a specifically appointed bicameral parliamentary committee (Vassallo 1998).[9] But the enormous qualitative differences between the phenomena that characterize the two periods are such that party responses have to be treated separately. For the pre-1992 period, we will consider party responses in terms of organization, target groups, policies, candidates, relations with the state and with state-regulated media, especially television. More attention will be dedicated to the system's dominant parties, the DC and the PCI, and to a lesser extent, the PSI and the MSI. Post-1992 responses will be treated in a less analytical fashion, given the difficulties in separating party from political system and even societal responses.

Party organization: membership and basic units

Italian parties were organized according to two dominant models after they were all (re)-founded in the aftermath of the Second World War. The four largest parties DC, PCI, PSI and even the MSI gave themselves organizational structures that, at least on paper, were consistent with the mass-integration model. The other three parties that survived for most of the postwar period, PLI, PRI and PSDI, could instead be characterized as elite-dominated opinion parties with a prevailing middle-class appeal and a very limited grass-roots or even intermediate organizational structure. The PRI did have a strong territorial rooting in some limited areas, most notably in the provinces of Ravenna and Forlì, but failed to extend its mass appeal to other parts of the country. Parties in this latter group were part of the governmental coalition for most of the pre-1992 period. In general, their responses to electoral dealignment were expressed mostly through action at the governmental level, by giving or denying the coalition support at crucial times. Alternatively, they took firm positions on key issues (PRI), and often privileged specific clienteles (especially PSDI and PLI), rather than effecting organizational adaptation. After just one unsuccessful election in 1968, the PSDI even reversed the 1966 decision to merge with the PSI to form the PSU. It was clearly more important for the party to secure a small portion of the electorate than to seek a more influential role by joining forces with another party. The significance of most of these organizational characteristics and the intended purpose of some of the changes cannot always be seen as responses to specific instances of electoral dealignment, however. Nevertheless, it is plausible to suggest that they may have resulted from parties' intentions to exploit what could be seen as natural fluctuations in electoral behaviour. Some of the shares of the electorate enjoyed by these parties were so small that they could shrink or expand enormously even in extremely stable elections.

The PSI never developed as a mass-integration party, and because of the importance of its intermediate structures (provincial federations), stratarchy and factionalism developed relatively early on, even if party factions and groups in civil society were always rather weakly connected. Factionalization was also experienced by the MSI during the 1970s, following attempts to broaden the party's appeal. Both parties saw a strengthening of their top leadership during the 1980s. In the PSI, Bettino Craxi's rule only concerned the party's national-level strategies and did not affect the provincial federation's independence. Such independence was perceived to be crucial to the party's bid for electoral primacy within the Left. It was felt that diversified local and regional strategies would allow it not only to extend its appeal to those regions, such as the southern ones, where its rival, the PCI, was never able to make significant electoral inroads, but also to attract support in the regional strongholds of Emilia-Romagna, Tuscany, Umbria, and Marche from those portions of the traditional leftist constituency, especially shopkeepers and small entrepreneurs, who were displaying growing unease with the PCI's rigidity in economic matters. Conversely, in the MSI, Giorgio Almirante's Caesarism (Ignazi 1989: 309) was clearly intended to re-establish party unity. The MSI was still at the margins of the party system and could not hope to attract permanent support from significant sectors of Italian society. Alleged links with external groups were thus perceived by the leadership as instruments for the strengthening of internal factions rather than as opportunities for the expansion of the party's electorate.

Dealignment emerges much more clearly as a cause of important organizational changes in the case of the two major parties, the DC and the PCI, than it does in the case of the smaller parties. Both major parties moved towards a catch-all organizational model in response to either electoral defeat (the DC) and/or in an explicit effort to attract voters who were becoming available outside the *classe gardée* (PCI). Following the 1953 electoral decline, and explicitly as a response to it, the new DC secretary Amintore Fanfani embarked on the building of an autonomous party organization (Poggi 1968: 216). In the first few years of its history the party had relied heavily on the Church and its secular organizations (such as Catholic Action). Fanfani intended to create a modern mass party with a strong internal leadership, a large membership, a central organization, and, above all, a diffuse peripheral structure, independent of the Church and of Catholic organizations: a party capable of expanding its appeal beyond the Catholic electorate. Although the most visible result of his effort was a massive growth in membership, the most important aspect of Fanfani's initiative was the building of an extensive network of independent territorial units that gave the party the potential to reach electors of every extraction in every part of the country. In reality many of these units (and members) existed only on paper, because Fanfani's successors did not pursue the same strategy. Ultimately Fanfani's organizational goals were defeated but most of his electoral objectives were achieved as a consequence of the same development: that is, the progressive and unstoppable process of party factionalization which made it impossible for the DC to become a cohesive party with a strongly integrated and dominant elite, but which also made it flexible enough to adapt to changing societal and cultural conditions in a way that limited potentially negative electoral trends.

The progressive modernization and secularization of Italy stimulated PCI attempts at organizational reform from the late 1950s onwards. In this case the party's preoccupation was to extend its appeal beyond the industrial electorate (Poggi 1968: 76). The most important organizational consequence of this decision was the disappearance of the cell as the basic organizational unit (Bardi and Morlino 1994). At the 1979 party congress only about 2,000 factory cells were represented, the territorial *sezione* having become the basic organizational unit. The disappearance of the cell marked the transition to a much more pragmatic posture (from mass-integration to catch-all party). At the same time, the notion of membership underwent a parallel evolution. During the 1940s every member was a militant and by the mid-1950s at least 350,000 Communists still had leadership functions (Ghini 1981: 241). By the late 1960s the bulk of party activities, including recruitment and campaigning, were carried out by a handful of members in each of the 12–13,000 branches (Galli 1976), while a decade later the outer circle in the PCI membership was described simply as *iscritti* (literally enrolled), easily switching from that status to 'sympathizers' or just 'voters' (Casciani 1981). These changes may have made the party's outer appearance more attractive, but they did not change its centralized power structure. Even later attempts in selected regions (notably Tuscany) to introduce primary elections for candidate selection purposes had no consequences, given the notorious discipline of the party rank and file.

Furthermore, both parties adapted their organizations in order to establish links with a variety of interest groups. The DC created *sezioni ambiente*, non-territorial branches meant to replace territorial units, still strongly identified with Catholic organizations, as party contacts with civil society. The *sezioni ambiente* were aimed at organizing 'members belonging to the same working environment, and to the same cultural, social, and associational centre' (Poggi 1968). They seem to have had little impact, however, and by 1991 accounted for little more than 5 percent of the 13,700 DC branches, even if more than half (230 vs. 211) were located in major cities. These attempts, as well as that to strengthen the party organization *tout court*, were in fact carried out with very ambivalent feelings by the party leadership. Although they were obviously intended to benefit the party as a whole, they often strengthened individual factions, thus weakening the central organization and altering the internal balance of power. In other words, the factions replaced the party as gate-keepers between civil society and the state. The only noteworthy response to this distortion took place in the second half of the 1980s, when, in an effort to weaken the regional rooting of the factions, party secretary Ciriaco De Mita tried to redistribute internal power in favour of the regional level by increasing the powers and responsibilities of the regional secretaries.

The PCI strategy to 'open up' to civil society was more subtle, given the party's reluctance to abandon the democratic-centralist model. In the early 1970s, all parties felt the need to 'open up' to potential members, and especially to potential voters, outside their subcultures. Hence their need to make their presence felt in society at large; hence their relentless efforts to organize 'cultural events' with a potentially broad appeal. The PCI was extremely active in this phase because of the expansionist posture it had in those years. The growing emphasis on party-related recreational and – broadly defined – cultural organizations was part of this strategy. Its efficacy remained doubtful, however. In fact, rather than an expression of political sympathy for the party, membership in these organizations was very often instrumental: members were usually entitled to discounts on cinema and theatre admission tickets. In some cases the interests of the cultural organization or of one of its sections were diametrically opposed to the party line.[10] The PCI also ended its privileged relationship with the unified workers' movement during the 1980s. However, this decision seemed forced upon the party by adverse political circumstances rather than reflecting an autonomous and deliberate decision by the leadership to make the party more available to other societal groups (Bardi and Morlino 1994).

The most important organizational change on the part of the PCI was, of course, its transformation into the PDS. Certainly it was made necessary by a much deeper crisis than simple electoral decline. The transformation of Italian society, in its transition to post-industrialism, this time played against the PCI, characterized as it was by the shrinkage of the working class and of its cultural hegemony. Moreover, the collapse of international Communism forced a long-delayed redefinition of the party's ideological references and objectives (Ignazi 1992). These two developments made the PCI's electoral appeal very question-able, and in this sense the transformation of the PCI into the PDS was also in part a response to the new make-up of the Italian electorate.

The new party's constituent phase saw the birth of over 1,000 'constituent committees', many of which were meant to bring new forces into the party. In reality, these were not allowed to participate in the re-establishment of the party. Very innovative proposals, however, came from within the party itself. Piero Fassino, then PCI organizational secretary, proposed the creation of a decentralized party structure based on regional autonomy, characterized by high levels of professionalization and by the attribution of greater responsibili-ties to externally recruited party leaders. The basic party units at the municipal level were to be completely autonomous in terms of locally relevant decisions and also in terms of financial resources, in order to bring 'the fundamental powers ... down below, close to the members and the electors' (Baccetti 1997). This could at least partially be seen as a response to the relatively successful PSI regional and local strategy. In fact, the PDS statute approved by the 20th Congress of the PCI in 1991 permits the creation of internal, potentially dis-senting, factions, while remaining close to the old organizational model in most other respects.

Party organization: target groups

Italy's major parties started reconsidering their target groups even before the dealignment and realignment of the last two decades. Such moves were consis-tent with their strategic organizational choices. As we have seen, both the DC and the PCI emerged from the Second World War with clear mass integration features and with, respectively, denomination and class-defined target groups. The same can be said at least in theory of the PSI, but its working-class con-stituency was progressively replaced by an inter-class, mainly secular, electo-rate. At the same time the PCI consolidated its within-bloc dominance. The huge success of the DC in 1948 objectively made it a potential catch-all party, even if this implication was not clearly perceived at first: after all, Italy was still a traditional, and above all a Catholic country. The catch-all vocation became progressively dominant as more sophisticated analyses indicated that many DC voters came from moderate to conservative secular social groups. This tendency became more pronounced with the progressive secularization of Italian society and with the parallel decline of some of its traditional sectors, especially in rural areas. Already in 1954, when Fanfani began his efforts to reorganize the DC, he aimed at building an inter-class party. This did not in itself mean precisely the same as catch-all, since religion in Italy cuts across social classes, but it did acquire that meaning from the late 1960s onwards, when no party could afford to ignore secular electors. Moreover, and in increasing numbers, Catholic voters were learning to separate their religious from their political beliefs and were turning to parties of the Left, especially the PCI. It thus became a paramount preoccupation for all DC leaders from the Fanfani secretariat onwards to secure as many moderate to conservative, albeit secular, voters as possible.

Whether the efforts to turn the DC into a catch-all party were successful is still an open question. This uncertainty is mainly due to the fact that most attempts to answer this question have been based on analyses of the social make-up of the party membership, and this, in turn, is complicated by two problems: first, the classification criteria used by the DC varied over time and were not compatible with existing official population statistics – this makes time-series and comparative analyses very difficult. Secondly, the party appears to be organized according to at least two different models (especially in terms of territorial rooting) in the north and the south of the country, with different implications for membership recruitment (Bardi, unpublished). Given these limits, we can only conclude with Fausto Anderlini (1989), that in the mid-1980s, the DC was a middle-class party with still strong Catholic features in the north (especially in the north-east) and in the centre/Red Belt regions, and was a more secular inter-class party in the south. A few years earlier Ignazi and Panebianco (1979) had found that a majority of DC members had secular conceptions of politics. However, the catch-all character of the DC was more evident if one looked at the composition of its electorate, whose profile was close to that of the population as a whole (Mannheimer and Sani 1987: 69).

The PCI's attempts to become a catch-all party were not as successful, as it remained for all of its existence *the* working-class party. This was also a result of the leadership's deep-rooted preoccupation with preventing a separation of the party's more orthodox component. If it is true that over the years the blue-collar workers and related categories declined from over 60 percent in 1946 (Poggi 1968: 373) to less than 40 percent of the PCI total membership in 1989, this was due mainly to a decline of the working class in the make-up of the Italian population. The actual ability of the party to encapsulate the working class remained very high, and actually increased enormously between 1971 and 1989. The declining catch-all potential of the PCI is also shown by the fact that pensioners and housewives made up the bulk (32 percent in total) of the remaining members in 1989 and that all other professional categories declined among PCI voters (Baccetti 1997). Even the PDS was unable to shed the working-class-party image, as it remained the surviving national party with the highest percentage of working-class electors: 25.8 percent in 1994, much like the practically defunct PSI. This was actually higher than the RC figure of 18.4 percent, but was less than that of the regional LN, at 30.1 percent (Calvi and Vannucci 1995). Ostensibly, the PDS is no longer the party of the industrial working class and tries to appeal to all sectors of Italian society, but the PCI's legacy is still present.

All other Italian parties kept relatively static postures until at least the mid- to late 1970s and in some cases even after that. This is especially true of the MSI, whose timid and ineffectual attempts in the 1970s to broaden its appeal beyond the traditional extreme-right and anti-system electorate were thwarted by Giorgio Almirante's decision to suppress internal factions. As noted above, this had the probably unintended consequence of preventing the establishment of potential new links with civil society. Whether intended or not, however, this did not seem to concern the party's leadership. No attempts were made to change the organizational structure in order to accommodate new societal components until two decades later, when Gianfranco Fini transformed the MSI into AN. The PLI also tried to maintain its privileged relationship with Italy's entrepreneurial groups long after these had decided to throw their weight behind more authoritative parties like the PRI, or more important ones, like the DC and even the PSI. The inability to establish links with other societal groups coupled with the decision to oppose centre Left coalitions for most of the 1960s and 1970s caused the near disappearance of the party in 1976 when it was barely able to pass the very low electoral threshold. Meanwhile, the PSDI lost all credibility as a reformist workers' party immediately after its decision to separate from the PSI, when in 1947 it was able to attract only 2 percent of Italy's main trade union confederation (CGIL) membership (Ignazi 1997: 55). On the other hand, 52 MPs out of 115 joined the party, giving it the top-heavy characteristics that permitted it to hold a disproportionate number of offices, especially at the regional and local levels, and to develop concentrated and loyal clienteles. These remained the electoral hard core of the party until its effective disappearance in 1994. The PRI, in turn, progressively lost most of its mass-territorial rooting to turn to an opinion electorate. The party's appeal resulted mainly from the extreme rigour with which its long-time leader, Ugo La Malfa, treated crucial policy questions, especially those dealing with public spending and state inefficiency. In the long run, however, these positions were not consistent with the support the party gave, against what appeared to be its better judgement, to those governments responsible for the very policies its leader criticized. Because of this, the PRI eventually suffered the same fate as the other traditional parties.

The most dramatic and probably only noteworthy change was perhaps that experienced by the PSI, whose working-class orientation had prevailed until the 1970s, even if in subordination to the PCI. From the early 1980s onwards the party tried to exploit societal changes caused by the progressive reduction of

the industrial sector and by the parallel expansion of the service sector to extend
its appeal to emerging social groups. The party soon lost all working-class
features. As is discussed at greater length below, this process was symbolically
and substantially marked by Craxi's decision to greatly reduce the effects of the
cost of living adjustment mechanisms. The expansionist economic policies of
the Craxi-led government, a booming stock market, and the uncontrollable
increase of clientelism, allowed the PSI to recover to its highest postwar electoral levels, only to collapse dramatically after 1992.

Party policies

Italian party policy positions are rather difficult to trace. This is due to the
vagueness of official party documents, often conditioned by internal conflicts
or coalition compromises, and to discrepancies in party behaviour in different
parliamentary situations (e.g. committee as opposed to plenary session voting).
Moreover an analysis of policies as responses to electoral concerns can be dis-
counted for a number of parties. The MSI, for one, consistently took positions
demonstrating its opposition to the government and even to the political system
as a whole, irrespective of electoral strategies. Similarly, the smaller parties of
the centre could not afford to modify their positions too visibly, as they were
primarily preoccupied with preserving their identities in order to maintain their
limited number of followers. Only the PSDI abandoned its vaguely reformist
positions during the 1980s, but this was more a consequence of the right-wing
direction impressed by Craxi on the PSI and the consequent erosion of the PSDI
political space. Consequently the only noteworthy changes concern Italy's
three major parties. In order to further simplify matters here we shall limit our
analysis to three types of policy: economic policies, foreign and defence policies, and policies with moral or religious implications.

The first and the third group are by far the most interesting for the DC. In fact
the DC was always the staunchest advocate of Italian pro-NATO and pro-
EC/EU choices, and rarely deviated from an orthodox defence of such positions. In general, it was felt that this was a necessary consequence of being part
of the developed free world, and that was enough for the Italian public. A more
nuanced, moderately pro-Arab, stance taken by the party in more recent years
on Mediterranean-related questions cannot be ascribed to electoral considerations. The party position changed considerably on the other two types of policy.
On economic matters, the DC started out as a defender of the interests of industry and of independent farmers. But very quickly, as its links with civil society
expanded and its electoral target groups multiplied, the party became an avenue
for the advancement of the economic interests of every relevant societal and
economic group. For example, the interests of industrial, and in general
salaried, workers were advanced in the early 1970s through the approval of
important labour laws and the development of a very sensitive wage indexation
system, while the interests of industrialists were still protected through various
forms of direct and indirect subsidies, and even by a high tolerance of corporate

tax evasion. Moral and religious matters were not very prominent in Italian politics for more than two decades, after the sweeping Catholic victory of 1948. The dominance of Catholic morality was not questioned until the late 1960s, when, also as a result of the reforms fostered by the Vatican II Ecumenical Council, demands emerged for policies more in tune with the growing secularization of Italian society, especially on matters such as divorce, birth-control, and abortion. Although somewhat divided internally, the party took very orthodox positions in defence of Catholic family and right-to-life values in the crucial battles on divorce and abortion of the 1970s and early 1980s. The two crushing defeats in the referenda that spelled the final word on both issues – in 1974 and 1981 respectively – eventually forced a change in the party posture. As noted above, both were interpreted as omens of the party's electoral decline. Especially during Ciriaco De Mita's long secretariat (1982–89), the party veered towards more secular positions and was outflanked on the Catholic side by fundamentalist groups such as Comunione e Liberazione. After the collapse of the DC and the recasting of its splinters as expressions of Italian Catholicism, we are witnessing a return to more orthodox positions, especially in the CCD and, during its short existence, the CDU.

The evolution of the PCI/PDS positions is more straightforward on economic and moral questions and more problematic than that of the DC on foreign policy. As we have seen, the PCI probably aspired to become a catch-all party, but was always very aware of the nature of its constituency. On economic matters, party policy changed more as a consequence of changes in that constituency than as a result of any strategy aimed towards electoral expansion. Indeed, during its 'expansionist' electoral phase, the party ostensibly advanced the interests of the working class and did not overtly favour other groups, consistent with a doctrine aimed at making the social objectives and values of the working class hegemonic in Italian society (Gruppi 1972).[11] As such, they would become compatible with the party's catch-all aspirations. It is true that from the 1960s onwards, and certainly during the national solidarity period, the PCI voted with the governmental coalition on most bills favouring other groups. The positive phase of the Italian economy made it seem that there were sufficient resources to accommodate requests from all relevant groups. Party interests also often converged on the idea that such concessions could help pacify what was becoming a very turbulent society. When its electoral fortunes started to decline, the party reverted to protecting and guarding its working-class constituency. This was evident in the obsessive preoccupation with the preservation of existing employment, even if this meant fewer opportunities for younger cohorts, who progressively became alienated from the party. The worst political defeat of this period was when the PCI came under attack from Prime Minister Craxi, who decided to modify by decree the cost-of-living adjustment mechanism. The PCI responded with the call for a referendum to repeal the decree that had been converted into law. The eventual defeat in this referendum marked the end of PCI hegemony over the workers' movement and appeared to make its decline irreversible.

The parallel evolution of the party's position on the other two sets of policies was not sufficient to compensate for these losses. On moral issues, the PCI position was always very cautious, even if the law that introduced divorce in Italy was approved in 1971 with the decisive support of the party. Following the two victorious referendums on divorce and abortion, the PCI greatly emphasized its own merits, trying to cash in electorally on the results. But the secularization of Italian society was not the making of the PCI and its electoral advantage did not last very long. Even less rewarding was the party's evolution in terms of foreign policy. The party's original rejection of NATO and of the EC was gradually modified to a full acceptance of both – first, through a recognition of the EC's contribution to Italian economic prosperity and eventually also through the affirmation of NATO's importance for national security. There is little evidence that this difficult transition brought many new voters to the party. To be fair, foreign affairs are usually not very important in determining electoral behaviour, and the modification of the PCI's original positions was aimed more at gaining credibility as a governmental coalition partner than at attracting new voting support.

It was the PSI, once again, that experienced the most dramatic changes in policy. The party's secular orientation on policies with moral and religious implications remained substantially unchanged even in the heyday of Craxi's alliance – known as CAF, after the initials of the surnames of those involved, Craxi and the DC leaders Giulio Andreotti and Arnaldo Forlani. The divorce law of the early 1970s and a secular family law must be included among the party's greatest achievements, and these were never repudiated even when positions on other policies were being modified profoundly. In fact, PSI positions on foreign policy and on economic issues underwent a visible evolution from the mid-1950s onwards, to reach a complete turnaround by the early to mid-1980s. Not all the change can be imputed to electoral considerations. At least initially, changes in foreign policy were a consequence of the party's yearning for identity and autonomy. As such, they can better be seen as part of a new strategic posture than as tactical adjustments to perceived changes in electoral orientations. The post-1956 shift in foreign policy, at first simply in an anti-Soviet, but very soon in a pro-EC and even pro-NATO direction, followed the 20th congress of the CPSU and the Soviet repression of the failed Hungarian insurrection. These events provided welcome reasons for the party to abandon a pro-Soviet stance that had, up to that point, been modelled on that of the PCI and that had greatly contributed to a loss of party identity. The change was a precondition of PSI entry into governmental coalitions from the early 1960s onwards. The successive evolution of PSI foreign policy was consistent with the party's new governmental role, but the strong rhetorical emphasis on differences with the PCI was clearly intended to attract those voters who, even from within the ranks of the Left, were becoming increasingly disenchanted with the Soviet myth. This attitude became almost obsessive during Craxi's secretariat when the main objective of the party was to overtake the PCI in the move towards consensus. As the PCI progressively softened its own anti-EC and anti-NATO positions during the 1970s and early 1980s, the PSI became arguably the most pro-American Italian party.

The evolution of PSI positions on economic questions was similar, although not as sudden. Throughout the 1950s the party's orientation was essentially working-class. At least ostensibly, this did not change substantially for more than a decade, even after the party joined the so-called governmental area of the Italian party system. This achievement was actually marked by nationalizations, and by a generally sharp increase in state involvement in the running of the economy, as well as by important innovations in labour and salary protection (through wage indexation) laws. In this case, however, the party's positions remained similar to those of the PCI, whose leadership was able to claim most of the credit as a consequence of that party's greater parliamentary weight. As this progressively deprived the PSI of its working-class following, it became easier for the leadership to shift position on economic issues in an attempt to attract voters from the ranks of emerging entrepreneurial and generally self-employed sectors of Italian society. In reality, for most of the 1970s and early 1980s, the change was more rhetorical than substantial. This was due to the inability, if not the unwillingness, of the party and of the rest of the governmental coalition to reduce the size of the state-owned sector within the Italian economy, as this still represented its greatest resource. Nevertheless, the inefficiency of the public sector imposed an enormous burden on the Italian treasury. This, coupled with the government's expansionist policies, supported strongly by the PSI, always keen to please its recently acquired constituents, prevented a serious fight against inflation. By the early 1980s, this problem became particularly pressing, and one partial solution was offered by the decision to revise the wage-indexation system. Craxi's decision to reduce the effects of the cost-of-living adjustment mechanisms reflected the PSI desire to attract voters from new and potentially expanding constituencies, even at the expense of traditional ones.

Candidates

Even with Italy's extremely proportional electoral system small parties could hope to win only a very limited number of seats at each election. This no doubt conditioned their approach to candidatures. In fact there were more potential candidates among the party leaders than the party could hope to see elected. This prevented the development of strategies that could eventually be modified to respond to changes in the electoral market. The situation was slightly different for the PSI and the MSI. For many years PSI candidate strategies were dominated by the desire to preserve the internal factional balance. A change was possible when Craxi's leadership and the party's parallel electoral expansion decreased the relative weight of factions, at least at the national level. This resulted in fewer party officials and more exponents of emerging civil society groups and media being put up for election. In the MSI, the prevalent mode of candidate recruitment through the party apparatus was supplemented in 1972 with the inclusion of 'notables' in the hope of widening the party's appeal in civil society. The eventual failure of this initiative resulted in a return to internal party recruitment.

Conversely, both the DC and the PCI modified their approaches to political candidatures partially in response to electoral concerns. For many years the DC was reluctant to force candidate turnover because of preferential voting. Preference voting actually gave electors a final say in the election. Given that at the time Italian electoral slates allowed for the nomination of many more candidates than any party could hope to have elected, it was possible for the DC to confirm all incumbents and also include a number of potential challengers, leaving the final outcome to the individual's ability to attract preference votes. This did allow for some turnover, but not enough, since the advantages of incumbency also hold in Italy. After the 1974 and 1975 electoral defeats (respectively in the divorce referendum and in regional and municipal elections) demands coming from disgruntled factions or even frustrated younger cohorts caused a radical reshuffling in the wake of the 1976 general election that produced a 37 percent turnover in the parliamentary party (Bardi and Morlino 1994). Later attempts, again by De Mita, to allow external personalities into the party had very limited success.

PCI attempts to recruit 'new' candidates were apparently more successful. Especially after the post-1968 emergence of new movements and demands seeking political expression, the party felt an urge to open up to the representation of non-working-class social groups and cultural positions. As we have seen, this had a very limited impact in terms of membership renewal. There was, however, a gradual increase in the number of independents elected as PCI candidates in parliamentary elections. But the electoral returns of this strategy were doubtful, as most such candidates were not very visible to the electorate. Many did not represent relevant groups in civil society but expressed relatively isolated, albeit highly respected, political or cultural positions that could not be incorporated into the still rigid ideological and organizational party structure.[12] In fact the candidature of independents was especially relevant in the Senate, where the electoral system made it easier to assign 'safe' seats even to candidates who were unknown to the party electorate. Few independents were elected during the first four postwar legislative terms, but already in 1968, the independents in the Senate were strong enough (eleven members and almost 11 percent of the PCI delegation) to form their own parliamentary group (Sinistra Indipendente, or Independent Left). An Independent Left group was founded in the Chamber of Deputies in 1983 when 20 independents were elected. The number of independents elected as PCI candidates in the Senate grew to almost 20 percent in 1976, a level equalled and even surpassed in 1983 and 1987, after a dip to less than 14 percent in 1979. The Independent Left was a relatively autonomous parliamentary party although its candidates were dependent on the PCI organization for re-election. The Independent Left was meant to make the PCI the hegemonic force of the Left by enlisting influential personalities who could not find a political space with their own resources or within their original parties and groups (Baldassarre 1981: 473). As such it cannot be seen as an effective instrument to attract voters from a broad range of groups.

External relations: the state

The relationship between Italian parties and the state is best described by the word *partitocrazia*, party rule, a now classic term that was used to describe the Italian political system from the late 1950s until at least 1994. *Partitocrazia* was a power system with an extremely solid and permanent structure, established by an almost total overlap or connivance between party, state (including the judiciary) and social elites, through which parties exercised their control. Any academic work intending to provide an accurate description of the Italian postwar political system should first and foremost tackle the daunting task of describing and explaining *partitocrazia*. But because it was a permanent power system, *partitocrazia* was not an instrument that could be fine-tuned by individual parties to respond to electoral change. As such, it will be dealt with only very cursorily in this chapter. At best we can say that, at least until the final crisis of the early 1990s, it helped suppress any demand coming from the electorate. This is mainly because its full development had the clear effect of making society and the state adapt to party needs (rather than vice versa). So party attitudes towards the state should not be seen as responses to electoral change, but as preventive measures to impede such change. The ubiquitous patronage system established by the Italian party-cartel, made possible by the availability of state-controlled resources (jobs, contracts, pensions, subsidies, low or no interest loans, low or no rent housing) was in fact for many years an element of stability (mainly favouring the DC) in Italian electoral behaviour (Parisi and Pasquino 1980). The institutional and organizational bases for the complex network of holding companies and their subsidiaries, banks, social security and welfare agencies (including a national health system created in 1978), which came under more or less direct party control, were created during the Fascist era. It was not until the mid-1950s, however, that the dominant position of the DC permitted Amintore Fanfani to acquire for his party direct control of the public sector of the economy. In this way, the DC obtained an autonomous power base, the continuous expansion of which permitted the party to share the benefits with other parties of the governmental coalition and even, to a limited extent, with the PCI. However, as access to state-owned or otherwise public resources was made available to other parties, it turned into a source of dealignment (Parisi and Pasquino 1980). For example, the crushing DC defeat in the 1975 regional and municipal elections was interpreted by many as the result of the PCI's ability to create its own patronage network, following the party's acquisition of control over some important newly established regional governments and administrations in 1970 (most notably Emilia-Romagna and Tuscany). Moreover, as a result of attempts by all the parties to secure more resources to exchange for electoral support, the process of party encroachment on the state was greatly strengthened. By the mid-1980s, state-owned companies accounted for about 30 percent of sales and 50 percent of investments, while state-controlled banks and savings banks accounted for at least three-quarters of Italian banking. DC dominance of public banking was demonstrated by its control of the presidencies of most public banks (70 percent in 1992). In more recent years, the country's fiscal crisis has greatly downsized Italy's public sector and with it party control over state resources, and the anticipation of this development may have been one of the factors involved in the 1992–94 realignment.

One important aspect of party–state relations concerns the control that parties, especially those belonging to the governmental coalition, could exercise for their electoral advantage over the media – both through legislation and/or through appointment of the top managers in the state-owned television networks. For a long time Italian parties had very precisely structured relations with the mass media. Indeed, the parties were among the leading news publishers. Besides publishing official party newspapers, during the 1950s the larger parties also acquired control of some key 'independent' newspapers. The moderate or even conservative line of many of these newspapers was guaranteed by the party-sponsored appointment of editors and journalists. But although Italian political parties never underestimated the importance of the media, for many years it was not at the centre of their electoral strategies. Italy's state-owned radio and television company, RAI, which was controlled by the DC, had just one channel until the early 1960s and only later developed two more channels. Consequently, just like other aspects of *partitocrazia*, party- (state-) owned media relations contributed to electoral stability, or at least to limiting dealignment. Even a 1976 Constitutional Court ruling that put an end to state monopoly of radio and television broadcasts did not immediately change the relationship between political parties and the media in any substantial way (Bardi and Morlino 1994). That ruling led to an overnight explosion in the number of private local TV stations which, by the mid-1980s, had become concentrated into three national networks owned by media tycoon Silvio Berlusconi. Berlusconi's successful attempt to go beyond the limits posed by the Constitutional Court was made possible by the political and personal support of the PSI and Bettino Craxi. In this way, Craxi redressed the party balance in TV network control which was at the time still heavily pro-DC. The DC controlled the presidency of the RAI organization and of RAI 1, the most popular channel, while the PSI controlled RAI 2. This partition was done with the approval of the PCI, which obtained control of RAI 3, the most recently created and least popular RAI channel. Even if about half of Italy's important television networks were now in private hands, they still supported parties belonging to the governmental coalition.

Post-1992 responses

The massive shift of the 1990s, as we have seen, was only partly a response to electoral dealignment; other, and more contingent factors (changes in the electoral law, exposure of political corruption, collapse of international Communism) were also directly responsible for the near-total disappearance or transformation of the established political parties. But by forcing unprecedented voter mobility and centripetal electoral dynamics, it gave all surviving or newly created political parties a new outlook on electoral marketing. Party responses were conditioned by the new importance of the media, and by the party system's new two-level structure. Both influenced party approaches to candidatures and target groups. Moreover, the former, as could be expected, affected parties' relationships with the media, whereas the latter demanded complex organizational and diversified policy responses.

Party organization

The new environmental conditions brought about by the collapse of many traditional parties and by electoral reform caused unexpected organizational change. The most important changes in party organization can be seen as responses to the development of a two-level party system: individual parties need lighter and more flexible organizations in order to respond to, and adapt to, the needs of coalitions. These are becoming more institutionalized, although still mutable in some of their components, and condition individual party leadership and candidate selection procedures and strategies. As we have seen, by the early 1990s Italian parties had already undertaken a substantial process of organizational adaptation. Most of them had in fact completely changed their organizational models (Bardi and Morlino 1994). The PDS remained closest to tradition: the party rules voted upon in 1991 gave it a formal structure resembling the mass party model, although by then factionalism and stratarchy were already developing. All other parties, including of course those founded after 1992, ostensibly adopted radically novel organizational models, in the belief that representation should be through non-party organizations. The FI in particular stressed their non-mass and non-territorial approach to membership by calling their basic units clubs. This may well have been the source of the initial difficulties experienced by the party in rooting itself firmly in Italian society as well as of those experienced by organizational secretary Scajola in his attempts to strengthen the membership structure. Other parties, especially those of the post-DC centre, relied on societal contacts with pre-existing political movements (such as that which had promoted the referendums that forced the electoral reform) to obviate the need for heavy organizational structures (Masi 1994). Progressively, the centre became populated by a plethora of parties of notables, or, perhaps more appropriately, of notable leaders, who had virtually no permanent organizational structures but were nonetheless capable of using their popularity (Antonio Di Pietro), reputed personal or political qualities (Romano Prodi, Lamberto Dini, Antonio Cossiga), previous labour-union connections (Sergio D'Antoni) or strong territorial connections (Clemente Mastella) to attract crucial, if small, portions of the electorate. In fact, the very transformation of the parties' organizational models and, even more importantly, the creation of new political parties, can in itself be seen at least in part as a systemic response to changed electoral market conditions. But, especially because of changes in the electoral law, the adaptation of individual parties' organizational models, even if concerning practically all parties in the system, was not enough. The new competition rules also required the creation of new structures, in addition to a reshaping of prevailing party models. The outcome of elections could no longer be determined irrespective of individual parties' results and mostly as a consequence of post-election coalition negotiations; elections now had to be actually won through voting strength. And since no party could hope to win on its own, coalitions had to be formed before elections. Moreover, these coalitions grew to become more than simple electoral alliances, for even if they do not have organizations independent of their separate party components, they nevertheless survive, at least as labels, between elections.[13] The success of coalitions, especially in terms of electoral appeal, requires more than just the sum of their parts.

Parties and the media

Even if skilful media use was at the basis of the LN electoral success in 1992, it was not until the 1994 general election and the emergence of Silvio Berlusconi's FI that the importance of media (especially television) access and control became paramount. In the event, the regulation of party–media relationships became one of Italy's key political problems and one to which a solution has yet to be reached. Official campaigning is now much more strictly regulated than before 1994, and an independent agency, the Authority for Telecommunications, has been created with the task of developing Italy's frequency plan, that is of determining criteria for attributing the necessary broadcasting licences to national networks and local stations alike. The benefits of new legislation remain in doubt. A plan to reduce to two the maximum number of land-based analogic broadcast networks controllable by one single private or public operator would have forced RAI and Berlusconi's Mediaset to transform respectively RAI 3 and Rete 4 into satellite stations, with a greatly reduced potential audience.[14] The plan was never implemented in the anticipation of a new law that would also regulate digital and satellite frequencies and that, in the intentions of the centre Right government, would permit the survival of RAI 3 and Rete 4. This is justified by use of the argument that digital broadcasting would increase the number of available frequencies and permit more pluralism and competition. Critics of this approach maintain that increasing the number of frequencies would not change conditions in an already saturated market, where other existing competitors, like the La 7, were never able to challenge the RAI–Mediaset duopoly. Once the new digital frequencies are assigned, the projected Gasparri law, named after the AN Minister for Telecommunications, would also allow TV operators to own national newspapers. Moreover, the so-called *par condicio* law that regulates party access to media during electoral campaigns only concerns advertising and explicitly dedicated programming (Mazzoleni 2000). News coverage and normal programming are excluded, even if at times they can be used to favour specific candidates (Marletti 2002). In the months leading to the 2001 election, an independent monitoring agency, Osservatorio di Pavia, observed that Berlusconi enjoyed preponderant coverage in his networks' news programming, whereas the Ulivo candidate, Rutelli, prevailed, if by a much less evident margin, in RAI's. Although parties in government still have a privileged relationship with RAI, the alternation the country has experienced with the last three elections makes their grip much weaker than the old DC–PSI axis. Now coalitions proceed to the replacement of most of RAI's top executives soon after their electoral victories. After the 2001 victory, for example, the Casa delle Libertà (CdL) (House of Freedoms), the new name for the Polo, went so far as to suppress programmes and to dismiss political commentators, most notably the highly respected doyen of Italian television journalism, Enzo Biagi, who had been critical of Berlusconi during the campaign. This kind of practice, however, has different consequences depending on whether the centre Left or the centre Right wins the election. When the centre Left is in power its questionable use of RAI's information programmes is counterbalanced by Berlusconi's control over Italy's most important private television networks. Although partisan use of public resources is considered illegitimate, information pluralism is preserved. When the centre Right wins the election the same obviously does not hold.[15] Even if the Polo's 1996 defeat seemed to have convinced many observers, and ostensibly even Silvio Berlusconi, that the Italian electorate is growing media-wary, the question of whether it is acceptable for a political leader or movement to own and use television for electoral purposes is still open.

Policies, target groups, and candidates

It would appear that the two-tier party system poses the need for diversified policy responses, especially as a result of the new electoral law. The new, prevalently centripetal competition rules prescribe the need for moderate and often generic postures on most policy questions. This is furthermore stressed by the heterogeneity of the two coalitions, something that does not permit the adoption of unequivocal positions on many crucial policies.[16] But at least two major parties, the DS and AN still rely on the support of relatively ideological voters, representing respectively the original post-Communist and post-Fascist constituencies. This makes it very difficult for them to limit their policy options to the middle-of-the-road positions required by centripetal electoral competition. Electoral success depends not only on the ability to attract moderate electors, but also on the capacity to preserve a sizeable hard core. This is true of other less traditional but still ideological parties, such as the Verdi, or value-oriented groups, such as the CCD. As a consequence, most parties try to maintain specific, and in some cases relatively radical, policy concerns while at the same time subscribing, especially in fiscal and economic matters, to the 'responsible' policy postures generally exhibited by coalitions. Failure to do so can cause a party's marginalization or even crisis, as was the case with RC, when its wish to privilege orthodox working-class oriented positions at the expense of over-arching coalition objectives sent it back into opposition after the dramatic PDCI secession. The LN is perhaps an exception in that it has a much greater con-tractual power than most other parties because of the great concentration of its electoral constituency. This obviously makes it a decisive element and prospec-tively an indispensable partner in future plurality elections. Among the smaller coalition parties, the LN is the only one that tries – sometimes successfully, as with the Bossi-Fini law on immigration – to force the whole coalition to adopt relatively radical positions.

Party relations with target groups are similarly undetermined: with the sole exception of RC, which remains faithful to its working-class/pensioners con-stituency, all Italian parties try to avoid being typecast as the privileged agents of any particular group. The potential appeal of most parties is thus very broad, even if in practice it is sometimes severely limited by their policy positions. Thus DS, the successor to the PDS, still attracts more workers than FI, which, in turn, is preferred by the self-employed. The PPI is more attractive to socially concerned Catholics, whereas the CCD is closer to Catholic fundamentalists. However, it is a consequence of the new situation brought about by realignment that a powerful group such as Confindustria, the association of Italian industri-alists, can alternately throw its weight behind the right-wing Polo coalition, as it did in 1994 and 2001, or the Ulivo, as it did in 1996.

Nevertheless, all of this is overshadowed by the need to attract the middle electorate. We have seen how coalitions have to be built to respond to changes that have affected the shape of Italy's political space. In 1994 for the first time centripetal electoral competition squeezed the centre parties and prevented them from obtaining satisfactory electoral results. The defeat was especially crushing for the PPI, whose electoral support – an already disappointing 15.7 percent of the popular vote shared with the other post-DC splinter, Patto Segni – yielded a combined total of just 46 seats for the two parties, only four of which were obtained in the plurality part of the election. The reactions to this outcome had two consequences. The immediate result of the election was a further shrinking of the centre core of the party system, with the formation of yet another post-DC splinter, the CDU, and the decision of all centre groups and parties to join one of the two electoral alliances (the CDU left the PPI to follow the CCD in the Polo, and the PPI itself became part of the Ulivo). The second, medium-term, effect was, and still is, a process of redefinition of the centres of the two alliances, accompanied by calls for the rebuilding of a centre party that would be independent of both alliances. The memory of the political centre's long dominance is still very vivid and many are convinced that a reunited centre could challenge the two existing alliances or even replace one of them. At the basis of this position is the other conviction that centre voters are still available and would be very happy to support a sufficiently strong centre party. But calls for a 'refoundation of the DC', as many independent observers refer to this idea, have not yet been very successful – not least because of attempts by the two electoral alliances to attract groups and/or leaders from among the moderates of the other side.

In fact, enlisting attractive candidates (individuals and/or groups) has become one of the most important strategic objectives of both coalitions. Following the 1993 electoral reform, it was felt that the new majoritarian competition would get more media attention and that well known personalities who were already favourites with the media would be at an advantage. Actors, pop stars, sports and television personalities (Berlusconi himself being both), found their way into the candidate list of every major party, and then into the parliamentary group – the exception was the LN. Even Antonio Di Pietro, the hero of the *Mani Pulite* (clean hands) investigations, was virtually forced to become a political personality – more because of his unequalled popularity than because of his political qualities or standing. Given that the most important organizational response to the new electoral rules was the formation of quasi-permanent coalitions, the need for 'national' leaders with a very broad appeal became all the more pressing. This was especially true for the leftist coalitions, where the lack and/or inadequacy of the leadership was blamed for the 1994 and 2001 defeats, and where Prodi's ability to reassure sizeable sectors of the moderate electorate was seen to contribute to the 1996 victory.

In some respects, the Ulivo has proved more successful than the Polo, particularly in attracting former Prime Minister (and former Berlusconi minister) Lamberto Dini, as well as Antonio Di Pietro. Both are known for their rightist or at least moderate political leanings, and were considered natural Polo exponents. Around them the Ulivo has tried to build centrist groups, respectively RI and Italia dei Valori (Italy of Values), capable of occupying that part of the centre that still appears to be relatively empty, or at least mutable. Another popular and charismatic personality, Antonio Cossiga, went on to form his own centre party, the UDR, by attracting MPs and groups (notably most of the CDU) from both coalitions with the clear intention of exploiting this new pivotal position and maximizing its political returns.[17] In fact, coalitions can hope to expand only by orienting towards the still evolving centre. But in a wide electoral market, as that in Italy remains, moving towards the centre is not sufficient to win elections. The centre has to be won without losing the extremes. Hence the resort to coalitions capable of attracting a vast gamut of voters, and hence the need for the two dominant coalitions to include centre groups or parties before they can hope to attract centre voters. A different strategy, such as modifying in a moderate sense the positions of the core parties in the coalitions, could be very dangerous. For example, the AN move towards the centre in 1996 alienated a small portion of the right-wing electorate who then turned to support MSI-FT, a shift which may well have been the crucial factor leading to the Polo's defeat (D'Alimonte and Bartolini 1997: 257). The Ulivo may face a similar problem in the future because of the potential alienation of RC voters.

But the battle is far from over, and the potential availability of the centre electorate will continue to condition party responses and party strategies.

Conclusions

After almost half a century of relative electoral and, broadly speaking, even political stability, Italy is currently undergoing a process of momentous political change with profound implications for the electoral market, now extremely unstable and unpredictable. As a result, party perceptions of, and responses to dealignment are much more diversified and sensitive than in the pre-1992 period. To be sure, significant electoral market changes are taking place in many European countries. Party decline, increasing media influence, growing personalization of politics, and in some cases the emergence of new issue dimensions or the resurgence of once-forgotten ones, are also all contributing to greater voter mobility in other systems. Nevertheless, the Italian transformation appears to be particularly radical and presents some quite distinctive characteristics. Whilst most of the more widespread factors have also been at work in Italy, two key structural changes and their continuing adjustments are responsible for the uniqueness of the Italian change. The sweeping transformation of the party system, but most of all its development on two levels, and an important electoral reform, are producing effects whose magnitude is easily indicated by an unparalleled level of volatility. What is even more important is the fact that the structural changes they have produced are far from having stabilized. The present electoral law is considered by many to be a dangerous hybrid in itself and one that needs further reform, and uncertainty as to the future rules of the game is adding to the fluctuation in the electoral market and helping to delay the consolidation of the new party system.

Italian parties have been trying to adjust to this situation. The limited and generally predictable dealignment that characterized the political system for more than 40 years had allowed parties to develop relatively durable responses, such as the DC patronage system or the PCI strategy of cultural hegemony. In the event, however, as long as the overall electoral balance confirmed the DC at the head of the governmental coalition and confined the PCI to opposition, dealignment did not really matter. By contrast, the new rules of the game and, more generally, the characteristics more generally of the new electoral market make every vote count, as indicated by the fact that the overall outcome of the 1996 election was determined by the attribution to the Ulivo of most marginal seats. Not only is voter mobility now greater and its direction more unpredictable, but its effects are also more important. Crucially, electoral market conditions are now similar for more or less all parties, and hence dealignment or voter mobility can represent both a threat and an opportunity for each of the actors involved in the electoral competition. Moreover, party responses have been forced in part by structural aspects of the change. For all these reasons, party response modalities are fairly uniform across the spectrum, even if individual responses can be extremely diverse. The various parties may use different policy positions to try to preserve or slightly increase the shares of the electorate they can win in the proportional part of the election, but they all place their bids for the acquisition of a majoritarian position in parliament by joining coalitions. The two-level party system is at one and the same time a feature of the electoral market and an organizational response to changed electoral conditions. Its existence influences all other policy, targeting, and recruitment responses. It is also unlikely that we will see a return to a single-level party system, at least in the near future. Theoretically a return to a fully proportional system of election could have the effect of restoring a multi-party single-level party system, but this prospect is now unthinkable. At the same time a simple electoral reform, or even a more comprehensive institutional one, is not enough to produce a single-level two-party system (or, at least, none of the proposed reforms promises to do so). Consequently, the present electoral market is likely to persist, with all its complexity and competitiveness.

Notes

1 For the meaning of this and all other party acronyms see Appendix A, p. 144.

2 The PDCI supported Prodi's successor, Massimo D'Alema, whereas RC moved to the opposition.

3 The CDU suffered a serious split as a result of the creation of the UDR, a centre party formed in 1997 by former President of the Republic, Francesco Cossiga. Besides incorporating most of the former CDU, the UDR also included former CCD and RI exponents. Upon its foundation, the UDR did not join either party coalition (see below). However, it did oppose the government led by Romano Prodi and voted against it in the crucial confidence vote that brought it down, but eventually supported and obtained two ministries in the government led by Massimo D'Alema. The UDR's heritage remains in the UDEUR, the already mentioned Margherita component. Another party formed by ex-DC exponents, DE, contested the 2001 elections with very poor results.

4 Ideally, electoral mobility should be measured with panel survey data. As such data is virtually non-existent, analysts have based their mobility estimates on aggregate electoral results (at the lowest possible level of aggregation, the polling station) using special techniques to reduce the well-known problems associated with ecological analysis (Schadee and Corbetta 1984).

5 The PPI's split forced a revision of the BV calculation criteria in order to include the Popolari per Prodi in the 1996 leftist bloc. Similarly, the Margherita was included in 2001.

6 For example, Bettino's Craxi's role as leader of the centre Left coalition for most of the 1980s was to a large extent the result of the support he received from DC exponents, most notably Giulio Andreotti and Arnaldo Forlani, who wanted to counter DC Secretary Ciriaco De Mita's hegemonic intentions.

7 D'Alema was also blamed for having been unable to exercise a decisive role in passing conflict of interest legislation and institutional reforms.

8 For example, the Greens obtained just under 5 percent of the seats in the Senate even though they claimed only about half that much of the popular vote.

9 The package of proposals drafted by the bicameral committee was never discussed by the Italian parliament ostensibly because of Berlusconi's dissatisfaction with the proposed electoral reform (namely the norm that would give the winning coalition a firm majority through a second vote). However, many observers believed that the decision was meant to embarrass Massimo

D'Alema, who had agreed to preside over the committee on the understanding that the proposals eventually drafted would win very strong support in parliament, including from Berlusconi's FI.

10 The most evident example of this was provided by the total lack of discipline of rural PCI supporters in connection with the 1990 referendum aimed at prohibiting private possession of firearms; the referendum, called by the environmentalist movement and half-heartedly supported by the PCI, was first and foremost meant to make hunting impossible, an objective in total contrast with the interests of the very powerful, and very strong in rural areas, hunting section of ARCI, the PCI cultural and recreational flanking organization.

11 The PCI's doctrinal position was confirmed by the widespread belief, even among intellectuals, that PCI values were indeed becoming hegemonic in Italian society (Alberoni 1976).

12 It would indeed have been difficult to attract well known and respected intellectuals such as, among many others, Luigi Spaventa, Mario Gozzini, and Gianfranco Pasquino, or such living icons as Euro-federalist Altiero Spinelli, unless they were excused from following the party's rigid membership and elected office rules.

13 For example, 'Ulivo' was also included in the names chosen for the parliamentary fractions of the Ulivo coalition's most important party components, the PDS and the PPI.

14 The number of families that have access to satellite television is 2.5 million, about one eighth of the total. Alternatively, RA13 could survive as a commercial-free land-based broadcast network.

15 In July 2003 the draft of the European Parliament's annual report on the respect of fundamental rights in the EU that was approved by the EP's Committee on Citizens' Freedoms and Rights, Justice and Home Affairs, criticized the growing concentration of media power in the hands of a few large conglomerates in Europe and used Italy as an example of this trend because of Silvio Berlusconi's unique position: as head of government he was able to control RAI while maintaining a quasi-monopoly of privately owned television.

The report implicitly recommended new conflict of interest norms that could help safeguard freedom and pluralism in information. Data reported in a national newspaper indicated that Italy's two major television concerns (RAI and Berlusconi's Mediaset) had a combined audience of 90 percent in 2001, as opposed to 74 percent for the equivalent two concerns in France, 66 percent in Germany and 65 percent in the UK (*La Repubblica*, 11 July 2003).

16 Both coalitions harbour secular and religious groups, something that does not allow clear positions on ethically laden questions. In the CdL, AN's pro-state tradition is at odds with the LN's devolutionary imperative.

17 Returns he clearly obtained when the UDR became part of the D'Alema governmental majority.

References

Alberoni, Francesco (1976). L'Italia in trasformazione. Bologna: Il Mulino.

Anderlini, Fausto (1989). 'La DC: iscritti e modello di partito.' *Polis* 3: 277–306.

Baccetti, Carlo (1997). *Il PDS. Verso un nuovo modello di partito?* Bologna: Il Mulino.

Baldassarre, Antonio (1981). 'I gruppi parlamentari comunisti.' In Massimo Ilardi and Aris Accornero (eds), *Il Partito Comunista Italiano: Struttura e storia dell'organizzazione 1921–1979*. Milan: Annali della Fondazione Feltrinelli, pp. 445–98.

Bardi, Luciano (unpublished). 'La DC: 1946–1993'. University of Pisa.

Bardi, Luciano (1996a). 'Anti-Party Sentiment and Party System Change in Italy.' *European Journal of Political Research* 29: 345–63.

Bardi, Luciano (1996b). 'Change in the Italian Party System.' *Congrips Newsletter*, 46: 9–23.

Bardi, Luciano and Leonardo Morlino (1994). 'Italy: Tracing the Roots of the Great Transformation.' In Richard S. Katz and Peter Mair (eds), *How Parties Organize: Adaptation and Change in Western Democracies*. London: Sage, pp. 242–77.

Bartolini, Stefano and Peter Mair (1990). *Identity, Competition, and Electoral Availability. The Stabilization of European Electorates 1885–1985*. Cambridge: Cambridge University Press.

Biorcio, Roberto and Paolo Natale (1989). 'La mobilità elettorale degli anni ottanta.' *Rivista Italiana di Scienza Politica* 19: 385–430.

Calvi, Gabriele and Andrea Vannucci (1995). *L'elettore sconosciuto*. Bologna: Il Mulino.

Casciani, Enrico (1981). 'Dieci anni di reclutamento nel PCI.' *Il Mulino* 30 (274): 310–26.

D'Alimonte, Roberto and Stefano Bartolini (eds) (1997). *Maggioritario per caso*. Bologna: Il Mulino.

Galli, Giorgio (1976). *Storia del PCI*. 2nd edn, Milan: Bompiani.

Ghini, Celso (1981). 'Gli iscritti al partito e alla FGCI. 1943/1979.' In Massimo Ilardi and Aris Accornero (eds), *Il Partito Comunista Italiano: Struttura e storia dell'organizzazione 1921–1979*. Milan: Annali della Fondazione Feltrinelli, pp. 227–92.

Gruppi, Luciano (1972). *Il concetto di egemonia in Gramsci*. Rome: Editori Riuniti.

Ignazi, Piero (1989). *Il Polo escluso. Profilo del Movimento Sociale Italiano*. Bologna: *Il* Mulino.

Ignazi, Piero (1997). *I partiti italiani*. Bologna: *Il* Mulino.

Ignazi, Piero (1992). *Dal PCI al PDS*. Bologna: Il Mulino.

Ignazi, Piero and Angelo Panebianco (1979). 'Laici e conservatori? I valori politici della base democristiana.' In Arturo Parisi (ed.), *Democristiani*. Bologna: Il Mulino, pp. 153–64.

Laakso, Markuu and Rein Taagepera (1979). ' "Effective" Number of Parties: A Measure with Applications to Western Europe.' *Comparative Political Studies* 12: 3–27.

Mannheimer, Renato (1989). *Capire il voto. Contributi per l'analisi del comportamento elettorale in Italia*. Milan: Angeli.

Mannheimer, Renato (1994). 'Il mercato elettorale dei partiti tra il vecchio e il nuovo.' In Renato Mannheimer and Giacomo Sani (eds), *La rivoluzione elettorale*. Milan: Anabasi, pp. 71–115.

Mannheimer, Renato and Giacomo Sani (1987). *Il mercato elettorale. Identikit dell'elettore italiano*. Bologna: Il Mulino.

Maraffi, Marco (2002). 'Per cosa si è votato il 13 maggio? Le mappe cognitive degli elettori italiani.' In Mario Caciagli and Piergiorgio Corbetta (eds), *Le ragioni dell'elettore*. Bologna: Il Mulino, pp. 301–38.

Marletti, Carlo (2002). 'La campagna elettorale, attori politici, media ed elettori.' In Paolo Bellucci and Martin Bull (eds), *Politica in Italia*. Bologna: Il Mulino, pp. 79–98.

Masi, Diego (1994). *Dal partito piovra al partito farfalla*. Milan: Lupetti.

Mazzoleni, Gianpietro (2000). 'The Italian Broadcasting System between Politics and the Market.' *Journal of Modern Italian Studies* 5: 157–68.

Nuvoli, Paolo and Alberto Spreafico (1990). 'Il partito del non voto.' In Mario Caciagli and Alberto Spreafico (eds), *Vent'anni di elezioni in Italia, 1968–1997*. Padova: Liviana Editrice, pp. 223–258.

Parisi, Arturo and Gianfranco Pasquino (1980). 'Changes in Italian Electoral Behavior: the Relationships between Parties and Voters.' In Peter Lange and Sidney Tarrow (eds), *Italy in Transition: Conflict and Consensus*. London: Frank Cass, pp. 49–68.

Poggi, Gianfranco (ed.) (1968). *L'organizzazione partitica del PCI e della DC*. Bologna: Il Mulino.

Rae, Douglas W. (1971). *The Political Consequences of Electoral Laws*. New Haven, CT: Yale University Press.

Schadee, Hans and Piergiorgio Corbetta (1984). *Metodi e modelli di analisi dei dati elettorali*. Bologna: Il Mulino.

Schmitt, Hermann and Sören Holmberg (1995). 'Political Parties in Decline?' In Klingemann, Hans Dieter and Fuchs, Dieter (eds), *Citizens and the State*. Oxford: Oxford University Press.

Vassallo, Salvatore (1998). 'The Third *Bicamerale*.' In Bardi, Luciano and Rhodes, Martin (eds), *Italian Politics. Mapping the Future*. Boulder: Westview Press, pp. 111–31.

Verzichelli, Luca (2002). 'I gruppi parlamentari della XIII e XIV legislatura. Verso la stabilità maggioritaria?' In Paolo Bellucci and Martin Bull (eds), *Politica in Italia*. Bologna: Il Mulino, pp. 141–62.

Appendix A: Party acronyms

AN:	Alleanza Nazionale/National Alliance
CCD:	Centro Cristiano Democratico/Christian Democratic Centre
CDU:	Cristiani Democratici Uniti/United Christian Democrats
DC:	Democrazia Cristiana/Christian Democracy
DE:	Democrazia Europea/European Democracy
DP:	Democratzia Proletaria/Proletarian Democracy
DS:	Democratici di Sinistra/Democrats of the Left
FI:	Forza Italia/'Let's go' Italy
IdV:	Italia dei valori/Italy of Values
LN:	Lega Nord/Northern League
MSI:	Movimento Sociale Italiano/Italian Social Movement
MSI-FT:	Movimento Sociale Italiano-Fiamma Tricolore/Italian Social Movement-Tricolor Flame
PCI:	Partito Comunista Italiano/Italian Communist Party
PDCI:	Partito dei Comunisti Italiani/Party of the Italian Communists
PDUP:	Partito di Unità Proletaria/Party of Proletarian Unity
PDIUM:	Partito Democratico Italiano di Unità Monarchica/Italian Democratic Party of Monarchic Unity
PDS:	Partito Democratico di Sinistra/Democratic Party of the Left
PLI:	Partito Liberale Italiano/Italian Liberal Party
PMP	Partito Monarchico Popolare/People's Monarchist Party
PNM:	Partito Nazionale Monarchico/Monarchist National Party
PPI:	Partito Popolare Italiano/Italian People's Party
PPST/SVP:	Partito Popolare Sud Tirolese/Südtiroler Volkspartei/South Tyrolean People's Party
PR:	Partito Radicale/Radical Party
PRI:	Partito Repubblicano Italiano/Italian Republican Party
PSdA:	Partito Sardo d'Azione/Sardinian Action Party
PSDI:	Partito Socialista Democratico Italiano/Italian Social Democratic Party
PSI:	Partito Socialista Italiano/Italian Socialist Party
PSIUP:	Partito Socialista Italiano di Unità Proletaria/Italian Socialist Party of Proletarian Unity
PSU:	Partito Socialista Unificato/Unified Socialist Party
RC:	Rifondazione Comunista/Communist Refoundation
RI:	Rinnovamento Italiano – Lista Dini/Italian Renewal – Dini List
UDC:	Unione Democratica Cristiana/Christian Democratic Union
UDEUR:	Unione Democratici per l'Europa/Union of Democrats for Europe
UDR:	Unione dei Democratici Riformisti/Union of Reformist Democrats
VER:	Verdi/Greens

SIX   Party Responses to the Erosion of Voter Loyalties in Austria: Weakness as an Advantage and Strength as a Handicap

Wolfgang C. Müller, Fritz Plasser, and Peter A. Ulram

From the heyday of the mass integration party, party strength has had a strong organizational dimension. A party with a dense net of local branches, many members and activists, in particular devoted ones, and strong organizational routines has been seen to have a competitive advantage over parties that lack these properties. While organizational routines stabilize the party and make it to some extent independent of its fate in the electoral arena, the other dimensions of organizational strength allow the party to communicate with its potential voters. The two traditional major Austrian political parties – the Social Democratic (Socialist until 1991) Party (SPÖ) and the Christian Democratic People's Party (ÖVP) – have long been world champions with regard to organizational strength. All three traditional political camps could rely on the loyalty of political subcultures (Luther 1999), but these subcultures were particularly large and well organized in the case of the Social Democrats and the People's Party. In contrast, the German national subculture, stronghold of the third traditional party, the Freedom Party (FPÖ), was relatively small and never produced an encompassing organization.

For most of the postwar period the Austrian party system displayed a remarkable degree of stability and concentration (Table 6.1). Until 1986 the SPÖ and ÖVP combined won between 82.7 and 94.4 percent of the valid votes. Despite the PR electoral formula, five of the twelve elections in the 1945–83 period resulted in absolute parliamentary majorities for single parties (in 1945 and 1966 for the ÖVP and in 1971, 1975, and 1979 for the SPÖ). The SPÖ and ÖVP have also mainly provided the country's government. Except for the all-party coalition that held office in the immediate postwar period and a short-lived coalition between the SPÖ and FPÖ in the 1980s, all governments until 2000 were either single-party or 'grand coalitions' of the SPÖ and ÖVP.

Between 1986 and 1999, however, the party system went through a process of de-concentration, leaving the two major parties with just 64 percent of the

Table 6.1 Austrian election results, 1950s–2002

Party	Votes Seats	1950s	1960s	1970s	1983	1986	1990	1994	1995	1999	2002
SPÖ	% votes	43.3	43.3	50.0	47.6	43.1	42.8	34.9	38.1	33.1	36.5
	% seats	45.5	45.5	50.7	49.2	43.7	43.7	35.5	38.8	35.5	37.7
ÖVP	% votes	43.8	46.9	43.2	43.2	41.3	32.1	27.7	28.3	26.9	42.3
	% seats	47.5	50.3	44.1	44.3	42.0	32.8	28.4	29.0	28.4	43.2
FPÖ[1]	% votes	8.4	6.2	5.6	5.0	9.7	16.6	22.5	21.9	26.9	10.0
	% seats	6.7	4.2	5.2	6.6	9.8	18.0	23.0	21.9	28.4	9.8
Greens	% votes	–	–	–	(3.3)[5]	4.8	4.8	7.3	4.8	7.4	9.5
	% seats	–	–	–	(0)	4.4	5.5	7.1	4.9	7.7	9.3
LF	% votes	–	–	–	–	–	–	6.0	5.5	3.7	1.0
	% seats	–	–	–	–	–	–	6.0	5.5	–	–
Others[2]	% votes	4.5	3.6	1.3	0.9	1.0	3.7	1.7	1.4	0.5	0.7
	% seats	1.4	–	–	–	–	–	–	–	–	–
Total[3]	Votes	100	100	100	100	100	100	100	100	100	100
	Seats	165	165	165/ 183[4]	183	183	183	183	183	183	183
Volatility[6]		4.0	3.9	2.7	4.7	9.7	9.7	15.5	3.8	9.0	21.1
Fractionalization[6]		0.61	0.59	0.56	0.58	0.63	0.68	0.74	0.72	0.74	0.67
Turnout %		95.3	93.8	92.5	92.6	90.5	86.1	81.9	86.0	80.4	84.3
Effective number of parties[6]		2.56	2.42	2.40	2.40	2.71	3.15	3.86	3.59	3.76	3.01

[1] VdU before 1956.

[2] Until 1962 mainly Communists; in 1966 mainly DFP, a splinter party of the SPÖ; in 1990 a Green splinter group; in 1994 and 1995 mainly the anti-EU group Nein.

[3] Due to rounding errors the seat and vote shares do not always add up to 100.

[4] 183 since 1971.

[5] Combined share of two Green groups, which later joined forces and won parliamentary representation in 1986.

[6] Excluding parties smaller than 0.5 percent.

Source: Bundesministerium für Inneres; own calculations.

parliamentary seats in 1999. The number of relevant parties increased from three (in 1983) to four when the Greens (in 1986) established themselves in parliament and temporarily to five (1993–99) when the Liberal Forum (LF) split from the FPÖ and was twice returned to parliament in elections. The single most important factor for bringing the SPÖ–ÖVP dominance to an end, however, was the rise of the FPÖ. This party increased dramatically, from slightly less than 5 percent of the vote in 1983 to 26.9 percent in 1999, taking a lead of 415 votes over the ÖVP. After coalition negotiations with the SPÖ came to nothing the ÖVP formed a coalition with the FPÖ in 2000. This coalition broke down in 2002 and early elections reversed much of the electoral shift that had taken place since the 1980s, making the ÖVP the strongest party (for the first time since 1970) with 42.3 percent and reducing the FPÖ to 10 percent, only marginally stronger than the Greens.

These electoral results clearly indicate that the traditional loyalties of voters to parties have disappeared to a considerable extent. This chapter studies how the two major victims of electoral dealignment, the SPÖ and ÖVP, and the prime beneficiary, the FPÖ, have behaved under and responded to electoral dealignment in the 1986–2000 period.

The main argument of this chapter, captured in its title, is that the enormous party organizations and links with established interest groups, which previously have been a source of strength, are a kind of liability under the new conditions of electoral competition. To be sure, they still constitute a stabilizing factor in the major parties' electoral performance (Müller 1996a), but they also reduce their manoeuvrability and slow down adaptation to changes in the party environment. In contrast, an absence of mass organization can allow parties to be more flexible, responsive, and effective (Mair 1997: 10–11).

Between 1987 and 2000 the SPÖ and ÖVP formed a grand coalition government and the FPÖ was in opposition. Their status as government parties exacerbated the SPÖ and ÖVP's situation while its opposition role helped the FPÖ. In 2000, the ÖVP chose to change coalition partners as a way out of its dilemma. By joining forces with the FPÖ it won the head of government position for itself and at the same time deprived the FPÖ of the 'opposition bonus'. Indeed, government participation of parties is associated with electoral losses more often than with electoral gains (Müller and Strøm 2000: 589). Governing often means making unpopular decisions, it deflects time and energy from electoral competition, and often it makes internal contradictions in parties more visible. This was indeed the case with the FPÖ after 2000. The extraordinary magnitude of its losses and ÖVP's gains in 2002 are the product of special circumstances. Yet, in its new role in the party system the FPÖ's traditional weakness was again in evidence.

Changes in the electoral markets

The Austrian electoral market has seen significant changes since the mid-1980s: these are summarized in Table 6.2. Although there are ups and downs,

Table 6.2 Indicators of party loyalty in Austria, 1954–2002

Year	Party identification (a)	Strong party attachment (b)	Core voters (c)	Floating voters (d)	Party shifters (e)	Party members (survey data)	Party members (membership statistics)
1954	73	71					27
1969	75	65				24	27
1972		61	76	8		23	26
1974	65	61					26
1979	63	56	66	16	7	22	26
1983	61	47			10		24
1986	60	39	58	26	16	23	23
1990	49	34			17	18	20
1994	44	31	44	44	19	15	17
1995	49	28			22		
1996	46	31	46	44		13	16
1997	47	28	43	45			
1998	51	25	43	46	18		
1999	51	26					15
2000	52	29					
2001	55	25	44	42		15	15
2002			41	53	24		
Change	−18	−46	−32	+34	+15	−9	−12

(a) Percentage of respondents with party identification.
(b) Percentage of respondents who say that they continue to vote for their party even if they are not entirely satisfied with the party.
(c) Percentage of respondents who say that they vote for the same party in every election.
(d) Percentage of respondents who say that they occasionally change their voting behaviour.
(e) Percentage of exit poll respondents who changed their voting behaviour compared to the previous general election.

Sources: FESSEL+GfK, Representative surveys (1954–2002), N = 1,000–2,000; Müller 1996b: 81, updated.

electoral participation has declined considerably. Party identification declined by 18 percent in the 1954–2002 period. In the late 1990s, there were signs of realignment (and an increase of party identification), with the FPÖ being the beneficiary, though this soon came to naught. The decline of party identification (macro-partisanship) was accompanied by a decline in its intensity and impact on voting behaviour. In the 1954–2001 period the share of voters who claim that they would continue to vote for their respective party even if they were not completely satisfied with it declined from 71 percent to 25 percent. This decline has been much more even throughout the postwar period than the decline of macro-partisanship. While party seems to play an ever diminishing role in the voting decisions of Austrians, an increasing number of voters claim that they base their voting decision on the characteristics of the parties' top candidates.

Since the 1970s the organizational grip of parties on the electorate has also been in decline. According to survey evidence, the number of party members fell from 24 percent of the eligible voters in 1969 to 15 percent in 2002. Party statistics display the same pattern: total party membership declined from 26 percent in 1970 to 15 percent in 2002. Again the period since the mid-1980s accounts for most of the decline. It is exclusively the party membership of the SPÖ and ÖVP that fell during this period, however, with membership in the FPÖ and the new parties increasing slightly.

The consequence of the decline in long-term party attachments is reflected in survey evidence of long-term patterns of individual voting. Thus the share of core voters, i.e. voters who claim that they always vote for the same party both in national and *Land* (provincial) elections, declined from 76 percent in 1972 to 41 percent in 2002. Likewise, the proportion of voters claiming to occasionally switch between parties (floating voters) increased from 8 to 53 percent in the same period. Nowadays, floating voters outnumber core voters.

In the early 1970s the proportion of party shifters in general elections was estimated as 3–5 percent. Since 1979, when 7 percent of the voters voted for a different party than in the previous general election, the percentage of party shifters has increased to about 20 percent of the voters in the 1990s (Plasser and Ulram 2003). Volatility has become a relevant pattern of individual voting behaviour in the once 'ultra-stable' Austrian electorate.

Since the 1980s the decline in party loyalty also affects the core groups of the SPÖ and ÖVP (Ulram 1990; Plasser *et al.* 1996; Plasser *et al.* 2000). Blue-collar workers, the traditional SPÖ core group, are a case in point. While only 2 percent of the trained blue-collar workers had voted for the FPÖ in 1983, 48 percent did so in 1999, considerably more than for the traditional party of this group, the SPÖ (which attracted a mere 31 percent). However, the FPÖ gains among the ÖVP core groups of shopkeepers and other self-employed were similarly spectacular. The FPÖ's inroads into the SPÖ and ÖVP core groups considerably reduced the manoeuvrability of these parties.

Finally, the attitudes of Austrians towards politics and parties have changed fundamentally since the 1980s. Alienation from politics has increased. This combines with aggressive attitudes towards politicians and the established political organizations and increasing dissatisfaction with political outputs (Plasser and Ulram 1993). In the late 1980s, disenchantment with parties and politicians was higher in Austria than in most other West European countries and best compared to the Italian level. Although the items contained in Table 6.3 are somewhat suggestive and therefore may overstate the case, it is clear there is a trend towards more negative attitudes since then (Plasser and Ulram 2002: 101–7).

To summarize the main points of our discussion of changes in the electoral markets: the changes in all indicators – party system concentration, party identification, party membership, short-term voting behaviour, and attitudes towards political parties – are consistent. They show that the major parties have been losing the strong electoral hold that was once so characteristic of modern Austrian politics. Although the 2002 election, resulting in combined gains for the ÖVP and SPÖ of 18.8 percent of the voters, indicates how much the FPÖ has discredited itself since 1999, it neither stops nor reverses the structural erosion of party–voter linkages in Austria.

Perceptions of parties

Social structural change following partisan dealignment was recognized by all parties in the 1960s or even earlier. The parties responded by further reducing their ideological baggage, by devoting more resources to propaganda efforts, by professionalizing their communications with the electorate and by placing more weight on the popular appeal of their leaders when selecting them. In short, they continued with the catch-all strategies as they were identified *in nuce* by Kirchheimer (1966). To be sure, the parties differed in their ability to identify changes in their environment and to adapt to them. These differences are reflected in their electoral fortunes in the 1960s and 1970s and they have been subject to a number of analyses (Müller 1993). In this section we will concentrate on the parties' perception of electoral dealignment since the mid-1980s.

The SPÖ received some early 'warning signals' of dealignment but did not decode them correctly. These were its defeat in the 1978 nuclear power referendum and, more specifically, the triumphal election by preference votes to parliament of Josef Cap, the leader of the Young Socialists, who had publicly criticized leading party functionaries because of their lifestyle and privileges, in 1983. With hindsight it is easy to identify Cap's election as the first major protest against the 'political class' in Austria that took place at the ballot box. A study by Traar and Birk (1987), completed before the 1986 general election, provided the first comprehensive survey evidence of disenchantment with political parties which was recognized by the SPÖ. At this time the scope of party weariness was judged 'modest' (Traar and Birk 1987: 9). On the basis of this study deputy party chairman Karl Blecha, the main interpreter of survey research in the leading party bodies, recognized three developments: first, that

Table 6.3   Disenchantment with parties and politicians in Austria, 1974–2001*

	1974	1984	1989	1993	1996	2001	Change (since first measurement)
Political parties are only interested in the votes of the people, but do not care about their opinions	69	–	69	75	79	73	+4
Politicians do not care much about what people like me think	67	–	69	–	73	75	+8
Once elected MPs quickly lose contact with the people	72	–	78	83	85	82	+10
Politicians care too much about maintaining their power rather than thinking about the real needs of the population	–	80	79	83	86	–	+6

*Percent of respondents who agree with the statements.

Sources: Political Action survey 1974; FESSEL+GfK, Representative surveys (1984–2001), N = 1,000–2,000.

structural dealignment was continuing; secondly, that a value change was taking place which would benefit Green groupings; and thirdly, that a potential for protest had developed in the electorate, mainly benefiting the oppositional ÖVP (comment in Traar and Birk 1987: 86). This consideration was supported by the second ballot victory (with 53.9 percent) of the first ever successful ÖVP candidate, Kurt Waldheim, in the 1986 presidential elections.

Since then, the SPÖ perspective has been that it has maintained considerable support in the electorate, but it is the floating vote that decides which party will be the strongest one. While a popular candidate – Bruno Kreisky – had provided the SPÖ's majority in the 1970s, other popular candidates – Franz Vranitzky and more recently Viktor Klima – were selected to provide the SPÖ's plurality in the 1980s and 1990s. Although the SPÖ had to face substantial losses in the 1986 general election, the goal of maintaining its plurality was achieved. In 1990, on other hand, it managed to transform the general election into a plebiscite over the question of who should be Federal Chancellor (Müller 1990; Müller and Plasser 1992), and while the ÖVP suffered dramatic losses, the SPÖ almost maintained its electoral strength. Though disturbed by the electoral success of the FPÖ in that election, the SPÖ did nevertheless feel more relaxed: it had roughly maintained its share of the vote and its plurality seemed safe, with the lead over the ÖVP increasing from three to 20 seats. Moreover, although the SPÖ lead over the FPÖ had been reduced, it still amounted to 47 seats. The reasons for the SPÖ success in the 1990 general election were correctly stated both by politicians and survey researchers working for the party. Deputy party chairman Heinz Fischer expressed it succinctly: the SPÖ had received many 'votes on credit,…votes for future expectations and not for past performance' (*Die Presse*, 12 October 1990) and, on the basis of survey evidence, Günther Ogris (1990) claimed that the people voted for Vranitzky because they wanted him to reform the SPÖ. Indeed some relevant attempts were made to meet these expectations in the following years (see p. 155 below). However, the SPÖ neither realized the (potential) scope of dealignment nor could it isolate itself from the effects of this process in the years to come. In 1994 the SPÖ suffered its then worst electoral defeat in the postwar period, losing 7.9 percent of the vote and fifteen seats. Now the SPÖ read the situation as follows: a new cleavage line between modernization winners and modernization losers has emerged. Modernization losers blame the government for their individual misery, abandon any party affiliation, and become easy victims for protest parties such as the FPÖ. The SPÖ had finally realized the scope and characteristics of the dealignment process. However, to understand dealignment is quite different from coming to grips with it, as was demonstrated by subsequent events.

In a similar vein to the SPÖ, the new quality of the dealignment process of the 1980s was not recognized by the ÖVP decision-makers. First analyses by party advisers of the early 1980s were ignored by politicians or dismissed as 'purely academic' (and hence not requiring a response from the party). Severe electoral losses for the SPÖ in the early 1980s at the *Land* level, in the 1984 Chamber of Labour elections, and in the general elections of 1983, in which the ÖVP was the main beneficiary, were interpreted with a strange bias. The underlying changes in the electorate were seen as affecting the SPÖ exclusively. This development came to a halt in 1986, when the ÖVP did not achieve the electoral breakthrough it had expected. Rather than winning additional vote shares, it lost almost 2 percent, and although the gap with the SPÖ narrowed, the ÖVP did not become the strongest party. Nevertheless, this election did bring the ÖVP back to government. Soon after it had joined the SPÖ in cabinet, however, it experienced a dramatic decline in the polls. The party reacted by resorting to the traditional remedy of replacing its chairman. It was only the débâcle of the 1990 general elections, when the ÖVP lost more than a fifth of its voters, that made clear to the party that it was not merely suffering from temporary fluctuations or the unpopularity of a particular leader. Leadership change nevertheless continued.

It is fair to summarize the SPÖ and ÖVP's perceptions of the dealignment process as follows: while the party elites had long been aware of social structural change and of its negative implications first for the ÖVP and later also for the SPÖ, they did not recognize the new dynamics of the dealignment process that emerged in the late 1970s. Both parties underestimated the level and seriousness of the changes which were occurring, and hence both believed that any problems could be dealt with by 'quick-fix' solutions: 'aspirin rather than penicillin', to borrow a phrase from Peter Mair. It was not until the 1990s that the SPÖ and ÖVP became aware of the scope and dynamics of partisan dealignment. This delay in recognizing changes is indicative of the major parties' complacency. Both were used to seeing the party system mainly in terms of themselves: if one side fails, the other side must benefit. This perspective was rooted in the fact that the SPÖ and ÖVP were the main contenders with regard to the most prominent cleavages – the socio-economic and religious ones (cf. Schattschneider 1960: 64–8). As we have already seen, the major parties were mistaken, at least concerning the *magnitude* of their capacity to structure electoral competition in the 1990s.

The FPÖ in the early 1980s perceived the changes in the electorate as both a challenge and an opportunity. On the one hand, the traditional German nationals, the party's core constituency, were dying out. On the other hand, increasing levels of education were seen as a chance for the FPÖ, which always had done relatively well among the better educated. Under the leadership of Friedrich Peter (until 1978) and Norbert Steger (1979–86), the FPÖ moved in the direction of becoming a liberal party, similar to the German FDP. FPÖ leaders believed that government participation would increase the party's electoral appeal. Government participation in turn was seen to be more plausible in a coalition with the SPÖ rather than the ÖVP. In this kind of coalition, the FPÖ, in a mid-term perspective, would attract voter groups previously tied to the ÖVP. New voters were expected to come from the professions, the business community, and certain sectors of the civil service. This strategy did not work out, however. Under the chairmanship of Norbert Steger, the FPÖ eventually became a government party but did not attract new voters. On the contrary, it became weaker and weaker. When Steger was replaced as party chairman in 1986, despite (or rather because of) its government participation, the FPÖ was smaller in the polls than the sampling error.

Within the FPÖ the perspective and strategy of renewing the party's appeal and electorate had not been accepted unanimously. Under party chairman Alexander Götz (1978–79) and in the Carinthian *Land* party organization the German national core was seen as more important and certainly as worth being preserved. In Götz's short period of office the party's electoral appeal was extended beyond the German national core by appealing to voters with rather diffuse but certainly anti-Socialist protest feelings. Jörg Haider worked in the same direction in the Carinthian *Land* party organization. When he assumed the office of national party chairman in 1986, the FPÖ was kicked out of government and immediately turned to a protest strategy. Initially, this may have been no more than an attempt to recapture the FPÖ traditional support that had been undermined by the party's participation in government. After its sensational election result of 1986 (almost doubling its vote share compared to 1983), however, the FPÖ recognized the scope of the dealignment process. In so doing, it took the lead over the SPÖ and ÖVP. Once the FPÖ had recognized the changes in the electorate, it adapted more quickly and radically to this process than did its main competitors. This was eased by the lack of a large group of party activists and members as well as by the weakness of the links between the FPÖ and the major interest groups and the party's powerless position in public sector institutions. The FPÖ's success was also related to the fact that it was not willing to respect any taboo when selecting and defining the issues to be used in political competition, and that it largely satisfied itself with building *negative* voter alliances (Müller 2002). As witnessed by the 2002 elections, the nature of its rise also made the FPÖ more vulnerable than its main competitors.

Party responses to electoral dealignment

Organizational responses

The party headquarters of both the SPÖ and ÖVP were aware long before our period of investigation that their existing mass organizations were deficient when it came to one of the main original purposes: to function as an instrument of communication with the general public. Rather than being outward-oriented they are self-centred. They absorb resources, including the time of politicians, and by nurturing traditionalist views and encouraging the stubborn representation of special interests they push and pull the party in directions that are not electorally viable. At the very least, their old-fashioned style is likely to create a negative image. To the extent that intra-party democracy works or the leaders are afraid of the members voting with their feet (and hence making mid-level party functionaries nervous) the traditional mass organizations reduce the parties' manoeuvrability. And given the decisive role of the mass organization in nominating candidates for elected public office, the party may field candidates who are not attractive to the general electorate and who, once elected, are likely to favour traditionalist policy proposals.

The SPÖ began to work on party organizational reform in the mid-1980s. According to the party leadership's analysis the main problems of the organization were that it isolated itself from the electorate by bureaucratic language and outdated organizational rituals and symbols (Müller 1996a). Therefore, the goal of party reform was to make the party organization more open and attractive to new groups and generations. Eventually such reform was introduced in 1991.

The reform allows for regional variation in the party organization. In addition to local party units, party units can be based on a concern for special issues. Such issue-based party units ('issue initiatives') are also open to non-members and indeed the expectation was that this would encourage the participation of people in the SPÖ who would never have thought of joining a traditional local party branch but would instead have engaged in single-issue or social movements. The rationale of this element of the reform is to reduce the isolation of the party organization from society and improve its image. The reformers' expectation was that issue initiatives would soon constitute a kind of parallel organization and would replace local organizations as the party's main building blocks in the long run. However, this element of the organizational reform failed to produce significant results. The idea of issue initiatives was never popular among the SPÖ's rank and file. Party activists argued that members of such initiatives would free-ride on the party organization without contributing to its maintenance. Consequently, emerging issue initiatives have not received a warm welcome from the party organization 'on the ground'. The party's general image problem, in turn, has kept the demand for new issue initiatives very modest, although the idea of such initiatives has proved more successful in the party's youth organization.

These attempts to make the party's mass organization more attractive were paralleled by the technical modernization and professionalization of the party organizational apparatus. Since the mid-1980s the party headquarters have made several attempts to speed up communication with party activists. For this purpose, a regular fax service was established. Beginning in 1987, the SPÖ tried new electronic means of internal communication. Since 1998 all organizational units down to the district (though not local) level have an internet connection. E-mail and mailboxes are increasingly used both in intra-party and external communication. As a special service, the SPÖ offers its members cheap and unlimited access to the internet (Volst and Voglmayr 1998: 221–8). The rationale of these attempts to speed up intra-party communication is to brief party activists before the mass media report on a topic. At a minimum, the party hopes to immunize the party activists against unfriendly interpretations; at best, it hopes that well-informed activists will counterbalance the mass media influence in their contacts with other people.

Following the débâcle of the 1994 general election, reformers in the SPÖ headquarters developed strategies to improve the party's communication capability. According to their plans, the SPÖ would improve its intelligence by engaging in the systematic observation of the communications of its political competitors. On the active side, the SPÖ planned to make use of linguistic analyses and the know-how of professional text writers, whose task would be to coin words and phrases which translate the jargon of professional politicians into colloquial German, easily accessible to 'ordinary people'. The SPÖ also recognized the amateurish nature of its communication style: too many statements by SPÖ politicians are uncoordinated and of a one-off character. This should be replaced by strategic communication, in which individual statements are part and parcel of an overall plan. In order to generate a competitive advantage from the SPÖ's disciplined mass organization it should be systematically involved in the party's communication by taking up SPÖ issues as phrased by the professionals and carrying them into the pubs. It is generally recognized that this 'campaign ability' is the most difficult goal to achieve. After the leadership change from Vranitzky to Klima, which was followed by a turnover in the relevant positions in the party headquarters, only an impoverished and vulgar version of these plans was realized. Klima's self-styled spin doctors concentrated their efforts on the party leader. They managed to streamline his public statements to an extent that made Klima look like a puppet, repeating the spin doctor's slogans time and again, even if it was obvious that they did not provide the appropriate answers to questions put to him. Despite his initial popularity, he was soon a spent force.

In order to increase the SPÖ's attractiveness for women, the party had introduced a 25 percent quota for all party and representative functions in 1985. In 1993 the quota clause was reformulated in a gender-neutral way, granting each sex a 40 percent quota, with the remaining 20 percent to be selected exclusively on the basis of qualification.

The ÖVP tried to modernize and professionalize its central organization since the early 1980s by devoting more resources to strategic planning, survey research, working out new party programmes, and computerizing the party headquarters. Public relations and campaigning were the party activities most affected by professionalization. In preparing the 'critical' media performances of the party leader (such as TV debates and party congress speeches) the ÖVP relied on external media consultants. Likewise, external experts and representatives of PR agencies increasingly became part and parcel of campaign planning.

The main weaknesses of the ÖVP organization, which to a large extent result from the indirect party structure, remained largely untouched by reform attempts (Müller 1997; Müller and Steininger 1994). They are similar to those of the SPÖ mass organization and include in particular a lack of ability to communicate with the general electorate. If the mass organization has any effect on the party strategy, it is largely to defend the interests of those groups that are over-represented in it, in particular farmers, shopkeepers, and civil servants. This, in turn, has not increased the ÖVP's appeal. The ÖVP return to government office at the national level in 1987 rather increased the problems with its mass organization. Now the 'party as organization' had to submit to the 'party in government'. However, since many government decisions were compromises with the SPÖ, or, for technical reasons, did not match the ÖVP proposals developed while in opposition, party activists and members were dissatisfied with much of what their leaders were doing in government. This gap could not be bridged by making use of technological innovations such as fax and e-mail. As in the SPÖ, these were intended to speed up intra-party communication in order to provide official interpretations of events as quickly as possible, thus to bring 'good news' before or simultaneously with the 'bad news' of the mass media.

In contrast to the SPÖ and ÖVP, the FPÖ party organization has traditionally been weak and not comprehensive in geographical terms (Müller 1994; Luther 1997). Therefore the new party leader Haider faced less in-built constraints when introducing thorough organizational changes. Moreover, the lean FPÖ organization is cheap both compared to those of the SPÖ and ÖVP and in relation to its electoral strength (until 2002). This, in turn, left a larger share of the party's budget for propaganda and election campaigns in particular.

Being aware of widespread anti-party feelings and indeed exploiting them when attacking the government parties, Haider could not leave the FPÖ an old-fashioned party. Instead he tried to stylize it as a 'movement for political renewal' and even 'thought aloud' about abolishing the party. In 1995 a party statute reform brought this process to a formal end. First, the FPÖ now officially called itself 'Die Freiheitlichen' (The Freedomites) and the word 'party' was also eliminated from the names of all (party) bodies.[1] This move parallels what the Italian parties did at about the same time. Secondly, a 'citizen movement' was established to supplement the traditional (party) structures. The main aim of this reform was to provide a structure for a closer link between the FPÖ and the million new voters it won in the 1986–99 period. Many of them share anti-party sentiments and therefore could hardly be approached via a 'classic' party organization. Indeed the growth of the FPÖ party organization in terms of members between 1986 and 1999 (+ 36 percent) remained small compared to the growth of its electorate (+ 438 percent, including the 1986 increase). Copying the organizational innovation of the Italian Lega Nord, the 'citizen movement' provided two additional levels of organizational attachment. They can best be seen as concentric circles around the remaining (party) organization. The outer circle comprised all those who took out an 'info card'. The holders of this card were entitled to get 'insider' information through the party. The inner circle comprised all those who took out an 'active card'. These card-holders were invited to party seminars, and they were entitled to participate in electoral conventions also introduced in 1995. According to the statute, their purpose is to elect the party's top candidates in each electoral district. However, by mid-1996, the 'citizen movement' had only recruited 461 active card-holders and 337 info card-holders (Luther 1997: 288, 290–2), and recruitment of these new types of party supporter did not improve much afterwards. Consequently, electoral conventions were never held and the 'citizen movement' was allowed to die silently. In 1999, the FPÖ made a strong move in the opposite direction (cf. Luther 2001), with central scrutiny of all candidates, including a practical test of their TV skills.

Irrespective of the possible long-term contribution of the organizational reform to achieving its stated goals, media coverage of its introduction certainly helped the FPÖ in its attempts to create the image of being 'special' and not an old-fashioned party. Other activities that aimed at this image were the foundation of 'F Clubs' and the organization of disco events. Part of this strategy was the generational turnover of party activists, which was pushed forward by the party leadership. Younger people who were first and foremost attracted by the image of the party leader, and indeed were quite often personally recruited by him, increasingly replaced the traditional FPÖ functionaries. This occasionally caused conflict in the party, which was typically solved by the party leader's call for loyalty.

Like the other parties, the FPÖ engaged in a strategy of professionalization by making use of external consultants. Advertising and campaigning were concentrated in an advertising agency founded and owed by the party. This agency, in turn, hired external consultants. It is worth mentioning that Haider's clothes, which cover a much broader range than is usual for politicians, are selected with the advice of a designer agency. Perhaps more than anything else, it is Haider's frequent change from one unconventional outfit to another, usually reported by the media, that symbolizes the nature of the game as change for change's sake, and hence as being about news and media attention.

The traditional weakness of the party organization not only facilitated its transformation, it also forced the FPÖ more than its main competitors to resort to other means of communicating with the general electorate. The party organization was largely used to provide the forum for events designed to attract media attention to the party and to its leader in particular. While this to some extent is true for all parties, the FPÖ has clearly taken the lead. The 1996 FPÖ party congress is a case in point. It was framed after the model of smooth running, 'made for TV' US conventions. The party leader appeared on a TV screen, engaged in a talk-show-like conversation with journalists. An internet connection to this event gave the impression of total accessibility.

Internal power distribution

In the SPÖ, the only formal change in the power structure since 1967 affected the recruitment for candidates to public office. The party leadership tried to break up the bureaucratic recruitment process, thereby producing candidates who have more electoral appeal by introducing intra-party primaries in 1993 (Nick 1995). Together with other organizational reforms these primaries were meant to be a signal of more openness, paralleling the aims of the electoral reform (see p. 168 below). According to the statute, all party members enjoy voting rights. The primaries are based on proposals of the relevant leadership body but party members can eliminate candidates, change their ranking in the party list, and write in new ones. The results of the primaries are binding if at least 50 percent of the party members participate. If the participation rate is below this mark the results only have the character of suggestions to the relevant leadership bodies. Primaries have so far been carried out just once at the national level, before the 1994 general election (Müller 1996a: 283–4).

Although a majority of party members welcomed the introduction of primaries, this reform has not been particularly popular in large parts of the party organization. Many party activists and particularly public office holders were lukewarm supporters or were even opponents of this selection method. As a consequence, efforts to mobilize the majority of passive party members remained modest. Only in the two smallest *Länder*, Burgenland and Vorarlberg, was participation sufficient to produce binding results and only two of the official candidates were rejected in 1994. In the late 1990s, the SPÖ internally considered abolishing the primaries, when working on further organizational reforms. It was primarily the anticipated negative image effects that prevented the party from doing so. Instead, it decided simply not to carry out further primaries.

While the formal power structure was not changed significantly, the informal power structure has seen interesting variations. Most interestingly, a gap has opened between the SPÖ's leadership and trade union wing (see p. 170 below).

In the ÖVP the party organization was only slightly more enthusiastic about the introduction of primaries than in the SPÖ. The national party leadership nevertheless pushed through primaries open to all voters. By so doing it intended to open the process of candidate recruitment. In the most optimistic scenario primaries were to eliminate unpopular politicians and allow for the breakthrough of political talents who were popular not only among party activists and members but in the electorate at large. Given the dominance of the three leagues in the ÖVP's recruitment process, the party has the problem that most of its candidates reflect the interests traditionally represented by one of them. Moreover, it was hoped, primaries would lead to extra efforts by the candidates that, in turn, would increase the party's communication with the electorate.

However, the price for the party organization's acceptance of primaries was that the primaries remained in the competence of the *Land* party organizations, some of which implemented primaries half-heartedly and were not ready to accept results which did not meet their expectations (Leitner and Mertens 1995). With hindsight the effects of the 1994 primaries can be evaluated rather sceptically. They neither had a significant effect on candidate selection (though more so than in the SPÖ), nor did they improve the ÖVP's communication with the general electorate (Nick 1995). Like the SPÖ, the ÖVP in 1999 silently ignored the statute clause that commits the party to holding primaries.

The ÖVP's attempts to attract new voter groups, in particular the new urban middle class, led to informal changes in the party's power structure. In developing its electoral strategy the national party leadership largely bypassed the traditional power centres of the party – the three leagues which organize farmers, other self-employed, and blue- and white-collar workers (in practice mainly civil servants). The leagues participated in the modernization strategy only in the form of a 'permissive consensus'. They were willing to grant the party leader and party headquarters a greater degree of autonomy in addressing the target groups and working out policy proposals in order to improve the party's electoral fortunes. Since this process was not accompanied by a change in the formal power structure, the leagues considered it easy to reverse. Moreover, party leader Alois Mock kept the leaders of the leagues and *Land* party organizations well informed and called for personal loyalty in the event of conflicting interests.

When it became clear that the modernization strategy had dramatically failed in the general election of 1990 (a loss of 9.2 percent of the vote and 17 seats), a formal change in the leadership bodies was introduced which formalized some of the behavioural changes and thus increased the autonomy of the party leadership (Müller 1997: 268–9). In subsequent policy decisions, the Business League in particular experienced a loss of intra-party power. The ÖVP's continued attempts to attract voters from the large constituency of employees increasingly frustrated the party's business wing. For a while the Business League developed plans to break away from the ÖVP and establish a separate business party. Eventually these plans were given up. The newly introduced 4 percent clause of the electoral law was considered a high risk factor, particularly since the Business League lacked a convincing electoral leader to push a new business party.

The centralization of power at the horizontal level – the party–leagues relationship – was paralleled by increased autonomy for the *Land* party organizations. Typical of the 1990s was a decoupling of the *Land* party organizations from the national party. The ÖVP *Land* party organizations had always been much more autonomous than those of the SPÖ. While the party was in opposition at the national level, they had generally done very well at *Land* elections, partly benefiting from voters' willingness to balance power between parties. Indeed there was an enormous asymmetry in the party's electoral strength in *Land* and national elections, which made the *Land* leaders' positions very safe (Dachs 1997). In 1989, however, the ÖVP began to experience a series of massive defeats at the *Land* level and the *Land* party organizations reacted by distancing themselves from the national party. They stressed their individual identity, to the extent of changing their name (e.g. Tyrolean rather than

Austrian People's Party). Until 2002 they concentrated their resources entirely on *Land* politics and even after their national party's triumph they still refuse to submit to national party strategy if this conflicts with their own goals. Nor do ÖVP *Land* party organizations refrain from criticizing the national party or ÖVP ministers when this can be expected to pay off in electoral terms at the *Land* level. Consequently, national-level politicians are sometimes told to stay out of the *Land* when a *Land* election is approaching. While this development bears some similarity to the stratarchy hypothesis of Katz and Mair (1995: 21), the underlying intra-party power relations and the locus of the initiative are different. It is the *Land* party organizations rather than the national party that have initiated this process, and an alliance of *Land* party organizations can still intervene successfully in national affairs. This was exemplified by the *Land* organizations' decision to remove the party leader in 1994 and their influence on the national party's decision to de-emphasize issues (such as NATO member-ship) which they did not consider electorally viable in the second half of the 1990s. Likewise, before the 2002 elections the *Land* organizations successfully demanded that the national party removes the commitment to purchase inter-ceptor jets from the government agenda.

The FPÖ has seen a thorough change of intra-party power relations since the election of Jörg Haider to the position of party leader (see Luther 1997: 290; Kräh 1996: 136–8). Traditionally the FPÖ party leader had much formal but little real power. Because of the FPÖ's electoral triumphs that not only occurred under his leadership but were also almost entirely due to his ability to shape the party's profile and attract voters, Haider managed to make use of the full range of his formal competences and even to gain power far beyond them. Until 2000 it was Haider who *de facto* made all important strategic and personnel decisions. Party bodies only ratified what had very often already been publicly announced. It is interesting to note that Haider's authoritarian leadership style was seen as an attractive element of the FPÖ by many of the party's voters.

In 1997 and 1998, limits to this leadership style and its effectiveness first became apparent. The FPÖ's Vienna and Lower Austria *Land* organizations did not submit to Haider when it came to electing a *Land* party leader or nominat-ing the party's top candidate for *Land* elections. The Salzburg FPÖ paralysed itself for months in an intense battle within the leadership. The national party intervened by removing 700 party functionaries from office and calling new intra-party elections, a move that was not well received by the rank and file. The most serious problem, however, resulted from massive fraud and economic incompetence in the Lower Austria party organization, almost leading to the *Land* party's bankruptcy. Haider responded by designing a private law contract between the FPÖ and its party and public functionaries, which gives the party the right to impose financial sanctions on those who are disloyal to it. All FPÖ functionaries had to choose between signing this contract or being expelled from the party. Although this led to the break-away of four *Land* diet deputies in Vienna, the overwhelming majority of FPÖ politicians did sign the contract. In addition, it was announced as a project to make FPÖ party finance totally transparent and its flows of money accessible via internet. Little action followed, but agenda management had been effective.

Initially, Haider's voluntary resignation from party leadership after the FPÖ's accession to government in 2000 did not affect intra-party power relations. It was just another trick, this time directed against those European leaders who had reacted to the FPÖ's government participation by introducing poorly thought out sanctions against Austria. With the chief bogeyman Haider reduced to the status of an 'ordinary party member', as he himself stated, there would be no rationale to maintain the sanctions. The move was also perhaps intended to allow Haider to dissociate himself from unpopular government policies while still pulling the levers of his party behind the scenes. In the event, however, the sanctions were not immediately lifted and a gulf gradually emerged between Haider, on the one hand, and the official party leadership and most of the government team, on the other.

Party outputs towards the electorate

Target groups

As the SPÖ was in a majority position in the early 1980s, this would have been sufficient to maintain its level of electoral support. The SPÖ at that time identified the educated urban middle class and younger people as the groups whose support was most endangered. The support of the educated middle class had to a large extent been due to the appeal of Bruno Kreisky and his liberal reforms. In the 1980s the SPÖ faced the double challenge of the ÖVP and the emerging Greens, both of which were particularly attractive alternatives for the educated middle class. Since Haider took over the leadership of the FPÖ, the SPÖ's core group of blue-collar workers has also become a problematic support group. Before the series of FPÖ electoral victories, almost two-thirds of blue-collar workers had supported the SPÖ, almost none the FPÖ. This proportion has changed dramatically, resulting in an FPÖ lead over the SPÖ with regard to support from blue-collar workers (see p. 149). In the mid-1990s, the SPÖ therefore made the defence and recapture of blue-collar support a major goal, which it spectacularly failed to achieve in the 1999 elections. Nevertheless, the SPÖ still follows a catch-all approach. The draft for the 1998 party programme (less so the final programme), for instance, made a deliberate attempt to appeal to the self-employed, a group which has never figured prominently among the SPÖ's target groups.

The ÖVP traditionally has represented farmers, the urban middle class of the self-employed, and those employees who have strong ties with the Catholic Church, in particular civil servants. These groups are organizationally expressed by the three Leagues of the ÖVP (Müller and Steininger 1994). Changes in the social structure put the ÖVP in a losing position: the share of self-employed (plus family members) in the population declined from more than a third in 1951 to less than a sixth in 1981. Since the early 1970s at the latest, the party leadership has been aware of the electoral disadvantages resulting from social structural change. As a consequence white-collar employees were recognized – at least symbolically – as the party's new prime target group. Employees were to be approached by giving the Workers' and Employees' League a stronger voice within the ÖVP and by broadening the appeal of the other two leagues. Accordingly, the Farmers' League should represent not only farmers but all people in the countryside and the Business League not only owners but also managers.

The ÖVP strategy was complicated by changes in value orientations. One aspect was the increasing importance of the environmental issue, which was accompanied by the emergence of Green parties. These were nurtured equally by former SPÖ and ÖVP voters. Before the Greens won parliamentary representation in 1986, one wing of the ÖVP wanted to send strong signals to this 'emerging market'. Opponents of this strategy argued that this would lower the barriers against ÖVP supporters voting for green parties (Kukacka 1984). In any case, it would have increased the already existing problem of intra-party cohesion tremendously.

Another relevant change in value orientations was secularization. To be sure, this was not a new phenomenon, but one of ever increasing relevance. As a Christian democratic party, the ÖVP could only suffer from it. By the 1980s, the core-Catholics were clearly only a fraction of those voters who already supported the ÖVP. Concentrating the party's appeal on this group would have been like preaching to the converted. The ÖVP therefore tried to keep a low profile in terms of religious issues or, even better, to keep them off the agenda. This also affected the party's relations with organized groups such as the Catholic student fraternity (Cartell-Verband). Party managers were keen, for instance, to avoid delegations of the student fraternity coming to the party headquarters in their colourful uniforms, because this was seen as the wrong signal to secularized urban voters.

Electoral defeats at the national and *Land* levels in the 1987–94 period raised the level of internal conflict in the ÖVP. The main line of conflict was between the so-called 'steel helmet faction', as this wing was soon labelled by journalists, and the party's moderately liberal wing. The 'steel helmet' wing comprised the organizational traditionalists who tended to share conservative Catholic views. The moderately liberal wing aimed at a more open party organization. Ideologically its members had a stronger free market outlook and a more pluralistic view of personal lifestyles. The ÖVP was wavering between two strategies, orienting itself towards the party's traditional core groups or trying to win (back) mobile voter groups. In so doing, the ÖVP sent out contradictory signals to its various target groups which were not well received by any of them. In the mid-1990s the ÖVP *de facto* accepted its new position as a middle-sized party and temporarily abandoned its electoral 'catch-all' approach. Now it gave priority to maintaining its remaining core voters. It tried to extend its appeal to mobile voter groups only to the extent that this did not conflict with the 'hold the core voters' strategy. However, when the FPÖ imploded in 2002 the ÖVP was quick to appeal to its former supporters and indeed was able to pick up the pieces, winning over a stunning 600,000 voters.

After the election of Jörg Haider to the FPÖ party leadership and the subsequent breakdown of the SPÖ–FPÖ coalition in 1986, the FPÖ changed its strategy fundamentally. Initially Haider returned to his party's heritage by mobilizing the remainder of the German national camp (which was mainly important for winning the internal leadership contest) and by subscribing to a protest strategy when addressing the general electorate. Since the formation of the SPÖ–ÖVP coalition seemed a foregone conclusion even during the 1986 election campaign, the FPÖ (while still represented in the government by its previous leaders) could take over the role of opposition and attract protest voters. In the 1986–90 period the FPÖ continued to 'collect' protest voters. They came from both major parties and they protested for different reasons. Most of these voters were relatively young.

After its success in the general election of 1990 the FPÖ assumed a more active role in setting the political agenda. It concentrated on 'modernization losers', i.e. on people who were affected by or afraid of the consequences of economic change (Betz 1994) and those who rejected recent cultural changes such as the emancipation of women and the trend towards a multi-cultural society. In socio-demographic terms the FPÖ target groups mainly comprise low-income pensioners and low-qualified workers in the internationally competitive sector (cf. Kitschelt 1995). Male voters are grossly over-represented. Most of the new FPÖ voters had previously voted for the SPÖ or have an SPÖ family background. In concentrating its efforts on this group the FPÖ was willing to risk losing some of the voters it had won in the first phase. The FPÖ was also willing to accept that its support base had changed in the direction of lower social classes and consequently moved towards promoting welfare state policies. After the general election of 1995 and in particular the European election of 1996 the FPÖ made special attempts to improve its appeal to female voters, who were strongly under-represented among the FPÖ electorate. For this purpose, it invented the 'children's cheque' (a monthly welfare benefit for each child payable to mothers) that figured prominently in the 1999 election campaign. In 2002, facing defeat in a desperate attempt to hold on to the working-class vote the FPÖ demanded a government-imposed 1,000 euro per month minimum wage and tax reductions for low-income earners.

Finally, it should be mentioned that the FPÖ makes extensive use of the instruments of plebiscitary democracy, in particular the people's initiative (Müller 1998). Technically, a people's initiative is nothing more than a legislative proposal that has the support of 100,000 citizens. Between 1986 and 2000, the FPÖ organized four of these initiatives (and supported two more) and threatened several times to introduce such an initiative if the government did not behave appropriately. The rationale of a parliamentary party in organizing a people's initiative is, of course, not to initiate legislation, but to get media attention and public recognition as the 'owner' of a specific issue, to influence the political agenda, and to mobilize party supporters (Müller 1999).

Mass media relations

The erosion of voter loyalties, the vanishing of the remainder of the party press in the 1980s, and the decline of the communication capability of the party organizations have increased the relevance of non-partisan mass media, in particular television. Indeed, the 'televisualization' of politics had reached new levels in the late 1980s and 1990s. Not only does TV news reach by far the largest audience and enjoy more credibility than the press, but it has proved possible to use TV to appeal to voter groups who could not be reached by traditional print media and who otherwise show little interest in politics. TV appearances of politicians are now more important than ever for image man-agement and electoral success. Campaigns have become television-centred, with critical media events – especially TV debates and 'confrontainments' – being of crucial importance for the evaluation of candidates. The share of candidate-oriented voters has increased by 15 percent within a decade, amounting to 52 percent in 1993, and this, in turn, has given professional media consultants a crucial role (Plasser 2000).

As already mentioned, all parties have tried hard to adapt to these changes in their environment by devoting more resources to and professionalizing their attempts to communicate with the voters. However, in so doing political parties aim at a moving target. The media coverage of politics has changed consider-ably over the last few years. In particular live 'duels' between pairs of party leaders have become a central feature of campaigns since 1994. Such 'duels' and 'critical' interviews cannot be prepared in the same way as the more official self-presentations which were typical of earlier periods. There are clear limits to what professional media training can do to improve the media skills of political leaders. Yet, their ability to exercise 'impression management' has been crucial to their performance in the more difficult TV arenas since the 1990s.

The risks of tele-politics can best be highlighted using the example of the ÖVP, whose pre-1995 leaders all turned out to be bad TV performers. This con-tributed significantly to the electoral decline of the ÖVP. In order to reverse this process, the ÖVP replaced its leaders frequently (in 1989, 1991, and 1995). Yet, each leadership deselection or selection caused severe intra-party conflicts that again contributed to the ÖVP's electoral decline.

The FPÖ under Haider constituted the most drastic contrast. He is an excel-lent TV performer and has managed to use his TV appearances for strategic agenda setting and image styling. It was mainly Haider's performance in TV discussions with political opponents that created the FPÖ's image as an effective opposition. In contrast to the representatives of the government parties, who try to behave like statesmen, Haider acts like a 'gladiator'. In TV discussions his style is offensive, his language largely colloquial. His contributions to TV confrontations typically consist of an endless stream of attacks, mostly not directly related to the contributions of his opponents. Haider's attacks largely do not focus on the 'big' issues as such. Rather they pick little details of highly symbolic relevance and link them to the points he wants to make. Since print media reports about Haider and the FPÖ usually have a distant or critical attitude, Haider's TV performances have been essential to the FPÖ's public appearance and electoral success.

Candidates

Given the increase in the share of voters who claim that their electoral decision depends on the appeal of the leading candidates, the parties have become even more concerned about the qualities of their leaders. While polls and the tone of media reports have proved good indicators of the electoral performance of personalities once they have assumed the office of party leader, this was not always true before their selection.

When Vranitzky was selected as Chancellor in 1996, he was an outsider who would previously never have been considered eligible for this office. When he became Chancellor, he had never held any party office before and he had been a cabinet minister for less than two years. Moreover, his policy positions were outside the then mainstream of the party. Vranitzky soon turned out to be an electoral asset for the SPÖ. Despite declining popularity, he remained the most popular party politician until his resignation, indeed the most popular one since regular monitoring by surveys began in the 1960s. When Vranitzky resigned in 1997, the selection of his successor Viktor Klima was a toned-down version of his own accession to power. Vranitzky had recruited Klima for his cabinet in 1992. At that time, Klima was a manager in a state-owned industry. He had a record as an active social democrat, but had never held any real political office. He managed to win support in the party while in cabinet, but it was Vranitzky who made him 'crown prince' by appointing him Minister of Finance in 1995 and eventually suggested him as his successor as Chancellor and party leader. Although the polls initially proved Vranitzky right, Klima, unlike his predecessor, led his party to electoral disaster and subsequent loss of government office. The SPÖ had a record in the 1980s and 1990s of appointing party political outsiders to cabinet office who later turned out to appeal to the electorate at large, such as Vranitzky and Klima, or to specific groups of voters, such as Ministers Rudolf Scholten and Caspar Einem. But although these ministers as a rule were nominated for safe seats in the elections following their appointment to cabinet, the SPÖ did not change its recruitment policy for parliamentary candidates.

While the 1993 party organizational reform did allow for candidates who were not party members – a clause which was heavily criticized by party activists and strong *Land* party organizations (such as the Vienna SPÖ) – not a single candidate was nominated in the 1994 and 1995 general elections who was not a card-carrying member, and only one non-member candidate was nominated in 1999. In the same year's European Parliament elections, the SPÖ leader nominated a well-known journalist as the top candidate, a move that caused a considerable amount of unrest in the party without leading to any compensating applause from the media. As an opposition party the SPÖ took a slightly more radical approach in 2002 and nominated three external candidates.

The ÖVP also recognized the importance of the electoral leader and engaged in a strategy of personalization from the early 1980s. At that time, ÖVP leader Alois Mock faced the ageing Kreisky and his hapless successor Sinowatz, making personalization a potentially viable electoral strategy. Concentrating its propaganda efforts on the party leader, however, had other purposes, too. It was intended to hide intra-party tensions, the lack of publicly perceived competence in crucial policy fields, and the fact that important ÖVP policy proposals did not withstand critical scrutiny. This concentration on the electoral leader increased the demands made on his media skills. Consequently, the ÖVP leaders' lack of TV skills offered a crucial argument for their deselection. Alois Mock was replaced in 1989 after a series of defeats in *Land* elections and with the expectation, based on polls, that a major defeat would follow at the national level in 1990 if things remained as they were. However, his successor, Josef Riegler, could not improve the ÖVP's position. He pre-empted his deselection after the 1990 electoral débâcle by his voluntary resignation in 1991. Riegler's successor, Erhard Busek, was deselected in 1995 after the 1994 electoral defeat. In all these cases the party leaders' lack of a positive media image and TV skills figured prominently among the arguments that fuelled the intra-party debate preceding their replacement. Busek's successor, Wolfgang Schüssel, could not prevent the FPÖ from winning more votes than the ÖVP in 1999, but leading his party back to the dominant position in government after 30 years (with the prospect of rolling back the FPÖ and benefiting from holding the head of government position) has kept him in office and indeed seems to allow him more intra-party power than any of his predecessors since the 1950s. Since the electoral triumph of 2002 he has been unassailable, but only as long as the ÖVP can hold on to governmental power.

It is interesting here to note that the ÖVP elites have drawn only *negative* conclusions from the dominating importance of TV skills, i.e. it has led to the deselection of unsuccessful leaders. They have not yet switched over to the offensive by broadening the range of potential candidates for the party chairmanship. Indeed, all party chairmen had been recruited from the core group of party leaders, with priority given to intra-party acceptability over image or image potential *vis-à-vis* the general electorate (Müller and Meth-Cohn 1991).

In contrast, such considerations have played a role in the selection of candidates for positions at the second or third level, for instance cabinet ministers or MPs. Since the late 1980s, the ÖVP has tried to send specific signals to its target groups by nominating outsiders as parliamentary candidates. The most prominent example occurred in the European election of 1996. Then the ÖVP nominated a popular female TV journalist as its top candidate, although she had been affiliated with the ÖVP only loosely and did not take out party membership when she was nominated. This nomination turned out to pay off electorally: for the first time since 1966 the ÖVP became the strongest party in a nationwide election (leaving aside the ÖVP-sponsored candidates in the post-1986 presidential elections).

From Haider's election to party leader until his party's entering government in 2000 (with Haider remaining outside cabinet) his and the FPÖ image were completely tied together. Haider dominated the public appearance of the FPÖ both in campaigns – even if he himself was not a candidate (as in most *Land* elections) – and in 'normal' times. Since Haider's TV skills are hardly matched by any other Austrian (and certainly no FPÖ) politician, he had a *de facto* monopoly on the FPÖ media presence (Plasser and Ulram 1995: 496; Müller *et al.* 2001: 389–91). Given the FPÖ strategy of presenting itself as a movement rather than a party and given also the limited choice the party's mass organization provides, the FPÖ turned to 'unconventional' candidates for many public offices (Höbelt 2003: 155–6). Haider also played a very active role here, helping to recruit outsiders from the free professions, journalism, and sports. To the discomfort of many party officials, these often jumped the queue. To provide a few examples: Haider nominated a retired female state prosecutor for a safe parliamentary seat after she had earned nationwide prominence for strong law and order statements in a TV news show. In order to undermine the long-standing accusation that the FPÖ would have an inappropriate relationship to Nazism, Haider nominated a Jewish journalist for a safe seat in the European elections. In order to win media attention in 1999 the FPÖ revealed its candidates for the national list one by one with a week's intermission, beginning with an Olympic champion in downhill skiing. Once elected, many of these candidates have not proved particularly qualified for actually carrying out their political job. However, their nominations hit the headlines and gave credibility to the FPÖ's claim to 'be different'.

External relations I: the state

The electoral system

The SPÖ and ÖVP introduced electoral reform in 1992 (against the votes of all the smaller opposition parties). It might be expected that the government parties would introduce an electoral system tailor-made for their needs. This was not the case, however (see Müller 1996c). While it is true that some aspects of the electoral system tend to favour large parties rather than small ones, its overall effect in the 1994 and 1995 elections has been an increase in the level of proportionality with respect to the previous (already very proportional) electoral system.[2] Nevertheless, the government parties had originally hoped to improve their relative positions through the new electoral system. A discussion of electoral reform had been pursued in Austria since the late 1970s, and it is interesting to note that in both major parties reformers considered the large electoral districts (comprising up to 1.1 million voters) as a (potential) source of popular dissatisfaction with political representation well before 'party weariness' was even mentioned in the academic or media discourse. When the emerging grand coalition met public criticism in 1986 for constituting too great a concentration of power and for bringing the country back to the 1950s (i.e. the 'old' grand coalition) in terms of democratic accountability, the SPÖ and ÖVP were quick to point out that their government would promote democracy. In particular, they would empower the voters and the parliamentary opposition by reforms of the electoral law and the parliamentary rules of procedure. Electoral reform from the very beginning was meant to strengthen the accountability of MPs while maintaining the current level of proportionality. The original plan was to introduce about 100 single-member districts and to have a second stage of seat distribution in order to adjust for proportionality. This plan failed in that it was rejected not only by the opposition parties but also by many of the government parties' own backbenchers. The government parties therefore resorted to the alternative of increasing the accountability of MPs by increasing the number of multi-member electoral districts (from 9 to 43) and by strengthening the preference voting system (Müller and Scheucher 1995).

As noted, the announcement of this reform was an attempt at agenda management: it aimed to take the wind out of the sails of the critics of the new grand coalition. However, the substance of the electoral reform was supposed to help the SPÖ and ÖVP in two ways. First, the reform was seen as a major contribution to fighting party weariness that, in turn, is much more a problem for the traditional parties in government than for the new or fundamentally transformed parties in opposition. Secondly, the SPÖ and ÖVP hoped (and the opposition parties were afraid) that the logic of personalized campaigns in the 43 electoral districts would automatically increase their vote. This is due to the fact that the SPÖ and ÖVP were initially expected to win almost all of the seats to be distributed at the first stage of the electoral system. Election campaigns that were personalized at the level of individual candidates (rather than at the level of party leaders) would also benefit the two traditional major parties since they have the larger reservoir of suitable candidates.

Although even before the introduction of the electoral reform individual MPs had come to be considered a more relevant factor by voters in making their electoral decision than was the case a decade earlier, and although the candidates' campaign behaviour has indeed changed under the new electoral system (Müller and Scheucher 1995), its effects on the electoral outcome were marginal at best.

Party finance

State funding of parties has been introduced in a piecemeal fashion since 1962. Major steps were taken at the time when partisan dealignment gained momentum. Public party finance may have helped to maintain party system stability until the mid-1980s because only parliamentary parties were entitled to substantial subsidies. However, once small parties establish themselves in parliament with five MPs, they receive relatively more money than big parties. This is because the funding consists of a fixed amount, equal for all parties, plus an amount proportional to the party's electoral strength.

These rules, and other rules which regulate contributions to political parties, have been subject to a number of changes, depending on the government–opposition constellation, with the government parties trying to make their own lives easier while making that of opposition more troublesome. This tradition has continued in recent years. As a response to the increase in the number and strength of opposition parties and their more radical style, the government parties substantially reduced the bias in favour of small parties in 1987. In 1990, they introduced the principle that parties have to apply formally for public funding, thus indicating that they actually want the money which they are entitled to receive. This was the government parties' response to the opposition parties' criticizing increases in state party finance but still taking advantage of them (see Müller 1992: 115–17; Sickinger 1997). In 1990, the FPÖ deliberately did not apply for public money. It thus accepted a competitive disadvantage in terms of resources in order to preserve its 'anti-privileges' image. However, in subsequent elections it did not find it worth the price.

External relations II: interest groups

Traditionally, the two major parties have had very close and good relations with the major interest groups (Müller 1996b: 76–8). While both parties have been represented in all major interest groups via their auxiliary organizations, those of the ÖVP have dominated farmers' and business organizations and the social democratic trade unionists have controlled the Trade Union Congress and the Chamber of Labour. The parliamentary groups of both the SPÖ and ÖVP are well staffed with interest group representatives.

From a comparative perspective, party–interest group relations are, without doubt, still intense and cosy. Nevertheless there have been changes since the late 1970s, which have their roots in the parties' responses to changes in the electoral market. Conflicts between the parties and interest groups emerged in the 1980s when the parties aimed at winning or maintaining 'Green' voters and hence were willing to compromise elements of the postwar economic growth consensus. The conflicts became more serious over the economic policies of the grand coalition, particularly between the SPÖ and the social democratic trade unionists. For electoral and coalitional reasons the party leadership had been willing to subscribe to policies the SPÖ had emphatically rejected only a few years earlier (for instance privatization and cutback of welfare policies) while the trade unionists acted as defenders of traditional social democratic values and aimed to minimize these policies. This conflict was most visible in coalition negotiations between the SPÖ and ÖVP. In 1994 leading social democratic trade unionists withdrew from the SPÖ delegation because they did not want to legitimize a cutback in welfare programmes. The conflict then was contained by the party leader Viktor Klima, but broke out again during the unsuccessful coalition negotiations in 1999–2000, when the leader of the social democratic trade unionists declared that he would not sign the policy programme that had been hammered out by the party leaders, and hence provided one good argument for the ÖVP to change its coalition partner. In 2002 trade unionists were no longer included in the SPÖ coalition negotiating team.

Likewise, the Business-League-dominated Chamber of Business tried to keep liberalization at bay, and joined forces with the trade unions when it came to liberalizing shop opening hours. In all these and other cases, the government parties were less willing to accept the policy proposals of the interest groups than they would have been in previous times. The parties' behaviour was triggered by the dictatorship of empty government coffers, policy conviction, and electoral logic. In the context of this chapter it is sufficient to elaborate on the last point, which itself has two components. First, there is an increasing part of the electorate that is interested in liberal reforms. Secondly, the major interest groups became more unpopular in the 1990s, partly because of scandals (Plasser and Ulram 1996b). This, in turn, has caused the government parties to intervene in the internal organization of the major public interest groups – the Chambers of Labour and Business. While it is true that the reforms which aim at restoring the credibility of the chambers were *negotiated* between interest group representatives and political parties, the chambers themselves would have been much more reluctant to endorse them.

The opposition parties had realized that they could gain votes by 'bashing' the major interest groups. Articulating protest within the chambers as well, the FPÖ has gained dramatically in chamber elections since the 1980s. In 1997 it founded a separate trade union, the first ever such attempt to split the all-party Trade Union Congress (ÖGB). However, this new trade union remained remarkably unsuccessful, failing even to attract shop stewards who were elected on FPÖ lists (*Profil* 40, 28 September 1998) and having recruited only a few thousand members by 2000 (compared to the 1.6 million members of the Trade Union Congress). Two *Land* organizations of the ÖVP decided in the 1990s to remove from parliament those of their MPs who also held chamber posts. Likewise, the new (as of 2000) president of both the ÖVP Business League and the Business Chamber, Christoph Leitl, has decided not to take a seat in parliament, in order to allow himself more room for manoeuvre as an interest group representative. While all this does not add up to a dramatic split between parties and the interest groups to which they were traditionally close, it is clear that relations have become less intimate and that the parties' behaviour has been triggered by, among other factors, pragmatic electoral considerations.

External relations III: other parties

In the 1980s, the SPÖ and ÖVP considered each other the main electoral competitor. This changed in the 1990s, when the FPÖ made considerable inroads in both their constituencies. At the same time, both major parties also proved vulnerable to the Greens and, in the 1994–99 period, the Liberal Forum. Although the SPÖ and ÖVP have tried to defend their electoral territory against these competitors, they have given preference to the fight against the FPÖ, simply because this involves a larger share of the vote. The FPÖ first concentrated on winning disappointed ÖVP voters. These were easy victims after the formation of the grand coalition, when the FPÖ could portray the ÖVP as a traitor to the cause of non-socialist politics. In the early 1990s, however, the FPÖ concentrated its fire on the SPÖ, with the aim of winning over blue-collar workers.

The competition for votes has been linked to the parties' coalition strategies. Since Haider's election as FPÖ leader, the SPÖ has ruled out any coalition with the FPÖ. The ÖVP was less clear in this respect. Although leading politicians as a rule have stated conditions a coalition partner would need to meet, which made it unlikely that the ÖVP would actually opt for the FPÖ, it was only in 1994 that a coalition with the FPÖ was explicitly ruled out 'with no ifs or buts', as ÖVP leader Busek put it. The result of this election was disappointing and the ÖVP thereafter refrained from committing itself in terms of future coalitions before elections. This, in turn, was an electoral advantage for the SPÖ. Both in 1990 and particularly in 1995, it made the fight against this kind of coalition an important campaign item, which, according to voting studies, proved quite effective (Ogris 1996; Plasser and Ulram 1996a: 20; Plasser *et al.* 1995: 84).

Eventually, in 2000, the ÖVP did form a government with the FPÖ. This move caused national and international uproar because of the 'nature' of the FPÖ. Yet, in forging the coalition, the ÖVP may have been employing its last real chance to use its pivotal position in the government formation process – not only to improve its share of government offices, but also to position itself relatively favourably with regard to elections. The formation of the ÖVP–FPÖ government introduced a new round of party adaptation, with the SPÖ and FPÖ facing the greatest challenges. While the SPÖ, after three decades in government, was forced to adapt to the role of opposition, the FPÖ challenge was that of learning to govern. And all three parties needed to cope with the challenge of how to increase or maintain electoral support under fundamentally changed conditions.

As it turned out, the SPÖ found it very hard to learn its new trade of opposition. Plagued by financial and personnel problems and burdened with both its own government record and what it had been willing to give away as the price for remaining in government (in failed coalition negotiations with the ÖVP) it did not constitute a very effective challenge to the government. Indeed, its electoral gains after one term in opposition were modest and its 2002 electoral result was the third worst of the postwar period.

While the FPÖ initially did better in terms of public performance, government participation made what traditionally had counted as weakness, and what had then proved a source of strength, a weakness once again. Not being rooted either in any of the major interest groups or in the civil service, and not having built up much policy-making capacity, made the party often appear incompetent. It was also heavily dependent on help from its coalition partner (e.g. for staffing the private offices of ministers and reviewing draft legislation). None of this matched well the inflated demands the FPÖ had created in building its negative electoral alliance. This raised the question of strategy: to what extent should the FPÖ aim at abandoning its heritage as populist opposition and try to become a responsible government party? Gradually the government team (including the formal party leader) and Haider began to differ about the answer to this question, and in the end the issue of leadership itself was at stake. This led to the resignation of the FPÖ leader and of the most prominent government members and, to the dismay of the FPÖ, Chancellor Schüssel called early elections. Ironically, the problem of having to choose between different strategies and different leaders caused the FPÖ to stumble into the 2002 elections without either – that is, without either a clear strategy or a clear leader. These issues were not resolved when the FPÖ renewed its government contract with the ÖVP in 2003 (see also Luther 2003; Heinisch 2003).

Conclusion

Since the late 1970s Austrian parties have faced a rapid and substantial process of electoral dealignment. The traditional parties – the SPÖ, ÖVP, and FPÖ – differed dramatically in their ability to understand this process and respond to it. In this process the strength of the past has become a liability and traditional weaknesses have turned out to be advantages.

By any standards, the FPÖ in the mid-1980s was a weak party. With less than 5 percent of the vote (in 1983), a further decline in the polls, and a shrinking number of core voters, the FPÖ was in a seemingly hopeless situation in electoral terms. Nor could it rely on the support of any major interest group. The FPÖ was also weak organizationally, certainly by the standards established by its main competitors. All this in turn meant it had no or few constraints in adapting to the changing environment. The weakness of the party mass organization and apparatus allowed the party leader to be flexible, responsive, and effective, once it was established that he would be an electoral asset. Indeed there is hardly any aspect of the party that was not fundamentally changed in the post-1986 period. As we have seen, the new FPÖ strategy paid off electorally for more than a decade. A party that had already been on its deathbed achieved levels of electoral support that no one could have imagined in the mid-1980s. The FPÖ came close to the ÖVP and SPÖ in national and particularly in European elections and eventually won more votes than the ÖVP in 1999. It also assumed the position of the strongest party in one *Land* and the second-strongest party in two more *Länder* (out of a total of nine). In short, the FPÖ maximized the opportunities afforded to it by electoral dealignment. However, as the 2002 elections demonstrated, the new electoral alliance that it built proved only as solid as quicksand.

In contrast, the ÖVP and particularly the SPÖ have been strong parties by most indicators. Their organizational scope and their penetration of both the government apparatus and society have been at a record level among Western democracies. The SPÖ and ÖVP have also been closely linked to the country's main interest groups on whose support they have been able to rely. Most important, however, has been the traditional loyalty of the vast majority of voters to either the SPÖ or ÖVP. But while all of these elements reinforced one another in a positive sense during the 'golden age' of 'two-party' politics in Austria, they have turned out since the 1980s to be constraints on the parties' capacities to adapt to a changing environment. The large number of party members and core voters constitute a clientele with vested interests that increasingly seem to conflict with those of the 'available' voters. The intra-party power structures make it hard to overcome these interests even if this would be electorally advantageous. Likewise, there is a strong bias in favour of the status quo when it comes to adapting the party organization to environmental changes. Intra-party groups and individual politicians are afraid of losing power, income, and comfort, and party activists have jealously defended the privileges of membership – after all, there seems little point in being a member if the party leadership blurs the distinction between members and non-members. Hence the SPÖ issue initiatives were resisted, the new party statute clause that allows the candidacy of non-members proved irrelevant in practice, and the primaries in both parties have become largely ineffective. In short, attempts to adapt have often been made too late, in a half-hearted way, and have not been credible. This has been reflected in the reform of the electoral law.

Until 2000, FPÖ success was largely contained in the electoral arena. While the party dramatically increased the number of its adherents who held elected office, it had been denied access to the most attractive political offices – those in the political executive. Quite simply, the FPÖ had not been seen as 'coalitionable' by other parties. The dramatic change that occurred in 2000 was partly the result of the FPÖ's attempt to become more respectable in the late 1990s, but partly also the result of ÖVP ambitions to realize more of its office, policy, and electoral goals. The ÖVP gamble was successful, at least in the short run.

As it turns out in the Austrian case, it is the relationships between political parties that can be identified as the most important factor in the parties' attempts to cope with the complexities and uncertainties of the electoral market. While the series of 'grand coalition' governments – apparently without a politically viable alternative – allowed the FPÖ to harvest frustrated voters with quite different motivations, the FPÖ's own participation in government triggered events that led to the collapse of this electoral alliance. Special circumstances, in turn, allowed the ÖVP to be the one that picked up the pieces. This is not to say, however, that other moves of the parties over the period covered here were irrelevant to this outcome. Clearly, the FPÖ could have been less effective (and perhaps more scrupulous) in approaching available voters, while the major parties might have been less hapless in their various attempts at adaptation. Yet, though facing different internal constraints, all parties have basically the same menu of choices. If, for instance, all parties hire external consultants, subject their politicians to intensive media training, and recruit unconventional candidates, one could expect that over time the effects would not vary dramatically from one party to another. In contrast, institutional manipulation and coalition politics allow changes in the structure of competition to be wrought in more discriminatory fashion, affecting various parties differently. But while institutional manipulation is often bound to fail for constitutional reasons, coalition politics is unique in that it critically shapes the roles of political parties in the party system. Although the roles of government and opposition certainly allow for variation and different interpretations, the basic script is already in place when the parties first begin to perform these roles.

Notes

1 The FPÖ has taken care, however, not to be 'too radical' and therefore endanger its claim to state party finance. Officially, the FPÖ has two names, its traditional one and 'Die Freiheitlichen'.

2 However, in 1999 the Liberal Forum fell out of parliament because it failed to win 4 percent of the votes while it would have survived as a parliamentary party under the old electoral system.

References

Betz, Hans Georg (1994). *Radical Right-Wing Populism in Western Europe*. New York: St Martin's Press.

Dachs, Herbert (1997). 'Parteiensysteme in den Bundesländern.' In Herbert Dachs *et al.* (eds), *Handbuch des politischen Systems Österreichs*. Vienna: Manz, pp. 877–94.

Heinisch, Reinhard (2003). 'Success in Opposition – Failure in Government: Explaining the Performance of Right-Wing Populist Parties in Public Office.' *West European Politics* 26 (3): 91–130.

Höbelt, Lothar (2003). *Defiant Populist. Jörg Haider and the Politics of Austria*. West Lafayette, IN: Purdue University Press.

Katz, Richard S. and Peter Mair (1995). 'Changing Models of Party Organization and Party Democracy: the Emergence of the Cartel Party.' *Party Politics* 1: 5–28.

Kirchheimer, Otto (1966). 'The Transformation of the Western European Party Systems.' In Joseph LaPalombara and Myron Weiner (eds), *Political Parties and Political Development*. Princeton: Princeton University Press, pp. 177–200.

Kitschelt, Herbert with Anthony J. McGann (1995). *The Radical Right in Western Europe*. Ann Arbor, MI: Michigan University Press.

Kräh, Gerd (1996). *Die Freiheitlichen unter Jörg Haider*. Frankfurt: Peter Lang.

Kukacka, Helmut (1984). 'Anpassung oder Abgrenzung? Anmerkungen zur "Grün-Strategie" der ÖVP.' *Österreichisches Jahrbuch für Politik*, 151–62.

Leitner, Lukas and Christian Mertens (1995). 'Die Vorwahlen der Österreichischen Volkspartei zur Nationalratswahl 1994: Analyse und Reformvorschläge.' In *Österreichisches Jahrbuch für Politik*, pp. 199–217.

Luther, Kurt Richard (1997). 'Die Freiheitlichen.' In Herbert Dachs *et al.* (eds), *Handbuch des politischen Systems Österreichs*. Vienna: Manz, pp. 286–303.

Luther, Kurt Richard (1999). 'Must What Goes Up Always Come Down?' In Kurt Richard Luther and Kris Deschouwer (eds), *Party Elites in Divided Societies*. London: Routledge, pp. 43–73.

Luther, Kurt Richard (2001). 'Parteistrategische Herausforderungen der Regierungsverant-wortung: Die FPÖ vor und nach ihrem Eintritt in die Bundesregierung.' In Ferdinand Karlhofer, Josef Melchior, and Hubert Sickinger (eds), *Anlassfall Österreich*. Baden-Baden: Nomos, pp. 69–88.

Luther, Kurt Richard (2003). 'The Self-Destruction of a Right-Wing Populist Party? The Austrian Parliamentary Elections of 2002.' *West European Politics* 26 (2): 136–52.

Mair, Peter (1997). *Party System Change*. Oxford: Oxford University Press.

Müller, Wolfgang C. (1990). 'Persönlichkeitswahl bei der Nationalratswahl 1990.' In *Österreichisches Jahrbuch für Politik*, pp. 261–82.

Müller, Wolfgang C. (1992). 'Austria (1945–1990).' In Richard S. Katz and Peter Mair (eds), *Party Organizations*. London: Sage, pp. 21–120.

Müller, Wolfgang C. (1993). 'After the "Golden Age": Research into Austrian Political Parties since the 1980s.' *European Journal of Political Research* 23: 439–63.

Müller, Wolfgang C. (1994). 'The Development of Austrian Party Organizations in the Postwar Period.' In Richard S. Katz and Peter Mair (eds), *How Parties Organize: Adaptation and Change in Party Organizations in Western Democracies*. London: Sage, pp. 51–79.

Müller, Wolfgang C. (1996a). 'Die Organisation der SPÖ, 1945–1995.' In Wolfgang Maderthaner and Wolfgang C. Müller (eds), *Die Organization der österreichischen Sozialdemokratie 1889–1995*. Vienna: Löcker, pp. 195–356.

Müller, Wolfgang C. (1996b). 'Political Parties.' In Volkmar Lauber (ed.), *Contemporary Austrian Politics*. Boulder, CO: Westview, pp. 59–102.

Müller, Wolfgang C. (1996c). 'Wahlsysteme und Parteiensystem in Österreich, 1945–1995.' In Fritz Plasser, Peter A. Ulram, and Günther Ogris (eds), *Wahlkampf und Wählerentscheidung. Analysen zur Nationalratswahl 1995*. Vienna: Signum, pp. 233–72.

Müller, Wolfgang C. (1997). 'Die Österreichische Volkspartei.' In Herbert Dachs *et al.* (eds), *Handbuch des politischen Systems Österreichs*. Vienna: Manz, pp. 265–85.

Müller, Wolfgang C. (1998). 'Party Competition and Plebiscitary Politics in Austria.' *Electoral Studies* 17: 21–43.

Müller, Wolfgang C. (1999). 'Plebiscitary Agenda-Setting and Party Strategies.' *Party Politics* 5: 305–17.

Müller, Wolfgang C. (2002). 'Evil or the "Engine of Democracy"? Populism and Party Competition in Austria.' In Yves Mény and Yves Surel (eds), *Populism in Western Democracies*. Houndmills: Palgrave-Macmillan, pp. 155–75.

Müller, Wolfgang C. and Barbara Steininger, (1994). 'Party Organization and Party Competitiveness: the Case of the Austrian People's Party.' *European Journal of Political Research* 26: 1–29.

Müller, Wolfgang C. and Christian Scheucher (1995). 'Persönlichkeitswahl bei der Nationalratswahl 1994.' In *Österreichisches Jahrbuch für Politik*, pp. 171–97.

Müller, Wolfgang C. and Delia Meth-Cohn (1991). 'The Selection of Party Chairmen in Austria: a Study of Intra-Party Decision-Making.' *European Journal of Political Research* 20: 39–61.

Müller, Wolfgang C. and Fritz Plasser (1992). 'Austria: the 1990 Campaign.' In Shoun Bowler and David Farrell (eds), *Electoral Strategies and Political Marketing*. London: Macmillan, pp. 24–42.

Müller, Wolfgang C. and Kaare Strøm (2000). 'Conclusion: Coalition Governance in Western Europe.' In Wolfgang C. Müller and Kaare Strøm (eds), *Coalition Governments in Western Europe*. Oxford: Oxford University Press, pp. 559–92.

Müller, Wolfgang C., Marcelo Jenny, Barbara Steininger, Martin Dolezal, Wilfried Philipp, and Sabine Preisl-Westphal (2001). *Die österreichischen Abgeordneten*. Vienna: WUV Universitätsverlag.

Nick, Rainer (1995). 'Die Wahl vor der Wahl: Kandidatennominierung und Vorwahlen.' In Wolfgang C. Müller, Fritz Plasser, and Peter A. Ulram (eds), *Wählerverhalten und Parteienwettbewerb. Analysen zur Nationalratswahl 1994*. Vienna: Signum, pp. 67–117.

Ogris, Günther (1990). 'Ebenbild oder Kontrastprogramm.' In *Österreichisches Jahrbuch für Politik*, pp. 151–70.

Ogris, Günther (1996). 'Kampagne-Effekte: eine Analyse von Panel-Daten aus dem Wahlkampf 1995.' In Fritz Plasser, Peter A. Ulram, and Günther Ogris (eds), *Wahlkampf und Wählerentscheidung. Analysen zur Nationalratswahl 1995*. Vienna: Signum, pp. 119–53.

Plasser, Fritz (2000). 'Medienzentrierte Politik: Die "Amerikanisierung" des politischen Wettbewerbs in Österreich.' In Anton Pelinka, Fritz Plasser, and Wolfgang Meixner (eds), *Die Zukunft der österreichischen Demokratie*. Vienna: Signum, pp. 203–30.

Plasser, Fritz, Gilg Seeber, and Peter A. Ulram (2000). 'Breaking the Mold: Politische Wettbewerbsräume und Wahlverhalten Ende der neunziger Jahre.' In Fritz Plasser, Peter A. Ulram, and Franz Sommer (eds), *Das österreichische Wahlverhalten*. Vienna: Signum, pp. 55–115.

Plasser, Fritz and Peter A. Ulram (1993). 'Politisch-kultureller Wandel in Österreich.' In Fritz Plasser and Peter A. Ulram (eds), *Staatsbürger oder Untertanen? Politische Kultur Deutschlands, Österreichs und der Schweiz im Vergleich*. Frankfurt: Lang, pp. 103–56.

Plasser, Fritz and Peter A. Ulram (1995). 'Wandel der politischen Konfliktdynamik. Radikaler Rechtspopulismus in Österreich.' In Wolfgang C. Müller, Fritz Plasser, and Peter A. Ulram (eds), *Wählerverhalten und Parteienwettbewerb. Analysen zur Nationalratswahl 1994*. Vienna: Signum, pp. 471–503.

Plasser, Fritz and Peter A. Ulram (1996a). 'Kampagnedynamik: Strategischer und thematischer Kontext der Wählerentscheidung.' In Fritz Plasser, Peter A. Ulram, and Günther Ogris (eds), *Wahlkampf und Wählerentscheidung. Analysen zur Nationalratswahl 1995*. Vienna: Signum, pp. 13–46.

Plasser, Fritz and Peter A. Ulram (1996b). 'Akzeptanz und Unterstützung sozialpartner-schaftlicher Interessenvertretung in Österreich.' In Anton Pelinka and Christian Smekal (eds), *Kammern auf dem Prüfstand*. Vienna: Signum, pp. 75–109.

Plasser, Fritz and Peter A. Ulram (2002). *Das österreichische Politikverständnis. Von der Konsens- zur Konfliktkultur?* Vienna: WUV Universitätsverlag.

Plasser, Fritz and Peter A. Ulram (eds) (2003). *Wahlverhalten in Bewegung. Analysen zur Nationalratswahl 2002*. Vienna: WUV Universitätsverlag.

Plasser, Fritz, Peter A. Ulram, and Franz Sommer (1995). 'Restabilisierung der Traditionsparteien oder nur scheinbare Konsolidierung?' In *Österreichisches Jahrbuch für Politik*, pp. 73–102.

Plasser, Fritz, Peter A. Ulram, and Günther Ogris (eds) (1996). *Wahlkampf und Wählerentscheidung. Analysen zur Nationalratswahl 1995*. Vienna: Signum.

Reiter, Erich (1994). 'Zur Entwicklung der FPÖ vor und nach der EU-Volksabstimmung.' In *Österreichisches Jahrbuch für Politik*, pp. 427–53.

Schattschneider, E. E. (1960). *The Semisovereign People*. New York: Holt, Rinehart and Winston.

Sickinger, Hubert (1997). *Politikfinanzierung in Österreich*. Thaur: Kulturverlag.

Traar, Kurt and Franz Birk (1987). 'Der durchleuchtete Wähler – in den achtziger Jahren.' *Journal für Sozialforschung* 27 (1).

Ulram, Peter A. (1990). *Hegemonie und Erosion: Politische Kultur und politischer Wandel in Österreich*. Vienna: Böhlau.

Volst, Angelika and Irmtraud Voglmayr (1998). *Politik Online. Der Umgang der Parteien mit dem Internet*. Krems: Donau-Universität Krems.

SEVEN   Political Parties and Their Reactions to the Erosion of Voter Loyalty in Belgium: Caught in a Trap

Kris Deschouwer

The desperate search for the wandering Belgian voter is not a new story. Electoral stability came to an end in 1965. Since that date the political parties, the party system and the political institutions have gone through dramatic changes. These changes are still going on. The debate about change and renewal of both parties and political institutions continues. Parties change their internal rules, try to change the logic of the party system, and try to develop new procedures of policy-making, to produce new policies, and to give new answers to new questions. The period of high volatility started in the 1960s, but especially since the 1990s a frantic search for change and renewal can be witnessed. Of the thirteen parties that were represented in parliament in 1991, six have adopted a new name. One has divided into two parties, one has simply disappeared, and one became part of a larger fusion party.

The Belgian parties mostly claim to understand the logic of the volatile voter. When they introduce change, they do so in a very confident way. But they undo the change a few years later with exactly the same level of confidence. In reality, the parties do not really know what to do. Their activities look very much like a strategy of trial and error. Their behaviour is that of a wounded animal, caught in a painful trap.

This chapter will try to make sense of this. It will try to produce a historical and analytical insight into the rather complex story of party politics in Belgium. It should make clear why it is indeed extremely difficult for the parties to communicate one single message or to move into the one and only winning direction. The Belgian story is one of increasing complexity, increasing fractionalization and decreasing legitimacy (Deschouwer 1998a, 1998b, 2002b; Elchardus and Derks 1996), and is also therefore a never-ending nightmare for the political parties. If they could, they would simply choose a new country (which they actually already have).

Electoral dealignment since the 1960s

Between the introduction of universal (male) suffrage in 1918 and the general election of 1961 – the last election before the 1965 earthquake – Belgium had a very stable and predictable party system. There were two major parties – the Catholics (Christian Democrats after 1945) and the Socialists – and a smaller Liberal Party. Two major cleavages had given birth to these three parties: Church versus State and Labour versus Capital (Van Haegendoren 1967). A third cleavage had however been politicized after the First World War (McRae 1987). A Flemish movement demanded a reform of the state that should do away with the linguistic domination of the French-speaking minority in Belgium and of the French-speaking elites in the Dutch-speaking northern part of the country (the area which is now called Flanders). The demographic and later also the economic weight of the north produced a reaction on the Francophone side, that also then defended the idea of having autonomous institutions to avoid being dominated within a Belgian unitary sturcture.

The 1965 elections were a real surprise. In 1961 the three traditional parties still controlled 91 percent of the votes: almost 42 percent for the Christian Democrats, 37 percent for the Socialists and 12 percent for the Liberals. In 1965 they polled 83 percent together. The Christian Democrats decreased from 42 to 34 percent, the Socialists from 37 to 28 and the Liberals went up from 12 to 22. This was only the beginning of a long period of change. Table 7.1 gives an overview of the electoral results between 1961 and 2003.

The figures in Table 7.1 show very clearly how things have changed dramatically. In particular, the evolution of the Christian Democrats is quite spectacular, but the Socialists have also known better times. The winners of the 1960s and 1970s are undoubtedly the regionalist movements, which reached their height in 1971. They had a very clear message: reform the unitary state into a federation that takes into account the drive towards autonomy from both the Flemish and the Walloon sides. At first sight this is an unambiguous message, to which the other traditional parties could easily respond. That was indeed what happened, and from 1974 on the votes for these new parties started dropping, and a substantial number of voters found their way back to the three traditional families.

The parties have responded to this regionalist challenge a bit awkwardly. In fact, they were unable to respond without dying (Deschouwer 1994a, 1996). None of the three traditional parties has been able to keep under control the regionalist cleavage that cut across them. The Christian Democrats fell apart in 1968, the Liberals in 1971 and the Socialists in 1978. Knowing this, the figures in Table 7.1 lose a lot of their meaning. They give electoral results for the country as a whole, while the parties no longer compete in the country as a whole. The regionalist tension has divided the parties, and therefore also the electoral party system. The Dutch-speaking parties only field candidates in the northern region called Flanders (and in the bilingual region of Brussels), while the Francophone parties only field candidates in the southern region called Wallonia (and in

Table 7.1 Electoral results in Belgium, 1961–2003

	1961	1965	1968	1971	1974	1977	1978	1981	1985	1987	1991	1995	1999	2003
CVP–PSC	42.3	34.8												
CVP (CD&V)			22.3	21.9	23.3	26.2	26.1	19.7	21.3	19.5	16.8	17.2	14.1	13.3
PSC (CDH)			9.4	9.0	9.1	9.8	10.1	6.7	8.0	8.0	7.7	7.7	5.9	5.5
BSP–PSB	36.7	28.2	28.0	27.2	26.7	27.1								
SP (SPa)							12.4	12.6	14.5	14.9	12.0	12.6	9.6	14.9
PS							13.0	12.6	13.8	15.7	13.5	11.9	10.1	13.0
PVV–PLP	12.3	21.6	20.9	16.5										
VLD					9.6	8.5	10.3	13.1	10.7	11.5	12.0	13.2	14.3	15.4
PRL (MR)					5.6	7.0	6.0	8.2	10.2	9.4	8.1	10.3	10.1	11.4
KPB–PCB	3.1	4.6	3.3	3.1	3.2	2.1	3.3	2.3	1.2	0.8	0.1	0.1	–	–
VU (N-VA)	3.5	6.4	9.8	11.1	10.2	10.0	7.0	9.9	8.0	8.0	5.9	4.7	5.6	3.1
FDF		1.3	2.5	4.5	5.1	4.3	4.2	2.5	1.2	1.2	1.5	–	–	–
RW		1.1	3.5	6.7	5.9	3.0	2.9	1.7	0.2	0.2	0.1	–	–	–
AGALEV (GROEN!)								2.3	3.7	4.5	4.9	4.4	7.0	2.5
ECOLO								2.2	2.5	2.6	5.1	4.0	7.3	3.1
VL. BLOK							1.4	1.1	1.4	1.9	6.6	7.8	9.9	11.6
FN											0.5	2.3	1.5	2.0
RAD-UDRT							0.9	2.7	1.1					
Rossem											3.2			
Others	2.1	2.1	0.3	0.0	1.3	2.0	2.4	2.4	2.2	1.7	2.0	3.8	4.6	4.2
Total	100.0	100.0	100.0	100.0	100.0	100.0	100.0	100.0	100.0	100.0	100.0	100.0	100.0	100.0
Turnout	92.3	91.6	90.0	91.5	90.3	95.1	94.8	94.6	93.6	93.4	92.7	91.2	90.7	91.6
Electorate	6036	6092	6170	6271	6322	6316	6366	6878	7001	7039	7144	7199	7343	7570
Fractionalization	0.67	0.75	0.81	0.82	0.84	0.82	0.87	0.89	0.88	0.88	0.90	0.89	0.90	0.86
Effective number of parties	3.1	3.9	5.2	5.6	6.1	5.6	7.4	8.9	8.1	8.1	9.8	9.3	9.8	6.5
Total volatility	4.8	16.1	7.1	6.5	3.5	6.1	6.0	14.4	10.0	4.5	12.2	7.7	10.8	12.8

For full details of party names and party families see Table 7.5, p. 201.

Brussels). This has far-reaching consequences for the topic of party responses to the electorate: the political parties in Belgium compete in two separate electoral arenas, and the story for each of these arenas is different, because the circumstances of the parties, and their perceptions, are also different.

Before the creation of the federal state (realized by a series of major constitutional reforms in 1970, 1980, 1988, 1993 and 2002), the parties were already acting within this logic of a double party system. To cut a long (and complicated) story short, we take a look at the electoral evolution by region in Tables 7.2 and 7.3, and add a few measurements of the party system by region in Table 7.4. The figures reveal different pictures for each part of the country. And since the parties compete in only one of these regions, their perceptions of the evolution and their eventual strategic reactions to it will be different.

The dominant party in Flanders has for a very long time been the Christian-Democratic CVP. Its dominance in Flanders used to be stronger than the dominance of the Socialists in Wallonia (CVP polled close to 60 percent of the votes in Flanders in 1950), but has declined rapidly. While the Francophone Socialist Party remains the strongest in Wallonia, the Flemish party landscape has become much more fragmented, with the Liberal Party being number one since the 1999 elections. Flanders still has a regionalist party, and also a right-wing extremist party, pleading for the full independence of Flanders. In Wallonia the landscape is less fragmented. The high scores of the Greens are striking, even after the major defeat of 2003. There is also one major trend common to both party systems: the gradual growth of the Liberal parties.

The problem of erosion of voter loyalty has been perceived and felt more and earlier by the parties in Flanders. The results of 1965 were dramatic on both sides (and the Belgian parties still existed at that time), but the elections of 1981 and 1991 were primarily critical in Flanders and led to a debate on political changes in Flanders alone. With the breakthrough of right-wing extremism, the 1991 elections were especially perceived as a major warning that things had to change. A number of corruption scandals hitting the Walloon Socialists in 1995, and the Dutroux case[1] in 1996 subsequently led to much more mobilization and loss of legitimacy in the Francophone part of the country. The 1999 elections showed a further decline of the Francophone Socialists, with the Liberals slowly closing the gap and the Greens taking third place. Since 1999 the search for change and renewal is also very central to the Francophone party system.

There does remain a difference though between the two parts of the country. The 1999 elections were not only critical because they changed the balance of power. They also led to the formation of a completely new type of government coalition including Liberals, Socialists and Greens of both language groups. The coalition was called 'purple-green' in Flanders and 'rainbow' in Francophone Belgium. This coalition change was more important for Flanders, since it meant the end of the dominance of the Christian Democrats. In the south the Socialists kept their leading position and remained solidly in power at all levels.

Table 7.2 Electoral results (federal elections) in the Region of Flanders since 1961

	1961	1965	1968	1971	1974	1977	1978	1981	1985	1987	1991	1995	1999	2003
CVP (CDdV)	50.9	43.8	39.1	37.8	39.7	43.8	43.5	32.3	34.6	31.4	27.0	27.8	22.2	21.3
SP (SPa)	29.7	24.6	25.7	24.2	22.0	22.3	20.9	20.6	23.7	24.2	19.6	20.3	15.0	23.9
VLD	11.6	16.6	16.2	16.3	17.2	14.4	17.2	21.1	17.4	18.5	19.1	21.1	22.6	24.6
VU (N-VA)	6.0	11.3	16.9	18.8	17.8	16.3	11.5	16.0	12.7	12.9	9.4	9.0	8.8	4.9
Agalev (GROEN!)								3.9	6.1	7.3	7.9	7.0	11.0	3.9
Vlaams Blok							2.1	1.8	2.2	3.0	10.4	12.7	15.3	18.1

Table 7.3 Electoral results (federal elections) in the Region of Wallonia since 1961

	1961	1965	1968	1971	1974	1977	1978	1981	1985	1987	1991	1995	1999	2003
PS	47.0	35.7	34.5	34.4	36.8	37.2	36.7	36.2	39.5	43.9	39.2	33.7	29.0	36.4
PSC (CDH)	30.5	23.7	20.9	20.5	22.6	25.8	26.9	19.6	22.6	23.2	22.5	22.5	16.7	15.4
PRL (MR)	11.7	25.5	26.7	17.7	15.1	18.8	17.5	21.7	24.1	22.2	19.8	23.9	24.5	28.4
PCB	6.3	10.5	6.9	5.8	5.7	5.4	5.9	4.2	2.5	1.6	0.3	1.0	1.0	
RW	0.2	3.4	10.5	20.9	18.5	9.0	9.2	7.1	0.6	0.8	1.2			
Ecolo						0.5	1.2	6.1	6.2	6.5	13.5	10.3	18.2	7.5
Extreme Right											2.4	6.4	5.0	5.6

Table 7.4 Characteristics of the Walloon and Flemish party systems since 1961

	Three[a]		Two[b]		Gap[c]		Frac[d]	
	FL	WL	FL	WL	FL	WL	FL	WL
1961	92.2	89.2	80.6	77.5	21.2	16.5	0.64	0.67
1965	85.0	84.9	68.4	61.2	19.2	10.2	0.71	0.74
1968	81.0	84.9	64.8	61.2	13.4	7.8	0.73	0.75
1971	78.3	75.4	62.0	54.9	13.6	13.9	0.74	0.76
1974	78.9	74.5	61.7	59.4	17.7	14.2	0.73	0.75
1977	80.5	81.8	66.1	63.0	20.8	11.4	0.71	0.75
1978	81.6	81.1	64.4	63.6	22.6	9.8	0.72	0.75
1981	74.0	77.5	52.9	57.9	11.7	14.5	0.78	0.77
1985	75.7	86.2	58.3	63.9	10.9	15.9	0.77	0.73
1987	74.1	81.3	55.6	67.1	7.2	20.7	0.79	0.70
1991	65.7	81.5	46.6	61.7	7.4	16.7	0.82	0.74
1995	69.2	80.1	48.9	57.6	6.7	9.8	0.81	0.76
1999	59.6	70.2	44.8	53.5	0.4	5.5	0.83	0.79
2003	69.8	80.2	48.5	64.8	0.7	8.0	0.80	0.75

[a]The sum of the three traditional parties.
[b]The sum of the two major parties.
[c]The gap between first and second party.
[d]Fractionalization in the electorate.

The first wave of change in the 1960s was clearly marked by the breakthrough of the regionalist parties. Both in Flanders and in Wallonia they gained up to 20 percent of the votes. In the region of Brussels – where all the parties compete – a Francophone autonomist party even polled 40 percent of the votes. The background and history of the regionalist tensions in Belgium is too long to be dealt with here (for more details see McRae 1987; Murphy 1995; Van Dyck 1996). For our purpose we can simply state that the electoral pressure produced by these new parties led to a gradual but far-reaching reform of the state. The unitary Belgian state has become a federation of two linguistic communities (the Dutch-speaking and the French-speaking) and of three regions (Francophone Wallonia, Dutch-speaking Flanders and bilingual Brussels). As a response to erosion of voter loyalty, this is quite a dramatic change.

At first no electoral majority wanted to go that far, but electoral pressure was of course very strong. Even if the 20 percent for the regionalist parties is very far from a majority, it was a real threat to the existing parties. The threat was however more fundamental and more structural than the mere electoral figures show. It is the falling apart of the old parties, which was the result of the appearance on the agenda of linguistic and regionalist tensions, that made the pressure even stronger. Without national political parties, there were no longer any moderating forces, and the debate on possible state reform became extremely centrifugal. It was not only the presence of relatively successful regionalist parties on each side that made pressure rise, but the fact that electoral competition on the issue became a competition between radicals and moderates of the same side (Deschouwer 1994b). On the electoral scene, even the moderate parties tended to overreact, and then had to negotiate with the parties of the other side under this (perceived) high pressure. In the end this made the new regionalist parties extremely successful. There are not too many parties that have been able, like the Belgian regionalist parties, to almost realize a radical programme on the reform of state institutions.

The pressure was (and still is) higher on the Flemish side. The Walloon Socialist Party took over the regionalist demands, and was able to completely absorb the Walloon regionalist movement. This movement was originally a leftist one, with a strong trade unionist flavour. It defended the idea of Walloon regional autonomy in order to be able to conduct an autonomous (i.e. more leftist) economic policy. When the Socialist Party split, the Walloon wing could easily follow that line. The Socialist Party in Wallonia was thus able to recover from the regionalist storm and to come back as the one and only dominant party in the south of the country.

On the Flemish side this strategy of incorporation did not pay off. The Flemish regionalist party entered the Belgian government in 1978, which immediately led to the creation of a new and radical nationalist party (the Vlaams Blok), and to protest by the many social and cultural organizations belonging to the broad 'Flemish movement'. After twice having been in the national government and twice in the Flemish regional government, the Flemish nationalist party Volksunie has fallen apart in 2002 (see also p. 196 below). The more radical party Vlaams Blok, which is now also a classical new right-wing party (anti-establishment and anti-immigration), polls a solid 18 percent. Flemish parties thus constantly feel this regionalist pressure and all of them therefore tend to defend the claims for more autonomy and extended financial means for the region. Election surveys show that the demand for greater Flemish autonomy is very low among the population, but politically it remains present and visible (Maddens *et al.* 1994).

The effects of the first wave of dealignment, related to the regionalist tensions, are still visible in the Belgian party system(s). After this first wave of the 1960s and 1970s, the system kept on changing in the 1980s and 1990s. In 1981 two Green parties gained representation: Agalev and Ecolo. These are not competing parties: each simply emerged within one of the two now-separated Belgian party systems. Since they are not the product of a party split, the two Green parties manage to work fairly closely together. They form a single group in the federal Parliament. The Flemish Green Party, Agalev, polls fairly 'normal' scores: between 5 and 10 percent, with a maximum of 11 percent in 1999 (but a meagre 4 percent in 2003). While these Green voters and militants came primarily from a Christian Democratic background, the Flemish Socialist party felt the need to react and to try to win them over. It has been trying since the late 1980s to present itself as a 'Red–Green' party, without much success.

The electoral results of the Francophone Greens of Ecolo are much more impressive, and indeed fairly high if one compares them with the scores of other Green parties in Europe. As early as 1999 Ecolo had climbed to an impressive 13.5 percent. While in Flanders the right-wing extremist party suddenly broke through, the protest votes in the Francophone part were mobilized and channelled by Ecolo. The reactions were totally different. In Flanders the election day was labelled 'Black Sunday' and it marked the beginning of a search for remedies against the further growth of right-wing extremism. In the south the gains of Ecolo were not perceived as dangerous or problematic. Its result in 1995 was a bit lower, but the best days of the party would come after 1995. When the Francophone Socialists appeared to be involved in financial scandals (accepting bribes from the Italian helicopter manufacturer Agusta), and especially when the shock of the Dutroux case confronted Belgian politics and politicians with high levels of distrust, Ecolo was again able to provide an outlet for the protest movement. In September 1996 some 300,000 people participated in the so-called 'White March', organized by the parents of the children who had been kidnapped and abused by Dutroux. While Flemish parents either tried to form a new political party or joined left-wing extremist parties, the Francophone parents openly declared their support for Ecolo, which was perceived as the only real non-system party, and therefore as the only party that could not be held responsible for the malfunctioning of the Belgian institutions and administration. Ecolo's score in 1999 was a fairly spectacular 18 percent, making it larger than the Christian Democrats in the south. Since the Socialists also lost quite heavily in 1999 – losing votes to Ecolo – the greening of the electorate confronted the traditional parties with the fundamental question of what to do to avoid further decline.

The enduring effects of the debates on regionalization and the more recent waves of Green and right-wing extremist success have thus created pressure on the older parties. They are confronted with a diminishing electorate and with the challenge of finding a response to these gradual but, in the long run, fairly dramatic changes. Before analysing the ways in which the parties have tried to react, we need to take a better look at the functioning of the new and federal Belgian institutions. The absence of federal parties in a federal country is indeed responsible for another type of pressure and challenges, to which it is not at all easy to respond.

A federal state without federal parties

The new federal Belgian state functions without Belgian federal parties (Deschouwer 1997). The parties first fell apart and consequently adapted the state. This reaction (or maybe overreaction) is now causing new problems for the legitimacy of Belgian institutions, which in turn influences trust in the parties. In the electoral arena there are two different party systems, but after the elections the parties of both sides have to come together to form a federal Belgian government. That is a constitutional obligation (which prevents in fact the Flemish majority from governing alone). But this obligation makes it very difficult to form a government that shows responsiveness to what happened at the polls.

First there are the different power relations in the two major regions. The Francophone Socialists are so strong in their own region that it is very difficult to form a federal government without them. Yet in Flanders the largest party has until 1999 always been the Christian Democratic Party, a party that held the second (and between 1999 and 2003 even the fourth) rank in Wallonia. This means that there has always been a normal, almost natural federal coalition: Christian Democrats and Socialists of both language groups, whatever the election result. This coalition has indeed often been formed (most recently between 1987 and 1999), and its very existence and persistence is one possible explanation for the lack of trust in the system, which can be vented by voting for other than these two large traditional families. A way to respond to this kind of defection is not easy to find. The two major party families were trapped in their dominating position.

Especially for the Flemish Christian Democrats this was a problem. Their domination in Flanders was less clear, but on the Belgian level they were clearly the largest party, because the Francophone population is smaller. The Flemish Christian Democrats have often been blamed for succumbing to the pressure of the 'red enemy' in the south, and they have paid for that at the polls. If they were more responsive to their own Flemish voters, they would eventually form another government or let other parties form a government. They could either blow up the Belgian system (which would make them lose a lot of power) or keep it alive (for which they were easily blamed in Flanders). Here is a textbook example of a dilemma.

Another problem is the fact that it is hardly possible to take into consideration the electoral changes when a new government is formed, since these fluctuations are not necessarily the same in both party systems. If one party wins votes in one region, the party of the same family might not win, or might even lose, votes in the other region. Government formation then does not (cannot) take into account short-term electoral changes. And this leads to erosion of the legitimacy of the system and eventually to more votes for alternative parties. It is not easy to find a strategy to respond to this kind of erosion of loyalty.

At first sight the easiest solution seems to be the decision to focus more on regional politics. At that level, the obligation to take the results of the other side into consideration is gone. After the reform of the state, leading to the now far-reaching autonomy of the regions and communities, this is a feasible and attractive strategy. There are however two drawbacks. The first is the lack of visibility of regional politics. As all parties are only regional, the same parties govern at the two levels, and they often transfer their political personnel from one level to the other (Deschouwer 2000). The normal multi-level game of party politics in federal states is absent. The regional parties make the two levels collapse into one very opaque power game.

The second problem is also related to the fact that the Belgian parties have to govern at two levels. So far the best way to keep this more or less under control has been the formation of so-called 'congruent' coalitions (the same coalition at all levels), and of 'symmetric' coalitions (keeping the parties of the same family together in or outside of government). The 1999 elections were both federal and regional elections, and produced a coalition of Liberals, Socialists and Greens. The combination of Liberals and Socialists held a majority in the Walloon region, but not at the federal level. At the federal level, the Greens were needed for a winning coalition without the Christian Democrats. In Flanders, where a coalition including the Christian Democrats would have been more comfortable, four parties were needed to exclude them: Liberals, Socialists, Greens and Volksunie. The last partner was a rather unreliable one, not only because it was a federal opposition party (the congruence was not complete), but also because the party was very divided. The bottom line is that Flanders got a complex and rather leftist government, while a more solid and more conservative coalition would have been possible. The latter would have disturbed the congruence with the federal level and with the Walloon region, however. The crucial point is that in the absence of federal parties coalition-making in the regions needs to be done simultaneously in all regions *and* at the federal level. If a party would only govern at one level, its coalition partner would be its opponent at the other level. The lesser of two evils is congruence and symmetry. The Belgian parties are not only caught in a trap, they seem to be painfully torn between two levels.

Until 1999 regional elections (held for the first time in 1995) and federal elections were held on the same day, allowing the parties to form all the coalitions in one major negotiation round. The 2003 elections were only federal, however, with the regional elections following in 2004. This marks the beginning of a new era, in which election results at one level can affect governments at the other level. In 2003 the Flemish Greens lost all their federal seats. The Greens are no longer needed at the federal level, but the Flemish Greens are absolutely necessary until 2004 for a majority without the Christian Democrats in the Flemish parliament. They remained – but extremely reluctantly – in the Flemish regional government. Elections at one level can thus easily lead to coalition changes at the other level, and that is a feature that will not add to the legitimacy of the Belgian political parties.

The parties in search of renewal

Christian Democrats, Socialists, Liberals, moderate Nationalists and Greens all tried to react to Black Sunday and later to the popular protest following the Dutroux case. They all tried to produce a response to the so-called 'warning of the voter'. Quite a bit of movement can be seen inside and between these parties. In this section we will discuss the changes that directly affect the political parties: adapting the party rules and internal organization, changing the name of the party, and trying to change the party landscape (Table 7.5).

The 'warning of the voter' has to a very large extent been interpreted as a request to change the internal functioning of the parties. The voter is perceived as wanting the parties to be real and open membership movements. This is a quite surprising interpretation. The 'winning' parties of the 1991 elections – Vlaams Blok and Rossem – were not and are not examples of that type of party. And the Greens did not score extremely well. Yet there are a number of possible and plausible explanations for this fixation on the inside of the party. The first is the most obvious: changing the party itself is fairly easy. The party's own internal rules are something that it can control completely and change at very short notice. Internal rules are an obvious target for a party that feels the pressure to show that it has received and understood the message, that it really wants to make a number of things change and that it wants to do it fast.

A second explanation refers to the fact that parties in general are indeed truly concerned about their internal organization. They constantly face the choice between efficient and centralized leadership on the one hand and open demo-cratic participation on the other. Especially since the rise and success of new social movements and new-politics parties, the awareness of this choice has risen. A perception of failure will therefore easily be seen as a request to move away from the old forms and to try more of the new forms, even if objective analysis shows that these new forms are not necessarily electorally profitable.

A third explanation refers to the dominant type of party organization in Belgium. The Belgian parties can be considered to be close to the ideal type of the mass party, especially the Christian Democrats and the Socialists (Deschouwer 1994b). These parties are the central pillar of a network of organi-zations, linked both to the party and to the state. This type of party is a logical type in a very consociational style of decision-making, which constantly rein-forces the pillarized network and the importance of its party (Deschouwer 1994c, 1998b; Dewachter 1987). The Belgian parties can be considered as securely locked into this old mass party type. They have not felt a lot of pres-sure to leave it. Even electoral decline did not cause pressure. The divided party system helps to explain this, as does the very fact that in a consociational system the amount of power and control exerted by a party is not directly a function of its electoral strength. This feature is being fiercely attacked by – among others – the new right-wing parties. In the 1960s and 1970s the regionalist parties also criticized the pillarization and the closed or cartelized procedures of decision-making, but this message was less clear (or less well understood and less taken into account) than their demands for a reform of the state structures. The Greens later blamed and still blame the traditional parties for the way they are locked into the state through their ancillary organizations, and therefore allow their internal decision-making to be led too much by these organizations and not enough by their individual members. The criticism is old enough to make the parties realize that changing something in this respect might be a successful answer to their loss of voters. It refers both to the internal party organi-zations and to the procedures of decision-making.

The parties thus believe that they have to change the way they function, and that is exactly what they do. The main direction of the changes is very obvious and clear: they try to rethink the way the party leadership is linked to the members. The results of this rethinking are also obvious and clear (and certainly not typically Belgian): the relations become more direct, leaving out a number of intermediary stages. Members receive the right to participate directly at the party congresses and can vote directly for the party leadership. Intermediate organs like party councils disappear or are linked to local rather than to constituency organs.

One other way to answer the perceived demand for change and renewal has been the introduction of new faces. All the parties try to attract new participants, not as ordinary members, but as potential candidates for the party. People have to be attracted back to politics (since voting for Vlaams Blok or Rossem was believed to be a move away from politics). These new faces must be potential winners of elections, and so have to be popular before they come to politics. The parties actively solicit journalists, actors, singers, TV personalities, writers, museum directors, fashion models, soccer players and others. Some of them have even been elected, which shows that the strategy pays.

This new form of recruitment is again sidelining the intermediate levels of the party organization. In order to attain a mandate for the party, one does not have to be an active militant at the lower levels any more. One enters through the main door, on the invitation of the central leadership. The effect of this style of recruitment on the motivation of the active militants who expect something substantial in return for their commitment remains to be seen.

Belgian parties also attempt to change the landscape, to change the party systems. They perceive fractionalization – especially on the Flemish side – as a real problem. They feel that there are too many parties (Huyse *et al.* 1992). This is disturbing for a number of different reasons. The first one is governability. At the Belgian level for most of the time it is impossible to form a winning coalition with fewer than five parties. Compromising and going on compromising is the only solution. But the electorate does not necessarily appreciate this. One complaint that can often be heard is that the Belgian parties are far too compromise-oriented. They avoid the real debates; they always go for the muddy middle (Platel 1993). If there were fewer parties, the need to negotiate and to compromise would be reduced, and parties could have a much sharper profile to show to the voters. That is the first reason why many believe that a reduction in the number of parties would be a good thing. The second reason is the relations between the regions. The Flemish party system is more fragmented than the Walloon one, which makes the Walloon parties stronger at the federal level. The largest party in Flanders might one day even become really smaller (in absolute numbers) than the largest party in Wallonia, and that would give too much weight to the smaller part of the country. A third reason is of course that in a fragmented landscape everybody is bound to be smaller. Any party wanting to win more votes can sell its argument by appealing to the general wish for a less fragmented party system. There have been a number of serious attempts to reduce the numbers.

In the following sections we will describe the major movements and changes that have occurred in the Belgian parties along the lines discussed above. First we look at the Flemish parties, where the changes started in the early 1990s.

Then we look at the Francophone parties, where change and adaptation are more recent phenomena. All changes are summarized in Table 7.5.

The Flemish parties

As noted above, the general elections of 24 November 1991 were experienced as a shock. After a four-year coalition of Christian Democrats and Socialists (with the Flemish Volksunie also on board) these governing parties were heavily punished. The three traditional parties now controlled only 66 percent of the votes in Flanders, while they still had almost 82 percent in Wallonia. The major Flemish (and Belgian) party, the CVP, dropped to 27 percent of the Flemish votes, its poorest result ever and less than half that of the 1950s.

In Flanders the Christian Democrats thus hit rock bottom, and the same goes for the Socialists. The latter did not even reach 20 percent. The Liberal Party did not profit from these losses. Even the Greens did not achieve the expected wins. The clear winner was the right-wing extremist party Vlaams Blok, with a (then) astonishing 10 percent. On top of that came the 5 percent of a 'libertarian' non-party 'Rossem', led by the eccentric and (apparently) wealthy Jean-Pierre Van Rossem, who had been accused of fraud and racketeering (he was in prison on election day and was sentenced to five years in 1997). Fractionalization was up to a record figure of 0.82 (0.74 in Wallonia). Election surveys showed later that one third of the voters had changed their mind between 1987 and 1991. The election day was soon baptized 'Black Sunday' and an animated debate started on the real meaning of this 'warning of the voter' (Swyngedouw *et al.* 1993; Frognier and Van Vaerenbergh 1994).

Black Sunday introduced in Flanders the awareness that the voters had lost their loyalty. This is rather surprising, because a quick look at the figures shows immediately that this was far from a new phenomenon. Yet the *perception* of it was new, and therefore the reactions to it only started at this time. Why did perception lag behind the real evolution? The explanation is fairly easy, at least when one is familiar with the Belgian state structure and with the double party system. The CVP is a powerful party. Since 1958 it was always in government and (almost) always leading the government.[2] This position was originally based on its overwhelming electoral strength in Belgium and in Flanders. But while the electoral basis eroded, the party did not lose power. Being the first party in Flanders meant (given the demographic weight of Flanders) being the first party in Belgium. The party was certainly aware of the fact that it was losing voters, but it did not perceive this as something dramatic. Some elections – like those of 1974, 1977 and 1985 – were even perceived as victories, because the party improved its previous score (and of course was still without doubt the Belgian and Flemish number one).

Before the 1991 elections the party leadership had announced that 30 percent of the Flemish votes were to be considered an absolute minimal level for the CVP. The coalition (with the Socialists) between 1987 and 1991 had been a difficult one, and the party was expecting problems. The result was 27 percent, which immediately led to the announcement that the party would not govern this time. The CVP wanted to save its own soul instead of saving the country at, yet again, a high electoral price. Socialists and Liberals tried to form a government, but this attempt failed after a few days. The end of the story was that the CVP had to govern again, with the same Socialist partner (De Ridder 1993). But now the party was extremely aware of the fact that it had to do something to avoid facing the same kind of problems in 1995. The party started to think about 'change' and 'renewal'. It wanted to respond now to the erosion of voter loyalty, but as long as it remained in power, nothing spectacular happened.

The Liberals: from PVV to VLD

The most interesting things at that time happened in the Liberal Party. It was totally trapped in the Belgian system. Being second in Flanders, with its Francophone counterpart also being second in the south, the Liberal family was almost automatically excluded from government. Guy Verhofstadt, the leader of the Flemish Liberal Party, PVV, decided that it was time for a radical change. Before the 1991 elections he had already published his '*Burgermanifest*' (Citizen Manifesto), in which he defended a more direct democracy and fulminated against the pillarized logic of Belgian politics and especially against the strong position of the Flemish Christian Democrats. Since Christian Democrats and Socialists just went on governing after the 1991 elections, Verhofstadt started with a deep reform of his own party, trying to find the means to break Christian Democratic dominance in Flanders.

The PVV was renamed VLD (Flemish Liberals and Democrats) and its internal organization was totally changed. The two most striking new features were the direct election of the party president and of the complete party executive, and the termination of all formal relationships with auxiliary Liberal organizations. By introducing these, the VLD showed that it wanted to be a model of the citizen democracy that it defended for society in general. During the process of party renewal, the president of the Flemish nationalist Volksunie had created a 'Centre for Political Renewal' that finally joined the new VLD. A few office-holders of the Volksunie followed the former party leader, but the idea of bringing together Liberals and Flemish nationalists into one larger movement was not realized.

The party reform was intensively advertised, and the VLD was perceived as the one and only party that was really promoting change and renewal and that wanted to change the system in depth. Polls predicted a great future, but at the European elections of 1994 the results were disappointing: only 18 percent of the Flemish vote. The general elections of 1995 – at which the outgoing coalition of Christian Democrats and Socialists announced that they wanted to continue together – were once more a disappointment. The new VLD polled 21 percent, which was a bit more than in 1991 but left the party lagging far behind the Flemish Christian Democrats. It had to wait until 1999 before it could finally seize the number one position, and then mainly because the Christian Democrats lost heavily again.

Since 1999 the VLD has been the leading party of Flanders and of the federal coalition. But it has remained aware of the fact that its position is far from secure, and therefore has continued trying to expand its electoral base. This has been achieved mainly by attracting people from other parties. One former president of the Flemish Christian Democrats – Johan Van Hecke – created a movement called NCD (New Christian Democracy). First intended as a discussion group within the Christian Democratic party, it finally joined the VLD in 2002. This was the second former president of another party to join the VLD. When the Volksunie finally collapsed in 2001, a number of office-holders (including two more former party presidents) went to the VLD. The party thus went to the 2003 elections with the firm will to consolidate its number one position and to lead the coalition formation talks in the future. It polled a reassuring but not spectacular 24.6 percent of the Flemish vote.

Christian Democrats: from CVP to CD&V

The VLD's major challenger is the Christian Democratic Party, which in 1999 found itself in opposition for the first time in 40 years. Its gradual decline at the polls had finally led to its removal from power. The new opposition role was very difficult to play, especially with a Liberal-Socialist government putting itself right in the centre position that has always been defended by Christian Democracy. Earlier there had been some attempts to refresh party ideology, and to rethink its (very solid) relations with the organizations of the Christian pillar. The party adopted new statutes in 1993, allowing all the members to participate in the election of the president via postal ballot. The first to be elected that way was Johan Van Hecke in 1993. He is today a member of the VLD.

A more radical change was realized in 2001 and 2002. As the Liberals had done before, the Flemish Christian Democrats changed their name in an attempt to be perceived as a new or renewed party, and no longer as the old and permanently governing party of the past. CVP thus became CD&V: Christen-Democratisch en Vlaams (Christian Democratic and Flemish). There had been long discussions about whether to keep the 'C' referring to Christian in the party name. The decision was indeed to keep it. Whether this is a good choice remains to be seen. The party is very much a party of churchgoers. Yet this section of the population is rapidly declining, which explains (part of) the electoral losses of the Christian Democrats (Deschouwer 2002b). The 2003 results only confirmed the Christian Democratic decline.

The Socialists: from SP to SPa

After the 1991 elections the Flemish Socialist Party was unhappy, too. Not only had it recorded its worst ever result, but it became very clear that it had been the main provider of voters for the successful right-wing extremist Vlaams Blok. Losing votes was not a new experience: it had happened several times before, but without really bothering the party. Its power in the Belgian system is a result not of its electoral strength but of its link with the dominating Walloon Socialist Party. The dominance of Socialism in the Walloon party system has automatically made the Flemish Socialists a partner in the federal government. This was again the case after 1991, but the success of the Vlaams Blok was both ideologically and electorally so frightening that the party started to think about 'change' and 'renewal'. It wanted to respond now to the erosion of voter loyalty.

In 1992 the SP abolished its party council – the intermediate congress that met a few times per year – and replaced it with a council of branch presidents and secretaries. The idea was to create a body closer to the ordinary members. Yet the major effect (and goal) was a strong reduction in the power of the larger constituency units, meaning that the central party leadership now has more effective power. The selection of the party president was also changed. In 1993 the president was elected for the first time by secret vote of all the congress members. In 1996 the SP adopted direct election (postal ballot) of the president by members. In practice however, the party leadership makes it clear who its candidate is, and this candidate is never defeated. In 1999 a totally new type of party president was selected: the spin doctor of the party was presented to the members as the (single) candidate, and was indeed elected.

In Flanders the three major parties now use direct election of the party president, copying the initiative of the VLD. Yet the VLD has had some very contested elections, with at least two candidates, and therefore with sometimes devastating effects on internal party cohesion. The other two parties now use a more direct procedure, but make sure that in fact the party leadership takes care of the selection of the president. The procedural change does not mean a lot, except maybe the strengthening of the legitimacy of the president inside the party, but that is more a perverse than an intended effect of the change.

The new Socialist Party leader – having a marketing background – tried very hard to get the party out of the disastrous position in which it had found itself after the 1999 elections. The SP polled only 15 percent of the votes, a little less than the right-wing extremist Vlaams Blok. Attempts to broaden the appeal of the party had clearly failed. After the 1991 elections an ambitious plan had been launched to bring together the Socialists, the Greens, the Christian Labour Movement and the progressive wing of the Flemish nationalist Volksunie. First it was announced as a project that should lead to a common list in 1995, then as the basis for a debate in the future that could lead to 'something' in common. But it did not work. The Greens did not feel like losing their identity. The Volksunie thought that the text was not Flemish enough, while many Socialists felt very uneasy because it was too Flemish. And the Christian Labour Movement felt very comfortable within the CVP.

The SP was thus on its own again. The most obvious partner for a common project is the Green Party, but Agalev keeps refusing invitations to create some sort of formal association. The SP also has the image of being an old and hierarchical party, very much the opposite of the kind of party the Greens would support. In 2001 the party decided to (slightly) change its name. It became SPa, where the 'a' stands for 'anders' or 'different'. The message is clear: 'anders' is also the first word of the name of the Greens (Anders Gaan Leven), and SPa is also the name of a successful association of Socialists and Greens in one of the Flemish cities.

The most important and risky change however was the decision to associate itself with Flemish nationalism. The Volksunie fell apart in 2002. The more leftist wing called itself SPIRIT, but opinion polls constantly gave it so few votes that it would probably not win a single seat on its own. For the federal elections of 2003, common lists were presented for SPa and SPIRIT. The results were quite spectacular: almost 24 percent of the votes. The fact that a high number of Green voters seem to have found their way to the Socialist lists refuelled the debate about an association between Red and Green.

Flemish nationalists: from Volksunie to N-VA and Spirit

The Flemish nationalists of the Volksunie were not very happy either with the 1991 result. Not only did they lose a lot of votes (as they had following their first governmental experience in 1978), but they now saw the xenophobic Vlaams Blok taking the electoral lead in the Flemish movement. The problem for Volksunie was that it had almost completely accomplished its programme. In 1991 only the direct election of the parliaments of regions and communities was needed to turn Belgium into a genuine federation. An agreement on this final step was reached in 1992. The party was then confronted with three major options. The first was to radicalize the nationalist programme, in order to counter the Vlaams Blok (which wants complete independence for Flanders). The second was to focus more on the non-regionalist aspects of its programme, which can be considered to be left-liberal. And the third option was simply to disappear.

The latter is what finally happened. The Volksunie had also introduced direct election of the president, and this clearly accelerated the internal division. Two camps of more or less the same size competed for the leadership and for the future of the party: a radical Flemish nationalist wing and a more moderate and left-liberal wing. They alternated at the head of the party until both groups decided that it was no use to try to go on together. The problem was a matter not only of ideology, but also of strategy. In 1999 the Volksunie had agreed to be part of the Flemish regional government (it was needed to form a coalition without Christian Democrats), but remained in the opposition at the federal level. This double position has proven lethal. When in 2001 and 2002 new changes in the Constitution had to be accepted, the negotiations were also conducted by the regional governments. The Flemish government with Volksunie had thus approved the proposals, but they had to be accepted in the federal parliament. At that level four of the eight MPs decided not to support the changes, while most of the Flemish regional MPs were ready to accept the compromises. The difference between the two wings of the party had more or less also become a difference within the party at two levels of the Belgian system, and was impossible to keep under control.

A referendum was organized among the members, to determine which group had the right to be the formal successor of the Volksunie. The rule was that the largest group would be the successor, and that it could keep the name if it gained at least 50 percent of the members' vote. The largest group was the Flemish nationalist wing, with 47 percent. It thus created a new party, named N-VA (Nieuw-Vlaamse Alliantie – New Flemish Alliance). It was backed by the majority of the members, but by a minority of the MPs at all levels. The smallest group in the membership was SPIRIT, with a clearly libertarian and economically more leftist programme. The majority of the MPs followed SPIRIT. As noted above, SPIRIT decided to draft common lists with the SPa for the federal elections of 2003. N-VA went to the polls alone, but secured just one seat in the Lower House.

Vlaams Blok and Agalev: the winning challengers

The Flemish Greens, 'Agalev', had a rather bad day on 24 November 1991. They polled reasonably well, but going up from 7.3 to 7.9 percent on a day when one third of the voters went looking for a new party was not very reassuring. Furthermore their Francophone counterpart Ecolo – with whom they closely cooperate – did extremely well. A number of left-libertarian votes in Flanders had clearly gone to Rossem (Swyngedouw *et al.* 1993). The Flemish Greens became concerned about their electoral strategy, about the way in which party leadership was organized (or avoided), and about the way in which they treated their members of Parliament. In other words they started to think about 'change' and 'renewal', to perform better in an electoral environment with less loyal voters. This basically resulted in a gradual professionalization of the party and in a better integration of the MPs in central decision-making. Gradually the party became ready to govern, which it did from 1999 onwards (Buelens and Deschouwer 2002). However, the disastrous results of 2003 have since put it back in the camp of the losers who need to think about ways to answer the challenge of non-loyal voters. Agaler changed its name into 'Groen!' in 2003.

It goes without saying that Rossem and Vlaams Blok felt good on 24 November. Rossem, however, did not survive this first legislature. It completely disintegrated and presented no candidates in 1995. Vlaams Blok on the contrary was still there in 1995 and in all the following elections, and at every one it improved its results. Vlaams Blok had a president for life (Karel Dillen), who resigned in 1996 and had the right to appoint his successor. That happened in a smooth way, with obviously no participation of the members at all. The other parties have decided to exclude Vlaams Blok from participation in power at all levels, including the local level. Yet the party used this so-called 'cordon sanitaire' to go on mobilizing with a strong and well-crafted populist discourse. The complex

Belgian system offers Vlaams Blok some extra ammunition. It can indeed show that – even if Flanders has received political autonomy – it still has to grant a veto to the Francophone minority in Belgium. And after 1999 Vlaams Blok kept on denouncing the fact that Flanders had a left-wing government because this was the type of coalition preferred in the south.

The Francophone parties

This 'Black Sunday' of 1991 and the sudden awareness of the erosion of voter loyalty was very much a Flemish phenomenon. The main reason – that is also why the Sunday was 'Black' – was of course the electoral success of Vlaams Blok. The real shock for the Francophone parties, on the other hand, came later, after August 1996. The arrest of Marc Dutroux quickly led to outbursts of popular indignation about the malfunctioning of the police forces. When in October 1996 the Court of Cassation decided to dismiss – for procedural errors – the judge who had arrested Dutroux, the movement became really political, blaming the system as a whole for being unable to deal with the real problems of the citizens. The 'White March' with its 300,000 participants was a clear illustration of the popular demand for change, although there was little specification of what exactly had to change and how.

This demand for change was certainly a national Belgian phenomenon, but it was deeper and more long-lasting in the Francophone part of the country (Hooghe 1997; Walgrave and Rihoux 1997). The obvious explanation is the fact that Dutroux was a Walloon, and so were (most of) his victims. Wallonia was the setting for the drama. The Francophone media paid much more attention to the case, and the parents of the victims became active participants in countless debates and rallies. The former Minister of Justice, the Francophone Christian Democrat Melchior Wathelet, who had taken the routine decision to release Dutroux a few years earlier, had committed the major political 'error'.

On the Francophone side we do not see the same amount of change as in Flanders. One reason is that direct election of the president was already established in the FDF in 1964, in the PSC in 1969 and in the PRL in 1979. We only see the Parti Socialiste introducing the direct election. It changed its statutes in 1997, and now uses a postal ballot, like PSC and PRL, to elect its president. In the FDF – a much smaller party, with only some 10,000 members – election of the president is the prerogative of the congress, in which all the members have the right to vote. That means in practice a few hundred people.

In 1999 the results polled by the PSC – the Francophone Christian Democrats – were disastrous, and the party became only number four in Francophone Belgium. It was now even smaller than the Greens. Together with the Flemish Christian Democrats it was removed from power. Already before the 1999 elections the party was going through a deep crisis. In 1995 the party president resigned. The election of a new president was extremely close, bringing the *éminence grise*, Nothomb, to office against the much younger Joëlle Milquet, who was the candidate of the outgoing president, Deprez. The latter then left the PSC and set up a 'citizens' movement for change' (MCC – Mouvement des Citoyens pour le Changement). This movement very rapidly formed an alliance with the Francophone Liberal Party, PRL, and they presented a common list at the 1999 elections. After these elections Joëlle Milquet did finally become president of the Francophone Christian Democrats, and decided to opt for a radical change. The old PSC was renamed the Humanist Democratic Centre (CDH – Centre Démocrate Humaniste). This change is remarkable since the party – unlike its Flemish counterpart – dropped the reference to Christianity from its name. The idea is that the religious cleavage is outdated and the party needs to reposition itself. It wants to be in the centre (beyond left and right) and it wants to defend the quality of life and the happiness of all the people. Classic Christian Democracy is far away, and this also means that the Flemish Christian Democrats are further away. It is now quite difficult to say that the two parts of the former Belgian Christian Democratic Party still belong to the same family. The 2003 elections were the first test for CDH, and it moved further down.

The Liberal PRL has not introduced important changes, but has first of all tried to become stronger. Like the Flemish Liberals, the PRL was trapped in the Belgian system. It is the second Francophone party, and it saw the first Francophone party (Socialists) governing with the much smaller Francophone Christian Democrats. In 1995 it was already presenting common lists with the Brussels Francophone regionalist FDF. This was a very smart move. The FDF is very strong in Brussels, and so is the PRL. Their association made them unavoidable for the formation of a Brussels regional government. It was a first step towards power.

The next step was an association with the Christian Democratic breakaway movement MCC. In 1999 common lists were presented, and the PRL–FDF–MCC association was able to become the first party of the French community (Walloon region and Francophones of the Brussels region), and close the gap with the PS in the Walloon region. The smartest move however had been the signing of an agreement with the PS in 1997, in which the two parties agreed that they would go together to the next government. This signature actually meant the end of the Christian Democrats in power, both in the south and in the north. With the Liberal family being the largest since 1999, and the Flemish Liberals the number one in Flanders, power relations in the Belgian party system(s) had been radically changed. PRL, MCC and FDF finally merged into one new party: the Reformist Movement (MR – Mouvement Réformiste). It did very well in 2003.

The two other Francophone parties – Greens and Socialists – have not changed a lot. For the Greens one can understand this: the party was doing – until 2003 – extremely well. The Parti Socialiste has been losing a lot. Yet – like the Flemish Christian Democrats in the past – it is well secured in power at all levels. Whether it polls 40 or 30 percent of the votes in the south does not really make a difference. The Parti Socialiste therefore does not change. It has introduced direct election of the party president, but keeps defending a very classical and traditional socialist discourse. With Ecolo it has created a 'pole of the leftist forces', but this does not mean a lot. It is not an agreement to present a common list, or to create one single political movement. In 2003 the PS did extremely well, while Ecolo lost heavily. For Ecolo (and for Agalev) the 2003 elections produced the 'warning of the voter' and thus the beginning of a search for change and renewal.

Changing the logic of decision making

Decision-making in Belgium is a complex and subtle thing (Dewachter 1992; De Winter 1996; Deschouwer 1999). Belgium's consociational character does not need to be explained here. However, its consequences are our concern. One of the consequences is a growing discontent with the way state and society are organized. As seen above, it is especially the Socialists and the Christian Democrats who have dominated the game and have divided large shares of state and society between them. When the two families controlled together 80 percent of the votes, this might have been reasonable and acceptable, but their share of the votes has constantly declined. Moreover, since the 1960s their role has been criticized, first by the regionalist parties, then by the Greens and by the right-wing parties.

How do these parties react to this system-related criticism? Can they react? Is it possible to move away from the consociational logic of power sharing, of elite consensus, of control over distribution of political outputs, of domination of parties over government, parliament and administration, of clientelism and corruption? It is certainly possible, although it is not easy. It is easier and moves faster in Flanders, for the simple reason that the old parties and structures there have already become much weaker and have been challenged for a longer time. Flanders is no longer the private garden of Christian Democracy, while Wallonia can still be considered much more a Socialist-controlled territory.

As far as their internal functioning is concerned, the parties did move. They have cut down radically on political clientelism, and they work hard on more objective criteria for nominations and promotions in the civil service and in the judicial organizations. They have also introduced a fairly stringent law on party financing. While in the 1980s almost everything was possible, especially in terms of gifts to the parties, the current law (introduced in 1991 and refined several times since then) completely forbids any gifts by organizations and reduces to a very small amount the gifts that can be accepted from individuals. This loss of income was compensated by the introduction of state funding for the central party organization and by a strict and controlled reduction of the expenses for electoral campaigns. This new law is, interestingly enough, not a reaction to the erosion of voter loyalty, but a reaction by the parties themselves. Parties realized that they had been crossing the line between acceptable and non-acceptable party finance, the latter being legally acceptable, but not morally. Of course the Agusta case[3] has affected voting behaviour, mainly leading to

Table 7.5 The changes in the Belgian party landscape

Family	Language	Old name	Change / New name	Date
Christian Democrats	Bilingual	CVP-PSC	Disappeared. Split up into CVP (Christelijke Volkspartij) and PSC (Parti Social Chrétien)	1968
Christian Democrats	Dutch	CVP	CD&V (Christen Democratisch en Vlaams)	2001
Christian Democrats	French	PSC	CDH (Centre Démocrate Humaniste)	2002
Liberals	Bilingual	PVV-PLP	Disappeared. Split into PVV (Partij voor Vrijheid en Vooruitgang) and PRL (Parti Réformateur Libéral)	1971
Liberals	Dutch	PVV	VLD (Vlaamse Liberalen en Democraten)	1992
Liberals	French	PRL	MR (Mouvement Réformateur) Fusion of PRL, FDF and MCC (breakaway from old PSC	2002
Socialists	Bilingual	BSP-PSB	Split into PS (Parti Socialiste) and SP (Socialistische Partij)	1978
Socialists	Dutch	SP	SP a (Socialistische Partij Anders)	2001
Socialists	French	PS	no change	
Regionalists	French	FDF	MR (Mouvement Réformateur) Fusion of PRL, FDF and MCC (breakaway from old PSC)	2002
Regionalists	Dutch	Volksunie	N-VA (Nieuw-Vlaamse Alliantie) Largest group after party split	2001
Regionalists	Dutch	Volksunie	Spirit (smaller group after party split; forms electoral Alliance with SPa in 2003)	2001
Greens	Dutch	Agalev	Groen!	
Greens	French	Ecolo	no change	2003
Right wing	Dutch	Vlaams Blok	no change (but many breakaways)	
Right wing	French	Front National	Only won parliamentary representation in 1991. Disappeared.	
Libertarian	Bilingual	Rossem		

electoral losses for the PS, but then the Agusta case occured in 1988–89, before the change in the law. The parties have reacted here even before the voters asked them to do so.

The complex and multi-layered logic of Belgian politics is here to stay. It means that decision-making will be – as long as Belgium exists – a matter of subtle and prudent leadership with high levels of quasi-diplomatic negotiations between governments and political parties at all levels. This would not really be a problem, if the parties at the Belgian level were not exactly the same as the regional parties. The absence of party federations to deal with federal politics makes it extremely difficult for the parties to send out the message that they have changed and that they have renewed themselves and the system. At the federal level an adversarial and majoritarian logic is out of the question. Only subtle consensus can keep the country with its two communities and three regions together. The parties playing the consensus game at that level are the same parties defending a more competitive logic at the level of the region. One needs a thorough analytical insight into the complex Belgian political institutions to understand that double game. The average voter is not supposed to be a political scientist, and the institutional logic remains a source of political frustration and protest (Deschouwer 2002b).

The Belgian institutions are complex indeed, and the complexity cannot be substantially reduced. Yet the idea that the complexity should be changed is very much alive among political elites. Reforms of the system are defended, especially as attempts to make the system more transparent. The Flemish Liberal VLD has very much defended the idea of 'citizen democracy' as an alternative to the existing cumbersome and opaque system. The party wanted in the first place the introduction of binding referendums. The Greens support this idea, but other parties are more reluctant. Organizing referendums at the federal level would indeed be difficult, because it would mean the use of a simple majoritarian device in a country where the very balance and survival of institutions is based on consociational negotiations and mutual vetoes. Nothing much has been accomplished. In 1996 the local municipalities and the provinces received the power to organize referendums (also on demand of the people), but the results are not binding.

The VLD has been defending the abolition of compulsory voting. Here the fiercest opponents are the Socialist parties. They fear – looking at election surveys – that they would pay most at the polls (Ackaert and De Winter 1993; Hooghe and Pelleriaux 1998). Christian Democrats are also unenthusiastic about the idea. Another VLD idea is to abolish or diminish the effect of the list vote. Belgian voters can either vote for the list as a whole or cast preference votes. Voting for the list actually means that one agrees with the list order. In practice it means that parties and not the voters are deciding who exactly will be elected. For the 2003 elections the effect of the list vote was reduced, to give more weight to the preference votes.

In 2002 a reform of the electoral law was accepted, and again defended as an attempt to simplify the political institutions. This reform is basically a reduction in the number of constituencies (from 20 to 11) and the introduction of an electoral threshold of 5 percent in 8 of these 11 constituencies (those with the size of a province). The request to do so mainly came from the Flemish parties, who hope the reform (especially the threshold) will reduce the number of parties represented in parliament. The level of fractionalization did indeed decline in 2003, but the effect of the electoral threshold was limited. Without the threshold Agalev would have had two seats and N-VA one.

Conclusions

The Belgian party system has been on the move since 1965. From that date on we can see the parties trying to reclaim the volatile voters. Yet the way the parties have responded to this early dealignment has created an institutional setting in which it is extremely difficult to react adequately to the challenge of decreasing legitimacy. The institutional setting has two major characteristics: the absence of national Belgian parties and the consociational federal state structure.

The absence of national parties is the primary and direct consequence of the electoral success of the new regionalist and ethnolinguistic parties in the 1960s. Their presence in the electoral landscape was an illustration of the growing salience of regionalist tensions, and at the same time it added to the salience. All three national parties fell apart, and new political parties created after the 1960s (Greens and right-wing extremist) appear twice, one for each language group. This has an important effect on the way parties react to volatility. Belgian parties compete in two separate party systems, and they look at the results only in their own language group. Except in Brussels, voters cannot be volatile across the language cleavage. In these two separate party systems, two different parties have dominated: the Christian-Democrats in the north and the Socialists in the south. Their regional leadership gives them more power than they would have in one single Belgian party system. It therefore reduces their vulnerability, or at least their awareness of vulnerability. Electoral losses are not a direct problem, as long as they keep their regional leadership, because that means almost guaranteed access to power. The smaller brothers of the two dominant parties – the Flemish Socialists and the Francophone Christian Democrats – are also in a rather comfortable position, since the force of the stronger partner of the ideological family secures their access to power. For the two Liberal parties however, the falling apart of the parties and of the party system has created a structural impasse. They feel extremely vulnerable, and have tried very hard to break the dominance of Christian Democrats in Flanders and of Socialists in Wallonia. They finally accomplished this goal in 1999, but only in Flanders.

A more indirect, yet extremely relevant, institutional effect of the linguistic and regionalist tensions has been the gradual reform of the Belgian state from a unitary structure into a federal one. In this newly created federal state, there are no federal parties, but only regional parties. This does not make the life of the parties easier. At the federal level, politics is very complex and requires subtle arrangements and the traditional Belgian consociational style. Of course this level is not very responsive, since electoral changes are not, and cannot be translated into real alternation in power. At the regional level, however, to which a large number of important competencies have been devolved, the parties have more room to manoeuvre. Here they can be more responsive and play a more competitive game. But that requires them to play a double game, which is not easy to explain to the electorate, and which is not improving their legitimacy. It creates a very visible tendency to focus on the regional level, to claim even more competencies at that level and – eventually – to completely forget about Belgium. For the parties this would dramatically reduce the complexity and allow them to be responsive. But unfortunately the Belgian population does not want to forget about Belgium. On the contrary: they do not really support this whole idea of federal devolution, which is to a large extent a solution to a (party-) political problem. Every answer then seems to be the wrong one.

Notes

1 Marc Dutroux was arrested in August 1996. He appeared to be responsible for the kidnapping of at least six girls. Four of them were killed, and two were rescued. He had been convicted of rape a few years earlier but was released early. Formally this decision had been taken by the Minister of Justice, Melchior Wathelet. The Dutroux case rapidly became a political one, in the sense that the judicial system, the public authorities in general and Wathelet in particular were blamed for the mistakes.

2 In 1972–73 a Francophone Socialist exceptionally held the position of Prime Minister.

3 Agusta is the name of the Italian company that has paid bribes to several top members of both Socialist Parties in order to sell helicopters to the Belgian army. Willy Claes had to resign as secretary general of NATO as a consequence of this Agusta scandal.

References

Ackaert, Johan and Lieven De Winter (1993). 'De afwezigen hebben andermaal ongelijk: De stemverzaking in Vlaanderen op 24 November 1991.' In Mark Swyngedouw, Jaak Billiet, *et al.* (eds), *Kiezen is verliezen. Onderzoek naar de politieke opvattingen van Vlamingen.* Leuven: Acco, pp. 67–82.

Buelens, Jo and Kris Deschouwer (2002). 'The Belgian Greens in Government.' In Ferdinand Müller-Rommel and Thomas Poguntke (eds), *Green Parties in National Governments.* Special issue of *Environmental Politics* 11 (1): 112–32.

De Ridder, Hugo (1993). *De strijd om de 16.* Tielt: Lannoo.

Deschouwer, Kris (1994a). 'The Decline of Consociationalism and the Reluctant Modernization of the Belgian Mass Parties.' In Richard Katz and Peter Mair (eds), *How Parties Organize: Adaptation and Change in Party Organizations in Western Democracies.* London: Sage, pp. 80–108.

Deschouwer, Kris (1994b). 'The Termination of Coalitions in Belgium.' *Res Publica* 36: 43–55.

Deschouwer, Kris (1994c). 'The Missing Link: Party Types and Consociational Democracy.' Paper presented at the ECPR Joint Sessions, Bordeaux.

Deschouwer, Kris (1996). 'Waiting for "the Big One": the Uncertain Survival of the Belgian Parties and Party Systems.' In Kris Deschouwer, Lieven De Winter, and Donatella Della Porta (eds), *Partitocracies between Crises and Reforms: the Cases of Italy and Belgium*. Special issue of *Res Publica* 38 (2): 295–306.

Deschouwer, Kris (1997). 'Une Fédération sans fédérations de parties.' In Serge Jaumain (ed.), *La Réforme de l'état ... et après. L'impact des débats institutionnels en Belgique et au Canada*. Brussels: Editions de l'ULB, pp. 77–83.

Deschouwer, Kris (1998a). 'Politieke partijen en de moeilijke democratie.' *Samenleving en Politiek* 5 (1): 4–17.

Deschouwer, Kris (1998b). 'Op verkenning in de kloof.' In Mark Elchardus (ed.), *Variaties op onbehagen en vertrouwen*. Brussels: VUB Press, pp. 77–100.

Deschouwer, Kris (1999). 'From Consociationalism to Federalism: How the Belgian Parties Won.' In Kurt Richard Luther and Kris Deschouwer (eds), *Party Elites in Divided Societies. Political Parties in Consociational Democracies*. Routledge: London, pp. 74–107.

Deschouwer, Kris (2000). 'Belgium's Quasi-Regional Elections of June 1999.' *Regional and Federal Studies* 10 (1): 125–32.

Deschouwer, Kris (2002a). 'The Colour Purple: the End of Predictable Politics in the Low Countries.' In Paul Webb, Ian Holliday, and David Farrell (eds), *Political Parties in Democratic Societies*. Oxford: Oxford University Press, pp. 151–80.

Deschouwer, Kris (2002b). 'Falling Apart Together: the Changing Nature of Belgian Consociationalism, 1961–2000.' In Jürg Steiner and Thomas Ertman (eds), *Consociationalism and Corporatism in Western Europe. Still the Politics of Accommodation?* Special issue of *Acta Politica* 37: 68–85.

Dewachter, Wilfried (1987). 'Changes in a Particratie: the Belgian System from 1944 to 1986.' In Hans Daalder (ed.), *Party Systems in Denmark, Austria, Switzerland, the Netherlands and Belgium*. London: Pinter, pp. 285–364.

Dewachter, Wilfried (1992). *Besluitvorming in politiek België*. Leuven: Acco.

De Winter, Lieven (1996). 'Party Encroachment on the Executive and Legislative Branch in the Belgian Polity.' In Kris Deschouwer, Lieven De Winter, and Donatella Della Porta (eds), *Partitocracies between Crises and Reforms: the Cases of Italy and Belgium*. Special issue of *Res Publica* 38 (2): 325–52.

Elchardus, Mark and Anton Derks (1996). 'Culture Conflict and its Consequences for the Legitimation Crisis.' In Kris Deschouwer, Lieven De Winter, and Donatella Della Porta (eds), *Partitocracies between Crises and Reforms: the Cases of Italy and Belgium*. Special issue of *Res Publica* 38 (2): 237–54.

Frognier, André-Paul and Anne-Marie Aish-Van Vaerenbergh (eds) (1994). *Elections: la fêlure? Enquête sur le comportement électoral des Wallons et des Francophones*. Brussels: De Boeck Université.

Hooghe, Marc (1997). *Het witte ongenoegen. Hoop en illusie van een uniek experiment*. Groot-Bijgaarden: Globe.

Hooghe, Marc and Koen Pelleriaux (1998). 'Compulsory Voting in Belgium'. *Electoral Studies* 17: 419–24.

Huyse, Luc *et al.* (1992). *23 November 1991. De betekenis van een verkiezingsuitslag*. Leuven: Kritak.

Maddens, Bart, Roeland Beerten, and Jaak Billiet (1994). *O dierbaar België. Het natiebewustzijn van Vlamingen en Walen*. Leuven: ISPO.

McRae, Kenneth (1987). *Conflict and Compromise in Multi-Lingual Societies: Belgium*. Ontario: Wilfrid Laurier Press.

Murphy, Alexander (1995). 'Belgium's Regional Divergence: Along the Road to Federation.' In Graham Smith (ed.), *Federalism. The Multiethnic Challenge*. London: Longman.

Platel, Mark (1993). *Het altaar van de politiek*. Leuven: Davidsfonds.

Swyngedouw, Marc, Jaak Billiet, An Carton, and Beerten Roeland (eds) (1993). *Kiezen is verliezen. Onderzoek naar de politieke opvattingen van Vlamingen*. Leuven: Acco.

Van Dyck, Ruth (1996). 'Divided We Stand: Regionalism, Federalism and Minority Rights in Belgium.' In Kris Deschouwer, Lieven De Winter, and Donatella Della Porta (eds), *Partitocracies between Crises and Reforms: the Cases of Italy and Belgium*. Special issue of *Res Publica* 38 (2): 429–46.

Van Haegendoren, Mieke (1967). 'Party and Opposition Formation in Belgium.' *Res Publica* 9: 413–36.

Walgrave, Stefaan and Benoît Rihoux (1997). *De Witte Mars. Eén jaar later. Van emotie tot politieke commotie*. Antwerpen: Van Halewijck.

EIGHT   Electoral Fortunes and Responses of the Social Democratic Party and Liberal Party in Denmark: Ups and Downs

Lars Bille and Karina Pedersen

Denmark is a constitutional monarchy with parliamentary democracy. Since 1920 the Crown has exercised a purely formal and symbolic role. The 1953 constitutional revision introduced a unicameral system. Parliament, the Folketing, has 179 seats, of which 175 are elected in Denmark, two in the Faroe Islands and two in Greenland. One important element that has to be taken into account in determining the magnitude of uncertainty of the parties in electorally competitive situations is that while the constitution stipulates a four-year election period, this is a maximum period. One of the most important prerogatives of prime ministers is that they are entitled to call a general election whenever they want. This means that the political parties never know when an election will be called.

The electoral system is a list system of proportional representation with provisions for effective preferential voting. Political parties which are represented in the Folketing when a general election is called automatically have the right to participate in the election. All other parties must present a list of signatures equivalent to a minimum of 1/175 of the total valid votes cast in the previous election (i.e. around 20,000 signatures). A party has to pass the electoral threshold of 2 percent of the valid votes cast in the election to be represented in the Folketing. There are no rules concerning the conduct of election campaigning in terms of the sums of money to be spent, the publication of the financial sources of the individual candidates, or the duration of the campaign. For technical reasons, however, the minimum duration of a campaign is three weeks.

Since the post-1973 party system consists of eight to eleven parties, a more in-depth analysis of the responses of all parties to the erosion of voter loyalties is impossible within the scope of this chapter. In the following, then, the main focus will be on the Social Democratic Party and the Liberal Party. They have been the two dominant parties in Danish politics and were the main adversaries throughout most of the twentieth century. The Social Democratic Party was in government most of the time, while the Liberal Party was leader of the opposition and the only realistic government alternative to the Social Democrats. In the 1980s, however, the Liberals were reduced to playing second fiddle among the bourgeois parties. During the same period, the Social Democrats were forced to play the role of opposition party. To both parties these positions were quite unfamiliar and 'unnatural'. This feeling of unease, as well as their perception of themselves as the traditional main pillars of the party system, their vacillating fate in the electoral arena, and their changing role as opposition and governing parties, all justify the selection of these two parties for an analysis of how parties respond to electoral challenges. Precisely these two parties, if any, might be expected to have undertaken initiatives to redress their 'unnatural' and unstable situation in a fluid electoral market.

By 1920 the format of the classic Danish party system was established, a system whose basic traits remained stable for the following 50 years. The classical party system was totally dominated by the four old parties: the Social Democratic Party (Socialdemokratiet), the Social-Liberal Party (Det Radikale Venstre), the Liberal Party (Venstre) and the Conservative People's Party (Det Konservative Folkeparti). Until 1973 these parties commanded around 85 to 95 percent of the electoral support. The ideological configuration and the high degree of cohesiveness and discipline prevailing in the parties (Pedersen 1967; Svensson 1982; Mikkelsen 1994), together with the fact that since 1909 no single party has held a majority in the Folketing, has created one of the most crucial features of Danish politics before 1973: its coalescent pattern of decision-making.

The simple one-dimensional model of the traditional Left–Right continuum provides the most adequate description of the relations between the parties. A relatively fixed pattern of cooperation and conflict existed between the parties in the old system, making it a kind of two-bloc system (Damgaard 1973). The Social Democratic Party and the Communist Party – replaced in 1960 by the Socialist People's Party (Socialistisk Folkeparti) – constituted the left-wing bloc. The Liberals and the Conservatives formed the right-wing bloc. These two blocs were of almost equal strength, leaving the role of the pivotal party to the Social Liberal Party. In the period prior to 1973 the Social Democrats were most successful in obtaining the support of the Social Liberal Party, and from 1945 to 1973 the right-wing parties were in office only three times, for a total of eight years.

Hence the pre-1973 Danish party system was a very stable system of moderate pluralism, characterized by a relatively high degree of predictability, a coalescent pattern of decision-making, norms of compromise and 'broad agreements' in parliament, and comprehensive collaboration between the parties and the various interest organizations (Pedersen 1987; Bille 1989).

The general election in 1973 resulted in a dramatic change. The format changed from a five-party system to a ten-party system. Since 1973, the number of relevant parties represented in parliament has not been fewer than eight. In Sartorian terms, the format of the party system changed permanently from limited pluralism to extreme pluralism (Bille 1989; Sartori 1976).

Table 8.1 Danish electoral results, 1971–2001*

	1971	1973	1975	1977	1979	1981	1984	1987	1988	1990	1994	1998	2001
Communist Party	1.4 (0)	3.6 (6)	4.2 (7)	3.7 (7)	1.9 (0)	1.1 (0)	0.7 (0)	0.9 (0)	0.8 (0)				
Left Socialists	1.6 (0)	1.5 (0)	2.1 (4)	2.7 (5)	3.7 (6)	2.6 (5)	2.7 (5)	1.4 (0)	0.6 (0)				
Red–Green Alliance										1.7 (0)	3.1 (6)	2.7 (5)	2.4 (4)
Socialist People's Party	9.1 (17)	6 (11)	5 (9)	3.9 (7)	5.9 (11)	11.3 (21)	11.5 (21)	14.6 (27)	13 (24)	8.3 (15)	7.3 (13)	7.5 (13)	6.4 (12)
Common Course								2.2 (4)	1.9 (0)	1.8 (0)			
Social Democratic Party	37.3 (70)	25.6 (46)	29.9 (53)	37 (65)	38.3 (68)	32.9 (59)	31.6 (56)	29.3 (54)	29.8 (55)	37.4 (69)	34.6 (62)	36.0 (63)	29.1 (52)
Total left wing	49.4 (87)	36.7 (63)	41.2 (73)	47.3 (84)	49.8 (85)	47.9 (85)	46.5 (82)	48.4 (85)	46.1 (79)	49.2 (84)	45 (81)	46.2 (81)	37.9 (68)
Social Liberal Party	14.3 (27)	11.2 (20)	7.1 (13)	3.6 (6)	5.4 (10)	5.1 (9)	5.5 (10)	6.2 (11)	5.6 (10)	3.5 (7)	4.6 (8)	3.9 (7)	5.2 (9)
Christian People's Party	2 (0)	4 (7)	5.3 (9)	3.4 (6)	2.6 (5)	2.3 (4)	2.7 (5)	2.4 (4)	2 (4)	2.3 (4)	1.8 (0)	2.5 (4)	2.3 (4)
Centre Democrats		7.8 (14)	2.2 (4)	6.4 (11)	3.2 (6)	8.3 (15)	4.6 (8)	4.8 (9)	4.7 (9)	5.1 (9)	2.8 (5)	4.3 (8)	1.8 (0)
Justice Party	1.7 (0)	2.9 (5)	1.8 (0)	3.3 (6)	2.6 (5)	1.4 (0)	1.5 (0)	0.5 (0)		0.5 (0)			
Total centre	18.0 (27)	25.9 (46)	16.4 (26)	16.7 (29)	13.8 (26)	17.1 (28)	14.3 (23)	13.9 (24)	12.3 (23)	11.4 (20)	9.2 (13)	10.7 (19)	9.3 (13)
Conservative People's Party	16.7 (31)	9.2 (16)	5.5 (10)	8.5 (15)	12.5 (22)	14.5 (26)	23.4 (42)	20.8 (38)	19.3 (35)	16 (30)	15 (27)	8.9 (16)	9.1 (16)
Liberal Party	15.6 (30)	12.3 (22)	23.3 (42)	12 (21)	12.5 (22)	11.3 (20)	12.1 (22)	10.5 (19)	11.8 (22)	15.8 (29)	23.3 (42)	24.0 (42)	31.2 (56)

(Continued)

Table 8.1 Continued

	1971	1973	1975	1977	1979	1981	1984	1987	1988	1990	1994	1998	2001
Progress Party		15.9 (28)	13.6 (24)	14.6 (26)	11 (20)	8.9 (16)	3.6 (6)	4.8 (9)	9 (16)	6.4 (12)	6.4 (11)	2.4 (4)	0.6 (0)
Danish People's Party												7.4 (13)	12.0 (22)
Total right wing	32.3 (61)	37.4 (66)	42.4 (76)	35.1 (62)	36 (64)	34.7 (62)	39.1 (70)	36.1 (66)	40.1 (73)	38.2 (71)	44.7 (80)	42.7 (75)	52.9 (94)
Others	0.2 (0)	0 (0)	0 (0)	0.9 (0)	0.4 (0)	0.2 (0)	0.1 (0)	1.7 (0)	1.4 (0)	1.2 (0)	1 (1)	0.4 (0)	0 (0)
Total	100 (175)	100 (175)	100 (175)	100 (175)	100 (175)	100 (175)	100 (175)	100 (175)	100 (175)	100 (175)	100 (175)	100 (175)	100 (175)
Turnout (percent)	87.2	88.7	88.2	88.7	85.6	83.3	88.4	86.7	85.7	82.8	84.3	86	87.1
Electorate (thousands)	3,332	3,461	3,478	3,523	3,731	3,775	3,829	3,907	3,912	3,941	3,989	3,997	3,999
Index of fractionalization	0.78	0.86	0.82	0.81	0.8	0.83	0.81	0.83	0.83	0.79	0.79	0.79	0.79
Effective number of parties	4.52	7.11	5.59	5.23	4.99	5.76	5.24	5.82	5.83	4.85	4.76	4.52	4.70
Total volatility	9.46	29.11	17.83	18.34	10.99	12.5	10.83	9.08	6.01	14.63	10.69	11.91	13.30

*Party share of electoral vote (percent), seats (numbers in brackets), index of electoral fractionalization.

Calculating the volatility in 1973, the Centre Democrats are assumed to be a new party, not a splinter party, since the party fulfilled all of the requirements in the electoral law to be officially recognized as a new party.

Source: Official election statistics

Table 8.2   Government composition in Denmark, 1968–2003

	Party of Prime Minister	Other parties	Status
1968–71	SLP	CoPP, LP	Majority
1971–73	SDP		Minority
1973–75	LP		Minority
1975–78	SDP		Minority
1978–79	SDP	LP	Minority
1979–82	SDP		Minority
1982–88	CoPP	LP, CD, ChPP	Minority
1988–90	CoPP	LP, SLP	Minority
1990–93	CoPP	LP	Minority
1993–94	SDP	SLP, CD, ChPP	Majority
1994–96	SDP	SLP, CD	Minority
1996–2001	SDP	SLP	Minority
2001–	LP	CoPP	Minority

CD: Centre Democrats; ChPP: Christian People's Party; CoPP: Conservative People's Party;
LP: Liberal Party; SDP: Social Democratic Party; SLP: Social Liberal Party.

The four old parties all experienced heavy losses, with their combined electoral support falling from around 85 percent in 1971 to 58 percent in 1973. Three brand new parties passed the electoral threshold of 2 percent: the Progress Party (Fremskridtspartiet), the Centre Democrats (Centrum-Demokraterne), and the Christian People's Party (Kristeligt Folkeparti). Two 'old timers', the Communist Party and the Justice Party, experienced a short revival in the 1970s but, unlike the three new parties, were not able to maintain their representation into the 1980s. The ideological space of the party system was expanded first and foremost by the entrance of the extreme right-wing protest party, the Progress Party, and the Communist Party on the extreme left wing.

The eruption of the electoral market seriously shook the four old parties and the old party system. In addition, economic recession contributed to the sense of crisis. Throughout the 1970s unemployment increased substantially, the state budget deficit grew, the balance of payments was negative and increasingly so, and inflation accelerated. This bleak economic situation in combination with the sudden change of the party system presented a tremendous challenge to the political parties.

Following the 1973 election, the shock was great, confusion among the established parties was immense, and the process of government formation became extremely complex. It became impossible to continue the two-bloc configuration from the previous years. None of the blocs commanded a majority in parliament. A Social Democratic government was only possible if, in addition to the Socialist People's Party and the Communist Party, the centre parties – the Social Liberal Party, the Centre Democrats and the Christian People's Party – decided to support it, and this was not the case. The latter two preferred a bourgeois government. In addition, discussion within the leadership of the Social Democratic Party indicated that, although opinions were divided on the issue, governmental responsibility was not what the party should aim at in the prevailing incalculable parliamentary and economic situation (Jørgensen 1989: 204ff.). The strategic considerations behind recommending what they anticipated to be a short period of recuperation in opposition include the following: the lowest electoral support for the party since 1920, the dim prospect of carrying through a Social Democratic policy in the new parliament, and the expectation that it would be revealed to the voters that the bourgeois parties could not agree with each other and the new parties on an effective and successful policy.

In the Liberal Party the perception of the situation was the opposite. The leadership perceived at an early stage of the government formation process that the situation offered an opportunity to regain in the minds of the electorate the position of undisputed prime ministerial party. The party decided to work for the formation of a single-party government, thereby disregarding the former coalition partners (Kaarsted 1988: 27ff.). The strategy of the Liberal Party in the 1970s was to regain and sustain its position as the leading bourgeois party.

The negotiations in 1973 resulted in the formation of a Liberal minority government based on only 22 seats out of the 179 in the Folketing. The government had to face opposition on both the Right and the Left – oppositions which were totally adversarial. Legislation was passed only after long, dramatic and complicated negotiations. In 1975, at a time when the opinion polls were very favourable to his party, the Prime Minister suddenly decided to call a general election, with the result that there was a doubling of his Liberal Party seats. The strategy had paid off in terms of voter support, and the party was now by far the largest bourgeois party. As regards parliamentary support, the victory was of little use, however, since the gains were at the expense of the supporting parties, which were very annoyed by the manoeuvre. Hence a vote of no confidence was passed at the first meeting of parliament after the election. Since a bourgeois majority existed, the strategy of the Liberal Party was to try to stay in office now by forming a minority coalition government with the Conservative People's Party, the Christian People's Party and the Centre Democrats. These negotiations succeeded, but the incoming government was not able to obtain an understanding with the Progress Party. Hence it failed at the last minute (Kaarsted 1988: 72ff.). In fact, the Progress Party blocked the formation of a bourgeois government for the rest of the decade and paved the way for the Social Democratic minority governments of 1975–78. Through a skilful strategy of dividing the Right these governments managed to compromise with the centre parties and, alternately, the Liberals and the Conservatives. As long as the centre parties decided to support the Social Democratic government instead of the Liberal alternative, the Social Democrats could stay in office.

In 1978 the parliamentary situation changed completely. The Social Democratic Party and the Liberal Party agreed to form a government and thereby created a coalition that was quite unique and astonishing: the two main adversaries in the political history of Denmark had decided to join forces. In itself this was proof of the unusual developments through which the party system had passed since 1973. This new approach was justified by the two parties' perception of the need for political stability in order to cope with the ever-growing problems of the economy and unemployment, as well as an attempt to improve the efficacy and esteem of the party system itself (FF 1979: 2f.). Furthermore, since neither of the two parties had been able to create a stable majority behind its policies and since the Liberal Party after its electoral defeat in 1977 was in danger of losing its position as the leading bourgeois party, they opted for a new strategy of cooperation. The calculation was that the voters would reward a successful economic policy at the expense of the other parties.

In practice, however, the coalition was incompatible. It was constantly troubled by internal disagreement and mistrust and it lasted only one year. It was followed by yet another Social Democratic minority government. In contradistinction to the previous Social Democratic governments of 1975–78, this government had to face a more stable pattern of cooperation between the Liberals and the Conservatives. Both bourgeois parties had reached the conclusion that neither gained from competing against the other: that this only encouraged the Social Democrats to play them off against each other. Competition sharpened between these two parties on one side and the government on the other as to which of them could win the support of the centre parties. As usual it was in the hands of the centre parties to determine whether the Left or the Right would take office.

It took another election in 1981, growth in the electoral support of the Socialist People's Party at the expense of the Social Democratic Party, a split between the Social Democratic Party and the Social Liberal Party due to disagreement on economic policy, continuously declining electoral support for the Liberals, and increasing support for the Conservative People's Party before this competition was settled to the advantage of the Right. Faced with ever-growing economic problems and a more united opposition centred on the Conservative–Liberal axis, the Social Democratic government resigned in September 1982 without calling a general election. According to the then Prime Minister, the strategic considerations behind the decision were that since it had become increasingly difficult to get vital elements of the party's policy through parliament, it was indefensible just to 'administer' a policy passed by the bourgeois majority, that an increasing number of voters would realize that a bourgeois policy was not in their interest, and that the bourgeois parties were unable to remain united once they had gained governmental power, i.e. a bourgeois government would be short-lived and the Social Democrats could quickly return to office in a stronger position. (Jørgensen 1990: 545; see also Callesen 1996: 48; Carlsen 1992: 48). But this time the Social Democratic 'bracket theory', i.e. a bourgeois government would not survive a general election, proved wrong.

A four-party minority government was formed by the Conservative People's Party, the Liberal Party, the Christian People's Party and the Centre Democrats. For the first time since 1901 a Conservative held the post of Prime Minister, meaning that the Liberal Party was no longer the leading bourgeois party. The government survived the 1984 election and for the first time since 1971 a government managed to stay in office for almost a full election period. This was achieved partly because of the fact that the bourgeois government could now form a majority without the support of the Progress Party, and partly because of the deliberate introduction of a new pattern in the relationship between government and opposition.

Since 1973, and particularly during the 1980s, there was a growing tendency for the government to stay in office even when it was defeated in parliamentary votes. Before 1973 there was a very limited range of issues on which a government would accept defeat without calling an election. By sheer necessity, however, the minority governments of the 1970s were obliged to become more tolerant. The four-party minority government was kept in office with the support of the Social Liberal Party. This party had bound itself to support the government only on confidence votes and on issues concerning general economic policy. In all other policy areas, however, the government could not take this party's support for granted. Thus an 'alternative majority' was manifested on a variety of issues on which the government tolerated a defeat without resigning. A completely new practice had been introduced (Damgaard and Svensson 1989). The governing parties believed this sort of arrangement was the only way to achieve some stability in the party system.

The 1987 election resulted in a strengthening of both the far left and the far right. The four-party government continued in office but the election resulted in a deadlock in parliament; the government had become dependent on the support of both the Progress Party and the Social Liberal Party, a centre party which had decided to cooperate with neither the far right nor the far left. The continuing gains of the Socialist People's Party set a limit on the extent to which the Social Democratic Party could move towards the centre. The Social Democrats viewed the Socialist People's Party as a serious competitor at this time and tried to eliminate its threat in two ways. The first was to launch a vigorous opposition to the government in an effort to outdo the Socialist People's Party and the second was to cooperate with the party in an effort to 'embrace' it. Centrifugal drives were at work, and the party system at the parliamentary level became paralysed. This is why the government decided to call a new general election just eight months after the previous contest.

The election of 1988 did not bring about a new distribution of power in parliament, and if the parties had maintained their pre-election positions a genuine deadlock would have ensued. In the event, however, a new tripartite minority government was formed by the Conservatives, the Liberals and the Social Liberals. The latter abandoned their hitherto genuine and forceful opposition to cooperation with the Progress Party, and the Progress Party proved more willing than before to cooperate with the government. For the first time since 1973 the centre and bourgeois parties were willing to encompass the extreme Right in forging a parliamentary basis for the government.

The basis for the tripartite government, however, proved far from stable and in 1990 the government called yet another general election. Despite the greatest postwar electoral victory for the Social Democratic Party based on a new centre-oriented and cooperative campaign strategy, the party was not able to gain governmental power since the centre parties decided to support the formation of a Conservative–Liberal minority government. The support in parliament for the government was indeed minimal, with none of the other parties committing itself to offer external support. The dominating feature of the legislative process was that the bills were passed by different majority formations in a pattern which proved even more fluid than before the 1990 election. The traditional reluctance of the centre parties to include the extreme Right and extreme Left in the legislative process was abandoned. This marked the introduction of a new practice as far as policy-based coalition building was concerned. Forced by the distribution of seats in parliament, the response of the parties was greater flexibility as regards policy alliances.

Two incidents changed the pattern of coalition building. First, increased electoral support had proved insufficient for the Social Democratic Party to regain governmental power. This caused increasing internal unrest. In 1992 the Social Democratic Party elected a new chairman since the centre parties did not regard the incumbent chairman as a trustworthy alternative to the Conservative Prime Minister Poul Schlüter. The party, then, had to come forward with a new chairman who could unite the party, cooperate with the centre parties and thereby pave the way for a change of cabinet. Ten years in opposition and the prospect of a further prolongation of this arrangement had proved traumatic for the Social Democrats.

Secondly, in 1993 the two-party government resigned following the decision of an independent court of inquiry that the government was guilty of the illegal administration of a law granting refugees the right to be reunited with their families in Denmark. In the subsequent government formation process the centre parties finally decided to change sides after more than a decade of continuous support for centre Right and right-wing governments. This decision was facilitated by a change of party leader in the Social Democratic Party. The result was the formation of the first majority government in Denmark since 1971, consisting of the Social Democratic Party, Social Liberal Party, Centre Democrats and Christian People's Party.

At the 1994 election the Liberal Party and the Conservative People's Party launched a strategy aimed at obtaining a majority for a bourgeois government without the support of one or more of the centre parties. This strategy of ideological confrontation paid off for the Liberal Party, which gained thirteen seats. But it failed to attain a pure bourgeois majority. The Liberal Party, however, continued the strategy and thereby created a more clear-cut line of ideological confrontation than was usual in Danish politics, thus squeezing the centre. At the 1994 election the confrontation had cost the representation of the Christian People's Party. The Social-Democratic-led government had to continue as a three-party minority government supported by the left-wing parties, including the Socialist People's Party and Red–Green Alliance (Enhedslisten). The new practice of including all parties in the policy coalition formation was further sustained.

In 1996 the Liberal Party's strategy of confrontation succeeded in encouraging the Centre Democrats to leave the government for fear of being the next victim of the squeezing of the centre. Thus, at the 1998 election the voters had a clear choice: either the continuation of the two-party minority government made up of the Social Democrats and Social Liberals with the support of the left-wing parties, or a bourgeois government headed by the Liberal Party. The incumbent government and its supporting parties won a majority by one seat only, and the government continued. Since the main objective of the confrontation strategy, an alteration of government, had failed once more, the leader of the Liberal Party resigned. The new party leadership launched a more centre-oriented strategy and tried to bring about a revival of the four-party government of the 1980s with the Liberal Party as the leading party instead of the Conservative People's Party.

By the end of the century the strategic situation of the Social Democratic Party and the Liberal Party was further complicated by the gains the Danish People's Party (Dansk Folkeparti) – formed in 1995 as splinter party of the Progress Party and represented in parliament with 13 seats in 1998–2001 and 22 after 2001 – had made on the basis of a nationalistic, xenophobic, anti-EU and populistic welfare state platform. Surveys indicated that the support for the new party came, to a large extent, from both traditional Social Democratic core voters and from Liberal voters. Hence both parties tried to adjust their policies to the new right-wing values prevailing among segments of the voters, first and foremost by tightening up their policies in the areas of refugees, immigrants and integration of people with a non-Danish ethnic background. This hampered their efforts to maintain or gain the support of the centre parties, traditionally the pivotal parties. A strategy of vote maximization could thus turn out to be detrimental to a strategy of maximization of parliamentary influence. This strategic dilemma has always been decisive in the Danish party system.

The centre-oriented strategy pursued after 1998 has been successful for the Liberal Party. In 2001 the alternative government was able to replace the incumbent Social Democratic-led government. The Liberal Party thus took office together with the Conservatives. Together with a supporting party, the electorally successful Danish People's Party, the government formed a majority and for the first time in many years it faced unilateral rather than bilateral opposition. As a result of the electoral defeat, a long process of renewal began in the Social Democratic Party. The former Prime Minister and party leader did not at first resign from the latter office but was pressured to do so about a year after the election. At this time the party had begun a process of organizational, political and 'image' renewal.

Voter loyalties

As mentioned above, the pre-1973 Danish party system was characterized by a relatively high degree of stability and predictability, based as it was on close bonds between social class and party choice. A process of structural dealignment began as a consequence of economic growth, a decline in the number of blue-collar workers and farmers (the core voters of the Social Democratic Party and the Liberal Party respectively), a rapid expansion of the public sector and an increase in the number of public employees – in other words, as a consequence of the fundamental social and economic transformation experienced by Danish society during the 1960s. Since then parties have had to operate under a high degree of uncertainty.

The rise in the level of electoral volatility has proved steady, however. From a low level, equivalent to most of the other West European democracies in the 1950s (Pedersen 1983), and a modest increase in the 1960s, volatility in the 1970s almost 'exploded' and in 1973 reached an all-time peak at 29 percent. The 1980s witnessed a return to the medium level of the 1960s with a low point at 6 percent in 1988 to be followed by a rise once again in the 1990s (see Table 8.1).

Regarding other indicators of party loyalty this situation of uncertainty is further exacerbated by evidence from survey data that since 1968 the average extent of party shifting has been 23 percent, again with 1973 as an all-time high of 40 percent. During the same period, another 15 to 20 percent of the voters actually considered voting for another party than at the previous election, but ended up voting for the same party once again. All in all, between 40 and 50 percent of the voters have been more or less available on the market during election campaigns. The importance of these campaigns is emphasized by the fact that on average 25 percent of the voters make the decision on which party to cast their vote for during the campaign itself (Worre 1987; Nielsen 1992; Borre and Goul Andersen 1997; Andersen *et al.* 1999).

Contrary to what could be expected on the basis of the level of electoral volatility and the percentage of party shifters, it is not possible to detect any significant change in the party identification of voters, either in the proportion of identifiers or in the proportion of strong identifiers. These indicators of electoral loyalty have been remarkably constant during the past 25 years, except for a minor momentary decline in 1973 (see Table 8.3). Throughout the period, surveys also indicated that the voters had a positive attitude towards the political parties, with at least nine out of ten electors who cast their vote having a positive attitude towards the party they voted for. Furthermore, turnout has been fairly stable at the 83 to 89 percent level, meaning that the option of expressing dissatisfaction with the whole range of parties by abstaining from voting has not been extensively exercised. Thus positive voting dominates negative voting by far. In general, anti-party sentiments have not prevailed among Danish voters. As a matter of fact, in the 1998 election, a quarter of the voters expressed a positive evaluation of at least two parties, whereas another quarter only differentiated slightly between their preferred parties. This means that voters do not choose among the lesser evils, but on the contrary, among the very best (Nielsen 1995, 1999).

From a competitive point of view this implied that not only did the left wing, centre and right wing compete against each other, but also that competition was directed as much, if not more so, against the neighbouring parties. For a

Table 8.3 Indicators of party loyalty in Denmark, 1971–98 (in percent)

	Party identification	Strong party identification	Party shifters	Decide during election campaign
1971	56	30	19	14
1973	47	24	40	33
1975	47	30	25	25
1977	50	30	21	27
1979	49	30	17	24
1981			20	29
1984	51	27	19	23
1987			26	24
1988			17	22
1990	54	27	19	20
1994			23	28
1998	50	23	29	29

No scientific survey was conducted before 1971. Questions on party identification were not included in the survey of the 1981 election and the elections after 1984, except 1990 and 1998. Data from the 2001 election are not available at the time of writing (March 2003).

Party identification: Question wording: 'Mange betragter sig som tilhængere af et bestemt politisk parti. Der findes også mange, der ikke føler sig som tilhængere af noget parti. Plejer De selv at betragte Dem som fx. socialdemokrat, radikal, konservativ, venstremand, SF'er eller noget andet, eller føler De Dem ikke som tilhænger af et af partierne? Hvis tilhænger, hvilket parti?' ('Many people identify with a particular party, but there are of course many who don't have any such identification with any of the parties. Do you usually think of yourself, for example, as a Social Democrat, a Social Liberal, a Conservative, a Liberal or something else, or do you not have any such identification with any of the parties? If you identify, which party?') 1998: 'Do you generally feel attached to a particular party?'

Strong party identification: Question wording: 'Hvis tilhænger: Nogle er stærkt overbeviste tilhængere af deres parti, mens andre ikke er så stærkt overbeviste. Betragter De Dem selv som stærkt overbevist tilhænger af Deres parti eller ikke stærkt overbevist?' (If you identify: Some think of themselves as strongly identified with their party while others are not so strongly identified. Do you think of yourself as strongly identified with your party or not so strongly?) 1998: 'If attached, do you feel very strong, quite strong, or not very strongly attached to this party?'

Party shifters: Percentage of voters who voted for another party than at the previous election.

Negative vote: Percentage of voters who have a negative evaluation of the party they voted for.

Source: Schmitt and Holmberg 1995: 128; Nielsen 1995: 14; Goul Andersen *et al.* 1998: 14

non-committed voter with basic bourgeois attitudes, the large number of parties at that end of the political spectrum provided a great variety to choose among. It was not a choice among basic values but among very specific issues. After all, to vote for either the Liberals or the Conservatives would not make that much difference since their basic programmes were relatively close to one other. What seemed to be decisive for a large proportion of the voters was the current performance and appearance of the party.

From the perspective of the parties this meant that their stand on very specific issues, their campaign strategy and techniques, their communication, their ability to respond to the actual mood of the electorate, and so on, were very important in convincing the electorate to vote precisely for this bourgeois party and not for another bourgeois party. This, and the stable proportion of party identifiers, might help to explain the stability of the distribution of votes between the socialist and the bourgeois blocs. If you occasionally changed your party vote, you only moved to a party for which you had an even more positive attitude, i.e. the adjoining party. This was the situation prior to the emergence of the Danish People's Party, which has attracted voters from the Social Democrats, Conservatives and Liberals (Nielsen 1999: 53), thus increasing bloc volatility.

This brief summary illustrates a mixed picture of high general volatility and low bloc volatility, with a large proportion of floating voters, lower levels of party loyalty, and a significant proportion of protest votes emerging in the 1970s, even with a more general absence of anti-party sentiments. This presents a challenging cocktail of uncertainty to the parties, not least to the Social Democratic Party and the Liberal Party, both of which for decades had the highest rate of committed core voters.

Perceptions of the parties

As a consequence of the economic and social transformation of Danish society, which took place during the 1960s, the traditional strong bonds between party and social class were loosened. The parties observed these changes and the effects they had on their electoral base. They perceived the moderate increase in volatility as a natural consequence of societal changes; changes that offered both threats and opportunities depending on how they adapted to the changing environment in which they had to operate in the future. The analysis by the party secretary of the Liberal Party in his report to the 1965 party conference (LP 1965) covers by and large the perception expressed in the reports of the secretaries from the other old parties as well. Among his conclusions were that the development in the occupational distribution of the population worked against the Liberals. The traditional electoral stronghold of the party, the rural population, had declined rapidly, while the party had gained voters in the urban districts. Furthermore, the structure of the mass media was changing. The influence of the non-partisan state television was increasing at the expense of the party press. The effects were a weakening of the parties' ability to monopolize information and to encapsulate 'their' voters. Political propaganda in general and election campaigning in particular had become more expensive and increasingly would become so. More resources for party-controlled communication and propaganda were needed (LP 1965: 69ff.). At the time, however, this process of change was not perceived by the parties as either dramatic in itself, or as threatening the parties or the functionality of the party system. This perception altered completely in 1973.

The election result of 1973 came as a shock to all the established parties. The fundamental change in format of the party system in 1973 coincided with the onset of an economic recession. Hence an atmosphere of crisis developed in Danish politics. During parliamentary debates, leading politicians of the Social

Democratic and Liberal Parties expressed the opinion that developments in the 1970s were threatening not only the established parties, but also the functioning of the party system more generally, and that they indicated a crisis of Danish democracy. At the systemic level, then, the established parties perceived the consequences of the new party system as leading to a loss of steering capacity and to diminishing efficacy. The legitimacy of the parties was jeopardized. Furthermore, this was seen as a challenge to the democratic regime as such and since they, not surprisingly, considered the established parties to be the building blocks upon which the democratic regime rested, this development was logically perceived as a threat to themselves as well:

> The parties' core voters – including the Liberal Party – are becoming fewer and fewer. This implies a risk of obliteration for the old established parties, but it also implies opportunities. The political battle will be severe as never seen before. It is no longer just a matter of losing or gaining a couple of seats. It is survival that is at stake. Nothing less. (LP 1975: 16)[1]

The general impression one gets from analysing internal reports and material produced by the established parties during the 1970s is one of instant bewilderment, disorientation and confusion. The parties did not know how to understand and how to react to the electoral upheaval other than by presenting themselves as accountable parties, sharpening the edges of their ideological profile and traditional policies, and streamlining their organizations (SDP 1977a: 12ff; LP 1975, 1980). They constantly stressed the need for increased activism by the rank-and-file party members. Besides admitting that they apparently had coped inadequately with the country's economic and social problems, they expressed the opinion that they had failed to communicate their platforms and policies to the electorate so that a large proportion of the voters had turned their backs to them in sheer protest. In their understanding, the support of the new parties was, first of all, an action of protest, misinformation and misunderstanding, and to a lesser extent was the result of the emergence of new cleavage dimensions leading to the transformation of the party system. In their own opinion, the established parties had failed in fulfilling some of their most important functions in the political system: the role as a channel for two-way communication between the electorate and the elected as well as their role in political education and socialization.

It seems fair to conclude that the perceptions of the established parties were threefold: concern for legitimacy of the democratic regime, concern for the party system's ability to solve the economic and political problems, and concern for their own fortunes in the electoral market. The established parties only gradually realized in earnest that the increased voter volatility and high degree of uncertainty in the electoral market was not just a temporary outburst of protest but a permanent phenomenon. The mood of shock, confusion and frustration was gradually replaced by more balanced reflections on how to respond to the challenge of the high level of electoral volatility, new political issues, a transformed party system, and a highly fractionalized parliament in the long run.

Party responses to electoral dealignment

Organizational responses

Since declining party activism and falling party membership were among the explanations given by the established parties as important causes of the increased electoral volatility and their own changing fortunes in the electoral market, several of the organizational adjustments were adopted to enhance internal party democracy, increase the formal influence of individual party members in the internal decision-making process, and improve communication internally between bottom and top within the party. The parties, then, were concerned with making their organizations better and more attractive to their members in order to maintain their existing memberships and even to attract new members. This, however, was not seen as an end in itself but as a way of improving communication with the public in general. At the congress of the Social Democratic Party it was stated in this way:

> The political strategy of the Social Democratic Party has as its prerequisite a large and comprehensive mass party. It has to be large because it must express the attitudes and the will of the people. It is not just about winning elections but also about a day-to-day effort to win people for our ideas. ...The purpose of having a membership organization...is to work out our policy, to communicate it, and to implement it at all levels of society. (SDP 1980)

Regarding candidate selection for national elections, the Social Democratic Party in 1969 introduced postal ballots among the party members. In 1973 the same procedure was adopted as an option in the Liberal Party (Bille 1993, 2001). In relation to the representation of individual members in the party conference or congress and in the executive bodies, the rule changes all pointed in the direction of slightly increasing their representation. The proportion of *ex officio* members of the leading bodies was slightly reduced to the advantage of officers elected by the lower party bodies (Bille 1994: 139ff, 1997: 86ff). In the 1980s and 1990s a trend of moderate decentralization of the membership party is perceptible.

The most important organizational change in the Social Democratic Party took place in 1996 at the 125th anniversary party congress when the delegates decided to cut the formal organizational linkage with the trade unions and the cooperative workers' movement. One of the explicitly stated intentions behind the abolition of the historic reciprocal representation in the executive organs of these organizations was to enhance the manoeuvrability of the party within the parliamentary and electoral arenas. In itself this can be seen as a relevant response to the unstable and fluid electoral market, as well as a response to the complicated pattern of competition, cooperation and conflict prevailing in the party system. The perception of the Social Democratic leadership was that the pattern of competition and the targeting of new voters required more room for prompt and flexible policy reactions by the party.

The parties also sought to enhance internal party democracy in the preparation of their basic programmes. In the 1970s and 1980s they introduced comprehensive hearing processes whereby proposals were circulated among party members before the final programme was adopted at the party conference (Bille 1994: 142ff.). It is possible to see here a deliberate effort by the parties to initiate and sustain a process of moderate decentralization of some of the important internal decisions.

Until the end of the 1980s the Danish parties were perceived by the public as well as by themselves as voluntary, autonomous and private associations. Amateurism, then, played for decades a predominant role in the functioning of the parties. This changed markedly in the Social Democratic Party and the Liberal Party from the 1980s and especially after the mid-1990s when a process of professionalisation took place. From a level of around 30 part-time and 15 full-time employees in the 1970s, there was a growth towards around 110 employees in both parties in 2000 (Bille 1997: 269ff.; SDP 2002; LP 2002). It is interesting to note that it is the staff employed by the parliamentary party (mostly secretaries for the MPs), which experienced by far the most expansion, indicating that this subsystem of the party has been professionalized to a larger extent than the membership party. On the other hand, the ratio of professionals to party members in the membership organization itself has also increased.

Reading the reports of the annual party conferences from the past three decades, one gets the impression that the two parties became more and more aware of the importance of communication, and of getting the 'right message' communicated to the public. However, this awareness did not result in any substantial increase in the employment of communications specialists, at least throughout the 1970s and 1980s when both parties had financial problems. Following the introduction in 1987 of state subsidies to the membership party, however, and a substantial increase in 1995 of the amounts paid to the parliamentary party and the membership party (see p. 238 below), the parties considerably expanded their communication capacity.

In addition to the increased manpower engaged by the parties, there has also been a recent introduction and rapid expansion in the use of computers and websites. The party leader of the Liberal Party was the first to publish a weekly electronic newsletter in 1995, a practice soon followed by the top politicians of the Social Democratic Party and the other parties. By the end of 1997 all parties had their own websites. Their quality and content vary but both the Liberals and the Social Democrats publish daily press releases, programmatic material and conference reports. They also offer voters the opportunity of an on-line dialogue with politicians. The new technology augmented the two parties' communication capacity and their ability to bypass the conventional media and communicate directly with voters and members. The internet became an integral part of the parties' communication strategy for the first time during the 1998 campaign and was further elaborated in the 2001 campaign.

One of the most significant signs of professionalization was the establishment of political-economic departments, founded by both the Social Democratic

Party and the Liberal Party in 1986. That of the Social Democrats was placed under the direct control of the party leader, and its main work was to undertake independent analyses of the economic and political situation, to elaborate appropriate strategies, to prepare major political initiatives and to participate in the planning and implementation of election campaigns. The political-economic department of the Liberal Party had similar functions and status. By the end of the century, each was staffed by some eight full-time academic employees. By Danish standards the increase in the professional expertise of these new and important party organs was quite substantial.

In sum, three trends support the conclusion that the responses of the Social Democratic Party and the Liberal Party to the erosion of voter loyalty and uncertainty of the electoral market included professionalization. First, the general increase in salaried manpower; secondly, the creation and expansion of departments of experts; and thirdly, an increase in the communication staff and new communication technology.

Traditionally, however, the Danish parties have been reluctant to make use of so-called 'modern' techniques. This has been reflected in their ambiguous attitude towards employing the expertise of professional advertising and marketing agencies, which have only been occasionally engaged by either the Social Democrats or the Liberals during inter-election periods to perform market research, voter surveys or promotions. When this has been done, it has tended to be on a purely *ad hoc* basis and cannot be seen as part of a coherent, deliberate and long-term strategy.

When it comes to election campaigning, the picture is somewhat different. Even though it is impossible to trace the use of advertising agencies in election campaigning systematically, sporadic information in the organizational reports of the two parties indicates that the parties have used such agencies since the beginning of the 1960s. The scattered information, however, also indicates that the use was never regularized. Since the mid-1980s, however, the Liberal Party has employed an advertising agency, which has been quite influential in determining the campaign style and appearance (Bille *et al.* 1992: 68). The practice of the Social Democratic Party points in the opposite direction. The use of professional consultants and market research agencies for the design of the party's 1987 election campaign was, in retrospect, considered too expensive and of little use. Thereafter the party's own strategists considered themselves to be the real experts on election campaigning – particularly since Denmark had held a general election almost every other year in the period from 1971 to 1990. They drew on their expertise, on feedback from the well-organized party network, on opinion polls in the newspapers, and on studies that had been produced by university researchers for general academic purposes. Instead of hiring advertising agencies, the Social Democratic Party relied on a partisan network of skilled lithographic artists, layout specialists and communication experts, all working on a voluntary basis (Bille *et al.* 1992: 65).

Although the use of advertising agencies by parties has long been the norm in campaigning (Bowler and Farrell 1992: 227), the Danish parties more generally have been hesitant in making full use of the campaign consultancy profession. A combination of money shortages and an ideological opposition to commercializing party competition have been among the reasons cited by the parties for this reluctance. After the substantial increase in the state subsidy to the parties, adopted in 1995, attitudes changed in this respect. Both parties have, to a larger extent than before, hired professional marketing expertise. They have also both experimented with and used focus groups and have hired professional experts for the election campaigns.

Nevertheless, throughout the period both parties attached great importance to, and depended heavily on, the voluntary labour of their party members – during the election campaigns themselves as well as during inter-election periods. The general trend has been towards a diminution in the parties' dependence on the voluntary work of amateurs, however. Until the mid-1990s, the costs of buying expertise 'in town' was considered to outweigh the benefits – as well as being seen as too 'American', and alien to the Danish political culture. However, by the turn of the millennium this attitude had changed. Focus groups, communication experts and the like are used to an increasing extent by the major parties, and primarily by the Social Democrats and Liberals. The parliamentary and extra-parliamentary party organizations have been professionalized and have increased their use of external expertise.

Programmatic, ideological and policy-oriented responses

Historically, organizing the labour movement in Denmark followed three paths. Parallel to the political organization in the party, the workers founded trade unions and cooperative firms, all of which were organizationally connected to one another. Since the Social Democratic movement was the driving force behind the creation of the Danish welfare state, this tightly knit organizational network and its political standpoints came under attack from two sides in the 1970s and 1980s. On the one hand, the extreme left-wing parties, experiencing a revival in the wake of the youth rebellion of the 1960s and the renaissance of Marxism, criticized the entire Social Democratic movement for being fossilized, too bourgeois and too reformist, and for not taking care of the real interests of the working class. The party had been confronted with that kind of criticism before, but competition on the electoral market for the Socialist voters became especially intense during the economic recession of the 1970s and early 1980s. On the other hand, the electoral success of the Progress Party in the 1970s also reflected a criticism of the Social Democratic Party, which in some ways was more serious than the usual attacks from the Left. The Progress Party constituted a special problem for the Social Democratic Party partly because it attacked the basic features of the Social Democratic model of the welfare state system, and partly because surveys demonstrated that, contrary to what one would expect from reading the Progress Party manifesto, a large proportion of the Progress Party's voters were drawn from the working class, and from among the traditionally committed voters of the Social Democratic Party.

This led to considerable soul-searching among the Social Democrats, and among the answers produced by the party was that the ideological education of the voters had been neglected. Too much emphasis had been put on providing material goods, and too little on the importance of cultivating solidarity, community spirit and solid information about the benefits ordinary people get in return for their taxes. The idea underlying the welfare system had not been sufficiently promoted, with the result that a party such as the Progress Party could succeed.

It is in this context of competition from both the Left and the Right that the content of a new basic programme adopted in 1977 is to be understood. Compared to the previous programme of 1961, this new platform marked a distinctive move to the left. Concepts derived from Marxist thinking were used in the description of the Danish capitalist society. Democracy was incomplete as long as key economic decisions were not under democratic control. Hence common ownership of all means of production was stated as the ultimate goal, a phrase which had been abolished in the 1961 programme. The qualities of solidarity, equality, brotherhood and cooperation were frequently contrasted with the drawbacks of selfishness, individual competition, alienation and self-centred consumerism. The responsibility of the community for care of the weak in society and the importance of comprehensive state regulation of the free market economy was emphasized. The public sector was not the enemy but the tool to create a harmonious society (SDP 1977b). In all, the 1977 programme was a move away from the rather catch-all manifesto of 1961 and a return to the traditional core values of the party. One of the ways by which the party tried to recapture and strengthen its electoral support was therefore through the adoption of a more distinct ideological platform.

Although this strategy proved a success in the second half of the 1970s, in the sense that the party regained some of its former electoral strength, it failed in the 1980s. Defeats at the 1981, 1984 and 1987 elections, a gain of only one seat in 1988, and persistence in opposition due to lack of support from the centre parties, gradually produced a situation in which a change of strategy was deemed necessary. The need for change was further underlined by the general transformation in the ideological climate that took place in the wake of the collapse of Communism in 1989. The competition from the extreme Left wing declined, as did competition from the Progress Party, which by now had been transformed into a small and ordinary opposition party. The result of this changing strategic environment paved the way for the adoption of a new basic programme in 1992.

This programme must be characterized as a catch-all programme, phrased in very short catchword-like sentences. Gone were the Marxist-inspired vocabulary and the lengthy analyses. Solidarity, community and brotherhood were still mentioned in the programme, but this time as prerequisites for individual freedom, for the right to choose, and for pluralism and happiness. Public regulation was replaced by public service, common ownership of the means of production by cooperation between the public sector and private enterprise, welfare state by welfare society, and so forth (SDP 1992). In short, it was now a Liberal ethic that prevailed, and the direction of the electoral competition was clearly centripetal.

The party succeeded in gaining governmental power in 1993 and managed to stay in office after the 1994 general election despite the loss of seven seats. This loss, together with decreasing support in opinion polls, the continuing decline in membership and the reform policy of the coalition government, aroused a heated debate in the party between 'traditionalists' and 'reformers'. The 'traditionalists' claimed that Liberalism was not the cure but the disease. They wanted an end to privatization and an increase rather than a cut in public spending. The reformers believed it was precisely such standpoints that had led to the weakening of electoral support. In their opinion such views were old fashioned, totally out of tune with contemporary realities, and had no chance of appealing to the new generations of volatile voters. The reformers did not regard the public sector as sacred and also had a more relaxed attitude towards privatization. What mattered was not who did the job, but how it was done, while the role of the public authorities was to lay down the general standards to be followed.

This intense discussion was part of the process of adjusting party policies to a changing cleavage structure. A 'New Politics' dimension of non-economic issue preferences had emerged in Denmark (Borre 1995). This confronted the Social Democratic Party with a serious challenge: how to maintain its support among the less educated, the low income groups and the pensioners yet gain support among the new groups and generations of better educated and well-off voters (Borre and Goul Andersen 1997). The catch-all 1992 manifesto, the historic change in party organization and the ongoing efforts to 'modernize' and change the entire culture and image of the Social Democratic movement from one of a 'combat army marching in step' to a dialogue-oriented, flexible and open movement have so far been among the responses to this challenge (SDP 1996: 28–33). The historical heritage is massive, however, and the public image of the party hard to change. The process of transformation at the end of the 1990s was therefore complex and difficult, and accelerated when the Social-Democratic-led government resigned following electoral defeat in 2001. This initiated both an organizational and a political process of debate and innovation.

By the beginning of the 1990s, the Liberal Party had completed the first part of its transformation. It had been a long process. Originally an agrarian party, the decline in the number of farmers, which has accelerated since the 1950s, had forced the party to appeal to voters from other segments of society. The constant decline in electoral support from 1957 to 1987 illustrates the magnitude of the difficulties that faced the party in this enterprise.

The party had to rethink its electoral target groups. It began to appeal to the wage earners, mainly in the private sector, and to the rapidly growing suburban middle-class population. In contrast to the Social Democratic Party, the Liberal Party was not constrained in its transformation by formal party rules linking it to any interest organization. The close cooperation with the agricultural organizations had always been based on personal overlapping membership. There were no formal ties to be cut. This facilitated the gradual build-up of relations to a variety of business and employers' associations.

Freedom, the rights of the individual versus the state and the supremacy of a free market economy have always been central to the Liberal Party's ideas. But in the basic programmes of 1963, 1970 and, to a lesser extent, that of 1979 (LP 1963, 1970, 1979), the importance of a well-functioning public sector, the obligations of the state, the continued build-up of a public social security net and a public-financed health and educational system were also stressed. As such, the party was not opposed to welfare systems as long as these systems did not excessively constrain the opportunities and the responsibilities of the individual. During this period, the actual positions adopted toward the welfare state were not so much a matter of differences in kind as of differences in degree. Paradoxically, the presence of a large Progress Party more or less forced the Liberals in the 1970s to be less critical of the public sector for fear of being lumped with the ultra-liberal, populist and protest attitudes of that party. During the 1960s and 1970s then, the Liberal Party pursued mainly a catch-all centre-oriented strategy with a liberal flavour.

This 'soft' strategy was abandoned during the 1980s – especially following the election in 1984 of Uffe Ellemann-Jensen as party chairman. Constant stress was laid on the ideological distinctiveness of the party's policy declarations, and in 1985 the central party organization published a proposal for discussion, *From Welfare State to Welfare Society* (LP 1985a), launching an attack on the Social Democratic welfare model. Due to this ideological offensive, the party was from time to time accused of simultaneously being in government and in opposition. A firm stand was taken in favour of cuts in the public sector, extensive privatization, a substantial increase in the opportunities, responsibilities and freedom of choice of the individual, and, of course, the free market economy. The title of the 1995 party manifesto is in itself telling: *The Person rather than the System* (LP 1995).

After the Liberal Party returned to opposition in 1993, it pursued an even more intense ideological battle against the Social Democratic Party and promoted the new liberalism with elements of libertarian positions. Electoral competition was certainly no longer centripetal. The party addressed no specific target group as such, other than those urban and suburban citizens who were generally favourable towards 'more liberalism and less social democracy'. Electorally, the party succeeded, and was able to regain the share of the electorate it had had during the 1950s. The ideological battle was downgraded following the election in 1998, however, when the Liberal-led alternative government just missed winning a majority of seats in the Folketing. This resulted in a change of strategy in the Liberal Party, which in the period up to the 2001 election pursued a new, centre-oriented strategy. This also proved successful, and for the first time since 1924 the Liberals became the largest party among the electorate, winning the position of Prime Minister in a joint coalition with the Conservatives.

Institutional responses

One of the most important responses to the volatile electoral market has been the decision to introduce state subsidies to the parties. Considering themselves private and financially autonomous bodies, the parties had been long-term opponents of any system offering direct public subventions to their extra-parliamentary organizations. Reluctance to introduce subsidies for the parliamentary party organization was less evident. Indeed, state subsidies to the parliamentary parties were introduced as early as 1965, with the law granting a direct state subsidy to the extra-parliamentary organization being passed only in 1986, with effect from 1987 onwards.

The rules regulating the allocation of money to individual parliamentary groups changed gradually, but the basic criterion was to allocate a fixed sum per group plus an additional sum per seat. The increase in the subsidy was modest prior to the 1980s, but was augmented in 1983, in 1986, and – substantially – in 1995. The reason given by the parties in 1965 for the introduction of a state subsidy was the need for the parliamentary groups to hire consultants and expert assistance in order to cope with the increasing complexity of legislation (FF 1966: 2369). This argument was repeated in the subsequent rounds of increases in the subsidy and was supplemented by the need for individual MPs to hire their own secretaries. These subsidies made possible the expansion of the manpower employed by the parliamentary groups as well as the establishment of the professionally staffed political-economic departments of the Social Democratic Party and the Liberal Party (see p. 222 above).The fact that it is the parties themselves that have awarded substantial increases in the amount of state subsidy to the parliamentary parties indicates the importance they attach to their performance in parliament, and to the effect of this on their success or failure in the electoral arena. In this sense, the system of state subsidies can be seen as a direct response to the volatility and uncertainty of electoral markets.

Another and related response has been the introduction of a state subsidy to the extra-parliamentary party. Since the beginning of the 1960s, and especially during the 1970s, there has been a drastic decline in party membership (Bille 1997: 68ff; Mair and van Biezen 2001). Because party members are assumed to be stable voters, paying their membership fees and at least occasionally providing voluntary manpower in the various party activities, the declining membership was correctly perceived by the parties as a destabilizing factor and as a loss of economic and human resources. Time and again, in a constant effort to turn the tide, the parties organized membership drives, but all in vain. Increasingly, the old parties felt that their position as the prime mobilizing and agenda-setting force in the democratic system was threatened by other actors such as powerful interest groups, the mass media and single issue movements – not to mention the fact that the new parties seemed able to mobilize voters without large party organizations. The parties desperately needed to find an alternative to the disappearing membership fees (Pedersen and Bille 1991: 156). This feeling intensified during the first half of 1980s, and not without reason. In 1984 the Social Democratic central party organization had a deficit of DDK 4.7 million. The party had to cut back on staff and limit its expenditure (SDP 1988: 73). The new measures that were adopted included a 30 percent cut in spending on training courses for party officials, as well as cessation of the publication of the membership journal (SDP 1988: 45, 59). The party secretary summarized the problem, and the solution, as follows:

> The economic and administrative demands on the party organizations are incessantly rising due to the accelerating development in society. As regards the Social Democratic Party, … the expenditures for various activities have increased immensely. So immensely that the budget could not keep up. The party's central committee and parliamentary group have been aware of this development for many years. That is why it has become a major issue for the party to pass a law granting public subsidy to the educational work and information activities of the parties. (SDP 1988: 37)

The secretary of the Liberal Party expressed similar opinions, and he too complained about the activities the party had to give up due to shortages of money (LP 1985b: 5).

In December 1986 an overwhelming majority in parliament finally passed a law granting a state subsidy to the party organizations. The legislation was carried through with the explicitly stated purpose of 'strengthening the most important part of Danish democracy', at the same time with the intention 'to avoid the tendency that the mass media becomes completely dominant in the process by which the parties present themselves to the citizens'. It was also intended to ensure that future political activities would become less dependent on 'donations from private business and from organizations' (FF 1986: 10395ff.). The spokesperson of the Liberal Party expressed the opinion of the majority as follows:

> what will be the consequences, if a still growing proportion of political opinion formation takes place within the framework of special interests and to an even lesser extent within the framework of the political parties… . Is it defensible in our democracy that the political parties become poorer and poorer compared to the power apparatus of the interest organizations, their swelling cash boxes and their potential for exerting influence? Hardly. (FF 1987: 2529)

The law imposes no organizational requirements whatsoever in terms of the rules for allocation of this subsidy. Rather, it is simply the number of votes that counts, and even a single candidate participating on his or her own in a national, county or municipality election is entitled to receive an annual sum of money from the state, the size of which depends on the number of votes received at the specific election.

The state subvention to the party organizations can hardly be seen as exclusively beneficial to the established parties. Nor does it shield them effectively from threats from the electoral market since the subsidy is also granted to parties which are not represented in parliament. This, of course, is not the case with the state subsidy to the parliamentary parties. In 2001 the direct state subvention to the central party organizations and parliamentary groups amounted to around DKK 175 million, of which the Social Democratic Party received DKK 54 million and the Liberal Party 39 million. The proportion of the total income of the central organization of the Social Democratic Party received from direct state subsidies was 40 percent in the election year 2001 and 55 percent in the non-election year 2000. In the Liberal Party, in 2001 the proportion was 44 percent and 54 percent in 2000 (2001 accounts of the two parties).

Concluding remarks

Although this chapter has looked at a limited number of possible responses to the erosion in voter loyalties in Denmark, and has focused on only two parties, the pattern which has emerged is probably typical of the full range of parties in the system as a whole. The first response to the difficulties that have faced the parties was the introduction of a state subsidy to the party organization in 1987 and a substantial increase in the subsidy that has been allocated to the parliamentary party since its introduction in 1965. This enabled the parties to improve their organizational capacity and communication capabilities, both of which were continually cited by the parties as being very important to their efforts to operate within a fluid electoral market and to maintain or even improve their position as a significant organizing force *vis-à-vis* other actors in the political system.

The second response is professionalization. The dependence on voluntary work by 'amateurs' was reduced, while the use of experts increased, first and foremost in the parliamentary section of the parties. While reliance on external expertise in campaigning has fluctuated, it nevertheless became a dominant element from the mid-1990s onwards. Coupled to this is a third response, which has involved a deliberate effort by the parties to initiate and sustain a process of moderate decentralization of some of the important internal decision-making procedures with the purpose of increasing activism among party members.

Both the Social Democratic Party and the Liberal Party have also been forced to rethink their electoral target groups due to the declining number of farmers, the weakening unity of the workers' organizations and the emerging complex value configuration of old and new politics. The party platforms that have been adopted indicate that, on the level of principles, the strategies of the two parties have vacillated, downgrading their ideological distinctiveness at one moment and reasserting it at another. In the late 1970s the Social Democrats succeeded in regaining electoral strength by upgrading their ideology, but this strategy then failed in the 1980s. For the Liberal Party, virtually the reverse occurred, in that the downplaying of its core ideology failed in the late 1970s and the first half of the 1980s. Then both parties shifted strategies once again. From the end of the 1980s, the Liberal Party succeeded in emphasizing a distinct Liberal ideological profile and in following a strategy of confrontation with the Social Democratic Party. The latter shifted at the beginning of the 1990s to a catch-all and centre-oriented strategy which paid off in the sense that its electoral support stabilized and the party regained governmental power after ten years in opposition. Part of the strategy was to break the formal ties with the trade unions, increasing the party's freedom of manoeuvre. The catch-all, centre-oriented strategy was also followed by the Liberal Party after their unsuccessful attempt in 1998 to win government.

These shifts in strategy have to be understood in the context of the composition of the party system itself. For all the electoral volatility which has taken place, the party system has been characterized by a remarkably stable distribution of seats in parliament between the bourgeois and non-bourgeois blocs. The relatively high turnover of seats in the period has mostly occurred inside each of the two blocs, leaving the centre to decide the majority formation. Neither the Social Democratic Party nor the Liberal Party was able to gain governmental power without the support of one or more of the centre parties, and hence the two parties oscillated between a centre-oriented strategy and a strategy of confrontation. Both tried to make the centre parties superfluous to the majority building in parliament, but never did so simultaneously before 2001.

The systemic properties, the way the parties themselves choose to compete, their willingness since the late 1980s to include all parties in the formation of policy coalitions, as well as the deep-rooted Danish tradition of compromise, cooperation, party cohesion and party discipline, served to foster a kind of stability in the party system itself – at least until 2001. This stability can also be seen as an effort by the parties to subdue a volatile electoral market. The story that begins with the 2001 election could well prove different, however, in that the centre parties are no longer needed for majority building, and hence no longer exercise their traditional moderating influence. How long this new configuration will last, and how it will impact upon the strategies of the parties and the properties of the system, remains to be seen.

Note

1 Here, as elsewhere unless otherwise stated, the translation is by the present authors.

References

Andersen, Johannes, Ole Borre, Jørgen Goul Andersen, and Hans Jørgen Nielsen (1999). *Vælgere med omtanke – en analyse af folketingsvalget 1998*. Århus: Systime.

Bille, Lars (1989). 'Denmark: The Oscillating Party System.' *West European Politics* 12 (4): 42–58.

Bille, Lars (1993). 'Candidate Selection for National Parliament in Denmark 1960–1990. An Analysis of the Party Rules.' In Tom Bryder (ed.), *Party Systems, Party Behaviour and Democracy*. Copenhagen: Copenhagen Political Studies Press, pp. 190–204.

Bille, Lars (1994). 'Denmark: the Decline of the Membership Party?' In Richard S. Katz and Peter Mair (eds), *How Parties Organize. Change and Adaptation in Party Organizations in Western Democracies*. London: Sage, pp. 134–57.

Bille, Lars (1997). *Partier i forandring. En analyse of otte danske partiorganisationers udvikling 1960–1995*. Odense: Odense Universitetsforlag.

Bille, Lars (2001). 'Democratizing a Democratic Procedure. Myth or Reality? Candidate Selection in Western Parties 1960–1990. '*Party Politics* 7: 363–80.

Bille, Lars, Jørgen Elklit, and Mikael V. Jakobsen (1992). 'Denmark: the 1990 Campaign.' In Shaun Bowler and David M. Farrell (eds), *Electoral Strategies and Political Marketing*. London: Macmillan, pp. 63–81.

Borre, Ole (1995). 'Old and New Politics in Denmark.' *Scandinavian Political Studies* 18: 187–205.

Borre, Ole and Jørgen Goul Andersen (1997). *Voting and Political Attitudes in Denmark. A Study of the 1994 Election*. Århus: Aarhus University Press.

Bowler, Shaun and David Farrell (1992). 'Conclusion: the Contemporary Election Campaign.' In Shaun Bowler and David Farrell (eds), *Electoral Strategies and Political Marketing*. London: Macmillan, pp. 223–35.

Callesen, Gerd (1996). 'Socialdemokratiets historie 1971–1996.' In Gerd Callesen, Steen Christensen, and Henning Grelle (eds), *Udfordring og omstilling. Bidrag til Socialdemokratiets historie 1971–1996*. Copenhagen: Fremad, pp. 1–109.

Carlsen, Erik Meier (1992). *Plads for dem alle? Strid og forvandling i Socialdemokratiet*. Haslev: Hovedland.

Damgaard, Erik (1973). 'Party Coalitions in Danish Lawmaking 1953–1970.' *European Journal of Political Research* 1: 35–66.

Damgaard, Erik and Palle Svensson (1989). 'Who Governs? Parties and Policies in Denmark.' *European Journal of Political Research* 17: 731–45.

FF (1966). *Folketingstidende 1965/66.*

FF (1979). *Folketingstidende, Folketingets forhandlinger, 1978/79.*

FF (1986). *Folketingstidende 1985/86, tillæg A.*

FF (1987). *Folketingstidende 1986/87, forhandlinger.*

Goul Andersen, Jørgen, Johannes Andersen, Ole Borre, and Hans Jørgen Nielsen (1998). *Danish Election Survey. Codebook and Marginals*. Århus: Aarhus Universitet.

Jørgensen, Anker (1989). *Bølgegang. Fra mine dagbøger 1972–1975*. Copenhagen: Fremad.

Jørgensen, Anker (1990). *Brændingen. Fra mine dagbøger 1978–1982*. Copenhagen: Fremad.

Kaarsted, Tage (1988). *Regeringen, vi aldrig fik. Regeringsdannelsen 1975 og dens baggrund*. Odense: Odense Universitetsforlag.

LP (1963). *Program for Venstre*, Danmarks liberale Party, 1963.

LP (1965). *Venstres Månedsblad* oktober 1965.

LP (1970). *Frem mod år 2000*. Programme for Venstre, Danmarks liberale Party, 1970.

LP (1975). *Venstre*. Organisationsberetning 1975.

LP (1979). *Det mener Venstre*. Programme for Venstre, Danmarks liberale Party, 1979.

LP (1980). *Styrk Folkestyret*. Landsmødeberetning 1980.

LP (1985a). *Fra Velfærdsstat til Velfærdssamfund*, 1985.

LP (1985b). *Beretning 1984/85.*

LP (1995). *Mennesket frem for systemet*. Principprogramme for Venstre, 1995.

LP (2002). Information from party headquarters.

Mair, Peter and Ingrid van Biezen (2001). 'Party Membership in Twenty European Democracies, 1980–2000.' *Party Politics* 7: 5–21.

Mikkelsen, Hans Christian (1994). 'Udviklingen i partisammenholdet.' *Politica*, 1: 25–31.

Nielsen, Hans Jørgen (1992). 'Valgkampen 1990.' In Lars Bille, Hans Jørgen Nielsen, and Steen Sauerberg, *De uregerlige vælgere. Valgkamp, medier og vælgere ved folketingsvalget 1990*. Copenhagen: Columbus.

Nielsen, Hans Jørgen (1995). 'Generel skepsis og konkret tillid. Vurderingen of danske politikere og partier 1971–1994.' Arbejdspapir 1995/12. Copenhagen: Institut for Statskundskab.

Nielsen, Hans Jørgen (1999). 'De individuelle forskydninger 1994–1998.' In Johannes Andersen, Ole Borre, Jørgen Goul Andersen, and Hans Jørgen Nielsen, *Vælgere med omtanke – en analyse af folketingsvalget 1998*. Århus: Systime, pp. 49–60.

Pedersen, Mogens N. (1967). 'Consensus and Conflict in the Danish Folketing 1945–65.' *Scandinavian Political Studies* (Old Series) 2: 143–66.

Pedersen, Mogens N. (1983). 'Changing Patterns of Electoral Volatility in European Party Systems, 1948–1977: Explorations in Explanations.' In Hans Daalder and Peter Mair (eds), *Western European Party Systems. Continuity and Change*. London: Sage, pp. 29–66.

Pedersen, Mogens N. (1987). 'The Danish "Working Multiparty System": Breakdown or Adaptation?' In Hans Daalder (ed.), *Party Systems in Denmark, Austria, Switzerland, the Netherlands and Belgium*. London: Frances Pinter, pp. 1–60.

Pedersen, Mogens N. and Lars Bille (1991). 'Public Financing and Public Control of Political Parties in Denmark.' In Matti Wiberg (ed.), *The Public Purse and Political Parties. Public Financing of Political Parties in Nordic Countries*. Helsinki: The Finnish Political Science Association, pp. 147–72.

Sartori, Giovanni (1976). *Parties and Party Systems. A Framework for Analysis*. Cambridge: Cambridge University Press.

Schmitt, Hermann and Søren Holmberg (1995). 'Political Parties in Decline?' In Hans-Dieter Klingemann and Dieter Fuchs (eds), *Citizens and the State*. Oxford: Oxford University Press, pp. 95–133.

SDP (1977a). Socialdemokratiet. Beretning politisk og organisatorisk 1973–1977.

SDP (1977b). Solidaritet, lighed og trivsel. Principprogram vedtaget på Socialdemokratiets 32. kongress september 1977.

SDP (1980). Organisatorisk beretning, 33. kongres 1980.

SDP (1988). Socialdemokratiets politisk-organizatoriske beretning 1984–88.

SDP (1992). Det ny århundrede. Socialdemokratiets principprogram, 1992.

SDP (1996). Socialdemokratiet. Kongresberetning, 1996.

SDP (2002). Information from party headquarters.

Svensson, Palle (1982). 'Party Cohesion in the Danish Parliament during the 1970s.' *Scandinavian Political Studies* 5 (1): 17–42.

Sørensen, Kurt (ed.) (1979). *Venstre. 50 år for folkestyret*. Holte: Forlaget Liberal.

Worre, Torben (1987) *Dansk vælgeradfærd*. København: Akademisk Forlag.

NINE   Political Parties in Electoral Markets in Postwar Ireland

Peter Mair and Michael Marsh

This chapter attempts to make sense of party responses to the changing electoral and party-systemic conditions in the Irish Republic. Notwithstanding evident long-term continuities in Irish politics, the situation that we analyse is multi-faceted and complex. Parties in Ireland have not just been obliged to adapt to changes in the electorate as such, and to new patterns of party–voter relationships, which is the main theme addressed by this volume, but they have also been obliged to reorient both their behaviour and their strategies within an environment that has become considerably more competitive. It is not only party–voter relationships that have been called into question, therefore, but also party–party relationships, with the system itself undergoing a series of major shifts in the structure of competition. Despite the complexities involved, however, we have opted for a very broad-ranging review in this chapter, highlighting a first wave of changes which took place from the late 1960s to the 1980s, when the parties made major efforts to professionalize their organizations and campaign techniques, and a second wave of changes which occurred during the late 1980s and 1990s, when many of the traditional political certainties appeared to evaporate. First we offer an overview of the long-term changes in the patterns of party competition. We then summarize the recent evidence of dealignment in a system in which there had never really been much evidence of long-term social group linkages. The following section reviews the shift from the stagnant political environment of the 1950s and 1960s to the more competitive and uncertain world that has developed since the 1970s, and identifies the principal lessons learned by all of the major parties as they sought to adapt. Our main focus here rests on the 1970s and 1980s, since it is in this period that the parties, at least at the organizational and campaigning level, did most to renew their approaches. The final section charts the parties' increasing reliance on state regulation and funding, while at the same time they attempt to remain as member-friendly as possible. We conclude by suggesting that however familiar the parties might appear, they are now having to respond to and cope with an increasingly unfamiliar political landscape, and that they therefore continue to tread very cautiously.

Changing patterns of party competition in postwar Ireland

For a country which was once classically defined as having a politics 'without social bases' (Whyte 1974), patterns of party politics in the Irish Republic for long proved remarkably stable – at least in the aggregate. During the 1930s, for example, when the parties as we now know them first took shape, the system had all the features of a two-and-a-half party format. Fianna Fáil, the biggest of the protagonists, then won an average vote of almost 48 percent. Fine Gael, the second major party, won almost 34 percent, and Labour, the 'half' party in the equation, won an average vote of little more than 8 percent. Half a century later, during the 1980s, the picture did not seem radically different, with Fianna Fáil winning an average vote of 45 percent, Fine Gael winning 34 percent, and with Labour still remaining on the margins with 9 percent.

Notwithstanding such aggregate electoral continuities, some fundamental shifts could be identified in the course of that half-century of party system development. The first and most obvious of these was in the broad ideological and programmatic orientation of the principal parties. This is hardly surprising, since it is really only through the regular adaptation of programmes and appeals that parties can hope to maintain an enduring presence over time. Fianna Fáil, which initially mobilized as radical nationalist alternative in pursuit of a more independent and self-sufficient Irish state, and which initially garnered most of its support from the more peripheral Irish constituencies, soon transformed itself into a centrist and quite conservative political force, intent on fostering economic growth and social harmony and reserving its more nationalist agenda for occasional rhetorical flourishes. Fine Gael also effectively reconstituted itself, eventually shedding a history which had involved close associations with the Blueshirts – the closest Ireland came to a continental-style Fascist move-ment in the 1930s – and promulgating a vision of a so-called 'Just Society' which saw its concerns in the late 1960s overlap increasingly with those of the moderately social-democratic Labour Party.

The second major transformation during these intervening years concerned the structure of competition. The initial alignment pitted Fianna Fáil against Fine Gael (the party political heirs to the protagonists in the short-lived civil war of 1922–23), leaving any remaining parties, including Labour, searching for a role. This was quickly transformed into a new and more enduring align-ment that pitted Fianna Fáil, on its own, against more or less *all* other parties taken together. This produced a structure of competition which bore many of the characteristics of a 'predominant-party system' (Sartori 1976), with Fianna Fáil winning most of the elections between 1932 and 1973. Thereafter, there emerged a more competitive, and usually bipolar system (see also Farrell 1994). In every one of the many elections held between 1973 and 2002, the incumbent government failed to be returned for a second consecutive period of office, and it was not until 2002, with the re-election of the Fianna Fáil–Progressive

Democrats coalition, that this sequence was finally broken. This newly competitive system was also marked by greater fragmentation and hence by a break with the traditional continuities, particularly from the late 1980s onwards. In 1987, the traditional parties were joined by the Progressive Democrats, a party that was originally set up by liberal Fianna Fáil dissidents, and in 1992 by the more radical Democratic Left, which began life in the early 1980s as an offshoot of the radical nationalist Sinn Féin party, and which eventually merged with Labour in 1999. The Green Party first entered the Dáil in 1989, and the new electoral emphasis of the old Sinn Féin party, which continues to be linked to the IRA, was rewarded when it won its first seat in 1997. By the start of the 1990s, therefore, the traditional party landscape seemed radically altered, with the increased fragmentation, and a sudden – if temporary – upsurge in Labour support in the early 1990s severely weakening the hold of the big two traditional parties (see Table 9.1).

Whereas Fianna Fáil and Fine Gael had often polled close to 80 percent of the votes from the 1930s through to the 1980s, their combined share fell to just 65 percent in the 1990s and to 64 percent in 2002. Newer and smaller parties, on the other hand, as well as an increased number of successful independent candidates, polled some 20 percent in the 1990s and over 25 percent in 2002. Turnout also fell quite dramatically at this time, and whereas Fianna Fáil and Fine Gael had been used to winning the votes of close to 60 percent of all registered voters, the combination of weakening support levels and the lower turnout left them with less than 44 percent of the electorate in the 1990s and only 40 percent in 2002. In short, an electoral market that had appeared relatively stagnant throughout the 1950s and 1960s, and which had become more competitive in the 1970s and 1980s, had, by the start of the twenty-first century, become substantially more open and disengaged. By then, few if any of the older certainties still remained.

A further change was also to be marked after 1989, in that government formation processes finally opened up to more innovative formulas. Prior to the late 1980s, and primarily because Fianna Fáil refused to consider entering coalition, insisting instead on its status as the only party which could plausibly promise the benefits of single-party (majority) government, competition was necessarily bipolar, with the only governing alternatives being either a Fianna Fáil single-party administration or a coalition of Fine Gael and Labour. All other options were closed off. This pattern was eventually broken, however, first by a Fianna Fáil–Progressive Democrats coalition in 1989 and then in 1992 by a Fianna Fáil–Labour coalition, followed by further alliances between Fianna Fáil and the Progressive Democrats in 1997 and 2002. An additional innovation was marked in 1994 when the Fianna Fáil–Labour government collapsed and when Fine Gael, Labour and the Democratic Left formed a three-party coalition, the first time a new government had been installed in the middle of a parliamentary term and without a prior election. These new patterns served to undermine the traditional structure of competition, and introduced a number of major uncertainties for both voters and party leaders. Not only had

Table 9.1 Irish election results, 1950s–2002

Party		50s	60s	70s	81	82i	82ii	87	89	92	97	02
Fianna Fáil	%Votes	46.0	45.7	48.4	45.3	47.3	45.2	44.1	44.1	39.1	39.3	41.5
	N Seats	71	72	77	78	81	75	81	77	68	77	81
Fine Gael	%Votes	28.1	33.4	32.9	36.5	37.3	39.2	27.1	29.3	24.5	28.0	22.5
	N Seats	43	48	49	65	63	70	51	55	45	54	31
Labour	%Votes	10.9	14.8	12.7	9.9	9.1	9.4	6.4	9.5	19.3	10.4	10.8
	N Seats	16	19	18	15	15	16	12	15	33	17	21
Sinn Fein	%Votes	2.8	1.0	–	2.5	1.0	–	1.9	1.2	1.6	2.6	6.5
	N Seats	1	0	–	2	0	–	0	0	0	1	5
Clann na Talmhan	%Votes	2.8	0.5	–	–	–	–	–	–	–	–	–
	N Seats	5	1	–	–	–	–	–	–	–	–	–
Clann na Poblachta	%Votes	3.2	0.6	–	–	–	–	–	–	–	–	–
	N Seats	2	1	–	–	–	–	–	–	–	–	–
Workers Party	%Votes	–	–	1.4	1.7	2.2	3.1	3.8	5.0	0.7	0.4	0.2
	N Seats	–	–	0	1	3	2	4	7	0	0	0
Democratic Left	%Votes	–	–	–	–	–	–	–	–	2.8	2.5	–
	N Seats	–	–	–	–	–	–	–	–	4	4	–
Progressive Democrats	%Votes	–	–	–	–	–	–	11.8	5.5	4.7	4.7	4.0
	N Seats	–	–	–	–	–	–	14	6	10	4	8
Greens	%Votes	–	–	–	–	–	–	0.4	1.5	1.4	2.8	3.8
	N Seats	–	–	–	–	–	–	0	1	1	2	6
Inds & Others	%Votes	7.2	4.0	4.8	4.1	3.2	3.1	4.5	3.9	5.9	9.4	10.7
	N Seats	9	4	3	5	4	3	4	5	5	7	14
Total	%Votes	100.0	100.0	100.0	100.0	100.0	100.0	100.0	100.0	100.0	100.0	100.0
	N Seats	147	144	146	166	166	166	166	166	166	166	166
Volatility		10.1	7.2	5.0	8.9	3.3	3.6	16.2	7.8	13.8	9.6	8.5
Fractionalization		0.69	0.65	0.64	0.65	0.63	0.63	0.71	0.70	0.74	0.74	0.75
Turnout (%)		74.3	73.8	76.5	76.2	73.8	72.9	73.3	68.5	68.5	65.5	61.9
Effective number of parties		3.2	2.9	2.8	2.9	2.7	2.7	3.5	3.4	3.9	3.9	3.9

Calculations of volatility and fractionalization exclude parties with less than 0.5 and treat Independents as a single bloc.

Sources: Mair 1987a; Sinnott 1995; Gallagher 1999, 2003

more or less all Irish parties now become 'coalitionable' by the 1990s, but, within still existing limits,[1] each seemed also capable of coalescing with more or less all other parties. This new openness clearly enhanced the level of competition, helping to create an electoral market that was even less predictable than might be indicated by changing party–voter relations alone.

Despite the evident longevity in the distribution of partisan preferences through to the 1980s, however, and the generally low aggregate volatility, there had never seemed much in the way of any 'objective' social anchoring of these preferences on which the various parties could rely. In this sense, the Irish party system has long been regarded as quite removed from the traditional patterns of alignments usually found in Western Europe. The two major parties, Fianna Fáil (the more radical faction) and Fine Gael (the more moderate faction), emerged from a split within the broad nationalist movement, Sinn Féin, which had mobilized against British control in the early part of the century. The split between these parties was intense, bitter and polarizing, with the result that the dimensions of conflict not absorbed within the burgeoning competition between Fine Gael and Fianna Fáil were effectively marginalized. Class politics certainly went that way. The split was also essentially political, and while initially it overlapped to a more or less significant extent with the opposition between the 'haves' (FG) and 'have-nots' (FF), and, even within Ireland itself, between 'centre' (FG) and 'periphery' (FF) (see especially Garvin 1974; Rumpf and Hepburn 1977); and although it initially generated quite strong senses of loyalty and identification with each of the competing parties (e.g. Sinnott 1978), there was no real sense in which it reflected an enduring and socially rooted cleavage structure. Moreover, the few social correlates that did emerge in the initial formation stage were quickly dissipated by Fianna Fáil's 'invasion of the centre' (Garvin 1974), and by its increasingly successful appeal to the electorate at large.[2]

The postwar period had therefore witnessed the consolidation of a party system built around socially amorphous electoral alliances. The electorate of Fianna Fáil was more or less a proportionate sample of the Irish electorate as a whole, and while Fine Gael tended to be more oriented towards the middle-class and richer farmer vote, with Labour being more oriented towards the working class, the two smaller parties' frequent reversion to a mutual coalition strategy acted to negate even these slight social biases. But while in other settings such poorly defined electoral constituencies might well have provoked flux and uncertainty, as well as a keenly fought competitive environment, in the Irish case they actually served to reinforce conservatism and caution.

These attitudes were also encouraged by the character of the electoral system. The Single Transferable Vote in multi-member constituencies encouraged the growth and consolidation of *intra*-party rivalries at the local level that often proved even more intense and closely fought than those at the inter-party level. This led to a situation in which there was no necessary correspondence between the interests of the party as such (here defined as maximizing the number of seats which it could win in any given national election) and the interests of its individual candidates (here defined as maximizing their own individual chances of election), a potential tension that was to place severe limits on the scope for national vote management strategies in the 1970s and 1980s (see p. 250 below). Local self-interest could not only block attempts to put forward new policies – as Labour discovered to its cost in 1969 (Gallagher 1982: 86–103) – but it could also prevent optimal candidate nomination strategies. Novelty tended to be frowned upon, and a conservative bias prevailed – both in terms of policy development and organizational strategy. It was only after the mid-1970s that this pattern was seriously challenged, albeit not always effectively.[3]

Moreover, none of the parties was willing to go out on a limb in terms of forging a distinct socio-political identity. Fianna Fáil made a virtue of its nationally representative support base, targeting distinct social groups only when it felt that these might be lost to another party (see, e.g. Bew and Patterson 1982; Gallagher 1982: 93–7). When Fine Gael worried, it was usually about its less than universal appeal. In 1961, for example, the complaint had been that voting support in suburban areas had been damaged 'by the fairly widespread belief that Fine Gael is primarily a farmers' party'.[4] Twenty years later the party secretaries explained to the annual conference that 'Our problem is that the bulk of [our] support comes from people with middle class backgrounds.'[5] Indeed both major parties seemed most intent on maintaining a sometimes quite delicate balancing act, with each expending its major efforts in the maintenance of an appeal which could traverse more or less all social boundaries. Even Labour was not immune to the demands of electoral catchallism. Especially from the mid-1960s onwards, its limited support base was characterized by an uneasy mix of urban radicalism and rural conservatism. The rural strongholds of the party were often little more than the fiefdoms of traditional Labour notables, and it was these elements that mounted the strongest resistance to the party leadership's attempts to move leftwards in the late 1960s.

The question of electoral dealignment

In this sense, therefore, and unlike in most European countries, the parties have always been forced to deal with a more or less 'dealigned' electorate – although Whyte's (1974) suggestion that Irish politics had almost no social basis whatsoever has been subject to much subsequent qualification (e.g. Mair 1979; Laver 1986a, 1986b; Laver *et al.* 1987; Sinnott 1995). These qualifications should not be exaggerated, however, especially when viewed from a comparative perspective. In the first place, although differences do exist, they tend to be quite small. Secondly, these social divisions tend not to coincide with what we have already described as the traditional political conflict, that between Fianna Fáil and Fine Gael. This is particularly true of class differences. Thirdly, and most importantly, they do not reflect organizational linkages between parties and social groups. For that reason, distinctiveness also fluctuates, sometimes quite considerably, from election to election (e.g. Marsh and Sinnott 1990).

However, social group linkages are simply one means by which the alignment of individuals is created. Above all, an aligned electorate is one in which a large proportion of voters is likely to remain loyal to the same party over time, and while specifying the basis of that loyalty is vital in an understanding of changes in voting behaviour, it is the loyalty itself which is critical in any assessment of alignment or dealignment. As far as voting analyses are concerned, such loyalty, and hence the evidence of alignment and/or dealignment, can be revealed in one of two ways. First, we can use survey questions that ask people whether they have some kind of enduring attachment to a particular party, and if so how strong that attachment is. This provides a direct measure. In the Eurobarometer polls taken since 1978, voters have been asked if they are 'close to any particular party', and, if so, whether they feel 'very close', 'fairly close', or merely 'sympathize'. The trend of these responses is shown in Table 9.2, and this demonstrates a clear decline in the number of those considering themselves to be 'close' to a party – the drop is over 25 percentage points in less than 20 years, with 64 percent claiming to be close to a party in 1978, as against less than 40 percent in 1994. This is in fact the biggest decline in this series in any EU country (Schmitt and Holmberg 1995).

In other words, while they may well think of politics and voting in terms of parties, Irish voters are much less likely to admit feeling close to any of those parties than they were twenty years ago. The decline in these figures was most pronounced in the early 1980s, with the percentage close to a party declining by 14 percentage points between 1980 and 1984, and a further 5 percentage points by 1986. There was another sharp drop of 5 points between 1990 and 1991, since when the decline appears to have levelled out. The Eurobarometer series ends in 1994 but there are observations after this point. The same question was asked in a 1999 telephone poll and less than 30 percent admitted any party attachment, indicating a further drop.[6] Almost exactly the same question was again asked in the 2002 Irish Election Study, and preliminary analysis indicates less than 25 percent admitted such party attachment, indicating a continuing decline.

A decline of around 35 percent in less than 25 years is certainly striking. But is this the full story, or might the decline have been even greater? Were the 1980s the start of the process, or would growing detachment have been found in the early 1970s, or in the 1960s had data been available? There is no direct evidence that we can call upon here, but we can make some assessment of long-term patterns by examining party loyalty across generations of voters. Figure 9.1 shows the growing detachment (percentage 'not close') across five sets of generations: those born in or after 1971, between 1961 and 1970, between 1951 and 1960, between 1941 and 1950, and those born in or before 1940. Essentially we are talking of those who first voted in the 1990s as against those who first voted in the 1980s, 1970s, 1960s, and in or before the 1950s.[7]

Figure 9.1 shows two separate processes of dealignment. First, and most important for our purposes, there is a generational effect. Each of these generations appears to be more dealigned than its predecessor. The various pre-1941

Table 9.2   Party attachment in Ireland, 1978–94

Year	Very close %	Fairly close %	Merely a sympathizer %	Not close at all %	Total %
1978	13.7	28.7	22.1	35.5	100
1979	9.6	26.3	26.6	37.5	100
1980	9.0	26.4	25.9	38.6	100
1981	8.7	23.4	28.3	39.7	100
1982	8.0	21.4	24.2	46.4	100
1983	7.5	22.3	23.8	46.4	100
1984	5.7	19.5	22.3	52.6	100
1985	7.8	18.9	21.0	52.3	100
1986	4.8	17.6	20.4	57.2	100
1987	7.7	19.1	17.9	55.3	100
1988	6.1	19.0	20.1	54.7	100
1989	6.0	16.4	18.8	58.8	100
1990	8.0	19.3	13.1	59.6	100
1991	8.0	15.3	11.9	64.8	100
1992	7.2	17.1	12.0	63.7	100
1993	6.3	14.6	15.5	63.6	100
1994	5.7	18.2	15.5	60.7	100

Source: Eurobarometers 1978–94. One 1978 and 1981 poll excluded due to different question wording

Figure 9.1   Increasing detachment from parties in Ireland by decade of birth (Eurobarometers 1978–94. One 1978 and 1981 poll excluded due to different question wording)

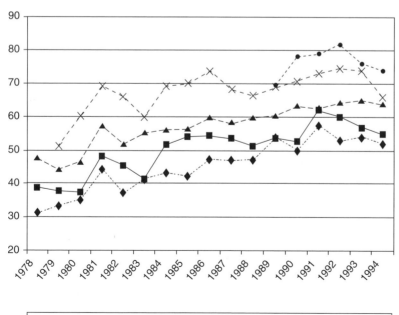

(ten-year) generations are amalgamated here because they do not differ from one another with any consistency. The classic model of socialization would of course predict this, since it asserts that attachment increases with time, with the early years of political experience in one's twenties being critical (Converse 1969). However, there is no sign here that the gaps between the generations are closing. The line for each generation shown here pursues a similar course, with almost no intertwining. The second process shown in the graph is a period effect under which all generations are dealigning steadily. By 1994, the pre-1940 generation was more dealigned than was the 1951–60 generation – its children perhaps – in 1978, and similar, if less striking, patterns can be observed for later generations. The whole picture is consistent with an argument that dealignment started some time in the 1960s or 1970s. The fact that the 1941–50 generation, first voting in the 1960s, looks somewhat different to its predecessor, and that the 1951–60 generation, voting first in the 1970s, is even more different, suggests that while the start of the process might be located in the 1960s, dealignment accelerated in the 1970s and after.[8]

Further evidence on dealignment comes from survey questions asking voters how likely is it that they would vote for each of the parties on offer. These data underline the fact that Irish voters are not committed to any one party but make a choice between two or more at any election (van der Eijk *et al.* 1996; Marsh 2004). The evidence from transfer patterns of the electorate's declining willingness to follow party labels when ranking preferences for candidates further confirms this (Gallagher 1999). Yet this does not mean there is wholesale change between elections. About one in five voters changes their vote between elections, a figure that has remained fairly stable since 1969 (Sinnott 1995; Marsh and Sinnott 1999; Garry *et al.* 2003).

This is underlined by the evidence of aggregate electoral change, that is, a measure that can be applied over a longer time period than that which is possible using survey evidence alone. Electoral change here is measured in two ways, each employing Pedersen's (1979) volatility index. The first measure contrasts party support at each successive pair of elections since 1937, giving the conventional measure of aggregate electoral volatility (see also the data in Table 9.1). The second contrasts party support at each successive election with party support at a fixed time point. Here we have taken 1937 as that fixed point, this being the first election in which both Fianna Fáil and Fine Gael participated under those names. While the first measure shows us the degree of short-term change in party support at each election, the latter shows us the extent of long-term change as measured against a fixed point in time. The results are shown in Figure 9.2.

While short-term and long-term changes do not necessarily coincide, the two series do track quite closely. The greatest departures from the 1930s party system have come about when volatility has been high, both in the 1940s and in the last decade. In between these times, volatility was quite low, and the party system returned to its 1930s form. Hence the volatility of the 1940s is quite consistent with a pattern of alignment in which the then new parties like

Figure 9.2 Volatility and system change in Ireland since 1937 (calculated from Donnelly 1997 and Marsh 2002. Volatility measured by Pedersen index taking last election as baseline; system change is volatility taking 1937 as the baseline. All parties never achieving 1 percent are included as 'others')

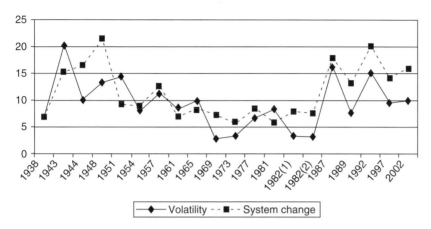

Clann na Poblachta and Clann na Talmhan in the 1940s and early 1950s are essentially 'flash' parties, mobilizing discontent but failing to redefine the party system itself. People simply return to their 'own' parties after the initial flurry of excitement. The survey data on dealignment considered above certainly support that view, since the generations which might have been expected to be most influenced by the turmoil in the party system in this period show no obvious traces of greater dealignment. More recent volatility may well be of a different character, however, since it coincides with a change in the character of the party system, and this, in turn, shows no clear signs of yet having reversed. It also coincides with declining turnout.

In sum, the direct evidence indicates that more than half of the electorate does not feel 'close' to any party, and that this figure has been declining progressively since at least 1980, although the evidence of the incidence of such closeness in different generations suggests the decline may have begun at least a decade earlier. Currently many voters claim to have a high likelihood of supporting more than one party in the future. The survey evidence of vote-switching, and the national-level aggregate data – which provide indirect evidence but within a longer time frame – indicate that although voting instability from election to election is not a new phenomenon, volatility has become higher in recent years. It also seems that these recent short-term fluctuations have had a greater impact on the party system.

One important reservation needs to be entered regarding the assumption that underlies most of these findings: this is that *party*, in terms of its leaders, policies, traditions or performance, is in some way the key factor in people's voting decision (see also Mair 1987a: 85–6; Marsh 2000). Under the Irish electoral system voters may, and often do, organize their ranking of candidates by party. But they may also choose to do so by gender, by locality, or even by alphabetical order. Moreover, individual candidates attract a very significant personal vote. As the US evidence on candidate-centred politics (e.g. Wattenberg 1991) illustrates, dealignment may well free voters to choose between parties, but it is not necessarily the case that it is parties which are eventually chosen. In other words, there is another dimension here, whereby dealignment, particularly in the Irish setting, can encourage the emergence and mobilization of independent, non-party candidates and issue-campaigns, further threatening the hold of the traditional parties on their voters and constraining their capacity to respond.

From complacency to competition

Prior to the late 1960s, the parties seemed to have met few if any of the sort of challenges that might have required a serious response. Fianna Fáil certainly expended little effort in either organizational or campaigning terms. For the most part, victory was taken for granted and laurels were rested upon. To be sure, the party was forced to engage in a substantial renewal of its leadership, with the old 'revolutionary elite' eventually giving way to a younger generation (Cohan 1972). It also engaged in substantial policy renewal, promoting the opening up of the formerly protected economy as well as a major expansion of welfare spending. But no specific electoral effort was expended, and in none of the elections until 1977 did the party even bother to publish an election manifesto. In other words, while some small and quite short-term efforts were made to revitalize the organization following the defeats in 1948 and again in 1954 (see O'Sullivan 1994: 122, 141–2), success was more or less taken for granted.

Fianna Fáil's complacency was encouraged by its opponents' lack of effort. Both Fine Gael and Labour scarcely functioned as campaigning organizations prior to the late 1960s (for details, see Mair 1987a: 119–27; see also the extensive analysis in Farrell 1993b). For these parties, it was defeat that was taken for granted, and there is little evidence to suggest that their leaders envisaged any possibility that Fianna Fáil predominance could be ended. The idea of coalition, which was really the only route to an alternative government, was ruled out in those years – at least in the medium term – and both parties were dominated by older generation of TDs (members of parliament) who seemed content to sit out their days in the Dáil without having to entertain any hopes or ambitions for the future. If the politics of the late 1950s and 1960s was to be briefly characterized, it would be as a process dominated by ageing TDs and by moribund political organizations, and one that was marked by more or less predetermined electoral outcomes.[9]

Already by the end of the 1960s, however, a greater dynamic was evident. The first change was that wrought by the rapid economic and social modernization in Ireland during the 1960s, which encouraged a quite widespread sense that many of the older and traditional moulds were breaking, including those of the political world.[10] Secondly, and perhaps even more importantly, the older parliamentary class began to be replaced by a younger, more educated and inevitably more ambitious cohort. Thirdly, there was the impact of events in neighbouring Britain, where consecutive Labour victories in 1964 and 1966 had ended thirteen years of Conservative government and had fuelled expectations that a similar change might yet spread westwards across the Irish Sea.

In practice, these and other 'background' features prompted two important and quite rapid changes in Irish political thinking. The first of these was a new sense of optimism within the leadership of the Irish Labour Party, where organizational renewal and the recruitment of new 'intellectual' cadres led to quite a sharp move to the left – at least rhetorically. Many of the newer elements within the party believed that theirs was finally the future, and that the last remnants of the traditional civil war politics would now rapidly disappear (e.g. Gallagher 1982: 67–85). Indeed, in 1969 some ambitious party posters called on voters 'to return a Labour government' (Gallagher 1982: 86). The second change was the greater voice given to younger and more progressive cohorts within the traditionally conservative Fine Gael. Their most notable achievement was the publication of the *Just Society* election programme in 1965, and its renewal in 1969, by means of which the party more or less aligned itself with Labour in a moderate social democratic opposition to the policies then being pursued by Fianna Fáil in government.[11] In other words, the basis for a new coalition – and hence, an alternative government – was being laid for the first time in more than a decade, although on this occasion it was driven at least as much by ideological affinity as by sheer political opportunism (Mair 1987a: 197–202).

In 1973, Labour and Fine Gael campaigned on a joint election programme, and won a clear Dáil majority. The change of government marked an important landmark in a number of respects, not least because it was not until almost 30 years later, in 2002, that a government won a second consecutive term. So 1973 ushered in a new and quite unprecedented period of alternation in government. It was also important, however, because success was built on the back of an *electoral* coalition rather than on the basis of *ad hoc* post-election bargaining. In addition, both Fine Gael and Labour had fought the election on the basis of a joint election manifesto, and this manifesto was then largely implemented during their term of office. This was a novelty 30 years ago, but it was quickly to become standard practice. Finally, the new coalition looked like being a winner. It was led by a relatively young, modern and professional cabinet, and it chalked up a number of early successes. More specifically, it also redesigned the electoral districts in a manner which looked likely to guarantee the two parties a second clear majority at the subsequent election.[12] That in itself would have been unprecedented, and there were those in Labour in particular who believed that Fianna Fáil would never recover from such ignominy: two consecutive periods in opposition would finally destroy Fianna Fáil's image as the natural party of government, it was believed, and would undermine its entire *raison d'être*. Thereafter, the party would collapse, and a wholesale realignment of Irish politics would ensue.[13] However, Fianna Fáil had also read this script and preferred to rewrite it by winning what turned out to be a most striking – and surprising – victory in 1977. Thereafter, instead of the expected realignment, there followed a series of pendulum swings, with each successive government being defeated and replaced by its opponents. A new pattern of government formation therefore quickly settled into place, and was to survive until the end of the 1980s: on the one hand, Fianna Fáil single-party governments; on the other hand, the periodically revived coalition of Fine Gael and Labour. Together, these two alternatives created a new two-party system in all but name.

Fianna Fáil had been very shaken by its 1973 defeat, which, because of the loss of a number of seats, and the loss of office, was perceived as a very serious setback.[14] In facing for the first time the prospect of two defeats in a row, the party therefore invested considerably in building up its organizational resources (see, for example, Manning 1978: 82–7). The veteran general secretary was replaced by a more dynamic national organizer; for the first time, a press officer was appointed; and, also for the first time, the party employed a full-time policy adviser. All three new appointees were in their twenties, and were clearly intended to breathe new life into an effectively moribund organization. They were to initiate a new style of campaigning in Irish politics, and were at least partly responsible for the publication of the party's first – and very glossy and voter-friendly – election manifesto in 1977. Rapidly, and quite abruptly, Fianna Fáil had therefore moved from being close to one organizational extreme, where the conduct and structure of its minimalist election campaigns were more or less left to the discretion of the local parties, to being close to the other extreme, where the key motor was provided by party central office, the national leadership and the national election programme. The fact that the unexpected victory that followed was perceived by both the party itself and its opponents as having resulted more or less directly from organizational renewal and centralization, was to dictate the future style of organization and campaign strategy across the party system as a whole.

Fine Gael, in turn, stunned by its surprising defeat in 1977, quickly emulated the new Fianna Fáil approach, and carried it even further (e.g. Mair 1987a: 127–9; O'Byrnes 1986: 16–29). A new leader, Garret FitzGerald, was elected, and he quickly arranged for the appointment of a new, and younger, general secretary. Press relations were professionalized, and control over local party activities was asserted, not least to ensure that the nomination of candidates would be designed to enhance the prospects of winning additional seats for the party as such rather than simply to protect the interests of the sitting TDs (O'Byrnes 1986). Party interest, at national level, was to take precedence over local interests. This new approach was extended to the organization of subsequent election campaigns, and most especially that of 1981 (see, for example, Farrell 1986). This revitalization of the party organization itself, as well as the campaign techniques, led to a record electoral success, with Fine Gael polling its highest vote and its largest percentage of Dáil seats since the end of the 1920s.

Thus, by 1981, the various party leaders, and the public at large, had witnessed two consecutive electoral successes – one by Fianna Fáil and one by Fine Gael – achieved on the back of large-scale organizational renewal and professionalization. Lessons for the future were thus learned, and two of these in particular were to feed through into more or less all of the parties in the subsequent decade. A third lesson would later become apparent in the 1990s in the wake of the new openness of the coalition formation process and the new electoral uncertainties.

Programmes and policy

The first lesson that was learned and to which the parties responded was that they were now 'required' to publish in advance their election manifestos and programmatic commitments; within the limits of the times available for the preparation of election campaigns, and the periods elapsing between elections, this has since become a standard part of Irish politics. From the 1970s onwards there has existed a plethora of lengthy, detailed, and especially glossy publications, often produced in very large quantities. Swamped by national messages, there now seemed to be little room within the national parties at least for attention to local issues. But what is also important to underline here is that this programmatic response has rarely taken a sharp ideological or even 'principled' colouring. Manifestos and campaign promises have now become crucial to electoral campaigning, but ever since the last major push towards ideological realignment – that which was reflected in the new social democratic emphases of both Fine Gael and Labour in the late 1960s – none of the policy profiles enunciated by the major parties has significantly deviated from the prevailing all-party consensus. In this sense, at least at the ideological level, there is rarely much of substance to choose between the principal protagonists.

This convergence marks not only social and economic policies, as might be expected, but also, and more strikingly, even those policies which touch upon issues involving Northern Ireland and public morality. In these latter areas, where sharp divisions were often highly visible in the past, the convergence of party stances has come about largely through the eventual adaptation of Fianna Fáil to a more secular consensus, with the party shifting quite markedly away from its traditionalist emphases. This change has undoubtedly been voter led, and has been prompted by the narrowing electoral base on which traditionalism came to rest. More to the point, however, and more notably, it was less a response to changes in the party's own electorate as such, which still retains a pronounced conservative bias, and more a response to changing attitudes within the electorate as a whole, including especially those voters who were seen to be 'in competition' and potentially available to all the parties involved. In other words, in an effort to extend its appeal to the more moderate and more volatile sectors of the electorate, Fianna Fáil has moved towards the centre ground in terms of these traditional issues, even though this carried the risk of alienating part of its own core support. The formerly hard-line policy on Northern Ireland was eventually moderated in the 1990s – if not wholly as a result of electoral pressure, at least in consequence of the commitments that were required as part of the burgeoning peace process in and about Northern Ireland (see also Sinnott 1995: 39–40). By the early 1990s Fianna Fáil was also concerned that it was losing potentially moderate support as a result of its traditional conservative stance on moral and religious issues. Indeed, it was largely this conservative stance which had prompted a small but prominent section of the leadership to split away and form the more liberal Progressive Democrats in 1985. By 1995, however, the party had come round to arguing in favour of legislation on divorce – a view opposed by a small majority of its own supporters (Girvin 1996) – while it was a Fianna Fáil minister in 1993 who finally introduced legislation decriminalizing homosexuality.

More importantly, perhaps, this new and more broad-ranging consensus on nationalist, cultural and moral issues, as well as most obviously within the social and economic domain, which has often been forged in the face of internal party critics in each of the major formations, also reflects the reluctance of any of the major parties to isolate itself from its opponents, particularly now that it may need one or more of those opponents as coalition allies. In this sense, and much as in the 1950s and early 1960s, although now for different reasons, policy competition in Ireland remains relatively closed, with none of the major protagonists being willing to go out on a limb in any ideological direction. When differences between the parties can be marked, it is usually only in the details, and especially in the competition by parties to outbid one another through specific appeals to a 'vote of exchange'. This leads to a tendency within the generalized consensus to enunciate new particularistic policies that are aimed at specific groups of voters, be these young people, women, farmers, car-owners, trade unionists or whoever, each of whom is seen as more or less available to be won by each of the major parties, and hence to be wooed with specific campaign pledges.[15] This is perhaps the most evident response to dealignment. Moreover, by focusing increasingly on the 'vote of exchange', the parties not only neglect any potential 'vote of opinion' but they may also be seen to be responding to, and indeed to be encouraging, the decline of any residual 'vote of belonging'.[16]

National organization

The second lesson that the parties learned, and perhaps inevitably so, is that they needed to improve their responsive capacity at the organizational level, and hence to accumulate more organizational resources at the national level and to direct these more explicitly towards ensuring electoral success (for details, see Farrell 1993a, 1993b, 1994). This was the lesson which had been learned from the record Fianna Fáil victory in 1977 and the record gains made by Fine Gael four years later. Voters were there for the winning. Between the late 1960s and the late 1990s, for example, the total numbers of staff employed in the party head offices of Fianna Fáil, Fine Gael and Labour more than doubled (Murphy and Farrell 2003). Moreover, although the parliamentary parties had effectively no employees at all in the late 1960s, by the late 1980s there were parliamentary staffs of 70, 56 and 12 respectively (see the figures in Farrell 1992: 408). Campaign staffs increased tenfold in the same period (e.g. Farrell 1993a, 1993b). When we then add to this the use of external consultants, market research and commercial advertising, then what we witness is a spiralling growth of the resources engaged at the centre (Murphy and Farrell 2003).

This expansion in national organizational resources has been accompanied by a growth in attention to the specifics of campaign strategy in the individual local constituencies, a factor which has become of utmost importance given that very small margins of victory at the local level can have a major impact on the potentially winning margins enjoyed by putative governments. Moreover, in winning these marginal constituency seats, and hence in possibly making the difference between incumbency and opposition, the distribution of even the smallest numbers of votes can prove crucial, particularly given that the average electoral quota – the number of votes required by a candidate to secure his or her election – is often fewer than 10,000, and given that the final seat in many districts is sometimes won on the basis of the transfer of relatively small numbers of lower-preferences.[17] In the Dublin South-Central four-seat constituency in the 1992 election, for example, Ben Briscoe of Fianna Fáil defeated Eric Byrne of the Democratic Left for the final seat by a margin of just five votes (6,526 vs. 6,521). Had Byrne won just six additional votes, whether in the form of first preferences or lower transfers, and therefore defeated Briscoe, the Democratic Left representation in the Dáil would have risen from 4 to 5, and that of Fianna Fáil would have fallen from 68 to 67, thus affording a possible Fine Gael–Labour–Democratic Left coalition precisely 50 percent of the seats, and an effectively winning margin (see also Laver and Shepsle 1996: 140). It is in this way that a fine-tuning of local electoral strategies can prove so crucial to eventual (national) party success.[18] Fianna Fáil had already devoted considerable effort to controlling local strategies in the hard-fought electoral contests of the 1920s and 1930s (see Dunphy 1995: 77–87), and such strategies were to find new favour again during the 1980s and 1990s as one of the few ways in which individual parties might still gain an edge at a time in which all protagonists had decided to invest significantly greater effort in national campaigning. In other words, the importance of local politics – as well as local issues and local candidate appeals – continued to be recognized, but now in a context in which the national parties sought to control these elements for national gains.

That said, it must be underlined that this particular approach has always remained most subject to centre–periphery tensions, and hence most resistant to central direction. Among the techniques used by the parties in this regard is simply the identification of constituencies where the chances are quite high that the party will win an additional seat or lose an existing seat; detailed local surveys of voting intentions are then often commissioned, and the campaign staff conduct careful analyses of previous distributions of the vote and the transfer patterns. This is itself not problematic, of course, especially if it implies the transfer of more campaign resources from the centre to these vulnerable localities. But this form of strategic vote management also implies more attention to the selection of potentially appealing candidates, including women candidates, whose personal appeals might gain the parties additional support, or particular local candidates who might appeal to an otherwise neglected bailiwick. The result is that in all the parties the national leadership has developed an increasingly interventionist stance as far as local strategy is concerned, with additional candidates sometimes being imposed on otherwise reluctant local parties and in the face of opposition from locally entrenched interests. Perhaps most importantly, greater attention also began to be paid in recent times to improving and making more effective the balance of support between the different party candidates in given constituencies, which sometimes meant that particular candidates were discouraged from accumulating too much individual support. And this, in turn, could expose some of these candidates to the risk of defeat. So greater candidate vulnerability was sometimes required if the chances of party success were to be enhanced – and this is where the problems began to arise. Already in 1982, for example, Fine Gael had demonstrated the benefits which could be gained by a more judicious distribution of first preferences between its own potentially competing candidates within a multimember constituency, with one now famous case involving two sitting Fine Gael TDs seeking to reduce their own personal levels of electoral support in order to boost (successfully, as it turned out) the support won by a third, aspiring candidate (for details, see Mair 1987b: 124–7). Centralization has not proceeded to the point where this strategy can be widely applied, however, as some more comprehensive assessments, which also point to strategic failures, make only too evident (see Gallagher 1993: 70–1; also Gallagher 1999, 2003). Particularly in this regard, it is clear that successful intervention from the centre requires not only a very detailed knowledge of local circumstances and likely voter reactions on the ground, which is difficult in itself, but also both the formal and active consent of sitting deputies and prospective candidates, so it is a strategy which will always be severely constrained.[19]

In sum, and in the space of little more than the twenty years that stretched from the mid- to late 1950s through to the mid- to late 1970s, Irish parties responded to the twin pressures of dealignment and competition by abandoning their relatively moribund and complacent organizational cultures, which had long survived within and even helped to sustain a largely uncompetitive party politics, and built instead aggressive, well-resourced and highly dynamic campaigning machines which were adapted to and even helped to promote a highly competitive and increasingly open political environment.[20]

We might even conclude that the parties have already gone about as far as they could go in this regard – in that apart from suddenly discovering some new and very appealing policy initiative, or some particularly novel means of communicating their message, they probably cannot take these new techniques much further than had already been done by the 1980s. In sum, parties have already developed into highly sophisticated and professional organizations, even though in some cases – as with Fine Gael in 2002 – they can end up running a seemingly incompetent campaign. To be sure, the continuing availability of financial resources can certainly make a difference in terms of the effectiveness of campaign techniques, and new laws on spending limits may well play an important role in the future (see p. 254 below); for now, however, the parties can do little more than simply refine and update the techniques they discovered in the 1970s and which they had more or less fully developed by the 1980s.[21]

The parties in the legislative arena

The possible exhaustion of the capacity for major innovation at the level of organizational and campaigning techniques, as well as the increasing uncertainties about the nature of electoral responses, serve to emphasize that a third lesson has also been learned by the parties, and this time more recently. This last lesson states that almost regardless of what happens in terms of electoral outcomes, which are themselves becoming less easy to predict, the parties now enjoy considerably greater freedom in building alliances within the legislative arena and in the government formation process. Since 1989, as noted above, this whole process has opened up more or less completely. Fianna Fáil is now willing to share government with other parties, and has already had experience of two different coalition formulas (joining with the Progressive Democrats on three occasions, and with Labour on one). Labour, for its part, and for the first time, enjoys a real choice of partners, and so it can now seek to play a pivotal role. Finally, the range of governing parties was broadened to include both the Progressive Democrats and the Democratic Left (now merged with Labour), while in the run up to the 2002 election it was also clear that the Green Party, which has maintained a presence in the Irish parliament since 1989, has become a possible partner, particularly in the context of a Fine Gael–Labour coalition.

The expansion of the parameters of the government formation process and the abandonment of the traditional norms of inter-party behaviour has clearly brought an entirely new dimension to Irish party politics. In the first place, it is evident that since 1989 in particular, electoral success can no longer be taken for granted, and that it no longer constitutes a prerequisite for winning a place in government – post-election bargaining has now become equally important, if not even more important. As happens in other countries, this could also mean that the parties would learn to endure electoral losses in situations where this might lead to potential gains in their post-election bargaining position. Secondly, precisely because it is in the various parties' interests to keep their post-election options open, they are now much more inclined to compete on their own, and without committing themselves to any pre-poll alliances. This response is also likely to be enhanced by the minimal constraints that are placed on governing alliances, in that all parties are now 'coalitionable', and each is also more or less capable of forming a credible alliance with almost any of the others. Thirdly, because the relevant arena for decision-making about government is increasingly the legislative arena, and less and less the electoral arena, voters find it more difficult to focus their party preferences on the likely governing alternatives. At least as far as government is concerned, they are voting in the dark, and this, in turn, may lead to greater volatility and to even more opportunities for local parties and/or single-issue candidates. In other words, if the governing dimension is largely removed from the electoral arena, the electoral response could well lead to greater fragmentation, instability and declining turnout. To be sure, the parties also know this, and so are aware of the risks that they run.

Fine Gael has been very explicit in noting the problems posed by this new situation. As an internal party report from 1993 noted,

> Until relatively recently, the perceived political role of the Party has been to provide a government whenever Fianna Fáil was defeated. The collapse of Fianna Fáil's dominant position, and the emergence of two successive Fianna Fáil led coalitions, brings an entirely new reality to Irish political life: defeat for Fianna Fáil no longer means that it ceases, automatically, to be in government. This stark reality, for which Fine Gael seemed unprepared in 1992, presents a challenge and an opportunity to the party. (Fine Gael 1993: 16)

It also presented a real danger, of course. As long as Fine Gael functioned as the basis for an alternative to Fianna Fáil, then the success of the latter more or less guaranteed the survival of the former. Once Fianna Fáil ceased to be dominant, however, and became 'just another party', the danger was that there would be less need for the Fine Gael alternative. Indeed, earlier in the same internal report the Fine Gael Commission had noted that 'the real issue for Fine Gael is re-establishing a distinct identity in a dramatically changing environment' (ibid.: 15).[22]

Whatever the likely consequences at the electoral level, however, it is evident that parties now enjoy the benefits of a new arena in which to develop their competitive behaviour. What this also means, of course, is that the parties are now more prepared to hedge their bets in pre-poll campaigning, at least to the extent that they often appear to give priority to post-election friendships in parliament rather than to the development of a distinct profile in the election itself. The 2002 election campaign provided an good example of this, for despite Fine Gael's best efforts, no other party was willing to commit itself before polling day to joining it in a post-election alliance. All the other parties, but most obviously Labour, kept open the option of government with Fianna Fáil.

A retreat to the institutions?

On one reading, this could be taken to imply that the parties have acquired a greater incentive to retreat into the legislative arena and to place less emphasis on their presence on the ground. Other factors that emerged during the 1990s have also appeared to encourage this response. In the first place, the extraordinary economic success which Ireland has experienced during the years of the so-called 'Celtic Tiger' has served to cement the cross-party policy consensus and to reduce many sources of inter-party tension (Crotty and Schmitt 1998). All parties are now more or less agreed on promoting low-tax and high-spending programmes. In this area, at least, there is little for which they or the voters can compete. In addition, the faltering success of the Northern Ireland peace process, and the signing of the Good Friday Agreement in 1998, as well as its subsequent approval by a massive majority in a referendum in the Irish Republic itself, has finally taken this lingering source of inter-party division more or less off the agenda. In policy terms, it is therefore almost impossible for the larger parties to develop distinct electoral profiles.

The parties have also been encouraged to retreat into the institutions as a result of the general dissatisfaction and distrust with which their activities are now viewed by a growing number of voters. One of the most striking developments during the 1990s was the series of financial scandals involving both parties and individual senior politicians that were brought into full public view, and that continue to be investigated by a number of tribunals of inquiry (see, for example, Collins 2000). With sometimes startling revelations of corruption in high places and evidence of illegal party financing being reported almost daily in the national media since the mid-1990s, and growing evidence that these practices have stretched almost right across the party spectrum, the standing of the parties among potential voters is very low.

Reflecting both the scandals and the hollowing out of political competition, the electorate is probably now more disengaged than at any comparable period in modern Irish history. As noted above, levels of party attachment have long fallen below the European average. The level of turnout in national elections has fallen below that in almost every other European country (Lyons and Sinnott 2003). Party membership now ranks among the lowest of all the long-established democracies in Western Europe (Mair and van Biezen 2001: 16; on Fine Gael in particular, see Gallagher and Marsh 2002: 57). Electoral support has grown for 'outsider' parties, including the Greens, which polled almost 4 percent of the vote and won six seats in 2002, and the nationalist Sinn Féin party, which polled 6.5 percent of the vote and won five seats. Support has also grown for independent and single-issue candidates, whose total vote rose to 11 percent in 2002, resulting in a record thirteen seats. Small wonder, then, that the mainstream parties find themselves orienting their strategies more and more towards the legislative arena, and that they retreat to the apparent security of the institutions.

Reaching out: the parties and their external relations

Formally speaking, Ireland has lagged far behind most of the European countries in establishing a system of public funding for political parties. The parties have also been remarkably free from regulation. In terms of resources, the parties have traditionally relied very heavily on membership fees and sub-scriptions, including the fee paid by the individual member, the subscription paid by the local branch and constituency organization in order to register with central office, and *ad hoc* collections and other fund-raising activities on the ground. And although, as non-regulated bodies, the published accounts of the parties often lacked detail, and sometimes even credibility – a point which became more than evident with the series of funding scandals that were revealed in Irish politics in the 1990s – it does nevertheless appear that they were, and still are, heavily dependent on their supporters for organizational resources. Even into the early 1990s, for example, Fianna Fáil accounts reported that some 45 percent of the total party income was derived from its annual national collection, while in the same period Fine Gael usually reported that some 80 percent of its income derived from membership fees and branch and constituency subscriptions (see the figures in Farrell 1992: 445–8). In addition, however, as recent headlines have amply testified, the parties – as well as individual politicians – have clearly enjoyed a substantial amount of largely undisclosed financial support from busi-ness corporations and property developers. The picture is further complicated by the existence of informal channels of state support, ranging from the Oireachtas (Parliament) grant and the party leader's allowance, which, like British 'Short money', is designed to support the parties in parliament, to various schemes allowing for the appointment of assistants, secretaries and youth officers, and those which also subsidize various expenses incurred by TDs.[23]

Although the character of the Irish electoral system and the premium which is placed on relatively close personal contacts between TDs and voters has always necessitated quite pronounced labour-intensive campaigning, the increased activity at the centre which was noted above, as well as the greater intensity of national campaign activities, has inevitably led to the rapid growth of capital-intensive techniques. The major costs incurred since the 1970s in revitalizing party organizations, and the heavy central office expenditures incurred during the seven Dáil election campaigns which have been held in the last twenty years (not to mention the presidential, local and European election campaigns, as well as the dozen or so referendum campaigns in the same period) combined to produce enormous indebtedness on the part of the parties by the mid-1990s, which was estimated by Farrell (1994: 234) at a total of some 5 million Irish pounds.

Given this situation, it was no surprise that in 1997 a formal system of state subvention for the party organizations was finally introduced (Electoral Act 1997), a system which also sought to set clear limits on total campaign expen-diture. However, this was very much a Labour (and Democratic Left) project which met with little manifest enthusiasm and even some hostility from Fianna Fáil, Fine Gael and the Progressive Democrats – and, indeed, from parts of the electorate. The new rules sought to limit campaign expenditure to a maximum of £18,000 per candidate (in a three-seat constituency, more in those with four and five seats), and guaranteed all candidates a subsidy of up to £5,000 for certified expenditure, subject only to their winning a given small percentage of the vote. In addition, £1 million was to be divided proportionally among all parties polling at least 2 percent of the vote, a sum which could be used by the parties for administrative, research and policy-making expenses, as well as for the promotion of the participation of women and young people. In exchange, as it were, parties were to be required to declare full details of donations in excess of £4,000 (with a limit of £500 for donations to individual candidates), and details of all anonymous donations of over £100 were to be forwarded to the Public Offices Commission (Laver and Marsh 1999).

These changes had several purposes. First, with the help of public subsidies, the parties hoped to ease some of their enormous financial burdens. In addition, the limits set by the Act(s) were intended to prevent a repeat of the spiralling costs of the 1980s, with the partial public financing somewhat easing the need for parties to raise funds themselves. The parties had come to realize that their activities would in future require much greater dependence on what the state can offer, a syndrome which has also recently been much in evidence in the increasing use of state resources by parties in government to fund the appointments of key political personnel. Secondly, the then government parties hoped these restraints would lessen the advantage accruing to Fianna Fáil as the richest party. Thirdly, by insisting on at least some transparency in funding, it was hoped to ease the sense of popular dissatisfaction with the parties which had grown in recent years, and which had been fuelled by the series of striking financial scandals and other revelations.[24]

Despite its initial criticisms of the legislation, which was enacted by its predecessor, and despite an initial promise to alter some of its provisions, the Fianna Fáil–Progressive Democrat government simply satisfied itself with tinkering about with the various financial limits involved. The Electoral (Amendment) Act 2001 doubled total state funding, raised the limits on election spending by over 10 percent, and capped donations to parties from individuals and organizations at £5,000 per year, and those to individual politicians at £2,000 per year. To benefit from the additional state funding, parties would be obliged to submit annual, independently audited accounts to the newly established Public Offices Commission. At the same time, Fine Gael and Labour, now in opposition, each committed themselves to an outright ban on corporate donations in an attempt to secure anti-sleaze votes at the next election. After the election, Fine Gael, even before a new leader was elected, subsequently moved away from this commitment, arguing that it placed too great a burden on party members to come up with the money to fund future campaigns, and handicapped the party unduly in the absence of a similar commitment by Fianna Fáil (*Irish Times*, 27 May 2002).

If the need to generate adequate funding has become one key concern for the parties since their shift into campaigning mode in the late 1970s, a second has become the need to maintain – or even rebuild – a sense of popular legitimacy. In 1993, for example, both Fine Gael and Fianna Fáil produced reports on organizational renewal which were clearly aimed at encouraging greater membership and at revitalizing their links with the wider society, with the former recommending the introduction of direct membership ballots for all senior positions inside the party,[25] as well as the creation of special action groups which would also be open to non-members.[26] Some years earlier, in 1989, Labour had also changed its rules in order to allow mass membership ballots in leadership elections (e.g. Farrell 1994: 232) – a system used again in 2002. Links to interest groups and varieties of social movements are also now strongly encouraged by the parties, but in the increasingly open electoral game these links tend to be of a short-term and *ad hoc* character, with both sets of actors being reluctant to establish any permanent ties, and with the parties being yet again unwilling to have themselves painted into a corner. As noted above, this is also indicative of the manner in which dealignment has occurred in the Irish case.[27]

Conclusion

In part, of course, the increasing problem of legitimacy to which Irish parties must respond derives from the changes that the parties themselves have brought about in response to the new sense of competitiveness. Expanding the role of the centre has inevitably led to a potential downgrading in the status of the local parties, and hence to a weakening of the most crucial link that exists between Irish parties and their voters. It has also tended to devalue the status of the local deputies themselves, who now often appear as ciphers within a larger, leadership-directed political game, and for this reason the parties have recently made great efforts to portray themselves as genuinely member-friendly (e.g. Fianna Fáil 1993; Fine Gael 1993). As the structure of competition has opened up, and as promiscuity in coalition formation has grown, the sense of a distinct partisan purpose has tended to erode even further. For the voters, as well as for the parties themselves, this makes it difficult to establish any enduring distinctions between friends and enemies. Irish parties are becoming office-seekers *par excellence*, and, as elsewhere in Western Europe, they appear to be increasingly ill-equipped to engage their electorates in any meaningful sense. As the recent headlines indicate, they are also sometimes office-abusers *par excellence*, and this makes the task of re-engaging the voters even more difficult.

By any standards, the sheer longevity of the apparently free-floating Irish party system has been quite remarkable. When we take into account the extraordinary degree of social, economic and even cultural change that has marked Ireland over the past decades, and particularly in the 1990s, this longevity appears even more striking. What it testifies to is the extraordinary adaptive capacity of the individual parties, as well as, perhaps, that of the system of which they are part. In the space of little more than 30 years, these parties have moved from operating within an essentially stagnant, complacent and largely non-competitive and predictable environment, to the stage where they are obliged to work extremely hard to hold their heads above water in a context which is now perhaps one of the most openly competitive, uncertain and vulnerable in Western Europe. Not only are Irish parties obliged to respond to a more pragmatic, individualized, and now also disillusioned electorate; and not only must they attempt to manage their support through an electoral system which allows voters easily to evade the principle of party; but they must also now learn to cope with a largely unstructured pattern of inter-party competition in which almost everything is possible and little is preordained.

By comparative West European standards, it is probably safe to say that the political parties in Ireland have proved among the most flexible and adaptive in the region. Once beyond the formative years of the state, there seemed little that could have tied them down, whether in ideological or in electoral terms. Socially amorphous, free from conventional cleavage ties, and with little organizational legacy to weigh down the new generations, they were indeed catch-all *avant la lettre* (Gallagher 1981). And as catch-all parties, they rarely experienced any major difficulty in responding to shifts in electoral markets.

This is not an unchanging story, however. For even if the parties have always remained more or less flexible and adaptive, the electoral market and the structures of competition were such that this capacity to respond was rarely tested, and hence during the early decades of the postwar period, the parties could afford to be complacent. There was little rattling of cages in those days. Since then, of course, the system has opened up completely, and now the parties are more or less obliged to work flat out to retain their traditional weight within the political system. The combination of widespread dealignment – reflected not least in the growing support for independent candidates and the sharp decline in turnout – and an almost completely open process of coalition formation, has left little or no anchoring of identity or strategy. Cues are increasingly hard to decipher, whether by the voters or their political leaders, and the parties themselves have become exceptionally vulnerable. However flexible and adaptive they might be, they are now finding that their responsive capacities are being stretched to the limit. In the new century, the most convincing image is therefore of some very familiar parties (as well as some new ones) operating in what is an unfamiliar and potentially inhospitable political landscape.

Notes

1 The chief limit is the continued refusal on either side to consider a Fianna Fáil–Fine Gael coalition, athough Fine Gael did support a minority Fianna Fáil government between 1987 and 1989 (see Marsh and Mitchell 1999). Combinations including both Progressive Democrats and Labour also seem extremely unlikely, but the lesson of the last few years is perhaps that even the unlikely has become accepted. For a general discussion of recent options see Laver (1999), Mair (1999) and Mitchell (2003). Currently the established parties have said that a coalition including Sinn Féin is out of the question until such time as the IRA is disbanded.

2 It goes almost without saying that religion, which is of course one of the key elements in the structuring of the vote in many other European countries, also traditionally played no role in the formation of alignments in Ireland. With a population long estimated to be 95 percent Catholic, of whom 90 to 95 percent were regular church attenders, at least until the 1980s, the promotion of Catholic values in politics was the norm, and was accepted as such. It is only recently, and as

a result of a limited secularization, a disaffection from church leaders and the emergence of issues such as divorce, contraception and abortion on the political agenda, that pro- vs. anti-Catholic sentiment has begun to play a role in electoral behaviour. Even along this dimension, however, the parties have begun to converge anew within a moderately secular consensus.

3 As late as 1993, for example, an internal Fianna Fáil report complained that 'the Cumann [i.e. local branch] is not always conducive to gaining new members and new ideas which will allow the organisation to grow and develop. Most Cumainn are quite active and well run but there are many more which exist principally for the purpose of maximising delegate voting at organisational level and at [candidate] selection conventions'. The problem still existed at the end of the decade, with an internal party committee criticizing so-called 'paper cumainn' which served 'only the interests of a power bloc' within constituency organizations (Rafter 1999). Similar complaints were voiced by some Fine Gael members in a study of the party carried out at the end of the 1990s (Gallagher and Marsh 2002).

4 Memorandum from party headquarters, 8 November 1961 (Fine Gael archive, University College Dublin, P39/BF34). Four years later, an unsigned internal evaluation of the party's performance in the general election of 1965 suggested that something more needed to be done for middle-class voters in particular, in that the party was seen to be taking the support of such voters for granted and to be offering them too little in return for this support (ibid.: P39/BF17(b)).

5 Honorary Secretaries' report to the 1981 *Árd Fheis* (mimeo: 2).

6 This was part of the 1999 European Election Study. The sample size was only 500.

7 Since the voting age has been 18 since 1977, some members of the 1971–80 generation would have first voted in 1989.

8 Each year's data in Figure 9.1 is based on two Eurobarometer polls of some 1,000 cases each, except for 1978 and 1981, which use only one poll, and 1989 and 1994 which each combine three. The number of cases on which each point is based is variable, but typically is between 300 and 500, smaller for 'new' generations. Obviously, with relatively small numbers the difference between points is commonly not statistically significant, and a typical confidence interval would be plus/minus some 5 percent. What gives the graph its credibility is the consistency of the differences. Moreover, if we take the set of polls between 1978 and 1994, overall differences between each of the generations displayed in Figure 9.1 are statistically significant ($p < 0.05$). Furthermore, there are no significant differences between each of the generations 1911–20, 1921–30 and 1931–40, although the generation 1901–10 is significantly less dealigned than any other ($p < 0.05$).

9 Basil Chubb (1959: 183) noted at the beginning of an analysis of the 1957 contest, for example, that 'Irish elections in these days are usually very dull, and this one was no exception.' Another seasoned observer was later to describe the 1961 contest as 'the dullest on record' (O'Leary 1979: 62).

10 See, for example, Thornley 1963; Brown 1981. Such arguments were also later revived and extensively cited by the Labour Party in a 1986 internal report on the need for organizational and strategic renewal (Labour Party 1986).

11 Garret FitzGerald, who was prominent among these reformers, and who went on to become leader of Fine Gael and Taoiseach, later recalled that: 'My own decision to enter politics and join Fine Gael was strongly motivated by a belief that a social democratic alternative to Fianna Fáil needed to be created through the coming together of Fine Gael and Labour in Coalition Governments. In the first half of the 1960s it became clear that Fianna Fáil, under Sean Lemass, was emerging as a "growth orientated" party, which while not insensitive to social needs was not likely to be orientated primarily towards social objectives' (personal communication, 7 March 1990).

12 The redistricting became known as the Tullymander, following the name of the responsible [Labour] Minister, James Tully. See also Mair 1986.

13 Such exceptional long-term strategic thinking was best reflected in an interview with the then general secretary of Labour, Brendan Halligan, midway through the government's term of office (see the *Irish Times*, 22 November 1975): 'our strategy now should be to beat Fianna Fáil in the next General Election, and to break up that party more or less in the same way that the Gaullist Party in France is beginning to break under the stress of electoral defeat … Fianna Fáil,

in the face of a second defeat, will clearly change its leader, will be subject to great internal stresses and will lose the monolithic image which they have had since 1932. This, I believe, will provide the Labour Party with a unique opportunity to win back the support which was robbed from it by the historical origins of this State.'

14 Perceptions are very important here, especially since, despite losing seats and office, Fianna Fáil had actually marginally increased its share of the vote in 1973 – from 45.7 percent in 1969 to 46.2 percent.

15 This particularistic targeting of groups of potentially available voters is also a feature of the often crucial by-election campaigns. In one important by-election in Dublin in the early 1980s, for example, the constituency in question won government promises for a new factory, new community centres, nine new schools, and £300,000 for a new sports centre. Countless new trees were also planted in the local housing estates, only to be uprooted and replanted elsewhere when the vote eventually went against the government (see Joyce and Murtagh 1983: 172–3).

16 For a discussion of these different types of voting links in an application to the Italian case, see Parisi and Pasquino 1977.

17 In practice, the last candidate to be elected in a multi-member constituency usually wins on the basis of fewer votes than the quota would indicate.

18 With reference to an earlier closely fought contest, Browne and Farrell (1981: 16) estimated that Fianna Fáil would have had enough seats to return to office in 1981 but for 260 votes – 94 in the constituency of Wexford, where a Labour candidate narrowly defeated a Fianna Fáil candidate for the last seat; and 166 in Dublin North, where a Fine Gael candidate narrowly won over Fianna Fáil.

19 We should not underestimate the importance of the candidate to the local effort by the party, however much electoral politics may have been nationalized in recent years. Candidates still bring vital resources of money and voluntary labour to the local campaign, and still canvass personally for votes on the basis of their own appeal and achievements. The national image may now loom larger than before, but the tradition of brokerage politics, as well as the nature of the electoral system itself, still places the individual candidate at the centre of the voting act.

20 For a very valuable and detailed nuts-and-bolts account of Labour's (often unsuccessful) attempts to build a modern party and campaigning machine, see Kavanagh 2001.

21 This was also more or less the conclusion which could be drawn from Fianna Fáil's own evaluation of its organization in the early 1990s, for example, in which all of the various recommendations were seen as being 'underlined by the need to bring a much stronger sense of professionalism to the way we work' (Fianna Fáil 1993: 8).

22 In 1998, the solution to this problem suggested by the then leader, John Bruton, was to develop policies that would 'marry the economically smart with the socially just'. In this way, he argued, Fine Gael would become the biggest party in parliament (Kennedy 1998). In the event, Bruton was removed from the leadership in 2001, and in the election of 2002 the party went on to record one of the worst results in its history. Following this last defeat, a party post-mortem identified the same problems as had been highlighted in 1993 (Fine Gael 2002).

23 Putting all these official sums together, Farrell (1994: 233–5) estimated that as early as 1989, when the parties were supposedly still being denied public subsidies, transfers from the state to the political parties amounted to some £4 million, a figure far in excess of the £2.7 million that was formally reported as the total income of all the parties taken together in that year. In the Fianna Fáil case, however, it seems that the party leader's allowance sometimes went directly into the party leader's private pocket – on one famous occasion, when collected by the now disgraced leader, the island-owning Charles Haughey, the allowance was used to buy a set of exceptionally expensive shirts in Paris.

24 This was the explicit reasoning employed by the then Prime Minister, Bertie Ahern, when he announced a new set of proposals for the regulation of political finance at the end of 2000 (See Ahern 2000).

25 The leadership resisted the recommendation for a directly elected leader but did accept 'one member one vote' procedures for the selection of election candidates.

26 Fine Gael in particular has been seriously concerned with its relations with the wider society: 'The Fine Gael organisation, nationally, is deeply internalised. It does not relate adequately to the general public or to other campaigning organisations with which it should have an affinity. The organisation, in this sense, is literally talking to itself … . A profound change of attitude is required. In order to thrive, local constituency organisations must actively invite outside influences and must actively cooperate with other campaigning organisations. We live in an age where increasing numbers of people find single issue pressure groups to be a more productive outlet than political parties. This is a phenomenon which must be recognised and acted upon' (Fine Gael 1993: 39–40).

27 In this regard it is worth noting the conclusions of a special Labour Party Commission on electoral strategy in the 1980s (Labour Party, 1986: 47–8), which highlighted the importance of the party's links with trade unions in the discussion of possible alliances with social actors, but which also emphasized the need for links with other groups and organizations, including tenants' and residents' associations, women, the unemployed, the poor, young people, charity groups, international groups, minorities, professional associations, and aid organizations. Nobody was to be left out.

References

Ahern, Bertie (2000). 'Politics Must be Credible and Clearly Accountable.' *Irish Times*, 4 December.

Bew, Paul and Henry Patterson (1982). *Séan Lemass and the Making of Modern Ireland, 1945–66*. Dublin: Gill & Macmillan.

Brown, Terence (1981). *Ireland: A Social and Cultural History, 1922–79*. London: Fontana.

Browne, Vincent and Michael Farrell (1981). *The Magill Book of Irish Politics*. Dublin: Magill Publications.

Chubb, Basil (1959). 'Ireland 1957.' In David E. Butler (ed.), *Elections Abroad*. London: Macmillan, pp. 183–226.

Cohan, A.S. (1972). *The Irish Political Elite*. Dublin: Gill & Macmillan.

Collins, Neil (2000). *Understanding Corruption in Irish Politics*. Cork: Cork University Press.

Converse, Philip E. (1969). 'Of Time and Partisan Stability.' *Comparative Political Studies* 2: 139–71.

Crotty, William and David E. Schmitt (eds) (1998). *Ireland and the Politics of Change*. Harlow: Longman.

Donnelly, Sean (1997). *Elections '97*. Dublin: Sean Donnelly.

Dunphy, Richard (1995). *The Making of Fianna Fáil Power in Ireland, 1923–1948*. Oxford: The Clarendon Press.

Farrell, David (1986). 'The Strategy to Market Fine Gael in 1981.' *Irish Political Studies* 1: 1–14.

Farrell, David (1992). 'Ireland.' In Richard S. Katz and Peter Mair (eds), *Party Organizations: A Data Handbook on Party Organizations in Western Democracies, 1960–90*. London: Sage, pp. 389–457.

Farrell, David (1993a). 'Campaign Strategies.' In Michael Gallagher and Michael Laver (eds), *How Ireland Voted 1992*. Dublin: Folens/PSAI Press, pp. 21–38.

Farrell, David (1993b). 'The Contemporary Irish Party: Campaign and Organizational Developments in a Changing Environment.' Florence: European University Institute, PhD thesis.

Farrell, David (1994). 'Ireland: Centralization, Professionalization, and Competitive Pressures.' In Richard S. Katz and Peter Mair (eds), *How Parties Organize: Change and Adaptation in Party Organizations in Western Democracies*. London: Sage, pp. 216–41.

Fianna Fáil (1993). *Commission on the Aims & Structures of Fianna Fáil: Final Report*. Dublin: Fianna Fáil.

Fine Gael (1993). *Our Country, Our Party, Our Future: Report of the Commission on Renewal of Fine Gael*. Dublin: Fine Gael.

Fine Gael (2002). *21st Century Fine Gael: Report of the Strategy Review Group*. Dublin: Fine Gael.

Gallagher, Michael (1981). 'Societal Change and Party Adaptation in the Republic of Ireland, 1960–1981.' *European Journal of Political Research* 9: 269–85.

Gallagher, Michael (1982). *The Irish Labour Party in Transition, 1957–82*. Manchester: Manchester University Press.

Gallagher, Michael (1993). 'The Election of the 27th Dáil.' In Michael Gallagher and Michael Laver (eds), *How Ireland Voted 1992*. Dublin: Folens/PSAI Press, pp. 57–78.

Gallagher, Michael (1999). 'The Results Analyzed.' In Michael Marsh and Paul Mitchell (eds), *How Ireland Voted 1997*. Boulder, CO: Westview, pp. 121–50.

Gallagher, Michael (2003). 'Stability and Turmoil: Analysis of the Results.' In Michael Gallagher, Michael Marsh, and Paul Mitchell (eds), *How Ireland Voted 2002*. London: Palgrave, pp. 88–118.

Gallagher, Michael and Michael Marsh (2002). *Days of Blue Loyalty: the Politics of Membership of the Fine Gael Party*. Dublin: PSAI Press.

Garry, John, Fiachra Kennedy, Michael Marsh, and Richard Sinnott (2003). 'What Decided the Election?' In Michael Gallagher, Michael Marsh, and Paul Mitchell (eds), *How Ireland Voted 2002*. London: Palgrave, pp. 119–42.

Garvin, Tom (1974). 'Political Cleavages, Party Politics, and Urbanisation in Ireland: the Case of the Periphery-Dominated Centre.' *European Journal of Political Research* 2: 307–27.

Girvin, Brian (1996). 'The Irish Divorce Referendum, November 1995.' *Irish Political Studies* 11: 174–81.

Joyce, Joe and Peter Murtagh (1983). *The Boss: Charles J. Haughey in Power*. Dublin: Poolbeg Press.

Kavanagh, Ray (2001). *Spring, Summer and Fall: The Rise and Fall of the Irish Labour Party, 1986–1999*. Dublin: Blackwater Press.

Kennedy, Geraldine (1998). 'Fine Gael devises agenda for climate of consensus', *Irish Times*, 23 September.

Labour Party (1986). *Report of the Commission on Electoral Strategy*. Dublin: The Labour Party.

Laver, Michael (1986a). 'Ireland: Politics with some Social Bases. An Interpretation based on Aggregate Data.' *Economic and Social Review* 17: 107–31.

Laver, Michael (1986b). 'Ireland: Politics with some Social Bases. An Interpretation based on Survey Data.' *Economic and Social Review* 17: 193–213.

Laver, Michael (1999). 'The Irish Party System Approaching the Millennium.' In Michael Marsh and Paul Mitchell (eds), *How Ireland Voted 1997*. Boulder, CO: Westview, pp. 264–76.

Laver, Michael and Michael Marsh (1999). 'Parties and Voters.' In John Coakley and Michael Gallagher (eds), *Politics in the Republic of Ireland*, 3rd edn. London and Dublin: Routledge and PSAI Press, pp. 152–76.

Laver, Michael and Keneth A. Shepsle (1996). *Making and Breaking Governments: Cabinets and Legislatures in Parliamentary Democracies*. Cambridge: Cambridge University Press.

Laver, Michael, Michael Marsh, and Richard Sinnott (1987). 'Patterns of Party Support.' In Michael Laver, Peter Mair, and Richard Sinnott (eds), *How Ireland Voted: The General Election of 1987*. Dublin: Poolbeg Press, pp. 99–140.

Lyons, Patrick and Richard Sinnott (2003). 'Voter Turnout in 2002 and Beyond.' In Michael Gallagher, Michael Marsh, and Paul Mitchell (eds), *How Ireland Voted 2002*. London: Palgrave, pp. 143–58.

Mair, Peter (1979). 'The Autonomy of the Political: the Development of the Irish Party System.' *Comparative Politics* 11: 445–65.

Mair, Peter (1986). 'Districting Choices under the Single-Transferable Vote.' In Bernard Grofman and Arend Lijphart (eds), *Electoral Laws and their Political Consequences*. New York: Agathon Press, pp. 289–307.

Mair, Peter (1987a). *The Changing Irish Party System: Organization, Ideology and Electoral Competition*. London: Pinter.

Mair, Peter (1987b). 'Party Organization, Vote Management and Candidate Selection: toward the Nationalization of Electoral Strategy in Ireland.' In Howard Penniman and Brian Farrell (eds),

Ireland at the Polls, 1981, 1982 and 1987: A Study of Four General Elections. Durham, NC: Duke University Press/American Enterprise Institute, pp. 104–30.

Mair, Peter (1999). 'Party Competition and the Changing Party System.' In John Coakley and Michael Gallagher (eds), *Politics in the Republic of Ireland*, 3rd edn. London and Dublin: Routledge and PSAI Press, pp. 127–51.

Mair, Peter and Ingrid van Biezen (2001). 'Party Membership in Twenty European Democracies, 1980–2000.' *Party Politics* 7: 5–21.

Manning, Maurice (1978). 'The Political Parties.' In Howard R. Penniman (ed.), *Ireland at the Polls: the Dáil Elections of 1977*. Washington, DC: American Enterprise Institute, pp. 69–95.

Marsh, Michael (2000). 'Party Wrapped but Candidate Centred.' In Shaun Bowler and Bernard Grofman (eds), *The Single Transferable Vote Electoral System: Studies of an Embedded Institution*. Ann Arbor, MI: University of Michigan Press.

Marsh, Michael (ed.) (2002). *The Sunday Tribune Guide to Irish Politics*. Dublin: Sunday Tribune.

Marsh, Michael (2004). 'Stability and Change in the Structure of Electoral Competition 1989–2002.' In John Garry, Niamh Hardiman, and Diane Payne (eds), *Facing Change in a New Ireland: an Analysis of Irish Social and Political Attitudes*. Dublin: Liffey Press.

Marsh, Michael and Paul Mitchell (1999). 'Office, Votes and then Policy: Hard Choices for Political Parties in the Republic of Ireland.' In Wolfgang C. Müller and Kaare Strom (eds), *Policy, Office, or Votes*? Cambridge: Cambridge University Press, pp. 36–62.

Marsh, Michael and Richard Sinnott (1990). 'How the Voters Decided.' In Michael Gallagher and Richard Sinnott (eds), *How Ireland Voted 1989*. Galway: Centre for the Study of Irish Elections, pp. 68–93.

Marsh, Michael and Richard Sinnott (1999). 'The Behaviour of the Irish Voter.' In Michael Marsh and Paul Mitchell (eds), *How Ireland Voted 1997*. Boulder, CO: Westview, pp. 151–80.

Mitchell, Paul (2003). 'Government Formation in 2002: You Can Have Any Kind as Long as It Is Fianna Fail.' In Michael Gallagher, Michael Marsh, and Paul Mitchell (eds), *How Ireland Voted 2002*. London: Palgrave, pp. 214–29.

Murphy, Ronan and David Farrell (2003). 'Party Politics in Ireland: Regularizing a Volatile System.' In Paul Webb, David Farrell, and Ian Holliday (eds), *Political Parties in Advanced Industrial Democracies*. Oxford: Oxford University Press, pp. 217–47.

O'Byrnes, Stephen (1986). *Hiding behind a Face: Fine Gael under FitzGerald*. Dublin: Gill & Macmillan.

O'Leary, Cornelius (1979). *Irish Elections, 1918–1977*. Dublin: Gill & Macmillan.

O'Sullivan, Michael (1994). *Seán Lemass: A Biography*. Dublin: Blackwater Press.

Parisi, Arturo and Gianfranco Pasquino (1977). 'Relazione partiti-elettori e tipo di voto.' In Arturo Parisi and Gianfranco Pasquino (eds), *Continuità e mutamento elettorale in Italia*. Bologna: Il Mulino, pp. 215–49.

Pedersen, Mogens N. (1979). 'The Dynamics of European Party Systems: Changing Patterns of Electoral Volatility.' *European Journal of Political Research* 7: 1–26.

Rafter, Kevin (1999). 'Fianna Fail Group Says Party Need Overhaul.' *Irish Times*, 23 September.

Rumpf, Erhard and A.C. Hepburn (1977). *Nationalism and Socialism in Twentieth-Century Ireland*. Liverpool: Liverpool University Press.

Sartori, Giovanni (1976). *Parties and Party Systems: a Framework for Analysis*. Cambridge: Cambridge University Press.

Schmitt, Hermann and Sören Holmberg (1995). 'Political Parties in Decline?' In Hans-Dieter Klingemann and Dieter Fuchs (eds), *Citizens and the State*. Oxford: Oxford University Press, pp. 95–133.

Sinnott, Richard (1978). 'The Electorate.' In Howard R. Penniman (ed.), *Ireland at the Polls: the Dáil Elections of 1977*. Washington, DC: American Enterprise Institute, pp. 35–67.

Sinnott, Richard (1995). *Irish Voters Decide: Voting Behaviour in Elections and Referendums since 1918*. Manchester: Manchester University Press.

Thornley, David (1963). 'What's Wrong With the Dáil? 4: the Image and the Machine.' *Irish Times*, 22 August.

Van der Eijk, Cees, Mark Franklin, *et al.* (1996). *Choosing Europe? The European Electorate and National Politics in the Face of the Union.* Ann Arbor, MI: University of Michigan Press.

Wattenberg, Martin (1991). *The Rise of Candidate-Centered Politics.* Cambridge, MA: Harvard University Press.

Whyte, John H. (1974). 'Ireland: Politics without Social Bases.' In Richard Rose (ed.), *Electoral Behaviour: a Comparative Handbook.* New York: The Free Press, pp. 619–51.

TEN Conclusion: Political Parties in Changing Electoral Markets

Peter Mair, Wolfgang C. Müller, and Fritz Plasser

Political parties can never afford to be completely complacent. In addition to the inevitable uncertainties that they face when competing in sometimes unpredictable electoral markets, parties also have to deal with uncertainties regarding their capacity to remain in public office, to make public policy, and to ensure continuing support within the party organization on the ground. Nonetheless, and at least with the benefit of hindsight, the analyses included in this volume are clear in suggesting that the grounds for complacency were stronger 30 years ago than they are today. Indeed, it is striking to note how many of the discussions of party responses that are included here begin by emphasizing how stability and predictability are now largely matters of the past. Nor is this shift solely attributable to what has happened within electoral markets as such, for it is also striking to note how many of these analyses document increasing party concern with the uncertainties involved in how parties relate to one another, and in how they interact within the parliamentary arena.

Parties begin with two goals: the first is survival, the second is success. Both are multi-faceted, and in different systems, as well as across different parties, the definition and ordering of these goals may vary significantly. Survival may be defined in electoral terms, but it may also be defined in terms of the party's role in public office. Survival is also relative: ticking along at just 5 or 10 percent of the votes is the most some parties can ever hope for; for others, being the dominant actor within the electoral arena seems almost a *sine qua non*. Success may also be measured differently: for some parties, even a single voice at a coalition cabinet table is the extreme ambition; for others, commanding that table is important; for yet others, it is not the office but the policy performance which counts (Müller and Strøm 1999). One obvious lesson to be drawn from these analyses is therefore that it is not only party responses that vary according to their perceptions, a point which is emphasized throughout the volume, but that these perceptions vary according to the different parties and the different contexts in which they compete.

Not everything is relative, however, and some changes seem more or less consistent across all systems, even if they fail to impact with equal effect on each and every party. These core changes have already been summarized in the Introduction, and are echoed not only in the different contributions to the volume, but also in most of the conventional literature on party–voter linkages in contemporary western democracies. They include the quite pervasive decline in the reach of traditional cleavage politics, whether measured at the level of the social structure or at the level of collective political identities; the weakening of partisan loyalties, a process which seems to be prompted as much by the new ways in which parties mobilize their support as by the increasing individualization and particularization of social behaviour; the emergence of new issues and the depoliticization of traditional alignments, this again being a function of both shifts in the political offer and a transformation of social demands; the emergence of new competitors, both within and without the traditional political arena; and, finally, the development of new possibilities for aggregating alliances and opposition.

The party response: commonalities

A number of the party responses to these changes appear also more or less consistent across all systems. One response in particular seems pervasive: faced with the demands of this new and uncertain environment, parties have begun to transform themselves more and more into centralized and professional campaigning organizations, in which the scope for the amateur politician has been curtailed, and in which the weight and direction of party strategy have tended increasingly to be located within the party leadership as such (see also Katz and Mair 2002). This is not to say that in the 1960s or 1970s it was necessarily the party rank and file which actively determined party strategies. However, the rank and file was much more influential via the 'law of anticipated reaction' (Friedrich 1941: 589), and the leadership had to be much more careful to ensure that party members and core voters accepted the party strategy. Today, however, despite often opening up leadership and candidate selection processes to the wider party membership, and sometimes even to supporters beyond the membership organization, parties are now increasingly leadership driven. Indeed, the opening up and democratization of the party organization has often resulted in a reduction in the power of party activists and in accumulation of more *de facto* control by the leadership.

One effect of this mode of response has been that party life outside parliament and head office has tended to wither away, so that it becomes less and less easy to distinguish a separate sense of party from that associated with the leadership in public office (cf. Downs 1957: 24–6). The parties become their leaders. What this also implies, of course, is that the party appears more undifferentiated and standardized, speaking with just one voice and imparting just one message to the broader public. Several parties have also created a new type of leadership which is attractive for the general electorate and the mass media but which may appeal less to those members who are still bound to the traditions of their party. Indeed, as was noted in the case of Germany, it is sometimes through new leaders and new candidates that the parties hope to distract attention from potentially divisive issues. As the chapters in this volume indicate, the parties are increasingly likely to widen the search for new leaders and candidates beyond the membership organization itself. They are also more and more likely to go beyond the conventional affiliate organizations, with the various contributions to this volume pointing to a weakening of the traditional organizational links between parties and interest groups, and particularly between the Left and the trade unions (see also Poguntke 1998).

There are good reasons for these shifts. In the first place, as is usually more than evident to the parties themselves, voter support can no longer be taken for granted, and traditional loyalties can no longer be easily assumed. What follows, therefore, is that traditional cues no longer suffice, and hence the parties have to work much harder to uncover the sort of strategy and appeal that could prove successful. Listening to voters becomes more important than listening to members, and this requires a substantial reallocation of organizational resources and the development of other competences. In terms of the valuable distinction first introduced by Parisi and Pasquino (1978), parties have learned to move from relying on a 'vote of belonging' to campaigning for a 'vote of opinion'.

Secondly, parties, or at least their leaderships, have had to learn to become more flexible and responsive. Not only are electorates proving to be more and more available, but they appear to remain so right up to polling day itself, with the allocation of political preferences proving ever more susceptible to the short-term considerations that emerge during the campaign itself. For this reason also party leaders have to remain on their toes, and to be ready to quickly adapt their message to new circumstances. Perhaps more importantly, however, flexibility is also required within the changing environment of party alignments at the elite level, especially with the opening up of traditionally closed processes of coalition formation. Parties must always be ready to forge new alliances, and all options must now be held open. In both the electoral and the parliamentary arenas, therefore, parties are struggling to free themselves from traditional constraints, and this struggle reinforces the need for greater leadership autonomy and versatility. As in Austria, for example, it is the parties with the ostensibly weaker organizations that can better respond to these new circumstances, whereas those that are conventionally seen as strong are also those that prove the more sluggish.

Moving towards such a top-down model of party organization does carry its risks, however. Being less rooted in the wider society, parties may also become more vulnerable in the longer term (see p. 273 below), and they may even leave themselves with fewer built-in defences against the more short-term ebbs and flows of popular opinion. On the one hand, it can be argued that they have no other option. Changes in the social structure alone appear to confirm that the days of the traditional mass party have passed, and, as Kirchheimer (1966) once predicted would be the case, it now appears impossible to pursue a strategy of electoral integration, even if such a strategy were still deemed desirable. On the other hand, vulnerability and the susceptibility to short-term losses are perhaps more than compensated by the potential to win new and additional electoral support, and certainly the top-down models which parties have developed are more suited to the needs of aggressive competition. Relying on brand loyalty may allow a party to survive, but marketing a new image may bring increased success. That said, the inevitable consequence of these shifts is that parties are obliged to work even harder to ensure that they succeed. Developing a more top-down strategy can therefore be viewed as both the cause and the consequence of declining voter loyalties. In this sense, the process by which parties adapt to looser electoral bonds will serve to loosen these bonds even further, thus perhaps obliging them to run faster and faster in order to remain in the same place.

Leadership flexibility, faster response times and top-down strategies are costly, however, and to meet the new needs, parties have inevitably been obliged to build up their resources, to expand their staffing levels, and to professionalize their organizations. In other words, and as was noted in the case of Denmark, the parties have had to learn to campaign more often and more intensively, and to invest more in competition. In many countries, and increasingly so, this new capital-intensive approach has become possible only as a result of quite generous state subventions – first, to the parliamentary party, and later to the party organization outside parliament. This too is one of the ways in which parties have responded to their changed circumstances, since it is the parties in government, in this case usually cooperating with the opposition, that are responsible for introducing public funding in the first place, as well as for ensuring that it is regularly increased to meet the ever-expanding demands of their organizations (see also Katz and Mair 1995).

To the extent that these processes are more or less common to all modern democracies and that they affect all mainstream parties within those democracies, they also imply that these parties grow to resemble one another. The way in which parties now respond to electoral markets encourages not only the convergence of organizational styles among the mainstream parties within each system, but also their convergence across systems. The peculiarities associated with different polities and different party types tend to erode in the face of similar transformations in electoral markets, and more or less common and predictable responses. Parties also learn from one another, of course, both within and across systems, such that contemporary West European politics is marked not only by the diffusion of political ideas – exemplified most recently by the contagion of the so-called 'Third Way' philosophy – but also by the diffusion of organizational and campaigning techniques (Plasser *et al.* 1999). In some respects, this is the inevitable consequence of the changes which are occurring at the various national levels. In electoral terms, and at national level, more and more voters are now potentially available to all parties. But at the same time, more and more parties are now potentially available to all voters, and the result is that, at national level, traditional differentiations fade into the background, and old shibboleths become undermined. And as these internal differentiations wane, so do the features which once distinguished one national political culture from another. Party histories remain specific, of course, as do the labels under which the parties campaign. But the ways in which they campaign, and the ways in which they seek to appeal to voters, are now becoming standardized across all the West European polities. This is another key lesson that may be derived from the various contributions included in this volume: not only there less certainty in contemporary European electoral markets, there are also fewer national specificities.

The party response: variations

Some national specificities still remain, of course. But what is perhaps most striking about the analyses included here is that these were once much more significant, and how they played a particularly important role in explaining variation in the *initial* responses by parties to the first real signs of increased uncertainty. Part of that initial response, to be sure, was sometimes almost negligible, or at best cosmetic. This too may be attributed to national specificities. In France, for example, it was the long-term familiarity with quite substantial electoral flux that appears to have inclined some party strategists to view even important shifts in the political alignments as part of the conventional land-scape. Responses tended therefore to be both inadequate and ineffectual, the party strategy equivalent of rounding up the usual suspects. Elsewhere, as in Belgium, for example, quick-fix solutions tended to be favoured, such as intro-ducing new leaders or new candidates. A more open approach to candidate selection also marked the strategy of the Italian PCI, one of whose relatively muted responses to the challenge of new social movements after 1968 was to include independent candidates on its lists – a sort of intra-party *trasformismo*. These were all largely cosmetic changes, similar to those traditionally seen in Fianna Fáil in Ireland, where candidate renewal was viewed as a substitute for party renewal more generally, and they appear to have had little lasting impact.

In part, and especially in hindsight, the resort to such 'easy' responses can be explained by the fact that the parties in question often underestimated the signifi-cance of the changes which were unfolding. Indeed, it is no coincidence that the reliance on easy solutions is primarily characteristic of the first wave of responses, that is, of a period in which complacency within the mainstream was most pro-nounced. It is evident that both of the major Austrian parties, for example, initially underestimated the level and seriousness of the challenge that they were facing, and hence both believed that their problems could be dealt with by quite short-term palliatives. Theirs was a prescription for aspirin rather than penicillin.

The responses to new electoral and systemic challenges also sometimes proved inadequate simply because the parties misunderstood or found difficulty in reading the messages that were being sent, and this, in turn, was often because the messages were themselves contradictory. The cautious response of the Danish Social Democrats to the electoral earthquake of 1973 – keeping their head down while waiting to see what would happen when the smoke finally cleared – offers a good case in point. But it is also important to recognize that problems arise simply because the parties themselves compete in a variety of different arenas – in the electoral arena, the parliamentary arena, and even the governing arena – and also because the structure of competition sometimes varies at different territorial levels. Problems in one arena may not be the same as those in another, and what works to the disadvantage of one party in one arena might well serve the interests of that same party in a different arena. In Germany, for example, the co-existence of federal and state elections, and the differing performances of the two main parties in each of these sectors, made for a situation in which, at one and the same time, each of the parties could see itself as both a loser (the CDU in the *Länder*, the SPD at federal level) and as a winner (the SPD in the *Länder*, the CDU at federal level). A similar pattern could be observed for a long time in Austria too, where the SPÖ was successful at the federal level and the ÖVP at the level of the *Länder*. Perceptions were going to be confusing, therefore, if not even misleading, and hence responses were likely to prove contradictory or even self-defeating. Parties are not unitary actors, and the same response will not necessarily suit each sub-unit equally. A similar conjuncture can be seen in Belgium, where ostensibly identical parties – parties that were actually once fused into one 'national' organization – compete in quite different sets of regional political circumstances, so that what appeared to be a major problem in one case proved quite irrelevant in the other.

The Italian case is also of particular interest here, since the confused transition from the First to the so-called Second Republic led to a temporal shift in the centre of gravity from the electoral to the parliamentary arena, and prompted entirely different sets of party preoccupations and hence also very different sets of perceptions of what mattered. Thus we see the PCI/PDS being concerned primarily with electoral developments through to 1991 (taking continued growth for granted up to 1976, then worrying about declining support – and declining turnout – in the 1980s) and later being concerned primarily with developments in the parliamentary and governing arenas. More generally, the Italian case reveals how the new situation modified perceptions of what was important to the parties and hence of what must be responded to and how the response was to be made. It could even be argued that a similar temporal shift from one arena to another was associated with the opening up of the government formation process in Ireland, although the Irish changes were clearly not so dramatic or fundamental as was the case in Italy. Nevertheless, in Ireland the parties also needed to learn to pay much more attention to what their opponents were likely to do in the parliamentary arena, in that many of the old certainties, which could often survive quite substantial electoral flux, had disappeared by the 1990s.

Those national specificities which were often strongest in the past, and which still remain even today, are those relating to the party system as such, and to the role of the individual party in that system. Two elements are important here.

First, and somewhat paradoxically, we learn from these analyses that the survival and success of individual parties may sometimes depend on the concurrent survival and success of others. In other words, party interests are neither necessarily exclusive nor autonomous. Again in both Italy and Ireland, we see parties concerned not only with their own fates, but also with those of their potential coalition allies. Being less competitive in the electoral arena, and even accepting electoral losses, may therefore be in a party's interest, since it facilitates the success of a possible parliamentary ally. In Ireland, in both the electoral arena (given the STV electoral system) and in the parliamentary arena, it was once clearly in the interests of Fine Gael to encourage support for Labour. Fighting together offered a much greater pay-off than sharp competition. In Italy, at least prior to the 1990s, it was also in the DC interest to ensure the survival and limited success of its erstwhile *pentapartito* allies. Going for broke on its own might well have yielded more votes and even more parliamentary seats, but it might also have spelled the end to the party's hegemonic control over government.

The German case is even more revealing in this regard, in that one of the more interesting developments in recent years has been the apparent decline in SPD worries about Green growth, as well as its awareness of a greater Green pragmatism which was eventually to facilitate a federal Red-Green coalition. Moreover, by going easy on the Greens, the SPD could focus more attention on attracting centrist voters, leaving the Greens to push for support on the Left. This might even imply that the SPD had won a position in which it could wage two distinct competitive strategies – the one in the electoral arena, where it aimed primarily at centrist voters, and the other in the parliamentary arena, where it aimed to build a centre Left coalition. This would also serve as a rather painless solution to the strategic dilemma that had otherwise badly troubled the party throughout the 1980s. France is also an interesting case here, since, as in Ireland, the nature of the electoral system encourages parties to work together in the electoral arena, even if relations between these parties are not always so easily managed in parliament itself. Perhaps ironically, we therefore see evidence of party responses which are sometimes geared towards supporting other parties in the system: depending on the party system concerned, the curtailment of electoral success need not necessarily damage a party's strategic advantage in post-electoral bargaining.

The second systemic feature that is important here follows immediately on from this, and relates to the competition for government. In brief, what we also learn from these analyses is that elections are not always pivotal, and so, within certain limits, electoral success or failure may not count for much. For this reason it need not require a particular party response. In Belgium, for example, the Flemish Christians were for a long time cushioned from the consequences of electoral erosion, since they were always the biggest party, and always in government. Like the Italian DC prior to the 1990s, or Fianna Fáil in Ireland prior to the 1970s, they could live with the losses, and it was only when these risked becoming unaffordable that they began to get worried. Applying the argument more generally, we should not read electoral erosion as being necessarily a problem for the party involved. Not all losses are experienced/perceived as problematic, while, equally, not all gains are necessarily perceived as being a success. Again in Belgium, the Flemish socialists seemed only to have begun to worry when the losses which they experienced fed into support for Vlaams Blok; in other circumstances, these losses could be afforded.

More generally, it might well be that in consociational-type systems electoral strength is not necessarily regarded as the leading indicator of a party's position: certainly, the individual parties may lose or gain a few percentage points, but this may not have any real effect on their overall standing, or on processes of government formation. What one party views as problematic may not be seen as problematic by another, and what emerges as a difficulty in one system might well be just a passing disturbance in another. It is in this sense that party perceptions matter, and particularly perceptions which go beyond the electoral arena alone. For this reason, we must also pay attention to the wider strategic environment, since, as the Italian and Irish cases easily demonstrate, a shift in patterns of coalition formation may introduce a new and enhanced level of competition which demands a much more careful and considered response by party leaders than does electoral change on its own.

Party strategists are far from infallible, of course, and this is also something that we learn from these various analyses. As noted above, strategists may misread or misunderstand the new situation which confronts them. They may also be set in their ways, being biased towards interpreting change in terms with which they are already familiar. This seems reasonably typical of all the established parties in Denmark in the immediate wake of 1973, for example. The Austrian case offers another useful example here, since the evidence suggests that the initial ÖVP response to the difficulties being experienced by the SPÖ in the 1980s was that this represented a real opportunity for its own advance. What we see here is more or less a form of tunnel vision, in which the ÖVP perceived the Austrian system in terms only of the SPÖ and itself, and hence believed that if one side failed the other would necessarily succeed. In fact, both parties eventually suffered while a third party, the FPÖ, reaped the benefits. As Schattschneider (1960) once emphasized, party systems involve not only conflicts between parties, but also conflicts between conflicts, such that there is an ongoing if often only implicit struggle existing between one set of parties whose mutual interests are bound up in the maintenance of one particular dimension of competition, and another party or set of parties that seeks to mobilize a wholly alternative dimension. Thus while party A competes with party B in an opposition that serves to keep the A–B dimension paramount, there are other parties, C, D, and so on, who wish to establish the primacy of other structures of competition. Inevitably, however, party A will almost always focus on party B, and vice versa, and hence each may fail to respond to shifts that threaten to condemn both to a marginal position. In other words, parties may be blind-sided.

The Belgian case offers a further example of parties being trapped within a traditional mode of thinking, and hence misreading the nature of the challenge they face. As Deschouwer notes, the parties initially responded to what they saw as a new electoral demand by effecting changes in their internal functioning. How this could have been seen to have been 'demanded' by the voter is unclear, but Deschouwer suggests that the parties were inclined to see this sort of response as being demanded since it was so easily implemented. Since the parties are internally oriented to begin with, and since they can make these changes quite easily, they were intrinsically biased in favour of seeing this as the source of the problem, even if it was not the problem at all. In the French case, Knapp suggests that the PS may have developed a pattern in its manner of responding to perceived new demands, which, while suitable in some past instances, might prove wholly inappropriate at a later stage. The party is inclined to read the present through the lens of past experience, and hence risks misjudging the situation entirely. Both Belgium and France also offer interesting examples of cultures – and hence traditions – in which institutional reform is readily seen as a potential palliative for changing electoral demands. In both systems, a lot of attention has been devoted to institutional reform over the years, and this is always an option which can also be considered by parties who perceive themselves to be in difficulty. In the United Kingdom, by contrast, where institutional sclerosis is much more characteristic, the attempt by New Labour to initiate a constitutional revolution marks a complete and very radical break with past traditions of political renewal.

Past and future challenges

As this volume has shown, the stability and predictability in electoral markets, which had been typical of most of the West European party systems for so long, no longer pertain. In particular, the contributions have shown that the parties are now fully aware of these changed circumstances, even though the learning process that was involved often occurred with a considerable delay.

As was noted in the Introduction, changes in electoral markets come about for a variety of reasons, and can be the result of changes in the social structure, in the political culture, and in the modes and techniques of political communication. Not all of these are wholly independent of the parties, of course, in that at least some of the ostensibly external shocks that have impacted on parties in recent years have their origin in the initial shift towards catch-allism. The catchall party may have been an effective vote-winner in what was becoming an increasingly open electoral market, but it was the promotion of catch-allism that served to reinforce that openness and to enhance the vulnerability of traditionally organized parties. This, at least, was the common experience in most of the West European polities from the 1960s or 1970s onwards, and while the party responses to the subsequent changes in electoral markets initially displayed marked national peculiarities, we now witness a strong convergence both within and between systems. This brings the parties closer to the status of centralized electoral machines, in which the leadership has a high degree of autonomy and in which the internal organization works according to the top-down principle. Meanwhile, how the parties present themselves in the electoral markets becomes more and more a matter for professional media consultants.

This is all a far cry from the days of the classic mass party. As many party leaders and strategists would argue, however, it is not only that a mass party strategy is now almost impossible to pursue in contemporary society, it is also ineffective. Voters have become more critical and self-sufficient, and parties, and their leaderships, need to be able to respond to their demands more quickly and more flexibly. Party leaderships also need to be quick on their feet when dealing with their counterparts, and they are not helped in this task when burdened by an unwieldy and bureaucratic mass membership organization. Traditional forms of party organization can prove counter-productive – slowing down rather than enhancing the party's capacity to respond.

But while this new flexibility might help the new-style campaign organizations and their leaders in dealing with electoral markets in the short term, it may well prove damaging to the parties in the long term. As the contributions to this volume show, parties have had to respond to different challenges over time. To begin with, as the mass party era drew to a close, they responded to greater uncertainty in the electoral market, and to the prospect of more or less unpredictable shifts in the traditional balance of support. Later, they were forced to respond to the emergence of new competitors, and sometimes also to the development of new dimensions of competition. Today, however, the most pressing challenge to which the mainstream parties have to respond is that posed by popular disengagement and disaffection – popular withdrawal from, or indifference to, conventional politics, on the one hand, or popular support for populist protest parties, on the other. As this book suggests, support for populist protest has already become quite marked in a variety of West European polities, including Austria, Belgium, Denmark, France, and Italy. In Britain and Ireland, by contrast, the concern is with growing disengagement. Some of this disaffection and protest is substantive – fuelled by relative deprivation, by xenophobia or racism, or by social discontent more generally. But some is also fuelled by resentment and hostility towards the political class, and hence towards the leadership of the political parties.

The timing here may not be coincidental. In moving beyond the mass party, in enhancing the power and flexibility of the party top, and in privileging their party organization through the provision of state resources and a more generalized form of *partitocrazia*, the political leaders may have responded effectively to the burgeoning uncertainties within electoral markets. At the same time, however, by so doing, they may have unwittingly exposed themselves to the criticisms of an increasingly disenchanted electorate. Moreover, by fudging lines of political conflict, and by giving perhaps more attention to the demands of party–party relationships than to party–voter relationships, they may have offered further impetus to those voters who feel neglected in representational terms. What this implies, then, is that the set of responses that parties developed in order to deal with a dealigned electoral market – the responses of well-resourced, professional campaign organizations – may be one of the factors that is currently stimulating the growth of anti-party sentiment. In other words, the party response to one set of problems may have provoked yet others, and these might well prove more difficult for the parties to resolve.

References

Downs, Anthony (1957). *An Economic Theory of Democracy*. New York: Harper & Row.
Friedrich, Carl J. (1941). *Constitutional Government and Democracy*. Boston, MA: Little, Brown.
Katz, Richard S. and Peter Mair (1995). 'Changing Models of Party Organization and Party Democracy: the Emergence of the Cartel Party.' *Party Politics* 1: 5–23.
Katz, Richard S. and Peter Mair (2002). 'The Ascendancy of the Party in Public Office: Party Organizational Change in Twentieth-Century Democracies.' In Richard Gunther, José Ramón Montero, and Juan J. Linz (eds), *Political Parties: Old Concepts and New Challenges*. Oxford: Oxford University Press, pp. 113–35.
Kirchheimer, Otto (1966). 'The Transformation of Western European Party Systems.' In Joseph LaPalombara and Myron Weiner (eds), *Political Parties and Political Development*. Princeton, NJ: Princeton University Press, pp. 177–200.
Müller, Wolfgang C. and Kaare Strøm (eds) (1999). *Policy, Office, or Votes? How Political Parties in Western Europe Make Hard Decisions*. Cambridge: Cambridge University Press.
Parisi, Arturo and Gianfranco Pasquino (1978). 'Relazioni partiti–elettori e tipi di voto.' In Arturo Parisi and Gianfranco Pasquino (eds), *Continuità e mutamento elettorale in Italia*. Bologna: Il Mulino, pp. 215–49.
Plasser, Fritz, Christian Scheucher and Christian Senft (1999). 'Is There a European Style of Political Marketing?' In Bruce I. Newman (ed.), *The Handbook of Political Marketing*. Thousand Oaks, CA: Sage, pp. 89–112.
Poguntke, Thomas (1998). 'Party Organizations.' In Jan W. van Deth (ed.), *Comparative Politics. The Problem of Equivalence*. London: Routledge, pp. 136–79.
Schattschneider, E. E. (1960). *The Semi-Sovereign People*. New York: Holt, Rinehart & Winston.

Index